THE LEAN YEARS

Politics in the Age of Scarcity

by

RICHARD J. BARNET

SIMON AND SCHUSTER
New York

Manufactured in the United States of America
1   2   3   4   5   6   7   8   9   10

Library of Congress Cataloging in Publication Data

Barnet, Richard J.
The lean years.

Bibliography: p.
Includes index.
1. Natural resources.   2. World politics—
1975–1985.   3. United States—Economic conditions
—1971–   I. Title.
HC55.B28   333.7′11   79-25578
ISBN 0-671-22460-3

Acknowledgments

MANY INDIVIDUALS have helped me with this book. Mary Waters was a brilliant research assistant, and Ann Wilcox, Rachel Fershko, and Lynn Kitzmiller worked devotedly on the manuscript at different stages. The following gave tirelessly of information, advice, or criticism: Eqbal Ahmad, Ann Barnet, Solon Barraclough, Philip M. Becker, Marjorie Craig Benton, Susan Berner, Herbert Bernstein, Hal Bernton, Brent Blackwelder, Robert Borosage, Joe Browder, Joseph Collins, Gail Daneker, Dave Danning, Arthur Domike, Erik Eckholm, Robert Engler, Richard Falk, Joseph Filner, Robert Goralski, Denis Goulet, Richard Grossman, Hazel Henderson, Mark Hertsgaard, Helen Hopps, Kent Hughes, Helen Ingram, Ed Janss, Gary Jefferson, Henry Kelly, Gordon Kingsley, Thomas J. Knight, Janet Kotler, Saul Landau, Eleanor LeCain, Joseph Legett, Mike Locker, Ted Lockwood, Jerry Macafee, Harry Magdoff, Lindsay Mathson, Michael Moffitt, Dan Morgan, Prexy Nesbitt, Jeremiah Novak, Nicki Perlas, Marcus Raskin, Steve Roday, Rustum Roy, John Saxe-Fernandez, Bill Schweke, John Sewell, W. Y. Smith, Paul Streeten, John Tilton, Louis Turner, Francis J. Vastola, Howard Wachtel, Daniel Walden, Bethany Weidner, David Weiman, Peter Weiss, Stanley Weiss, Jack Willis, Rex Wingate, Jayne Wood, and Michael Zimmerman.

William Shawn encouraged me from the beginning, and Alice Mayhew provided inspired help at exactly the right moments. Without the intellectual support of the Institute for Policy Studies and its director, Robert Borosage, this book could not have been completed.

FOR DAD

Contents

PART ONE

THE COMING OF THE POSTPETROLEUM WORLD

CHAPTER I

The Scarcity Puzzle

THE PROMISE OF THE INDUSTRIAL age has been tempered by many disappointments, but none so devastating as the growing belief that our civilization is out of control. By every conventional measure the postwar world born in 1945 was a huge success. More goods were produced and sold than ever before. More people were working; the standard of living had never been higher. Yet as the suspicion grows that the era is ending, there is a pervasive sense that something is deeply wrong. We are used to rapid change, but there is a new and uncomfortable feeling that we are in a racing car without a driver.

The new mood is no conventional pessimism, but rather a loss of faith rooted in a sense of betrayal. We worked hard. We educated our children. We believed in the future. We followed all the rules of success. And, somehow, it has turned out wrong. As the postwar era began, economists promised a managed prosperity through "fine-tuning" of the economy, and as it ended, they threw up their hands. The remedy for galloping inflation and nagging unemployment had yet to be discovered. Economists catalogued reality in a series of exchange transactions, counted them up, and arrived at an astronomical figure they called the "gross national product." It was big enough to make anyone feel rich. But much of what they counted—the automobile accident industry, the cancer economy, the costs of pollution, crime, and welfare—though they put money in a variety of pockets, made the society poorer, not richer. As *The Wall Street Journal* summed it up, "The economic ideas and policies employed during the Great Depression and through a long era of Post World War II prosperity seem to have worn out."

Scientists had promised to break the bonds of human finitude, to open the secrets of the cell, and to unveil the mystery of the planets. Instead of the boundless horizons they had promised, limits popped up everywhere. The symbol of the new world without options was the Energy Crisis.

Burn gasoline, and cities choke in fumes. Burn coal, and the delicate ecological balance of the earth is jeopardized. Take the nuclear route, and you court catastrophe. Mechanize agriculture to make it efficient, and it takes forty calories to produce and deliver a calorie of food. Develop miracle pesticides, and you produce miracle pests who seem to thrive on them. There is a misfit between politics and the natural order which neither economists nor scientists nor corporate executives nor government bureaucrats quite understand. To be sure, it is not written anywhere that leaders understand, much less have vision. But the contemporary crop of leaders, surely as bright and as well schooled as any, seem to lack even the competence to manage disasters well.

Twenty years ago it was fashionable, in the United States at least, to worry about being rich. Liberals and conservatives had different notions about the perils of abundance. Liberals worried about "public squalor" and "pockets of poverty" in the midst of affluence. Conservatives took heart that any moral or political problems associated with private wealth could be solved by having more of it. For both, the answer was escalating growth and indiscriminate consumption. In the first twenty-five years after the surrender of Germany and Japan the industrial world used more petroleum and nonfuel minerals than had been consumed in all previous human history. The United States bent, burned, or melted about 40 percent of the world's nonrenewable materials in those years—an appetite, Richard Nixon assured the American people, that was a badge of greatness.

During the 1970s, however, a rapid succession of shocks ushered in a politics of austerity. Suddenly the word on every lip was *scarcity*. The world monetary system designed at Bretton Woods toward the end of the war collapsed and with it America's unique role as world banker. U.S. forces withdrew in defeat from Vietnam. From nowhere, so it seemed, faraway people, whose traditional role was to be conquered, bought, or ignored, acquired the power to produce panic in the industrial world. The Arab producers raised the price of oil fivefold, and the Affluent Society found itself with cold houses and gasoline lines. Nothing dramatized more effectively the dependence of industrial society on the world resource systems or the reality that control was shifting. The sense of leaderless drift, particularly acute in the world's most powerful nation, stemmed in no small way from the new consciousness of a resource squeeze.

Cheap food had gone the way of cheap energy. Across the world a billion people were on the edge of starvation, and in the United States, supermarket prices jumped 60 percent in five years. Water was a growing problem everywhere, with droughts in the West and floods in the East. The Global Factory, a miraculous machine for turning natural resources into mass consumption goods, was in a permanent state of malfunction.

Unemployment was growing; for the first time in the postwar period it was becoming a serious problem throughout the industrial world, and in the Third World the unemployed and the cruelly underpaid made up 40 percent of the work force. As if to symbolize the crisis of production in the United States, more cars were recalled for defects in 1977 than were made.

This is a book about physical resources and political power. Whoever controls world resources controls the world in a way that mere occupation of territory cannot match. When vital materials are in heavy demand and short supply, that fact alone gives power to some people over others. Even the illusion of scarcity creates power. Indeed, the market operates almost totally on illusion. As a variety of materials become scarcer and more expensive, estimating their future availability becomes a political act. Every estimate published by governments and corporations has a purpose. Figuring out the purpose is often a good starting point for solving the puzzle.

Two questions impelled me to write this book. One was whether the world was really running out of everything, as it seemed. I wanted a better sense of the human prospect. Were the gloomy predictions of the Club of Rome computer, that we would be out of this or that in so many years, to be taken seriously? Was the world ignoring, at its peril, the growing chorus of Cassandras? Or were the baleful prophesies themselves merely symptoms of the gathering pessimism, cries of anguish dressed as science? Are we running out? On the answer to that question hangs the whole future of politics. A world of scarcity is a world of inevitable struggle.

The other question has to do with the *control* of resources. Who decides what resources are developed, what they cost, where they go? Clearly, the two questions are related. Whether there is scarcity or abundance of particular materials at particular times and places depends on human decisions. I wanted to know how these decisions are made. The power to make them was shifting. Certainly this was true in the case of oil.

The planet is indeed finite. There is only so much copper, phosphates, zinc, or petroleum buried in the earth and only so much land on which to grow food. We will try to make a rough inventory of five critical resource systems—energy, nonfuel minerals, food, water, and human skill. All these resources have become increasingly integrated into global systems of control. How these systems of control operate determines which people in which parts of the world are hungry, cold, or out of work. Our interest is in who controls them, how they developed, and by what plans they are operated.

We will look at the strategies of the great oil companies, the metals processors, the global food conglomerates, and other multinational corporations, in uneasy partnership with governments, for maintaining control over the major resource systems. What plans do the owners and managers of the global resource systems have for navigating the great transition from the oil economy, on which the prosperity of the last one hundred years has been based, to a civilization resting on a new set of fuels and materials?

I am neither geologist, agronomist, limnologist, demographer, nor economist. Before beginning research on multinational corporations ten years ago, my contact with the energy and food systems began and ended at the local shopping center. My acquaintance with the water system was somewhat deeper because I have a well that goes dry periodically. Minerals were of no interest at all; I was barely conscious of using any. During the research for an earlier book, *Global Reach,* I came to realize that labor was being organized into a world resource system.

To try to understand one global resource system is a lifetime job in itself. Whatever would possess one to take on five? My only defense is a feeling of being driven to it by the two overarching questions: Is scarcity real? How is the control over resources in the post-OPEC era changing and what does it mean? These seem to me inescapable issues, and they defy being cut up into digestible parts. A political analysis that skirts them is not worth much. Citizens without an informed view of the basic resource choices have taken themselves out of the democratic process. Their only role is to be part of the nightly television audience that the networks rent to advertisers, and politicians court with smiles.

Any canvas for portraying resource systems must try to be global, but this inquiry emphasizes American use of world resources. Whether Americans have enough is a question intimately related to the scarcity that faces people in Europe, Japan, and the Third World. One could start with a different angle of vision and emphasize the problems of Europe or the Third World. But in this book global scarcity is the backdrop for considering what is happening to the world's richest people. Properly diffident at first about not being a card-carrying resource expert, I soon came to realize that anyone who is making national policy in the executive branch or in the Congress cannot avoid basic decisions about the availability and control of resources, and neither can those who put them in office. The mountains of documents grew—estimates and counterestimates, claims and counterclaims. This book is one citizen's effort to make sense out of it all. In a bibliographical chapter at the end of the book I review the material on which the book is based.

The five systems are so interrelated that to examine them separately is somewhat arbitrary. Food cannot be grown without water. Electrical energy cannot be generated without copper, aluminum, or some other metallic wire. To understand scarcity we need to see how the systems fit together. The most crucial resource is of course energy, for it is the key to all the others, including human energy. If energy were unlimited, it could be used to produce limitless quantities of drinkable water from the sea, to synthesize food for billions of people, or to excavate rich mineral deposits at the very depths of the earth or in outer space. It is the resource for gaining access to all the other resources.

What resources the world contains is still largely veiled. What one finds depends upon what one looks for, how hard one looks, and where one looks. A good part of the world economy runs on guesswork about resources. Considerable money rides on whether the pushers of nuclear power or the antinuclear activists prevail, whether a major effort to develop solar energy is undertaken, whether government-funded international grain reserves are created, whether coal-fired systems are deemed safe enough to be developed, and a host of other questions.

Every generation is by definition an era of transition, but our own time portends bigger changes in the organization of the planet than we have had for at least five hundred years. A crisis of values has swept across both the capitalist and socialist worlds. The rapid process of decolonization following four hundred years of imperial conquest in Asia, Africa, and Latin America is far from completed. Profound struggles are taking place or are in the offing—between rich and poor nations over their share of the world product, within the industrial world over sharing resources and markets, and between cities and regions within nations over access to food, fuel, minerals, and water. The world is already in the midst of a transition to a postpetroleum civilization.

We do not yet know what the material base of that civilization is to be or whether the alternative materials to sustain the present industrial order can be developed in time. A global struggle over resource distribution is already underway. A key political question is whether the holders of power over the present resource systems will control the next. War has been a favorite way for great nations to meet their resource needs. If there is another world war, the conflict will most likely be over what the industrial states have come to regard as the elements of survival. Oil, of course, but also iron, copper, uranium, cobalt, wheat, and water.

The age of scarcity has speeded up the global division of labor. The rise of the multinational corporation has created the Global Factory. These changes in world production have transformed the nature of power itself, including military power. The world continues to spend $400 billion or so a year on armaments; statesmen still make a religion of "national security." The headlines read like a travelogue of horror—Iran, Angola,

Chad, Nicaragua, Zaire, Lebanon, Vietnam, and other distant battle-fields. Behind it all, the riches of the earth are being bought up, milled, melted, canned, shipped, dammed, and piped. More than diplomatic talk or chronic warfare, these activities are shaping our civilization and our future.

CHAPTER II

Oil: Enough for What?

1.

THE CURRENT DEBATE about energy confuses three crucial questions: Is industrial civilization running out? Who or what is responsible? What can be done about it? For affluent societies, running out is so new an idea that it is easier to deny than to understand. Adjusting to a chronic energy shortage is especially difficult because oil, the blood of industrial civilization, has always been so cheap. It still costs less than a penny a gallon to drill, pump, and transport Arabian oil to a Persian Gulf port. At that point the 7,000 percent markup begins. Suspicion runs high, since governments and oil companies regularly use panic to persuade the public to support all manner of disagreeable ideas, such as rationing, high prices, and subsidies to giant energy corporations. The side effects of panic are treated with doses of complacency. It is all a way of making things ''clearer than truth,'' as Dean Acheson once put it, explaining how one sold foreign policy. But having been used so long as a marketing aid, panic has lost the power to shock. Instead of inducing people to curb the suicidal impulses of modern civilization, the hysteria about energy has caused cynicism and emotional paralysis.

How can people who wait in line at gas stations assess what is happening? Bombarded by experts who agree on nothing except that each alone is right, citizens have lost control of the resources that shape their lives. This chapter is a personal effort to understand the oil crisis. The next chapter is an effort to understand what the governments and the oil companies are up to, and the third is a look at alternative energy sources and where the politics of the postpetroleum era are leading.

The world uses 30,000 gallons of petroleum every second; about 10,000 gallons a second are consumed somewhere in the United States. The multinational companies that still control almost 40 percent of the world's oil-flow act as world rationers, distributing oil to various parts of the world as profits and politics dictate. They are by default the energy planners for the United States.

In most "free enterprise" economies the state has limited administrative powers to control consumption, to develop energy sources, and to choose sources of supply. But such governmental planning powers are primitive in the United States. The government is not in the energy business. It gives concessions to private companies on its own oil lands much in the manner of the sheiks of Kuwait in the good old days. It cannot determine where its imported oil will come from. The market's invisible hand—a complex network of executives of major oil companies, traders on telephones making "spot sales," tanker fleet owners, pipeline companies, independents, jobbers, and a large supporting cast—determines the fate and the route of particular barrels of oil.

The President can cajole, the secretary of energy can establish regulations, but oil entrepreneurs in collaboration with oil sheiks and oil technocrats determine the petroleum traffic.

Oil was the answer to a peculiarly American prayer, for it made possible the world's first society in perpetual motion. To achieve greatness the United States spent oil as the empires of the past spent blood. Oil fitted the requirements of modern industrial society and the American continent in particular because of four characteristics. It was cheap, easily transportable, readily available to anyone prepared to spend energy to get energy, and relatively clean. These advantages could serve the national mania for motion. In a perceptive essay George W. Pierson of Yale identified the decisive element in American history as the "M-Factor." What made Americans different was their mobility. With the end of the frontier the whole country became a place to wander in. Once the oil began to flow and the internal combustion engine was invented to burn it up, the restlessness of the American spirit was packaged for sale.

The energy industry is built on the technology of selling trips. It was not so long ago that oil companies sponsored "take to the road for fun" campaigns and invited every American to join the "getaway people." About 53 percent of America's oil goes for motion of one sort of another, compared with 28 percent among Europeans. We assume that what some have called our motion sickness is a consequence of being spread across a large expanse of earth. There must be something to this, but Russians and Chinese, who live in even huger land empires, are not on the move like Americans. Motion is a basic American need growing out of the national character. We are a nation of go-getters, comers, movers, shakers, ever contemptuous of the "stick-in-the-mud" and always ready to respond to political slogans like John F. Kennedy's promise to "get the country moving again."

The celebrated American love affair with the automobile led to a host of progeny. The Interstate Highway and Defense System, a $27 billion program to transform the face of the country, to take one example, was as much an expression of manifest destiny as the push to the frontier. This essential playground for the nation's cars was originally sold as a civil defense measure. (Why target populations would be better off at one end of the road than at the other was never clear, and the pretense that the high-speed highways would save lives rather than take them began to look foolish.) But highways and motor vehicles, as the president of the American Association of State Highway Officials put it, had become "the keystone of the American way of life."

Buying highways meant buying motels, quick food eateries, extra hospitals to service the victims of highway mayhem, an outdoor life and sporting industry, and the culture of suburbia. The roads cut up cities, sped by farms, and connected markets. The highway system was the nation's only physical plan, and more than anything else it determined the appearance of cities and the stretches in between. In choosing the automobile as the engine of growth, the highway and automotive planners scrapped mass transit. General Motors, Exxon (then Esso), and the Goodyear Tire Company bought up the San Francisco trolley, tore up the track, and replaced it with Esso-drinking buses rolling on Goodyears. In the name of progress, GM, Firestone, and Standard Oil of California ripped up the Los Angeles interurban train system. In all, 100 electric railway systems in forty-five cities were destroyed as a result of similar conspiracies. (General Motor's treasurer, H. C. Grossman, was fined one dollar for sacrificing the antitrust laws to the automobile.)

The petroleum industry accounts for a fifth of the entire capital investment of the country, and it has lubricated our politics. "Oil controlled the Republican convention of 1920," William Allen White wrote a few years later. "It worked through the Senate cabal, led by the irreconcilables— who were so busy hating Wilson that they became easy victims of the greed of oil." Oil money catapulted to national leadership such recent major political figures as Sam Rayburn, Lyndon Johnson, Robert Kerr, and Russell Long, who faithfully looked after the interests of the industry. "I represent oil," Oklahoma Senator Robert S. Kerr, who made millions in drilling, stated flatly in 1962. So also does his successor, Russell B. Long, who, though more modestly oil-rich (through oil leases in his home state of Louisiana), looks after industry taxes as chairman of the Senate Finance Committee. An oilman, Sid Richardson, participated in the meeting in Paris in 1952 at which Dwight Eisenhower decided to run for the Presidency. (After Ike returned to private life, three oilmen, including W. Alton Jones, head of Cities Service, bought him his farm in Gettysburg.) Lyndon Johnson, another petroleum-propelled politician, dominated

American politics more than any other single individual in the Eisenhower years.

Richard Nixon launched his national political career with a "secret fund," a modest gratuity from a few oilmen, which he was forced to defend with the celebrated "Checkers" speech, and twenty years later he looked to the oil industry to finance his last campaign. The Committee to Re-Elect the President received $5 million from oil sources, including illegal contributions of $100,00 each from Gulf, Phillips, and Ashland, and another $5.7 million from 413 individuals connected with the oil business. (Between 1967 and 1972, Gulf dispensed a $10 million secret fund to political campaigns. Even a small company like Ashland invested $800,000 in similar ways.) The high oil company executive traveling with large sums to some discreet monetary laundry became for a time an American folk figure.

So also the oil-rich eccentric who spreads his political largesse in launching right-wing crusades (H. L. Hunt) or bankrolling joint ventures with the intelligence services (Howard Hughes). The man who is reputed to be the sole surviving billionaire, Daniel K. Ludwig, made most of his money in tankers, a crucial corner of the oil system which made Aristotle Onassis rich enough for Jacqueline Kennedy. John J. McCloy, the quintessential Wall Street Lawyer, symbol of patriotic service for two generations—High Commissioner to Germany, Disarmament Advisor, special envoy to Krushchev, key figure in the Cuban missile crisis—has the distinction of representing all the major oil companies and in this capacity calling on every attorney general from Kennedy on to urge relaxation of the antitrust laws so that his clients could get together and plan a common strategy in the Middle East. "The trouble with this country," Franklin D. Roosevelt once said, "is that you can't win an election without the oil bloc, and you can't govern with it."

Oil has been the key to political power in the U.S. because the automotive-petroleum complex has dominated the economy as nowhere else. It derives its power from a set of deeply rooted American fantasies that the dream packagers of Madison Avenue have put to effective use. They have been selling the car to three generations of Americans as a means to escape boredom and exercise vicarious power. The annual trade-in has been fueled by a never-ending "horsepower gap," which renders last year's model hopelessly sluggish. Until the Energy Crisis, the promise each year was more power, speed, and fierceness and more models named for tigers, cougars, cobras, barracudas, and other symbols of the fast getaway. The fact that Americans are so eagerly seduced into viewing steel boxes with splashes of chrome as a sex object or talisman on which to lavish love, water, and carwax has kept two generations of sociologists busy. "Why on earth do you need to study what's changing about this country?" a man in Muncie, Indiana, asked Robert and Helen Lynd in 1925 when they were doing research for their study *Middletown.* "I can tell you in just four letters: A U T O."

Woodrow Wilson thought the automobile was "spreading socialist feeling in this country." The traffic jam did become an equalizer of a sort, pinning bank presidents and plumbers alike in the same creeping caravans to their respective places of work. But in fact the car reinforced isolation, the breakdown of community, and competitive individualism. From private house to family car to place of work, it was possible to avoid all human encounters. The suburbs grew. Shopping centers became shopping malls. A detached house and a patch of lawn became the indispensable symbol of having left the ranks of the poor. The automobile was the chisel for cutting a new face for the American continent.

2.

In the process, the automotive-petroleum complex also came to dominate the economy. Making money from the automobile accounts for 4.2 percent of the gross national product. One out of every six men and women in the work force is engaged in a line of work directly related to the automobile. Almost 90 percent of long-distance hauling is by truck, and this fact has created another oil-based empire, the Teamsters Union. The dominance of oil put its peculiar stamp on the economic system. The government-oil nexus has been a model for the planning system that now operates in the other strategic heights of the U.S. economy dominated by the multinational corporations.

As John Blair has shown so effectively in his study *The Control of Oil,* the industry is concentrated. Indeed, oil has been a way to keep private wealth concentrated, not only in the same corporate enterprises but in the same families. The peculiar characteristic of oil, its mobility—or fugacity, as geologists call it—makes it a substance easy to monopolize and to control from oil well to gas station. Exercising such control requires huge amounts of capital and relatively few people, and this happy circumstance has produced extraordinary profits. In the last century large landowners became the new oil-rich because the gushers were on their property. To be sure, not everyone who tapped oil struck it rich. Edwin Drake, who brought in the first oil well in the United States in 1859, died a pauper. The year his well started producing, the price per barrel was twenty dollars; a year later it was ten cents. But those who survived created the greatest fortunes in the country.

The petroleum industry, dominated by a few families, took a lease on 25 percent of all the privately owned land in the country. The descendants of the nineteenth-century oil barons have for the most part consolidated their family wealth by diversifying their holdings into the greater petroleum economy. Thus the Rockefeller family still owns about 2 percent of Exxon but has expanded its economic power by heavy investment in other products made possible by oil: petrochemicals, automobiles, aerospace, resorts, the computers that keep track of a nation on the move, and the banks that financed the explosive growth. So also the Rockefeller partners and employees, such as Charles Pratt and Edward Harkness of Jersey Standard and Henry Clay Folger of Socony (now Mobil), who became the social arbiters and philanthropists of the twentieth century as the railroad, shipping, and cotton kings had been seventy-five years before. The Mellons, who still own about 16 percent of Gulf, have kept their fortune intact in much the same way. Their names are engraved on such monuments of American civilization as Pratt House in New York City, where the Council on Foreign Relations meets; Harkness Tower at Yale; and the Folger Shakespeare Library and the Mellon Collection in Washington. The great oil companies these families founded became the pioneer multinationals and the models of the modern conglomerate.

The power of the oil companies would be quite sufficient in itself to arouse public suspicion even if they were all run by St. Francis or Mother Theresa. But when prices go up and lines form at the gas station, suspicion gives way to fury. Exxon is spending 78 percent of its annual $18 million network-TV and magazine advertising budget to promote itself rather than its products, and it is doing so because 69 percent of the public, according to a 1979 CBS–*New York Times* poll, thinks the companies are profiteering on the energy crisis. Gulf's profits in the first quarter of 1979 jumped 61 percent and Texaco's 81 percent, and those of Standard Oil of Ohio, which has a large share of the Alaska North Slope, increased 303 percent. In 1978 the seven major oil companies were selling about 38 percent of all the oil moving in world trade, about the same proportion as in the days of cheap oil. Return on investment capital was higher than in the years before the oil-producing nations joined forces to create OPEC and to engineer the 400 percent increase in the price of oil.

Some of the giants are of course doing better than others. Mobil increased its profits 16 percent in the first half of 1978, mostly from its nonenergy business and phenomenal luck in bringing in wells in the Gulf of Mexico, while Texaco's fell 28 percent (because of its dependence upon domestic wells and an excess of overly expensive, antiquated gas stations). Annual statements are somewhat misleading. Exxon's profits in 1977 were a mere $2.4 billion, an 8 percent drop from the year before, but most of the decline was due to the weakness of the dollar, which made payoff of foreign debts more expensive. In the first quarter of 1979, Exxon's profit for three months was almost $1 billion, a gain of 7.4 percent over the previous year. The company plans a $24 billion capital expansion program, virtually all of it to be financed over four years with its own cash. As C. C. Pocock, a Shell director, exclaimed in a 1978 interview with *Time,* "There's no business like oil business."

Ever since the Energy Crisis achieved the status of a national myth in 1973—it must now be capitalized in the middle of a sentence like Free World or American Dream—the tide of anger against the oil companies has ebbed and flowed. For a brief political moment in 1974 the public fury was so intense that the oil companies became good populist targets. Senator Henry Jackson launched his 1976 Presidential campaign by treating the country's leading oil company executives to the sort of television scourging formerly reserved for Hollywood Communists and labor racketeers; forty-five senators lifted their finger to the wind and voted to break up the oil companies. It was folk wisdom that the crisis was exaggerated, that the 50 percent rise in heating bills and the doubling of gasoline prices was making the companies rich, that the companies were in league with the sheiks against the consumer—and it was all true. But by 1978 the problem of the oil companies was neither nationalization nor divestiture but what to do with their spare cash.

Exxon, Senator Edward M. Kennedy pointed out, "could tomorrow buy J.C. Penny, Du Pont, Goodyear, and Anheuser-Busch using only its accumulated cash and liquid assets." At one point, according to Mobil Chairman Rawleigh Warner, "there were 3,000 bills in the hopper in the Congress, all of them aimed directly at doing something dreadful to the oil industry." But by 1979 nothing more dreadful than deregulation and profitable price hikes had occurred. To be sure, after the fall of the Shah of Iran there was a new surge of anger. The new Iranian government dramatically cut oil exports, and prices at the gas pump rose to more than one dollar a gallon. U.S. officials accused the companies of stepping up the price well above what the increase in the cost of a barrel of crude oil warranted. The companies had overcharged the public some $2 billion, the Department of Energy charged. Howard Baker, the Republican leader of the Senate, warned the companies that they were again in danger of being nationalized. But so far the vehicle for expressing public anger has not been legislation.

How are we to explain this? Is anger simply a function of time spent waiting in gas station lines? The 1979 shortage witnessed the same hysterical behavior as in the 1973–74 crisis—screams, threats, assaults (including one on a pregnant woman) and an occasional shooting. Public relations have played a crucial role in diffusing public anger. The same oil companies that had sponsored years of "take to the road for fun" campaigns and other celebrations of carefree consumption—"The U.S.A. and its 205 million people use all we can get" ran a full-page advertisement in *The New York Times* by the American Petroleum Institute in April 1971—became self-serving Cassandras. Oil would run out unless there were new tax incentives to encourage exploitation. Profits were just not large enough, Charles E. Spahr, chairman of Standard Oil of Ohio, testified before Congress, to meet the huge capital needs of the coming era. A variety of other special interests also saw the crisis as opportunity. It was time to deregulate natural gas, to build the Alaska pipeline, which had been stoutly opposed by environmentalists, to eliminate unprofitable airline routes, to permit the trucking industry to operate longer and heavier vehicles. The new conservationists in the House of Representatives voted to ban the use of fuel in busing programs to achieve racially balanced schools.

The oil companies became the Medicis of television, patrons of operas, ballets, and entertainment "specials." Mobil had a weekly message on the Op-Ed page of *The New York Times* castigating environmentalists, sheiks, labor unions, and other sinister forces that were obstructing the flow of oil. "We think we're adding some gaiety and sparkle to American life," its public relations manager explained. "And we're also helping ourselves get a hearing with opinion leaders." It was a triumph in what the companies call "communication."

The incorporated oil fortunes, known as the Seven Sisters—Exxon, Gulf, Mobil, Shell, Texaco, BP, and Socal—were built by gamblers and buccaneers. In an age that longs for stability and prizes social planning as an ideal if not as policy, the robber baron image is something worth a great deal of money to expunge. Yet it would be a mistake to ascribe the paralysis of public policy in energy matters to the wizardry of Madison Avenue alone. Petroleum moguls would seem to make excellent political scapegoats, but they have escaped unscathed so far because too many other interests in the country are too deeply enmeshed in the petroleum economy to risk disturbing it.

By cooperating with oil companies all sorts of money is to be made. According to a 1977 report of the Senate Committee on Foreign Economic Policy, U.S. banks have on deposit in the U.S. and overseas some $50 billion in "petrodollars." Sheik Rashid of Dubai borrowed $230 million from a syndicate of seventy banks to finance a natural gas project. Qatar, another Gulf oil sheikdom, took out a $350 million loan from Chase Manhattan's London subsidiary and two other banks. In all, there is more than $12 billion on loan from U.S. banks to OPEC governments, most of which are thought to be much better risks than New York City.

Construction companies are participating profitably in the oil economy and have no interest in seeing it changed. Harbert Construction of Birmingham, Alabama, and the Paul N. Howard Company of Greensboro, North Carolina, have a $50 million contract in Abu Dhabi; Foster Wheeler, a $70 million refinery expansion project in Kuwait; and J.A. Jones, $385 million in construction projects in Saudi Arabia. A Las Vegas firm is putting up housing for 27,000 "guest workers" for the Saudis, and Brown and Root had a contract to build a $2 billion port facility for the Shah of Iran. Lawyers, lobbyists, public opinion consultants, public relations specialists, and other lubricators of the wheels of commerce, having picked up considerable business since 1973, see no reason to disturb either the oil companies or their delicate relations with the producing countries. The potential coalition of political forces that could curb the power of the oil companies or make them publicly accountable has not yet emerged.

3.

The principal reason why the United States and the rest of the industrial world have not developed a serious response to the Energy Crisis is that the crisis is not taken seriously. The prevailing public attitude is that there is really plenty of oil, that the companies have been creating an artificial shortage in order to keep control of supplies and to keep prices and profits high. As we shall soon explore, these suspicions are not groundless. In the wake of the Iranian crisis, companies held back supplies to "build up our reserves" and sold oil from Caribbean refineries normally destined for the U.S. on the "spot market" for double the OPEC price. All of this raised prices at the gas station even higher.

Is there plenty of oil? The real question is, Plenty for what? There are trillions of barrels of oil in the ground, perhaps as many as 6 trillion, but much of it is like a fortune in a locked safe without a key. Unless oil is actually produced and made available on a schedule to meet the demand of industrial civilization, a crisis cannot be averted. There are technical, economic, and, above all, political reasons why oil in the ground cannot be automatically translated into trips, hot showers, or air-cooled offices.

To enter the arcane world of the professional oil guessers, one must learn the language of the industry. Oilmen distinguish between "proven reserves"—pools of oil "recoverable at current prices and with current technology"—and "ultimately recoverable reserves"—oil that could be extracted from the earth with new technologies and higher prices. Cassandras talk about the one and Panglosses emphasize the other. The World Energy Conference that met in September 1977 and included twenty-nine specialists employed by major oil companies decided that the "ultimately recoverable reserves" are somewhere between 1.8 trillion and 2.2 trillion barrels. About three-fifths of all this oil has been found, but less than one-fifth of it has been produced. As Steven A. Schneider of the Institute for International Studies at Berkeley points out, "For every barrel of oil consumed during the 118-year oil era, there are four barrels of oil—discovered and undiscovered—still in the ground." Since one barrel of oil (42 gallons) will run a car about 500 miles or heat a house in the Boston area at 70 degrees for three or four winter days, and since the whole world in 1977 used only 16.9 billion barrels, it would seem that reports of the impending death of the petroleum era are at least premature.

Moreover, the ultimately recoverable reserves, recent surveys by institutes in Austria, France, and the Soviet Union suggest, may in fact considerably exceed the standard consensus. Mexico, which in 1971 was credited with 3.6 billion barrels, now turns out, perhaps, to have more than 100 billion. The estimate for Iraq's oil reserves has been more than doubled. Peter Odell, energy consultant to the British Government, thinks the petroleum era has at least two generations to go. "The so-called 'generally accepted oil shortage,' " he says, "is the outcome of commercially oriented interests rather than a statement of the essential realities of the oil resources of the world."

The extent of proven reserves is information in the exclusive control of oil companies. Reserves increase whenever and wherever companies choose to drill and are lucky. Oil may be known to exist in great abundance in particular beds of porous rock deep in the ground, but if no company thinks it can make a satisfactory profit recovering it, the oil never becomes part of the world's proven reserves. An 18 to 20 percent return on investment is the key to unlocking oil.

The state of world reserves is far more a matter of economics and politics than geology. Proven reserves are created only when companies actually recover oil. Where drilling is done has no relationship to the level of ultimately recoverable reserves. Thus, Latin America has 166 billion barrels, three-quarters of which are still in the ground. Africa has 160 billion, Asia 131 billion, and the Middle East 663 billion; in each case 90 percent or more are waiting for the drill. Two-thirds of the active oil rigs in the world operate in the United States; there are twice as many oil wells in Kansas as in the entire continent of South America, and three times as many in Arkansas as in all of Africa. The digging of the United States is well advanced. Half of the ultimately recoverable reserves are already gone.

Since the 1950s, U.S. companies have shifted their investment from the American continent to the Middle East. Backed by the military might of the United States and America's controlling voice in the world economy, the case for putting their capital into cheap Middle East oil instead of tired oil fields back home was obvious. In 1956, 16,000 wells were drilled in the U.S.; by 1971 the number had fallen to 7,000. Because of the abundance and cheapness of Middle East oil and the willingness of the sheiks to make only modest demands for a share of the profits, the expenditures per barrel of oil had fallen 25 percent.

There are two kinds of oil fields, as Steven Schneider puts it, "subsistence fields, which you get along on, and bonanza fields, which make you rich." Only 1 percent of the world's oil fields, he calculates, are in the bonanza category, but those that are "account for three-quarters of the world's resources." The bonanza fields in Texas and Oklahoma were discovered in the 1920s. Twenty years ago M. King Hubbert, a leading oil geologist, warned that the United States was about to run out of oil because new oil was becoming harder and harder to recover. The "continuously diminishing returns in the amount of oil discovered," Hubbert argued, means that "the inference can hardly be avoided that the pond is fished out." Barry Commoner, reviewing other estimates, especially a 1970 report of a study committee of the National Petroleum Council, blames falling production and reserves in the U.S. on the lack of effort of the oil companies rather than on the accelerating stinginess of nature. In fact, both factors are involved—increasingly unfavorable geological conditions for finding new oil as the bonanza fields are depleted, and deliberate company choices about where they want to spend their money drilling or whether indeed they want to drill at all.

In the years following the Energy Crisis of 1973–74, the large oil companies doubled their debt, ostensibly in order to invest in domestic oil and gas. According to the Office of Energy Policy and Planning in the White House, the top 18 U.S. oil companies increased their cash reserves from $1.9 billion at the end of 1973 to $4.9 billion by the end of 1976. But reserves and production for the industry as a whole fell 10 percent between 1973 and 1978. In 1978, however, according to a study by energy analysts at Salomon Brothers, the industry spent $11.6 billion drilling for oil and gas and added some 1.3 billion barrels to the proven reserves.

The issues are these: Given the national energy emergency, why aren't the oil companies doing enough to cope with it? What would it take to induce them to fulfill the national need? Is this a price Americans should pay? It is financially risky to dig new holes. Exxon, Mobil, and Champlin, for example, spent almost one billion dollars drilling off the Florida coast in 1974, and five companies spent $150 million drilling in the Gulf of Alaska. Most of this drilling has now been abandoned. Oil companies prefer to pump oil from old holes that suddenly became "economic" because of higher prices, but when they do this they are depleting reserves rather than increasing them. They are using up what has already been counted rather than adding to the overall supply.

Whether drilling is economically attractive thus depends upon the cost of finding oil in a particular place, the chances of keeping it if you find it, and the allure of alternative investments. Andrew R. Flower, an analyst for British Petroleum who was a member of the Massachusetts Institute of Technology Workshop on Alternative Energy Strategies, a study group of oilmen and economists, explains why the costs of oil recovery can vary so widely:

> Actually oil is found in small spaces in porous rock, somewhat like water in a sponge. It seeps slowly through the porous material until it is trapped by impervious rock, often as a layer between water and gas. The oil is usually under pressure, and a well releases that pressure; the oil flows into the well, where it either rises to the surface (if the pressure in the field is sufficient) or is pumped out. Oil recovery under natural pressure is considered "primary" production, and in the U.S. today such production recovers on the average about 25 percent of the oil in a reservoir. "Secondary" recovery is achieved, in fields where it is feasible, by pumping water or gas into the reservoir to produce more pressure on the oil. "Tertiary" recovery, not yet widely applied, can sometimes be achieved if the viscosity of the oil is lowered so that it flows more easily, either by heating the oil (by injecting steam, for example) or by injecting chemicals into the reservoir. Secondary or tertiary methods have increased recovery in the U.S. from about 25 percent of the oil in place in the 1940's to about 32 percent now. Most of the world's oil is produced from conventional fields by these methods and by the recovery of natural-gas liquids as a by-product of natural gas.

Whether there is oil scarcity or glut at any moment or in any place depends more upon what wells are drilled, where pipelines are located, which customers are preferred, than upon what maps and photographs of the earth's crust may show. Some countries are surveyed and some are not. Such choices are rather more likely to be made because of the political leanings of the regime than because of the qualities of the local rock formations. A number of Third World countries that import oil are believed to have ample petroleum to meet a substantial portion of their needs. Jamaica, for example, one of many poor countries close to bankruptcy because of the high cost of importing oil, is supposed to have enough to meet 50 percent of its requirements. But oil companies avoid "unstable" regimes, and none is more unstable than one that might nationalize foreign-owned wells. Only recently has the World Bank begun a major program to finance the development of Third World oil fields. Exxon's president, while his public relations department was warning of the worldwide energy crisis, tried to stop the program. The development of new sources outside company control threatened to weaken the control of the world oil supply by the Seven Sisters.

Ultimately, determining future oil prospects hinges on predictions about the behavior of companies and governments rather than on guesses about the contents of the earth. Will the Russians have to import oil and thus cut into the world supply, as the CIA has warned? Will the OPEC nations produce enough oil to meet the growing dependence of the West? Companies control the immense global pipelines through which more than 45 million barrels of oil flow every day from producer to consumer. At any of a number of points, business decisions and political decisions can intervene to slow down or speed up the flow or to divert it from one place to another. These business and political decisions affect the estimating process itself. John Blair, who for many years studied the oil companies for the Senate, argued in *The Control of Oil* that the oil giants engage in "planned and systematic restriction of output at home and abroad" in order to maintain control of supply and to keep prices high. The estimating process is part of the strategy of control.

It is an exercise of power because it is designed to influence behavior. Like unemployment and inflation rates, which are a form of government advertising designed to reassure investors and encourage patriotism, petroleum estimates are designed to affect the psychology of consumers and governments, eliciting resignation to high prices from the one and subsidies from the other.

Estimates rise and fall depending upon what is in the interests of the companies to disclose. No independent evaluation of their accuracy exists. In general, companies have had an interest in understating reserves to keep prices up. After World War II, for example, Christopher Rand, a former oil company executive, tells us, the companies not only refused to follow up on promising geological leads in Iraq but "kept the information it had acquired regarding the nation's oil potential largely secret from the Iraqi government." In 1950, *Oil and Gas Journal* estimated world proven reserves (outside the socialist countries) at 72 billion barrels. But in fact we now know that 230 billion barrels of oil discovered before 1950 never found their way into the 1950 estimate. Part of the explanation is a complex calculating procedure under which discoveries are backdated to the year of discovery so that as a field proves to be more productive than originally assumed the year of discovery is given credit for the additional oil. But, as the MIT workshop on alternative energy reports, there was a surplus in oil production capacity in the 1950s and hence "little incentive for oil explorers to speed the evaluation of new reserves." Sometimes the oil companies have an incentive to err on the optimistic side. A few years ago the Library of Congress sent a questionnaire to the fifteen largest energy companies asking them to assume a number of political events devoutly wished for by oil and gas producers, such as decontrol of oil and gas prices and no divestiture of the energy companies. All twelve companies who responded projected an increase in production in 1990 over what they produced in 1975.

Much of the public misunderstanding about energy scarcity arises from a failure to distinguish between the problem of short-term shortages and the historic prospect of petroleum exhaustion. The former is a function of a world market which is neither free nor perfectly controlled and which often operates in jerky and disruptive ways. Oil does not get to where it is needed because jobbers may be stockpiling it, waiting for higher prices. "Daisy chain" resales of shipments of crude oil from one part of a corporate enterprise to another to increase profits or to shelter profits from taxes, according to a staff report of the House Subcommittee on Oversight and Investigations, are "an area of real abuse." Oil companies reduce refinery runs when, as in 1978, world oil prices weaken, and the consequences are exaggerated shortages such as occurred a year later. The U.S. Government diverts large amounts of oil to the Strategic Petroleum Reserve, and this increases the shortage. When Iran cut its exports 90 percent in 1979, the companies held on to their stocks, claiming that "prudent management" required them to. But despite the sharp drop in Iranian production, world production was up 4.7 percent over the previous year, and U.S. imports and domestic production were up more than 6 percent.

Targets for finger pointing abound. The oil companies hoard and divert. Jobbers engage in price gouging. Drivers "top off" their tanks, another form of hoarding. Sheiks, ayatollahs, and incompetent administrators from the Department of Energy who send the companies conflicting signals all contribute to the short-term shortage. There is a certain amount of conspiracy that goes on all the time in the oil business. A variety of actors try to maximize their profits or assure long-term supplies, and the consequences are disastrous.

The world oil system operates according to plan, but the planning system works for the companies, not for the public. The issue is not whether oil company profits are "too high." In a multinational corporation the opportunities via transfer pricing, tax havens, and other cosmetic miracles of the accountant's art are so rich that profit and loss statements are impressionistic at best. An argument about what a "just profit" is has the aura of a medieval debate. The important point about profits is that, whatever the level, they do not seem to get oil delivered where it is needed at prices people can afford.

Let us return to the matter of proven world resources. Consider the chart below:

TOTAL WORLD—RESERVES AND CUMULATIVE PRODUCTION TO THE END OF 1975

	Remaining proven reserves (billion barrels)	Cumulative production to end of 1975 (billion barrels)
OPEC: Saudi Arabia	152	23
Other Middle East	208	61
Other OPEC	90	55
Total OPEC	450	139
North America	40	133
Western Europe	25	2
Rest of the WOCA*	40	17
Total Non-OPEC	105	152
Total WOCA	555	291
Communist Countries	103	50
Total World	658	341

(Source: *Oil and Gas Journal,* Dec. 29, 1975)
* World Outside Communist Areas

This particular chart has caused a good deal of alarm. In 1975 the MIT Workshop on Alternative Energy Strategies concluded on the strength of such information that "the supply of oil will fail to meet increasing demand before the year 2000, most probably between 1975 and 1995. . . ." Predictions of blackouts and brownouts all across North America in the early 1980s are becoming commonplace. Such pessimistic judgments are arrived at by comparing the rate at which oil from proven reserves can be produced with the rate of projected demand.

For most people, myself included, exponential growth is a mystifying notion. I am normally skeptical about catastrophes predicted on the basis of graphs in which demand curves shoot out of reach of supply curves. I share the prevailing suspicion about the manipulation of information on the crisis, particularly by the oil companies. Nonetheless, I line up with the Cassandras. The reason is that demand and supply appear to be seriously out of phase. As much oil was produced and consumed in the 1960s as was produced up to that point since drilling began in Rumania in 1857.* Within the existing political framework of the world it does not appear to be possible for the industrial world to turn the trillions of barrels in the earth into kilowatts and gallons of gas fast enough. A bonanza field such as Mexico's is barely sufficient to keep the industrial world going for ten years. And there is no reason whatever to believe that the huge oil deposits in Third World countries are going to be developed on a schedule to suit the gas-guzzling nations. Because of the enormous escalation of demand, we have come, in the so-called developed world at least, to the end of the age of oil.

Exponential growth is explained to French schoolchildren with the riddle of the lily pond. Every day the number of leaves floating on the pond doubles—two leaves the second day, four the third, and so on. The pond is completely filled with leaves on the thirtieth day. On what day was the pond half full? The twenty-ninth day. Schoolchildren are dazzled by the thought that it all happens so fast.

Those who talk about exponential growth often confuse matters by attributing it to the "population explosion," but the population problem has little to do with the crisis that the industrial world faces in the 1980s. In 1976 the United States, with 5 percent of the world's population, used 29 percent of all the petroleum. Between 1975 and 1979 the annual increase in consumption ranged between 5.5 and 8 percent. The millions of new inhabitants of the earth in Asia, Africa, and Latin America consumed very little of the world supply even when their leaders undertook heroic efforts to industrialize. China, for example, increased its petroleum consumption 30 percent from 1975 to 1976 and still, with almost one billion people, managed to take only 2.5 percent of the world supply.

Energy consumption in the U.S. is no longer growing exponentially as in the early years of the century, but it is still growing fast. In 1974, as a result of the recession, energy consumption in the U.S., as elsewhere in the industrial world, declined. When recovery came, the United States slowed its increase somewhat. The gross national product increased faster than the rate of energy consumption, a fact that economists make much of but one that did not keep the U.S. from importing $45 billion worth of oil in 1978 and $55 billion in 1979. Thus, while it is fair to say that in the years since the "oil shock" the U.S. has not done significantly worse than other countries in improving its conservation efforts, it started from a plateau of profligate energy use unmatched by any other society.

---

* Actually the first oil well was probably dug on the island of Sante in 400 B.C., and the Burmese were drilling around A.D. 100. Long before the Spaniards arrived the Aztecs had discovered Mexico's petroleum riches. They burned it as incense, caulked their boats with it, and made use of it as medicine, dye, and glue.

The Swedes, by some measures, have a "higher" standard of living (per capita income, higher hourly wages, education level, etc.), but they are much less extravagant in energy use.

In the U.S. most of the reduced energy demand in the years immediately following the Energy Crisis was attributable to the reduced demand for goods in the recession. Insulation and the holding down of thermostats caused home consumption of energy to fall about 2 percent in a year. However, according to a study of the American Institute of Architects, between 25 to 50 percent of energy in old buildings and up to 80 percent in new ones is wasted. The AIA estimates that the U.S. could save one-third of its entire energy consumption by installing energy-efficient systems.

Increased use of hydroelectric power and natural gas and a 16 percent cut in energy use in the energy industry itself were among the principal factors responsible for keeping the rate of increased consumption relatively low once recovery began in 1976. But for all the talk of small cars and speed limits, the consumption of gasoline soared well over 12 percent in the mid-1970s and began to decline only after the second round of price hikes at the end of the decade.

At some point in this generation and possibly in this decade the oil era is coming to an end. This does not mean that it will all disappear, but rather that the demand for oil will exceed the *available* supply. A crisis of industrial civilization may well occur long before global supplies are exhausted or even before the day consumption overtakes production. The key to the problem is timing. Reserves may still be high, but a situation in which oil cannot be delivered to ultimate users in time to keep factories running, cars moving, and homes heated, is the definition of a crisis. In such a crisis the issue is not the number of barrels in the earth or how much oil can be produced in five years but who gets the oil that is available now. The situation is not unlike that of a large house occupied by a large family. There may, theoretically, be an inexhaustible supply of hot water because the tank can be refilled and reheated, but not everyone can take a shower at the same time.

CHAPTER III

Oil: The Politics of Transition

THE POWER OF OIL COMPANIES is rooted in their ability to control the flow of oil. For this they need not only physical access to the exploitable petroleum pool around the world but the political power to decide when and on what terms it should be pumped and distributed. Let us look at the three crucial objects of control—supply, prices, and markets—and briefly trace how in each case the power of the companies and the techniques of control are shifting.

The traditional means for controlling supply was the oil concession, a system of renting oil-rich land for sixty years or so, sometimes in perpetuity. The rentals also covered the sheiks, viziers, shahs, and other officials useful for accomplishing the orderly depletion of the local wells. The story of the early oil concessions of the Middle East is a drama of adventure, gluttony, and skulduggery with dozens of lusty characters: the Armenian Alexander Mantachof, who carried a whip, flaunted his appetite for wine and women, and dismissed criticism with an aphorism: "Only the weak are good because they are not strong enough to be bad"; Calouste Gulbenkian, who engineered the carve-up of the richest oil fields in the world by drawing a red line across a map and using it to organize a cartel of the major oil companies for exploiting the oil of the old Ottoman Empire, and received 5 percent for his efforts; T. E. Ward of Gulf, who, after meticulously accounting to the company for modest bribes for the Sheik of Kuwait (about 70,000 rupees and a Sunbeam automobile), worked out an arrangement to rent Kuwait for $35,000 a year; Ibn-Saud, the bedouin conqueror of Saudi Arabia who liked to describe how he personally chopped the limbs off his enemies with a jeweled sword, a fabled libertine who from the age of eleven until a few weeks before his death at seventy-two had sexual relations with a different woman every night save during battles and pilgrimages. He supported his high style by giving a concession of 200 million acres of oil fields to Socal for $170,000.

The old strategy of controlling supply, prices, and markets was a judicious mixture of cartelization, bribery, and flim-flam. Mostly the companies were on their own, either individually or in collaboration, but at critical moments they could count on help from friends in Whitehall or the State Department. In the Middle East, there was no national consciousness. The concessions were family affairs and hinged greatly on personal relationships. As the sheiks grew more sophisticated or greedy, the companies warmed to one another, carving out areas of cooperation, even as they competed savagely elsewhere.

The public, a variety of opinion polls keep showing, suspects the oil companies of manufacturing the Energy Crisis and of being engaged in a conspiracy of one sort or another. The companies profess an inability to understand where all the suspicion comes from. The official explanation is "atavistic fears" of bigness. But the 1920s and '30s oil company chieftains fulfilled all the legal requirements of conspiracy. They met and made agreements in clear violation of law, policy, and the free market rhetoric that fell so comfortably from their lips. One such famous occasion was the conclusion of the Achnacarry Agreement, the outgrowth of a grouse-hunting weekend in Scotland at the home of Sir Henri Deterding, chairman of Royal Dutch Shell, at which the two guests, Walter Teagle, president of Standard Oil, and Sir John Cadman, president of Anglo-Persian (now BP), drew up a far-reaching set of understandings for controlling the petroleum market. John Blair in his authoritative study *The Control of Oil* summarizes the agreement:

> 1. Accepting and maintaining as their share of markets the status quo of each member; 2. making existing facilities available to competitors on a favorable basis, but not at less than actual cost to the owner; 3. adding new facilities only as actually needed to supply increased requirements of consumers; 4. maintaining for each producing area the financial advantage of its geographical location; 5. drawing supplies from the nearest producing area; and 6. preventing any surplus production in a given geographical area from upsetting the price structure in any other area. . . . From the outset it was emphasized that the purpose of the overall agreement was to achieve a consensus among the three on general principles which would serve as "enduring" guides for the operation of "local" cartels to be set up in the various consuming countries.

Other cartel arrangements of that era included the formation of Aramco in 1947. It was a partnership of Exxon, Mobil, Texaco, and Socal in Saudi Arabia which had the double advantage for Exxon, the industry giant, of buying off its new partners, limiting their impact on international price stability, and of keeping out altogether any troublesome newcomers. In

Blair's words, "the joint venture provided a handy alternative to compe-titon." A similar arrangement was established in Iran. After Premier Mos-saddeq's attempt to nationalize Iranian oil was foiled by a CIA-supported coup, the formerly British oil preserve was divided up: 40 percent for BP; 40 percent for the five American majors; 14 percent for Shell; 6 percent for the French company CFP. The consortium would control the market-ing, while the fields would remain technically nationalized. This event marked the beginning of "oligopolistic interdependence." Old-fashioned collusion was replaced by a more complex structure for keeping prices from falling and production from rising unduly. The secret formula under which the uneasy partners operated came to light only in 1974 at the Senate Multinational Hearings. It was called Aggregate Programmed Quantity, a neat calculation for restricting the total annual production for Iran to what was wanted by the companies most abundantly supplied elsewhere. The collusive formula was more civilized then collusive meet-ings and was much easier to keep secret, but when the Shah finally dis-covered how petroleum production of his country was determined, the humiliation spurred him to become the most aggressive spokesman in OPEC for making the West pay.

Thus in their golden years the Seven Sisters, as the Federal Trade Commission study *The International Petroleum Cartel* summed it up in 1952, "controlled all the principal oil-producing areas outside the U.S., all foreign refineries, patents, and refinery technology . . . they divided the world markets between [*sic*] them, and shared pipelines and tankers thoughout the world. . . ." The whole elaborate structure made it pos-sible to maintain "artificially high prices for oil."

Two historic developments intervened to bring the old structure of control to an end. One was the intrusion, despite the elaborate alliances of the major oil companies to prevent it, of newcomers, the so-called independents. Among them was Jean Paul Getty, the owner of two inde-pendent oil companies, Tidewater and Getty oil, who in 1949 bought a concession in Saudi Arabia for a $10.5 million down payment. A shrewd oilman, Getty was well on his way to amassing a billion dollar personal fortune. The entry of a successful loner into an area once the exclusive preserve of the majors shook old relationships. Other independents quickly arrived on the scene. Most important, the eagerness of the late-comers to buy in caused the Saudi Royal Family to overcome their tradi-tional reticence about oil pricing. If Getty would pay $10.5 million before a single barrel of oil had been produced, why was Aramco paying only $28 million in a year in which oil was flowing at an unprecedented rate? Why was Aramco paying only 21 cents a barrel when Getty was offering 55 cents? Then Enrico Mattel, who ran ENI, the Italian state oil company, began undercutting the Seven Sisters in European markets, using cheap oil from the Soviet Union, which also had an interest in humbling the majors. Earlier, he had cut away at their dominance in Iran. By the late 1950s, the Japanese had arrived. Remarkably adaptable to local customs, they produced a businesslike agreement for bribing the brother-in-law of the Crown Prince of Saudi Arabia:

> Whereas the Japan Petroleum Trading Company Ltd. desires to obtain a concession from the Saudi Arabian Government that gives her the right to search and prospect oil in the Saudi Arabian territory, Mr. Taro Yamashita, president of the Japan Petroleum Trading Company Ltd. and His Excellency Kamal Adham have agreed the following:
> 1. That Mr. Hassan Khalifa agrees to cooperate with Mr. Taro Yamashita to promote the exploitation plan under the supervision of His Excellency Kamal Adham.
> 2. That the contract regarding the said concession is to be concluded between Mr. Taro Yamashita, as president of the Japan Petroleum Trading Company Ltd., and the Saudi Arabian Government. . . .
> 3. That in case the above mentioned concession is granted by the Saudi Arabian Government . . . Mr. Taro Yamashita . . . undertakes to pay His Excellency Kamal Adham two percent (2%) yearly of the share of the total net profit accruing from the said concession. . . .
> 4. That Mr. Taro Yamashita . . . will pay Two Hundred and Fifty Thousand U.S. dollars (U.S. $250,000) to His Excellency Kamal Adham within one month after the conclusion of said contract . . . and Seven Hundred and Fifty Thousand U.S. dollars (U.S. $750,000) upon sufficient amount of petroleum be [*sic*] found as to permit sound business enterprise. . . .

The Japanese were willing not only to reward cooperative individuals in the old tradition but were prepared to offer much more favorable terms for extracting and buying oil—joint ventures with minority participation instead of the old royalty arrangements or the now common 50/50 deals. All this did not help the bargaining power of the oil giants.

The second and by far the more important development was the rise of nationalism. If the dramatic quadrupling of oil prices in 1973 and the seizure of control of pricing by the oil-producing countries is viewed as the climactic encounter that changed the oil system, it was a culmination of a sixty-five-year worldwide struggle. It all began in Russia. The Bolsheviks nationalized Jersey's and Shell's oil fields. (Unaccountably Jersey, now Exxon, bought its interest in Russia from the Nobel brothers *after* the Revolution—of all its deals "one of the most ill-considered ever made," company historians conclude.) The nationalist impulse to control domestic resources spread to Latin America in the 1930s. Uruguay, Peru, Bolivia, and Mexico expropriated oil fields and set up national companies. Venezuela began demanding a greater share of revenues. Because of the huge need for oil in war and the preoccupation of the governments of the oil-consuming countries, chiefly the U.S. and Britain, in fighting Hitler and the Japanese, small countries were able to modify the rules of the game in small steps. By the end of the war the international climate had changed. State companies for controlling and exploiting resources were appearing in all sorts of places, not only in the expanded socialist world but in some of the newly independent Third World nations.

In the Middle East the decline of the old order of oil was hastened by the rise of Arab nationalism, a historic divide symbolized by Nasser's closing of the Suez Canal and the disastrous failure of the Anglo-French-Israeli invasion. The successive disappearance of the good friends of international oil—Nuri as-Said of Iraq in 1958, Marcos Jiménez of Venezuela the same year, and King Idris of Libya in 1969—brought regimes that were prepared to bargain hard with the companies. (Under King Idris the Libyans had permitted Exxon, Mobil, Texaco, Socal, and BP to make an outrageously favorable contract that cost the country millions.)

The oil giants themselves accelerated this whole process by losing a measure of control over the world oil supply. Their elaborate planning structure for keeping prices stable was beginning to crack. By the late 1950s more oil was coming onto the international market than could be channeled at satisfactory profit. Russian oil, new oil from Algeria and Libya, and the increasing production of the independents was adding to the glut. This was the era of frenetic advertising to persuade Americans and, increasingly, Europeans to keep moving.

But there was still too much oil. In 1950 the U.S. passed mandatory import quotas to keep cheap oil from ruining the U.S. market, a step that a former chief economist at the Bureau of Mines estimated cost U.S. taxpayers about $5 billion.

Monroe Rathbone, chief executive of Exxon, now had a problem. Under the 50/50 agreements, which were then standard, the producing countries would be paid a royalty based on the "posted price," but in times of glut that figure was being undercut. To keep the Indian market against Russian competiton, three of the majors had to cut their prices. They still had plenty of money to finance expansion at about 8 percent a year, as Edith Penrose concludes in her study *The International Petroleum Industry*. But in response to the world oversupply they cut the "posted price" in the Middle East 18 cents a barrel, a move that cost the producing countries $132 million in revenue. A year later the oil companies dropped the price another 10 cents. It seemed at the time like a normal business decision in response to new market conditions. But it was a historic blunder. The double price-cut galvanized the oil-producing countries into forming what the Venezuelan oil minister termed "a very exclusive club." OPEC was born in Bagdad in 1960.

In the tradition of all empires confronted with colonial rebellions the first reaction of the oil giants was to try the tactic of nonrecognition. Refusing to deal with "this so-called OPEC," the majors continued to make their arrangements with individual governments, all the while loudly and confidently predicting the demise of the cartel that controlled 80 percent of world production. But they were sufficiently concerned to hire John J. McCloy to make the case to President Kennedy that the antitrust laws should be waived so that OPEC could be confronted in the name of "national security." Only if the producer countries were faced with a common company strategy could they be kept in line. As it turned out, about all OPEC accomplished in the 1960s was to prevent further reductions in the price. Because Saudi Arabia refused to restrict its production, there was little leverage for raising them.

OPEC's opportunity was created in Libya. Oil from Libya began flowing in the early sixties, and by 1969 it was supplying one-quarter of Europe's needs. Much of it was being produced by independents who did not share the interests of the majors in the delicate arrangements for balancing supplies and controlling the world oil flow. In 1966, Armand Hammer, who had built a pencil factory for Lenin and procured Russian oil for the Germans in the 1920s, appeared in Libya with a new kind of offer. For oil concessions Hammer offered an agricultural development project and an ammonia plant to be run as a joint venture between the governments and Occidental. He soon discovered fabulous amounts of oil and for a time was the biggest producer in Libya. Then on September 1, 1969, Colonel Muammar Qadaffi and a group of younger army officers removed the oil companies' favorite, King Idris, and began a campaign to recover what he had given away. Qadaffi negotiated with Moscow to sell his oil in the East and, with the help of the prime minister, Dr. Suleiman Maghrabi, who had once worked as a lawyer for Exxon, started playing the independents off against the majors. He ordered Hammer to cut production from 680,000 to 500,000 barrels a day and thereby made the historic point that by exercising the control over production he intended to control the price. Hammer flew to see J. Kenneth Jamieson, chairman of Exxon, to persuade the giant company to replace the oil Qadaffi was withholding at cost in order to strengthen Occidental's hand at the negotiations. But the residual contempt of the major for the upstart was stronger than its obvious interest in building a common front against the radical government. Without replacement oil, Hammer promptly acceded

to the Libyan's demand, and the old price structure was breached forever.

2.

As early as the Libyan cave-in, some oil experts voiced the suspicion
that the majors didn't mind all that much about their new relationship
with the producing countries. MIT petroleum specialist Morris Adelman
accused the majors of being "agents of a foreign power." Surely they
were, as Eric Drake, then chairman of BP, put it, "tax collecting agencies" for the OPEC nations. But neither were the companies simple tools
of the producing countries, nor had they merely merged one cartel with
another.

The conspiracy theory is easy to state: The companies did not resist
the tax increases with the traditional vigor of a Deterding or a Rockefeller.
The largest international banks that have profited from the huge investment of "petrodollars" are, as the British historian Geoffrey Barraclough
puts it, "the driving force behind the soft line toward OPEC." From 1967
to mid-1972, before the new relationship with OPEC, oil company profits
rose a mere 9 percent a year. Between the third quarter of 1972 and the
second quarter of 1974 they increased about 150 percent. Before the rise
of OPEC there was a stubborn problem of oversupply which continually
threatened company profits. After OPEC the internationally controlled
price kept profits high even in moments of temporary glut.

The whole story of what the oil companies were saying to the producing
countries during the critical months preceding the stunning price rise is
not known and may never be known. Oil companies are less bothered by
whistleblowers than is the CIA. Company archives never become available to independent historians, although a scholar with a proper sense of
awe may be shown a file or two.

Nonetheless, we do know that the companies put up considerable resistance to the demands of Saudi Arabia and the others. In 1972 the chief
executive of Exxon called on Nixon to put pressure on the Saudis, which
the President did. A few months later Secretary of the Treasury John B.
Connally warned that the government would have to intervene in support
of corporations that were negotiating for critical natural resources. The
Saudis pressed on in the negotiations nevertheless, and extracted an
agreement that would give them a steeply increasing share of the oil
concessions and a high price.

The new relationship that emerged between the oil companies, producer governments, home governments, and consumers revealed the ex-

traordinary power and adaptability of the giant oil companies. Within a few months they had demonstrated that they could shift to the consumers of the industrial world and to the Third World nations, some of whom were brought to the edge of bankruptcy by the price rise, the costs and burdens of OPEC's new power. Neither so bright nor so farseeing as some critics gave them credit for, so powerful was their hold over the world energy system that they could reap unprecedented profits from their own failures.

The style of the Seven Sisters in the Middle East is now more that of the Harvard Business School than Lawrence of Arabia. "We are spending a great deal of time and effort developing programs that are attractive to the Saudis," says Mobil Chairman Rawleigh Warner in explaining the spectacular new prosperity of old Standard Oil of New York. The company is selling technology to the desert kingdom—building a refinery in Juddah in which it retains a 30 percent interest, enlarging a blending plant, and managing the construction of a 750-mile, $1.2 billion pipeline from one coast of Saudi Arabia to the other. A few years ago euphoric predictions emanated from the Persian Gulf (reinforced by the panic of oil investors in New York) that refineries and gas stations throughout the world would soon be controlled by the oil-rich sheiks of the Middle East. This did not happen, because the majors have held on tightly to the principal source of their power—technology. Single pieces of technology are for sale, but the integration of it into a global marketing and distribution system is a feat now well beyond even fabulously rich underdeveloped countries. No country can match Exxon's global monitoring and marketing system. On the twenty-fourth floor of the company's international headquarters is a row of TV screens linked to giant computers and terminals in Houston, London, and Tokyo. This "Logistics Information and Communications Systems" (LOGICS) records the daily movement of 500 Exxon ships from 115 loading ports to 270 destinations, carrying 160 different kinds of Exxon oil between 65 countries. This sort of competitive advantage convinced the oil-producing countries that they could not compete in such "downstream" operations as retail marketing and transportation. By the late 1970s the Saudi and Iranian strategy was instead to develop a large local refining capacity and a petrochemicals industry for long-term exports.

The producer countries sell at roughly the same price to all the major oil companies, although some discounts are given, but the crucial issue for a company is having uninterrupted access in times of shortage. The Saudis have told us, Warner reports, "that those companies which are interested in developing the Saudi economy will have a better chance of securing some oil." The companies are trying to shift older and less profitable petrochemical and refining operations to the Middle East while retaining control over the most complex and profitable processes and the generation of new technology.

The companies have tried in different ways to ingratiate themselves with producing countries by performing political services for them as well. On May 23, 1973, the King of Saudi Arabia met secretly in Geneva with executives of Mobil, Exxon, Texaco, and Socal, the Aramco partners, and told them that "time was running out" and that they could "lose everything." On October 12 the indispensable John J. McCloy delivered a memorandum to the President to Nixon's chief of staff, General Alexander Haig:

> We have been told that the Saudis will impose some cutback in crude oil production as a result of the United States position taken thus far. A further and much more substantial move will be taken by Saudi Arabia and Kuwait in the event of further evidence of increased U.S. support of the Israeli position.
>
> We are convinced of the seriousness of the intentions of the Saudis and Kuwaitis and that any actions of the U.S. government at this time in terms of increased military aid to Israel will have a critical and adverse effect on our relations with the moderate Arab [oil] producing countries.

The chief executive of Socal included in his annual report to the stockholders a plea for a more "evenhanded," i.e., less supportive, policy on Israel. Gulf secretly funneled $50,000 to International Affairs Associates, Inc., through its Bahamas subsidiary, the Beirut branch of Citibank, and the bank account of an international lawyer to subsidize pro-Arab publications. Another $2.2 million went to American Near East Refugee Aid, Inc., which promotes various Arab causes. Aramco put up $86,000 to get Americans for Middle East Understanding, Inc., into operation. AMEU distributes *The Link,* a newsletter that presents the oil-producing countries in a sympathetic light and tries to combat the strong anti-Arab propaganda that swept the United States in the wake of the embargo. Advertisements of the Arab League are reprinted and distributed to key figures in the oil economy such as interstate trucking companies and service station owners. But the biggest political service of all was of course the willingness of the companies to help police the 1973 oil boycott even to the point of refusing to deliver oil to the U.S. Mediterranean Fleet.

The Middle East kingdoms want to penetrate U.S. and European markets for an increasing share of petrochemical products they plan to make. How much leverage they have to help them realize their ambitions for industrialization depends upon three principal factors; the world supply of crude, the ability of the companies to diversify their sources, and the success of the companies in cooperating with one another to maintain the international flow of petroleum.

Thus even as they accommodate and service the sheiks they once controlled, the oil companies are working hard to break free of them by finding new oil in new places. Accommodation is the essential short-term strategy, but diversification is the key to the long-term health of the firms. Mobil has been exploring energetically in the Gulf of Mexico since 1973 and is the largest nongovernmental shareholder in the Statjord Field near Norway in the North Sea. Exploratory talks with China are underway. Exxon is a 25 percent owner of the Prudhoe Bay fields in Alaska and also has a big share of the North Sea operations. Socal, the first to obtain a concession in Saudi Arabia, is the only major oil company to increase its domestic oil production significantly. (Two-thirds of its exploration money is going into the U.S.) In addition, it made a major find in Alberta, Canada, in 1977. The company has been unusually lucky in finding natural gas deposits in Wyoming and in the Gulf of Mexico and has found new oil in such places as Spain, Chad, and Sudan.

Increasingly, oil companies have come to look upon themselves as banks, bundles of money in pursuit of the safest and surest growth investments on the frontier of technology. The nature of the oil business itself is pushing the companies toward high technology. Traditionally, oil rigs and drilling equipment involved relatively simple technology. The oil giants made their money from a combination of monopoly power, persistence, and luck, not ultrasophisticated knowledge. But as offshore drilling and deep drilling become more important, advanced technology is assuming an ever more crucial role in their strategy of control. Keeping drilling platforms stable, for example, requires highly sophisticated computers to calculate and compensate for minute and rapid changes in the sea. Offshore drilling platforms with the latest technology now cost about $1 billion each. Mastery of this new technology (along with continued control of retail markets) explains why oil company executives are almost universally welcome even in China and Vietnam.

The principal target of the diversification campaign, as we shall see in the next chapter, has been the control of the alternative energy systems that will determine the postpetroleum civilization. However, as the reality has become apparent that control of the energy system requires reliable access to minerals, water, computers, and all sorts of other essentials for an integrated global operation, the oil companies have been investing heavily outside the energy field. In 1977, Exxon bought a Chilean copper company, and Arco acquired Anaconda. Since 1974, Texaco, Gulf, Shell,

Ashland, Occidental, and others have purchased petrochemical companies.

Arco is buying British newspapers, and Tenneco is now in the insurance business. Only because it was embroiled in a bribery scandal did Gulf drop its option to buy the Ringling Brothers circus. Exxon is experimenting with advanced electric typewriters, computer printout machines, telecopiers, and titanium disulfide button batteries for watches and calculators, and someday, its executives believe, electric cars.

3.

There has been a government–oil company partnership of sorts in the U.S. since the beginning of the petroleum economy. The companies for a long time have been called private governments. They have acted in a sovereign way but outside the law. But with the advent of the Energy Crisis the control of oil and gas required the majors to step up their planning efforts on a world scale, and this called for closer relations with government. The emergency allocation program to shift oil to targets of any future boycott that was established after the 1973 crisis requires and legitimates an international planning role for the companies. The creation of new international forums, such as the International Energy Agency and the Conference on International Economic Cooperation, affords opportunities for the participating oil companies to share information and to develop common strategies. Sharing oil resources is now government policy among all the nonsocialist industrial countries.

The legal relationship with government is changing in ways that give official recognition to an industry-government partnership. Industry officials are ambivalent about the partnership. Everyone is happy to see the government fund research and development for new energy sources, finance expansion of production, and establish a floor price on new energy products; but "once the technology is known," as Mobil Vice Chairman Herman J. Schmidt puts it, "we think the American enterprise system, including the financing, should be called upon." Others, such as former Exxon executive Richard J. Gonzales, think the best of all possible worlds in which the government bears the serious risks and the company reaps the profits may be a relic of the past. "It's like asking the fox to finance the hen house." Jerry McAfee, the chairman of Gulf, believes that the government must "participate" as a shareholder in financially risky enterprises for developing new energy sources. (The company has Canadian Government partners for its synthetic crude operations in Alberta.) Thornton Bradshaw of Atlantic Richfield, an advocate of national economic planning, is convinced that "the oil industry will have to forge a partnership with government."

Of course, the partnership has existed for a long time. Regulation, subsidies, leasing of federal lands, and tax write-offs are part of the national landscape. The Washington revolving door that facilitates the oilman's easy passage from energy companies to energy agencies obscures any possible conflict between patriotism and profits. A 1976 study by Common Cause of the top 139 employees of ERDA (the predecessor of the Department of Energy) revealed that more than half came from private energy companies, mostly ERDA contractors.

In Europe and Japan the role of government is larger and more explicit. The British Government has been the controlling shareholder of British Petroleum since Winston Churchill bought half the stock in 1914. The French have had a wholly owned state petroleum company, Elf-ERAP, since 1966. The Japanese Government is directly involved in supply contracts, drilling operations, and other strategies for assuring uninterrupted supply.

The relative lack of control by the U.S. Government over energy supply and energy use in the world's biggest energy consumer is a source of serious tension among the industrial nations. Despite periodic declarations of energy independence and loose talk of "self-sufficiency," the United States, which accounts for fully half of all the energy consumed by the nonsocialist industrial countries, has *increased* its oil imports significantly since the days of the "oil shock" of 1973. Imports represent 25 percent of total U.S. energy use. In 1977, 47 percent of the oil consumed in the U.S. was imported, up from 28 percent in 1972. (Thirty-eight percent of the 1977 imports were from OPEC.) The Europeans, who use much less energy and use it more efficiently, reduced their oil imports 1.7 million barrels a day in the same period. In 1978 the U.S. imported from various sources the equivalent of 75 percent of all the oil exported that year by Saudi Arabia and Iran.

The Europeans and the Japanese care how much oil the U.S. uses—for obvious reasons. They are far more dependent upon oil imports than the U.S. Germany imports 51 percent of its energy needs, France 74 percent, United Kingdom 42 percent, and Japan 74 percent (1976 figures). These countries have fewer alternatives than the U.S. Ironically, their present dependence on imported oil is a consequence of American munificence. After World War II the Marshall Plan financed West Europe's conversion from coal to oil. Seldom has there been a happier convergence of American national security and commercial interests. Europe's coal, on which her prewar industry almost totally depended, was in large measure in the hands of Communist unions. A highly labor-intensive industry, coal was thus a weak link in a strategy to keep Europe from going Left, which was of course precisely what the Marshall Plan was. Oil production and delivery took relatively little labor. All the work involved in shipping barrels from the Middle East and in setting up pipelines and refineries on the Continent could be done by American companies (with British participation, if necessary) and without employing Communist workers. The whole idea of introducing an oil economy would, as James Forrestal, the first secretary of defense, noted in his diary, "produce greater efficiency at lower cost (and would have various political advantages.)" In its first two and a half years, the Marshall Plan subsidized $384 million of American-produced oil from the Middle East for the factories of Europe. When the factories of France and Germany were going full blast again, they were powered by oil instead of coal. By 1950, Western Europe was dependent upon the Middle East for 85 percent of its crude oil and over the next twenty years was using imported oil to meet 55 percent of its energy needs. Behind the new energy system were the five U.S. majors, who now had a good share of every West European market. Behind the new power of the U.S. companies in the Middle East were the power and indulgence of the American Government.

Germany and France still have coal, but having converted substantially to oil, it is difficult and expensive to switch back. The antinuclear movement has slowed the building of reactors. So Europe is dependent upon foreign oil for years to come. Bidding against the United States for finite supplies opens the way to further price rises and further inflation in the 1980s. Many European economists are skeptical that in a price rise, temporary shortage, or in another politically inspired oil boycott, the emergency allocation plans hastily prepared after the 1973 boycott will really work. In a power struggle for supplies, the U.S. would "inevitably crowd other contenders for the limited oil reserves from the market," says Guido Brunner, the European Community's energy commissioner, "because the U.S. oil companies control most of the international production."

The Europeans and the Japanese are also concerned about the level of U.S. consumption and U.S. imports because of the sickness of the dollar. The etiology of dollar decline is a complex case history having to do with years of heavy overseas military payments, European and Japanese recovery, the Vietnam War, and the decline of American productivity. All of this set the stage, but the enormous and spiraling oil imports of the 1970s triggered the action. The weakened dollar is still the world's reserve currency, which means that Europeans and Japanese (not to mention the OPEC Arabs) are saddled with billions of dollars that keep losing value. While it is a source of nationalistic satisfaction to see the precipitous decline of the once almighty dollar—some German taxi drivers exact a one-to-one exchange rate from hapless American tourists, who not so many years ago thought of a mark as a quarter—the decline is not good for the health of European economies. Their exports to the U.S., still the world's biggest market, become much more expensive. U.S. companies that compete with them for exports abroad, notably auto manufacturers, can raise their prices without losing their share of the market.

However, the decline of the dollar became so precipitous that on November 1, 1978, the Federal Reserve raised interest rates to defend the currency. "The international position of the dollar suddenly became a burden," as a *Business Week* analyst put it, "adversely affecting domestic policy rather than an advantage helping it." The long era during which the U.S. Government could expand the economy by simply printing dollars and forcing other countries to take them whether they wanted them or not, was over. A unique perquisite of the number one nation was gone. From now on the U.S. economy would be swept by the same economic winds as the rest of the industrial world. Germany and France were building a European Monetary System to extricate themselves from dependence upon the dollar. The revival of competitive regional blocs threatened to bring on a "new mercantilism." As Arnold E. Safer, a vice president of the Irving Trust Company, warned:

> . . . chronic international payments deficits can set off a vicious devaluation-inflation cycle, which in turn brings about high unemployment or increased protectionism—key symptoms of the failure of the economic adjustment process. Lest the seriousness of this problem be too lightly dismissed, it is important to remember that most economic historians feel that the failure of the international economic and financial system was a principal element in the Great Depression of the 1930's.

Because the chronic U.S. balance of payments deficit casts a grim shadow over the world economy, a new ritual has developed. Every few months or so, high U.S. officials travel to Europe or Japan with promises to cut oil imports and are greeted with a skepticism that invariably turns out to be justified. In 1978, Secretary of Energy James R. Schlesinger promised to cut back current oil imports more than 2 million barrels a day by 1985, and President Carter committed the country to major cuts at the Tokyo Summit the following year. But the Europeans, who know the dependence of the U.S. economy on oil and are aware that many years elapse between the discovery and development of alternative sources, are understandably suspicious. The General Accounting Office predicts that the 1985 import level will be at least 2 million barrels a day higher than in 1978, and other estimates project even more substantial imports.

Oil imports are a major factor in the record $27 billion 1977 U.S. trade deficit, which has shrunk the dollar and made imports more expensive. The high price of imported oil, all by itself, according to econometric research of Joel Popkin of the National Bureau of Economic Research, was responsible for a 7 percent rise in consumer prices in the years 1973–75. Lawrence R. Klein, former president of the American Economic Association and an early advisor to President Carter, calculated that, because of the high price of OPEC oil, the world inflation rate is about one-third higher than it would otherwise be, and this was before the huge price hikes of 1979. Why then is the government of the most powerful nation in the world so impotent in the face of such economic and political danger?

From the days of Nixon's "Project Independence," raising prices has been the centerpiece of American energy policy. But when gasoline went from 40 cents to almost $1.00 a gallon, consumption in the U.S. actually increased. The reason for this defiance of sound economic theory is that most gasoline usage is not discretionary. For millions of workers there is no other way to get to the job. Trucking dominates the transportation system. The amenities of suburban life, the running of farms, and the survival of the travel and leisure industry all depend upon gas guzzling. An argument other than conservation for making oil and gas expensive is that fossil fuels must rise in price to the point where renewable energy sources, such as solar energy, become competitive. It is a theory with its own politics, for, like most austerity notions, it taxes the poor. In the 1973–75 oil crisis the price rises reduced the disposable income of poor families 4.8 percent, according to a report of the National Council of Churches of Christ, while the rich suffered a 0.5 percent loss. Alternative energy systems such as solar panels require high initial capital investment. Even middle-class families cannot afford these without subsidy. The consequence, then, is that the rich are able to manage the transition to ultimately low-cost, renewable energy, while the poor continue to pay the inflated prices for gas and oil that are the "signal" to the solar energy industry that its time has come.

After the Iranian Revolution dramatically cut world supply the demand became more insistent that domestically produced oil in the U.S. be decontrolled. The argument is that while the world price of a barrel of oil after the Iranian shutoff reached $15.75, because of controls domestic oil was only $11.20 and some of it as low as $5.50. Taking off controls and allowing U.S. prices to rise to the world level would, the economic writer John Berry predicted, cost $13 billion and add a percentage point to consumer prices, but it would encourage domestic production and decrease the dependence upon ever more expensive imports. However, partial decontrol has already helped oil prices to jump 30 percent in six months following the OPEC price rise of 1979. Domestic oil prices rose more than 9 percent in one month. The cost of decontrol to an average family is almost ten times what it was calculated to be when decontrols were instituted.

Unless decontrol were a part of a comprehensive program to develop new energy sources and to spread the cost fairly, rewarding the faster draining of America's dwindling oil reserves does not sound like an intellectual breakthrough. Some reform of the price system is obviously needed, but rationing by price alone is unfair. Subsidizing oil company profits by allowing them to take full advantage of their control over the world's dwindling oil supply produces more inflation than oil.

If conservation were to be a significant factor in reducing dependence on foreign oil, moralistic exhortation would have to give way to sensible planning—increased effort to develop renewable energy sources, public transportation, redesign of buildings, etc., subsidies to those who cannot afford high energy prices, and public control of oil imports and allocation. All of this requires, contrary to the popular political slogan of the day, more government, not less.

Other countries with less domestic supply and a more modest imperial reach are more obviously desperate about oil. It is worth recalling that the Japanese went to war for it in 1941. Seven years earlier, the presidents of Standard Oil of New Jersey and Royal Dutch Shell reported to Secretary of the Interior Harold Ickes that the Japanese were insisting that the companies, virtually the sole suppliers of the island empire, keep six months' supply ashore in Japan. The companies called upon the U.S. to threaten boycott to relieve the pressure, but President Roosevelt was afraid that cutting off oil shipments would push the Japanese militarists into an invasion of the Netherlands East Indies. Thus the Japanese were permitted to import crude up until four months before the attack on Pearl Harbor. The prize the Japanese sought in their audacious campaign was the oil-rich area of Malaya and the East Indies. The Germans, too, were desperate for oil. They sent Marshal Rommel into the desert and invaded the Caucasus in the hope of capturing what they needed. But the Allies controlled 86 percent of the world's supply, and when the synthetic fuel plants on which the Germans so heavily depended by the end of the war were bombed, they were finished. "It was the Nazis' lack of gasoline, not the loss of plane production, that gave us air superiority," the Strategic Bombing Survey concluded at the end of the war.

In recent years in Europe there has been a small dip in consumption and imports but little success in developing a coordinated continental energy policy. Most energy production is state-owned, and government has, by and large, much greater powers of intervention into the economy than in the U.S. Some countries have conserved petroleum by using cheap local natural gas (Holland) or burning significant amounts of wood (Austria, West Germany, and Italy). The price rise for gasoline has been less steep in Europe because it was so high already, although this varies greatly from country to country. (Motorists in West Germany were paying only 2.7 percent more for a gallon of gas in 1977 than in 1973, Italians 32 percent more, Belgians 8 percent *less*.) The price rises have little effect on demand, for the reasons just discussed, and also because governments have deliberately cushioned the effects for both industry and consumers by reducing their tax take when the price of crude oil rose. Japan is able to control demand more effectively because a high percentage of energy use is industrial rather than individual and the government has wide powers of intervention into the industrial economy. But conservation can plan only a small role in reducing Japan's energy needs.

Why have conservation efforts in the U.S. amounted to so little? There are two principal reasons. One is the psychological resistance of the public. The other is reluctance of the companies to make costly investments or to give up the profits to be made from technologies in place, however wasteful. A call to change comfortable habits or to abandon wasteful pleasures does not stir the heart like a war or a moon shot. It is not the moral equivalent of war, because people cannot visualize defeat. But the economic reasons are decisive. To replace energy-wasting technology requires the assembling of large amounts of capital for retooling, redesigning, and developing alternative energy sources. Corporations, banks, and governments are dragging their feet in making these shifts, because they are locked into existing capital investments on which they have yet to realize a full return.

Conservation makes good long-term economic sense but not good short-term profits. Electric utilities, for example, are permitted to set their rates according to the capital they invest. Thus they obviously prefer to build capital-intensive nuclear or coal-fired electric generating plants. But it is possible to obtain heat and electricity for the home from natural gas, an abundant energy source, by using a simple engine that runs an electric generator called a "cogenerator." The more people turn to this alternative source of home heat and electricity, the less capacity Consolidated Edison can use, the more it must raise its rates to make a profit, and the more customers it loses. Con Ed is understandably unenthusiastic.

Strategies to encourage domestic production encounter the same problems. Capital investment in U.S. energy development grew at about 10 percent a year in the years 1973–77 and the number of wells drilled went up almost 14 percent a year. But domestic production declined dramatically. It began to increase the next year, but the ever larger oil imports are almost entirely due to the prolonged dip in domestic production. How did it happen that in the years when the oil companies began to increase their investment in U.S. oil fields after abandoning them for so many years, the results were so disappointing? One problem is the long lead time in energy development. The big Prudhoe Bay find was discovered in 1968, and the oil did not begin to flow until 1977. Five- to ten-year lead times are common in the Middle East. As oil becomes harder to find and the search moves to deep water—Shell's Cognac Field in the Gulf of Mexico is 900 feet deep—the lead times stretch. It is also true that finding bonanza fields (10 billion barrels or more), which are the delight of the oil companies, is becoming much harder. Only nineteen of them have been found in the last hundred years. Extensive geological surveys suggest that there is little prospect of unearthing more of them within the continental United States.

Since 1918, according to *Business Week,* "the federal government has spent as much as 151 billion to stimulate oil, gas, coal, nuclear and other forms of electrical energy production." Some put the figure at $500 billion. Most of it has been spent in the last few decades in the form of depletion allowances, investment tax credits, accelerated depreciation, federal assumption of nuclear liability, federal subsidization of the uranium fuel cycle, rural electrification programs, etc. Up to now, virtually all of it has gone to fossil fuels and nuclear energy. For example, the solar energy research budget was $1 million in 1971. But times appear to be changing. The solar research budget in 1978 was $300 million and is about $1 billion in 1980. Congress has appropriated $15 million for Sunsat, a plan for sixty or so solar satellites circling the earth by the year 2025 at a projected cost of $1 trillion. Sunsat is an aerospace consortium of Grumman, Westinghouse, GE, Boeing, Lockheed, Martin Marietta, McDonnell Douglas, MIT, RCA, and other high technology firms. A few small research grants to individuals and small businesses for wind technology and other alternative energy experiments have been granted. But the major government research funds are, according to a Citizens Energy Project survey, directed to high technology and aerospace companies. For example, in 1977 only 2.6 percent of all money awarded for solar research and development went to small businesses.

The governments of West Europe and Japan have traditionally taken a more aggressive role in seeking to control energy supply, but these efforts too have been confined mostly to fossil and nuclear fuels. While heavy government investment has gone into developing North Sea oil in Britain and Norway and into natural gas in Holland, most of the nonsocialist industrialized world is still more than 50 percent dependent on imports. In the late 1960s, France, Germany, and Japan became increasingly concerned about their dependence upon the U.S.- and British-controlled oil majors for their petroleum supply. The French strengthened their own state oil company, and the Germans and Japanese started exploration companies. All three tried to develop secure nationally controlled sources. The French concentrated on their former colonies in North Africa, where they still maintained influence. The Japanese sent missions all over the world to make long-term supply contracts. Even before the 1973 war, France and Japan, mindful of how dependent they were on oil from the Gulf of Arabia, became noticeably more "evenhanded" in their support of Israel.

When the "oil shock" came, the governments of West Europe talked of developing a common policy as a counterweight to the U.S. claims on world oil, but they were unable to do so, because energy-rich countries such as Norway, Britain, and the Netherlands did not have the same interests as energy-poor countries like France, Italy, and Belgium. All of them tried to reduce import dependence by building up alternative domestic energy sources. Originally, nuclear energy was to have been the major new source. Two multinational consortiums, one French-led (EURODIF) and the second made up of Britain, West Germany, and the Netherlands (URENCO), built two large uranium enrichment facilities. Ambitious plans were laid for a huge nuclear power program. Europe's technological lead in developing the fast breeder reactor would be exploited. But the nuclear vision proved to be a trap.

Strong grass-roots opposition in France, Germany, Britain, Italy, and elsewhere (in Austria a reactor was voted down in a national referendum), technical difficulties, rising doubts about the economics of nuclear energy, higher costs, increased safety standards, and concern over environmental hazards such as waste disposal combined to cripple the program. Work still continues on the fast breeder reactor. Germany is moving cautiously ahead with nuclear energy. Under the Conservatives, Britain has developed enthusiasm for it, which the French continue to share. But the projections of nuclear power use in Europe which were made right after the 1973 crisis have been cut in half. In Japan, too, the hope had been that nuclear energy would supply about 10 percent of its energy needs by 1985. Because of intense opposition in the world's only nation to have been a nuclear target in war, the program is proceeding at about one-third the projected pace.

Similar problems beset the development of coal. Although the International Energy Agency is coordinating a research project on the promising technology of fluidized bed combustion, the social, environmental, and economic costs of increasing coal production were seriously underestimated. Thus, coal production in 1976 was below 1973 levels, although it is expected to rise in the 1980s as a result of the increased investment of the last few years. European energy plans also call for increased use of natural gas, but this will not decrease the dependence of the Continent on imports. Most of it is slated to come from Iran, Algeria, and the Soviet Union.

All this means that the European efforts to loosen their dependence on Middle East oil are only marginally more successful than the U.S. program. There is confusion as to direction in both Japan and West Europe. The result is continued dependence upon OPEC oil and increasing conflict between the U.S. and the rest of the industrial world for this crucial share of the world's energy reserves.

4.

In the complex set of strategies for assuring the world oil supply and keeping oil prices in line during the transition to the postpetroleum civilization, Saudi Arabia is the pivot. No matter what the energy system of the future will look like, no matter how promising the petroleum reserves of Mexico, Nigeria, or China appear to be, the industrial world faces a critical transitional period when the level of Saudi oil production and the price the Saudis choose to put on that oil can spell the difference between economic stability and economic chaos.

Saudi Arabia has fewer than five million people, most of them nomads or small farmers. They are illiterate, young (perhaps 50 percent of the population is under 20) and, increasingly, non-Arabian. About 40 percent of the population, according to a 1977 study prepared for the Senate Committee on Energy and Natural Resources, is made up of foreign workers—Yemenis, Sudanese, Pakistanis, Indians, and Africans. The country is run by the descendants of Ibn-Saud, the desert conqueror who proclaimed the Kingdom of Saudi Arabia in 1932, after thirty years of struggle, and left 40 sons to carry on his work. The Royal Family now numbers perhaps 5,000 members. The King is the final arbiter but tries to rule by maintaining a fragile consensus of tribes, religious leaders, and members of his family who represent a range of diverse interests. It is perhaps the supreme irony of the twentieth century that the most complex civilization ever built rests on a tenuous relationship with a desert kingdom from another age.

For the last ten years or so that relationship has seemed secure. Arabian oil was controlled by American-trained technocrats bound to the United States by a deep anticommunism rooted in Islam and strong old school ties. A deputy minister explained to the writer George Goodman how the technocrats in Riyadh, the Saudi capital, use their common Berkeley connections:

> We have a lot to learn, but it's not so bad, because we all know each other. For example, I went to USC. I think USC is probably the most popular school for Saudis. And if I want to get something done at Planning, I know a guy who was down the hall from me at USC, the guy at Finance was my roommate at USC, and we know the ringer from Ohio State because he is married to my roommate's sister. You know, the Saudi cabinet has more American-trained Ph.D.'s than the US cabinet.

For all the talk of conservation and the development of alternative energy sources, Middle East diplomacy has been the principal energy strategy of the last three administrations. This has meant a much closer relationship between the government and the oil companies than in the past. In his study *Oil Companies in the International System*, Louis Turner of the Royal Institute of International Affairs traces the cyclical nature of that relationship. By and large, governments used to leave the management of the world oil supply to the majors, intervening periodically in crises such as the Iranian nationalization and the CIA coup against Mosaddeq in 1953, or giving diplomatic support to the companies in their fight to scrap the Red Line agreement and other barriers to U.S. penetration into the Middle East. There were oil issues in a number of diplomatic crises in which the U.S. Government became highly involved. Oil nationalization was the immediate precipitating crisis leading to the break in relations with Castro. Oil was a consideration in U.S. involvement in the Nigerian Civil War of 1967 and in Angola. But oil did not dominate U.S. foreign policy. The support of Israel served larger strategic and domestic political purposes. The State Department was aware from 1948 on that support of a Jewish enclave in the heart of the Arab world was not good resource politics. (James Forrestal violently opposed the recognition of Israel, warning that this policy would force the country into four-cylinder cars.)

Even after the Energy Crisis, geopolitical goals and cold war rivalries continue to predominate over strictly energy objectives in foreign policy. Thus in 1978 the United States Government expressed its displeasure with the Soviet Union by refusing to allow the Dressler Company to sell them sophisticated drilling equipment. This was an extraordinary decision, given the fact that the CIA a year earlier had predicted a world oil shortage of crisis proportions because the USSR lacked the technology to exploit its vast oil reserves and was becoming a major importer.

In the early 1970s the relationship with Saudi Arabia and, to a lesser degree, Iran, became the crucial leg of the national energy policy, absorbing more governmental attention and guaranteeing a closer relationship between corporations and the state than ever before. Industry and government officials alike describe the U.S.–Saudi relationship as "big brother to little brother." The United States is a protector of the Royal Family. Over the last ten years American taxpayers have supplied it with $18.6 billions of sophisticated military hardware. In turn, the Saudis have invested more than $40 billion in the U.S. (According to U.S. Treasury officials 70 percent of the surplus funds in the hands of the OPEC countries have been invested in dollars, 25 percent of that in the U.S.) Thus the nightmare scenarios that excited financial writers and analysts after 1973, in which the newly rich Arabs used their dollar holdings to trigger the financial collapse of the industrial world, have so far failed to materialize. The rulers of Saudi Arabia understand that their interests are tied to the West. In a violent shake-up of the world economy they themselves would probably be swept away by a radical regime. More deeply and consistently anti-Communist than any regime in the West, the Saudi rulers, whose legitimacy is based on being defenders of the Wahhabi faith (the outgrowth of a seventh-century reformist movement in Islam) wish to do nothing that would play into the hands of godless communism.

"The Saudis know," as a U.S. foreign service officer explained in a "backgrounder" for the Washington *Post,* "that the prospect of radicals overthrowing the family and putting their foot on the lifeline of oil to American markets is just unacceptable to Washington, which would have to take drastic action. For them, American policy toward Saudi Arabia is defined by what American policy toward the family is." The entire kingdom of Saudi Arabia is a Royal Family Corporation. Herein lies the explanation for "the deep sense of cooperation" which President Carter has said is exceeded in no other diplomatic relationship. Here also is the reason for the extreme vulnerability of that relationship and of the oil lifeline that depends on it.

As pro-American as the oil technocrats are, they have a sophisticated understanding of where their interests diverge from those of the global giant that has made itself so dependent upon the continued draining of their country. "All we need to pump is 3 million barrels a day," the governor of the Saudi Arabian Monetary Fund points out to American visitors. "That will take care of us. Everything over 3 million barrels a day is a gift." The Saudis now pump 8.5 million. Were they to reduce the flow to 3 million, the West would be in panic. The price of a barrel would double. The fight over who would get the 3 million would be intense. The inflation would be catastrophic. Thus whether there will be enough oil in the next few years depends upon political decisions by the controllers of oil, and that now means the sheiks of Arabia.

The Saudis have strong economic reasons to restrict production. They cannot use for current development the revenue that the present production level creates, much less the 24 million barrels a day the CIA once said the Saudis will have to produce by 1985 to keep the West in business. If they spread out the production, the price will rise, their total take will be larger, and the development process more orderly. Explosive increases in revenue cause a huge inflation. (The *rent* in Riyadh for the equivalent of a nice suburban house fit for a middling corporate executive is $100,000 a year.) Beyond certain levels they must flare the natural gas, which is a by-product of the oil, because they do not have the facilities now to capture and to transport it.

But the Royal Family has larger political reasons for cooperating with the West. They have used some of their excess revenue to buy political influence. They poured $200 million into Somalia and induced that country to break its tie with the Soviet Union. Their underwriting of Egypt has kept Sadat anti-Soviet. By canceling their aid after the Camp David settlements with Israel, the Saudis preserved a role for themselves in Middle East diplomacy. They have sought to bolster governments facing Eurocommunism by giving the national oil companies of France, Italy, and Spain oil discounts. They do the same for Taiwan and did formerly for the Saigon regime in Vietnam.

The problem for the United States in Saudi Arabia, as a Trilateral Commission report puts it, is how to "justify production increases that are not consistent with Saudi economic interests." One way is to expand the Saudi definitions of economic interests to identify them ever more closely with the economic health of the West. The OPEC countries have almost $100 billion invested in American money. It is, as the president of OPEC put it, the only currency that can support investments on such a scale. Therefore, they share an interest with the United States, Europe, and Japan in keeping the industrial economy expanding. By expanding their investments in the U.S. and by setting up their own financing machinery—the OPEC Special Fund, the Arab Bank for Economic Development in Africa, the Saudi Fund for Development, the Kuwait Fund for Arab Economic Development, the Islamic Development Bank, and the Arab Fund for Economic and Social Development—they "recycle" dollars to poor countries that need them to import food and manufactured goods from the West. (In 1976, OPEC countries, led of course by the Saudis, made $5.2 billion available as grants for "soft" loans. This was more than 2 percent of their GNP; the "advanced" countries were giving about 0.7 percent in aid.)

To encourage Saudi restraint the Carter Administration, continuing Kissinger's policy, proposed further cultivation of the "special relationship" with the Royal Family. The deal is simple. The Saudis will within very broad limits get whatever sophisticated military hardware they fancy. They will get technology to help them develop their own petrochemicals and refining industry. They will get all sorts of advice. (The former CIA station chief in Riyadh, Raymond H. Close, went to work on his retirement for Kamal Adham, the Saudi intelligence chief who runs a profitable commission business on Saudi arms purchases on the side.) They will receive assurance of access to the markets of the West when their infant industries are developed. The Europeans and Japanese, more dependent on Saudi oil than the Americans, will compete for the privilege of assisting the industrialization of the Gulf and will assure markets for the Saudis in the developed societies in return for secure supplies of crude. All this requires some substantial, but manageable, rearrangement for the petroleum industry.

The problem, however, is the sinking value of the dollar. Until the Iranian Resolution the Saudis resisted raising the prices substantially beyond the 1973 levels, because of the danger of economic collapse in the West. In these years the real price of oil was shrinking, because the producers were being paid in dollars that were constantly worth less. Only in 1979 did the price of oil move ahead of the inflation rate. The Saudi strategy, as Petroleum Minister Yamani put it as early as 1969, was to develop an orderly alliance with the majors against consumers. "For our part, we do not want the majors to lose their power and be forced to abandon their role as a buffer element between the producers and the consumers. We want the present setup to continue as long as possible and at all costs to avoid any disastrous clash of interests which would shake the foundations of the whole oil industry." Yet the declining dollar, which is the currency for 65 percent of the world's reserves, is causing the sheikdom to lose vast sums and has prompted a search for alternatives, a new monetary unit represented by a "basket" of the major world currencies or Special Drawing Rights issued by the International Monetary Fund. But all are pegged one way or another to the dollar, and the strategy of extrication from the world's only reserve currency without triggering global panic is not apparent.

The biggest hold the U.S. has over Saudi Arabia is the dependence of the Royal Family on U.S. military power for their physical security. From World War II until 1962 the United States had a military airbase at Dhahran, and when it was closed President Kennedy sent a letter to the King assuring him of America's continued commitment to Saudi Arabia's "independence and territorial integrity." From the perspective of the Saudi rulers the world is a dangerous place. Radical regimes from Libya to Yemen which are committed to Arab nationalism with a Marxist cast are a clear threat to the regime. The Arab-Israeli conflict is also a threat because it feeds Arab radicalism. One element of Saudi dependence upon the U.S. Government, therefore, is the U.S. influence over a settlement. The power of Iran, the home of the other principal Muslim sect, the Shiites, for many years another recipient of U.S. military aid, has also been a worry. Indeed, for a while it was a worry that the United States subtly encouraged. In the days of the Shah semiofficial gossip circulated from time to time about an invasion of the Arabian peninsula by the Shah backed by the U.S. to keep the oil flowing in the event the Royal Family decided to hoard it.

The sophisticated military hardware that has arrived in Arabia is so much junk without extensive training of Saudi personnel by the U.S. corporations supplying the equipment. Thus in 1978, Northrop Corporation, in connection with the delivery of 110 F-5E and F-5F jet fighters had 1,134 contract personnel at Saudi airbases. Grumman had another 1,000 engineers and weapons experts to service the delivery of F-14 Tomcats. When these personnel arrived they expected to stay into the 1990s. In all, there are well over 30,000 Americans performing critical advisory roles for the Saudi Royal Family and its far-flung enterprises. All of this creates a dependence that affects the economic relationship.

What happened in Saudi Arabia is reminiscent of what happened in India in the nineteenth century. Aramco, like the British East India Company, operated for many years as a private government in the desert kingdom with only the shadow of state power in the background. But as local political forces became stronger or acquired new consciousness, in Arabia as in India, the military power of the state became increasingly more visible and more important.

Whether it can all work is another matter. Will the arrangements for maintaining secure access to Saudi oil last during the critical period of increasing U.S. dependence? The danger is that a radical regime will overthrow the Royal Family and institute a development policy more in tune with Arabian needs than with the requirements of world capitalism —3 million barrels a day for export instead of 8 or 12 million, or the 24 million the CIA said the U.S. would need in the mid-1980s. It is hard to think of a more vulnerable regime. It is a country as large as the United States east of the Mississippi with a population less than that of Chicago. Its army is a bit smaller than Peru's. In an age when the political watchword around the world is development, the more anachronistic a regime, the more unstable it is. Even in a world where so many countries are in the hands of fossilized autocrats, Saudi Arabia stands out as a political throwback. Slavery was officially abolished in 1962. Less than twenty years ago hand-choppings in the public square were regular Friday afternoon events; they still occur from time to time. The superficial modernization of the last few years—Hilton Hotels, New York banks, sophisticated drilling rigs, and the rest—unsettles but does not transform.

Within the Royal Family, there are divisions of opinion as to the pace and direction of industrialization, as to whether the traditional values, such as the total exclusion of women from public and economic life, should be or can be maintained. There are, according to a report submitted to the Deputy Secretary of Defense, Robert F. Ellsworth, by a former Exxon executive, Melvin A. Conant, rivalries for power between those who represent "traditional tribal and religious forces . . . who are appalled by the effects of oil wealth and the influx of foreigners on the society" and the oil technocrats whose fortunes, power, and status depend upon modernization. The modernization process is creating new class interests that appear to be at odds with those of the old ruling elite. That tension was an important factor in the Iranian Revolution. As the report suggests, the magnitude of the prize, the weakness of the state, and the rising tension between traditionalists and modernizers make "a military coup perhaps even inspired by a faction of the royal family" a distinct possibility.

Saudi Arabia, the pivot of American energy policy, was vulnerable even when the Shah of Iran looked like the most stable ruler in the Middle East, but the political storms that welled up in 1978 and forced the Shahinshah from the Peacock Throne cannot help having a destabilizing effect on the royal autocracy of Arabia. Within weeks the King had opened discussions for establishing relations with the Soviet Union, and reports of deepening splits inside the Royal Family circulated in the West.

The involvement of the U.S. Government with Iran was longer and deeper than its "special relationship" with Saudi Arabia. Even in the Shah's time only 3 percent of the oil imported into the U.S. came from the ancient Persian kingdom, but Iran played a vital role in the strategic planning of the West because it supplied two states in which the United States has a crucial interest—South Africa and Israel. Under the Shah, Iran provided South Africa with about 90 percent of its oil, and was also Israel's major source. Revolutionary Iran refuses to supply either. Both states, for political reasons, have trouble finding the oil they need. Both are important in U.S. global strategy, Israel for its strategic location and historic ties and South Africa because of its minerals.

America's relationship to Iran dates from the Second World War.

Under Lend-Lease the U.S. reorganized the Iranian army. The British and Russians had occupied Iran after throwing out the present Shah's father, who was pro-Hitler. "This is a fine country," General Greely, the first Intendant General of the Iranian army, wrote in 1942, "with a virile people, and more could be done with it than MacArthur did with the Philippines. . . ." Colonel H. Norman Schwartzkopf, head of the New Jersey state police and for years the narrator of the radio program "Gangbusters," arrived shortly afterward to take charge of the Imperial Gendarmerie. For Franklin Roosevelt, who sent James M. Landis, the dean of the Harvard Law School, to Tehran on an economic mission, Iran was to be the model for postwar relationships with developing countries. "I was rather thrilled with the idea of using Iran as an example of what we could do by an unselfish American policy."

In the intervening years the American involvement became deeper and deeper. In 1953 the CIA dispensed several million dollars to rent the mob that helped bring down Premier Mosaddeq, the wispy nationalist who had dared to take government control of Iranian oil. (One check for $390,000 cashed by an American agent was produced at Mosaddeq's trial.) The U.S. military mission did its part too:

> . . . when this crisis came on and the thing was about to collapse, we violated our normal criteria and among other things we did, we provided the army immediately on an emergency basis blankets, boots, uniforms, electric generators, and medical supplies that permitted and created an atmosphere in which they could support the Shah. . . . The guns they had in their hands, the trucks that they drove through the streets, and the radio communications that permitted their control, were all furnished through the military defense assistance program . . . had it not been for this program, a government unfriendly to the United States probably would now be in power.

Thereupon followed about $2 billion in U.S. aid, the establishment of SAVAK, the Iranian secret police, by the CIA, and a succession of economic and technical missions. Prominent Americans such as David Lilienthal, the first chairman of the Atomic Energy Commission, became enthusiasts of the Shah's White Revolution—and beneficiaries of profitable consulting contracts. (The Shah, according to a batch of photostated checks submitted to Senator John McClellan's Committee on Government Operations in 1963, used the considerable resources of the Pahlavi Foundation, some of which appear to have come from U.S. aid funds, to encourage the enthusiasm of influential Americans. Among those receiving unexplained disbursements from account #214895.20 of Union Bank of Switzerland, Geneva, were Mrs. Loy Henderson, wife of the former U.S. ambassador ($1,000,000); Henry Luce, publisher of *Time* ($1,000,000); and $1,000,000 each to two former U.S. ambassadors and the director of the Point Four aid program in the mid-1950s.

In 1978, large-scale riots erupted throughout Iran, and the Shah cut back drastically on his modernization program and imposed military rule. When the Revolution began, religious revolutionaries circulated leaflets in the American community:

> O cursed Yonky, you know about Shah-monarchism and his general massacres but while all liberal people condemn the executioner you and your domned President support him. This is the reason that all the Iranian people hate you. Viva Islam!

The simple message and the genuine hurt and surprise it evoked among the Americans capture the essential bankruptcy of forty years of naive *realpolitik*. To keep a secure footing in the Middle East and access to strategic real estate, what would make more sense than to support a non-Arab kingdom in the midst of the Arab world which invited private investment and was prepared to sell oil to America's friends irrespective of ideology? After all, Iran was a country, unlike Saudi Arabia, that had to sell all the oil it could comfortably produce to pay for development. The 41,000 Americans, including 25,000 weapons technicians, stationed in Iran when the Revolution came were a living symbol of the U.S. commitment. In the midst of the Teheran riots in September 1978 the director of the National Foreign Estimate of the CIA, Robert Bowie, appeared before the Senate Foreign Relations Committee to give an optimistic report; the intelligence services, as in Vietnam, consistently exaggerated the stability of the regime—and for the same reason. The "customers" in Washington did not want to hear that one of the principal pillars of Nixon's "structure of peace" and a crucial link in America's energy strategy was about to fall.

CHAPTER IV

Energy: What Is to Be Done?

1.

THE WORLD'S CONSUMPTION of energy for industrial purposes has been doubling approximately once every decade. "It is difficult for people living now, who have become accustomed to the steady exponential growth in the consumption of energy from fossil fuels to realize how transitory the fossil-fuel epoch will eventually prove to be when it is viewed over a longer span of human history," notes M. King Hubbert, the oil geologist who predicted the oil shortage of the 1970s twenty years ago. The era of fossil fuels, which he defines as the period in which human beings burned up 80 percent of the total supply of oil, gas, and coal, will turn out to last, he calculates, about 300 years. Some coal was burned over 2,000 years ago and some oil may still be burned 2,000 years hence, but these are infinitesimal quantities given the energy requirements of the present and the projected industrial civilization.

What then is to be done? There is wide agreement that the postpetroleum civilization should be run on renewable energy resources. Whether the principle source is to be nuclear energy or solar energy is a matter of controversy in every industrial country. The choice of a strategy of transition—how to convert an oil-based energy system into one or the other—is eliciting one of the major political struggles of the century. Whether, for example, a society chooses as its principle transition fuel coal, natural gas, or some others such as shale oil will make and unmake fortunes and change the face of nations.

Barry Commoner, one of the leading advocates of solar energy in the United States, argues that natural gas is the best "bridging fuel" to a solar system that, he states, can be fully in place in fifty years. The closest cousin to oil, natural gas is a mixture of methane, ethane, propane, and butane gases. As early as 1000 B.C. the Chinese were digging wells 3,000 feet deep for natural gas. The first commercial use in the U.S. was in Fredonia, New York. In 1821, local entrepreneurs dug a 27-foot pit to a concentration of seeping gas, constructed a crude pipeline, and began selling the gas to the town for street lamps and to the local inn. The Marquis de Lafayette stopped there four years later for a gas-cooked dinner.

About one-third of proved natural gas reserves are found together with crude oil in the same reservoirs. Until around 1920, the gas was regarded as a dangerous impurity to be burned off to keep the oil pristine, although it was piped from local oil wells in the West and Southwest for the heating of a few homes. Cooking with the fuel was dangerous, and more than one cook was blown up by leaking gas, which in its natural state is odorless. For the most part it was too expensive to produce and to transport as a commercial fuel. Today, natural gas accounts for more than a quarter of the total U.S. energy consumption, and more than half of the energy used in running factories and heating homes. In the last several years, it has quadrupled in price despite government regulation. By the end of 1975 natural gas in an amount equivalent to 520 billion barrels of oil had been discovered around the world and about 123 billion barrels had been consumed. The "proven reserves" are estimated to be about a quarter to half of the "ultimately recoverable reserves." The U.S. Bureau of Mines report, *Mineral Facts and Problems,* estimates world resources of natural gas to be "at least 10 times current proved resources." Of the roughly 400 billion barrels estimated to be available shortly after the embargo of 1973, 137 billion are in the OPEC countries, 46 billion in the U.S., 31 billion in Western Europe, 28 billion in Mexico, Canada, and elsewhere in the Western Hemisphere, and in Asia and Africa, and 144 billion in the Soviet Union, China, and the rest of the socialist world. Estimates of "ultimately recoverable" reserves have been dramatically increased in recent years.

By the mid-1920s big oil companies were using natural gas to run their Gulf Coast refineries. Methane, the primary ingredient of natural gas, turned out to be the key to the huge petrochemical industry, because it could be used to produce miraculous transformations; by one process it could become a solvent, by another a fiber or adhesive or rubbery substance. Petrochemicals derived principally from natural gas are now used in more than 3,000 chemical products, including plastic-coated aluminum siding, synthetic rubber, lacquers, aerosol propellants, anesthetics, detergents, and fertilizers. Some of the famous brand names are Dacron, Orlon, and nylon. By the early 1970s petrochemicals were taking about 5 percent of the natural gas produced.

But the biggest use was for heating, cooling, and cooking, and this depends upon an underground network of pipelines bigger than the railroad system. Though less visible, it has had a comparable impact upon the country. In the 1930s the development of welded pipe that could withstand high pressure made long-distance gas pipelines possible. Within a decade pipelines reached as far as St. Louis, Chicago, and Minneapolis and, by the end of World War II, to the Northeast as well. Handsome profits were now flowing to the gas producers, who bought Texas gas for five or ten cents per 1,000 cubic feet and sold it in New Jersey for thirty cents. Much of the pipeline system was owned by oil companies. There are 8,000 producers of natural gas, but 80 of them control about two-thirds of the interstate market. They competed fiercely for the most profitable lines, bugging each others' telephones from time to time and bribing local politicians for franchises where necessary. The face of suburbia changed. Gone were the early morning furnace stokings, fumes, ashcans dragged down icy walkways, and grime, which were the hallmarks of coal civilization. "Gas Heats Best" became the slogan of the utilities, and millions of new customers agreed. The new boom fuel also invaded the lair of its competitors. Machinery for strip mining in Appalachia now operated on natural gas instead of coal. Half of all natural gas produced went to industry, most of it to fire boilers. Industrial use was heavily concentrated in the Far West. Interstate traffic was regulated; the Federal Power Commission guaranteed a 12 percent return. But gas sold locally could fetch much higher prices, and by 1971, 40 percent of all gas produced was sold in a market developed to escape federal regulation. Indeed, 90 percent of gas from new wells was "intrastate" gas, and much of it was being used by electric utilities instead of coal. Making electricity is a particularly inefficient use of gas, a waste for profit of a versatile energy resource which Lee White, former FPC chairman, terms a "national scandal."

The perennial argument of gas companies is that federal regulation discourages the search for gas. The 1960s were the boom years when the utilities and suburban households converted to gas, but between 1956 and 1971 the number of natural gas wells dropped by half, exploratory drilling declined 50 percent, and more than 450 drilling firms went out of business. No new bonanza fields had been found, and the costs of deep drilling to find new gas rose to beween $3.5 million and $15 million per well. (Old-fashioned wells cost about $300,000.) Much of the new gas was offshore, risky as well as costly to produce. By 1985, because of the passage of the bitterly contested natural gas bill, the industry will be free of federal price control altogether. Indeed, controls on gas from especially deep and expensive wells have already been lifted.

Recent history does not lend much support for the euphoric predictions that high gas prices will produce enough gas to reduce imports of Arab oil significantly. Between 1969 and 1976 the price of "new" gas rose from 18 cents per 1,000 cubic feet to $1.45, and less and less gas was being produced. The companies say of course that the price wasn't high enough, but a Congressional Budget Office study estimates that total deregulation —the industry panacea that will send the price up to between $4 and $5 by 1985—would result in only a 5 percent increase in production. The cost to consumers of complete deregulation will be an additional $10 billion a year. A disproportionate share of that $10 billion is being paid by the working poor and middle class, who can do without the furnace or the stove even less than they can do without the car.

In 1973–74 there was an acute natural gas shortage. In 22 states companies refused to accept new customers. In California, Pacific Lighting curtailed its gas shipments to such major employers as Kaiser Steel, Lockheed, and fertilizer and canning companies, forcing users to switch to alternative fuels, usually the more expensive propane or diesel. Tri-Valley Growers, a California canning company, for example, estimated the cost of converting its seven canneries to diesel at $3.5 million even without the necessary environmental safeguards and other expenses. The gas companies resorted to fire and brimstone techniques to dramatize the shortage and to point the way to salvation—deregulation and higher prices. Joseph Rensch, President of Pacific Lighting, as part of a $3 million public relations campaign, predicted that without a new pricing policy 38,000 small businesses in California would face cutoffs; the Stanford Research Institute concluded that the gas shortage would cost California 800,000 jobs by 1981. Two years later the Federal Power Commission estimated a "shortfall" of 1.6 trillion cubic feet.

But by mid-1978, immediately after the deregulation bill was finally passed, the prospect of natural gas in great abundance suddenly materialized. "The gas industry is entering an entirely new era," said American Gas Association President George Lawrence. With prices headed for $4 per 1,000 cubic feet—up from 29 cents for "old" regulated gas—a dramatic upsurge in drilling loomed. Plans for new rigs in the Tuscaloosa Trend, a gas-rich geological formation in southeastern Louisiana, were announced. For years, industry spokesmen had been warning of falling reserves, but once the deregulation bill passed, the world looked completely different. "It wouldn't surprise me if new deep production in the U.S. reached 8 trillion cubic feet by the year 2000," Robert A. Hefner, an Oklahoma City deep driller, told *Newsweek*. The estimates by gasmen of unconventional sources of natural gas were dizzying. In the Northeast, there were perhaps 600 trillion cubic feet locked in shale deposits dating back to the Devonian age. All it takes to get it are massive amounts of capital and new technology. There are 600 trillion more in beds of sandstone in the West, but figuring out how to release them is a problem. (One government-sponsored experiment tried breaking up the sandstone with nuclear bombs, but they melted the rock formation and sealed in the gas even more tightly.) There are huge amounts of methane gas in coal mines. A Russian scientist thinks world reserves of methane below the ocean floor amount to 35 million trillion cubic feet.

Statistics are effective political weapons because they can be counted on to mesmerize some part of the electorate into agreement with any proposition and to produce a certain torpor among the rest. Estimates of natural gas are political statements or scientific fantasies. The information about huge new gas reserves was as available to industry spokesmen when they were playing Cassandra as it was when the prospect of new riches from unregulated gas converted them into instant Panglosses. Because of widespread suspicion of the industry the matter of natural gas pricing produced a considerable public anger in the late 1970s. The issue provoked a two-week filibuster and nearly strangled President Carter's energy plan in its cradle. But the industry prevailed because most people find it easier to heap their anger upon government than upon the gas company. The gas industry's battle for deregulation has been going on for more than a generation, and information about gas supplies has been the principal weapon. Company reserves began to fall precipitously immediately after the industry lost an important case in the Supreme Court challenging the rate set for interstate gas by the Federal Power Commission. The companies are in exclusive possession of information on reserves. They make available what they wish to the industry trade association, the American Gas Association, which assembles the data for use by federal regulators who make it the basis of the official natural gas inventory. Professor Philip Areeda of Harvard Law School, who was serving as staff director to a cabinet task force on energy in the Nixon Administration, reports that a high company official told him how much he regretted having given us "the optimistic-pessimistic data as distinct from the pessimistic-pessimistic data. In other words, he had drawersful of data. . . ."

Actually, according to the Federal Trade Commission, the gas companies keep three estimates of reserves, one for the Internal Revenue Service, one for the American Gas Association, and another that is held within the company for management and planning purposes. In March 1975 the Bureau of Competition of the Federal Trade Commission charged that "AGA reporting procedures are tantamount to price rigging," and the House Subcommittee on Oversight and Investigations found enormous discrepancies between the reserves on company books and what they had reported to the AGA. The U.S. Geological Survey, after subpoenaing AGA records, found that for federal lands where the Survey can get accurate data (unlike data on reserves held on private lands) the AGA reported 8.8 trillion cubic feet less than the government estimate. An FPC staff investigation found that the companies could have made available an additional 300 billion cubic feet—enough, as Senate energy expert Bethany Weidner notes, "to reduce by one-third the curtailment suffered by consumers, schools, and factories" during the bitter winter of 1976.

"There is little doubt," as Weidner concludes, "that the industry has delayed production and withheld available gas." Shell Oil had in 1976 a reserve of more than 2 trillion cubic feet deliberately kept out of production, known as "shut-in wells," and defended its action by claiming that more couldn't be produced because additional production facilities, drilling, or new pipelines were needed. Yet these bottlenecks were not natural disasters but the results of previous company decisions not to invest. "It is easy to look at raw statistics and jump to erroneous conclusions," G. C. Bankson, vice president for production, told *Business Week.* But there is no question that Shell could produce more gas had it not curtailed production in anticipation of deregulation and higher prices.

Natural gas is a good transition fuel, Commoner argues, because the vast pipeline system can be used to carry methane from manure, timber, and other renewable sources. New gas from biomass, as it is called, can be used to supplement the old gas from prehistoric ages that is locked deep in the ground. The gas company in Chicago has contracted with a feed lot in Oklahoma to buy the methane produced from their ever-growing mountain of manure. The same could be done, he says, with Louisiana sugar cane residues or Ozark timber. It is a form of solar energy, since animals and plants convert the rays of the sun in their life cycle and their wastes become a natural storehouse.

The idea of using grain for producing fuel has been around since Henry Ford's Model A, which had an adjustable carburetor to permit the use of alcohol mixtures. During the depression, crop prices were so low and gas prices so high that gasoline-alcohol blends were widely used. At one point 2,000 co-ops and service stations were selling it throughout the Midwest. Ford himself helped finance an alcohol fuel plant in Kansas. Other countries proceeded to develop alcohol fuels as a significant supplement to their fossil fuels. Brazil, which has a major alcohol production program using its huge sugar cane wastes, runs its cars on an alcohol mixture and expects eventually to replace petroleum altogether with an agricultural-based fuel. Exxon and Texaco are selling 20 percent alcohol blends to Brazilian motorists.

In the United States the fuel alcohol movement that swept across the plains in the 1930s was stopped cold by the oil companies. The American Petroleum Institute and the American Automobile Association ran highly publicized tests to prove that "gasoline and alcohol don't mix." As cheap Middle East oil flowed ever more abundantly and alcohol taxes rose, the fuel alcohol effort declined. Most European countries made mixing gasoline and alcohol mandatory, and some, like the French, provided ammunition to the oil industry by concocting almost unusable mixtures.

After the 1973 price rise the cry from the Farm Belt for a national effort to produce fuel alcohol was heard again. Once again the oil companies disparaged the idea. Gulf Oil said, "It simply would not be in the best interest of our country," but it quietly perfected a process for breaking down cellulose into fermentable sugars. Chevron attacked the Farm Belt proponents and the growing number of supporters among scientists for "scraping the cobwebs off an idea that failed 40 years ago." The principal objection, as Mobil Oil puts it, is that "growing, fermenting, and distilling grain consumes more energy than it produces." Mobil is developing a process for turning alcohol into gasoline.

The story of the alcohol battle has been told in fascinating detail by Hal Bernton, a reporter with Jack Anderson. It is an account of jousting experts, oil company propaganda campaigns, extravagant claims of alcohol enthusiasts, and of approaching vindication for alcohol. Even the oil companies are shifting their positions in the face of scientific evidence, successful experience from other countries, and the ever tighter squeeze on oil.

Serious questions remain. Whether alcohol production can provide a significant net energy gain depends upon the technology used. Small-scale stills can produce 150- to 190-proof alcohol using a wood fire. The process yields a nutritious residue that can be fed to cows and chickens. The more alcohol technology can be integrated into renewable farm operations, the greater energy savings there will be. But as in every alternative energy source there is the other technology route—big distilleries with centralized production controlled by big energy companies or corporate farms. Which one receives government support will help determine the shape of American agriculture.

Alcohol is no panacea. Limits operate here too. At some point, use of the land for fuel competes with the food supply for humans and feeds the inflation in supermarket prices. If alcohol fuels become profitable, even more disastrous soil exhaustion and soil erosion than we now have could result. As Bernton warns, when the temptation to sell corn stocks to the distillery becomes irresistible, they will no longer be used as organic fertilizer or animal feed. Then the farmer will have to use energy-intensive artificial fertilizers and feeds. But there are a growing number of encouraging examples of sensible resource planning in the use of organic substances for fuel.

2.

When we talk about this as the age of fossil fuels we let our ethnocentrism show. Nine-tenths of the people in the poor countries where most of the world's population is concentrated use no fossil fuels at all. For the most part they burn wood. They are now faced with a scarcity of a different order from that facing the disappointed weekend motorist in the United States.

The average villager in the Indian state of Madhya Pradesh, the Indian forestry specialist R. Chakravarty points out, is still in the wood age. His house, his furniture, many of his implements, are made of wood. About 80 percent of the wood in the Third World is used for cooking fuel. Wood is thus an indispensable component of the food system, and it is in very short supply. John Spears of the World Bank estimates that at present planting rates there will be only 10 percent of the wood needed in the Third World by the year 2000.

Most of the wood burned in poor countries never passes through a commercial market. It is foraged and scavenged. Although poor countries are utterly dependent on wood, most of the world's commercial forest products are grown and consumed in the rich countries. The United States and the Soviet Union are exporters of wood. Each year, Erik Eckholm of Worldwatch Institute reports, "the average American consumes about as much wood in the form of paper as the average resident in many Third World countries burns as cooking fuel."

The world is becoming rapidly denuded of trees. Forests present the same problem as the other energy sources. Like oil or coal deposits, they must be sufficiently concentrated to be commercially exploitable. Commercial operations need dense forests, and these are disappearing. According to the Swedish analyst Reidar Persson, who has made rough calculations based on aerial surveys by satellite, in 1950 one-fourth of the earth's surface was covered by dense forests. Twenty-five years later less than one-fifth was good forestland. Because of the worldwide wood shortage, costs have skyrocketed, particularly in poor countries. In the early 1970s the price of firewood rose 300 percent in twenty-four months in Katmandu, the capital of Nepal. In Upper Volta a manual laborer, Eck holm reports, spends 20 to 30 percent of his income on wood. In Pakistani towns foragers strip the bark off trees lining the streets. A single board is twice as expensive in Pakistan as in the U.S., where the average income is 46 times the Pakistani average. Because of the shortage of firewood in India hundreds of millions of tons of cow dung, although desperately needed for fertilizer, are being burned as fuel. "The use of cow dung as a source of non-commercial fuel is virtually a crime," the Indian National Commission of Agriculture declares. But the practice is growing, not only in India but in Africa and in parts of Latin America. As timber prices rise, the rush to cut down trees is causing erosion and other serious forms of ecological damage.

About one-third of the world's industrial wood is traded internationally, but more and more, the products of tropical forests are entering world commerce. Multinational corporations "cream" trees of commercial value, leaving the rest of the foliage and surrounding soil in bad condition. One study of Indonesian forests revealed that one-third of the trees left behind after a timber operation by a multinational company died. Eckholm describes what is happening:

> Of the scores of Indonesian, Japanese, Philippine, Korean, American, and other companies cutting and exporting Indonesian timber, Weyer-haeuser is the only one that is even experimenting with plantations on a small portion of the land it logs. Only a few companies are building sawmills so that more of the jobs and profits associated with the use of its timber can be kept in Indonesia. The companies and many individual Indonesians are getting rich off the timber trade, and the national government is taking in huge royalties that in theory can help finance the nation's economic development. But as log output begins to fall off. many Indonesians may begin wondering how much of lasting value the majority have received from the feverishly paced, largely unregulated exploitation of what is, under current modes of extraction, virtually a nonrenewable natural resource.

Multinational corporations, however, are not the only practitioners of forest plunder. The Soviet Union, as Solzhenitsyn pointed out, is systematically destroying the woods of Siberia near Yakutsk.

The raping of forests has insidious effects on other resource systems. Silt deposits from denuded land ruin freshwater sources and shorten the useful life of expensive dams. In cold climates tree removal takes away a needed protective belt for crops. The forestry expert Norman Myers warns that many species of animal and plant life in tropical forests used for drugs, food, and industrial products will be gone forever if the jungles continue to be decimated. What could be the biggest problem of all is the enormous increase in the carbon dioxide levels due to deforestation and wood burning. Like the risks of nuclear energy, no one knows for sure, but there are disturbing indications that this could produce a warming trend sufficient to melt the Arctic icecap and cause severe floods in the Western Hemisphere.

Brazil's rain forest has been called the lungs of the earth. Through photosynthesis it supplies, Harold Sioli, director of the Max Planck Institute of Limnology, has calculated, 50 percent of the world's annual production of oxygen. According to a number of scientists Brazil's plans to "develop" the Amazon jungle could imperil the oxygen supply and dangerously raise the carbon dioxide levels. Despite considerable pressure, Brazil has refused to file an environmental impact statement with the United Nations. The principal executioner of the assault on the Amazon is Daniel K. Ludwig, reputedly the richest man in the Americas. Having purchased 500,000 acres of the Amazon forest, Ludwig has set up a $400 million paper mill in the midst of the jungle. The plant was built in Japan and towed by barge on a 15,000-mile, 93-day journey to an Amazon tributary 250 miles inland. By 1981 the plant is expected to produce 750 metric tons of wood pulp a day, which is enough, *Time* magazine has discovered, "to make a single strand of toilet paper stretching more than 6½ times around the world." The intent, quite clearly, is to corner the world's bonanza forest at a time when timber products are increasingly used as fuel and prices are rising even faster than for oil. (Two barrels of petroleum substitute can be made from a ton of wood.) At risk is a third of Ludwig's $3 billion personal fortune. But, according to Sioli, much more is hanging in the balance. Even if the catastrophe he predicts does not occur, "the future of colorful, captivating life forms of our beautiful planet" are being sacrificed "to the momentary and trivial benefit of our materialistic civilization."

3.

Because it is dirty, hard to mine, and inconvenient to transport, coal is everyone's least favorite fuel. Because it is incredibly abundant, it keeps making a comeback after the convenient fuels have been exhausted. About three-fourths of all fossil fuel reserves in the U.S. are coal, and these reserves constitute perhaps a quarter of the world supply. Chinese mandarins began using coal for cooking about 4,000 years ago. According to Robert Lindsay Galloway, the historian of British mining, Romans in Britain burned it. We know that by 1200 coal was being exported from England to the Continent. In 1236 the monks of Newminster Abbey, near Morpeth in Northumberland, received a grant from the Crown entitling them to take "sea coal wherever it might be found." But the coal trade did not become significant until the eighteenth century when the British and French discovered that they had burned up their firewood.

Coal is making another comeback now in the United States, where it has been produced since miners first began digging near Richmond, Virginia, in 1701. George Washington recorded a visit to a coal mine in his diary for 1770, but until the Revolution most coal was imported from England or Newfoundland. It was the shock of war and the cutting off of the English supply that led to the growth of the American mining industry. In 1810 a huge deposit was discovered near Pittsburgh, and some of it was shipped by rafts and barges as far as Washington. But the age of coal did not really begin until the latter half of the nineteenth century. As late as 1850 the U.S. was burning ten times as much firewood as coal. With the advent of the railroads and the steel industry, coal became the dominant fuel in the country. The steam turbine developed in the 1880s to make electricity devoured a great quantity, and an enormous new market was born. By the end of World War I about 680 million tons were produced a year.

The coal age in America was short—or so it seemed until recently. From the time of Woodrow Wilson to Richard Nixon the use of coal declined from 70 percent to about 17 percent of total energy consumption. An even more precipitous decline occurred with respect to anthracite, hard coal used widely a generation ago for heating homes. One hundred million tons were produced in 1917; 6 million in 1975. The abandonment of coal was not hard to understand. Oil and natural gas became more available and easily transportable. The environmental hazards and risks to miners, the dirt, the recurring tragedy of collapsing mines, the threat of strikes, and the memories of labor violence—all contributed to the image of coal as a primitive commodity to be transcended as quickly as possible. Steven A. Schneider summarizes the danger this way:

> Deep mining is the nation's most hazardous occupation. Since 1970, 125,000 miners have been injured and 216 killed in major mine disasters. Each miner has a one in eight chance of suffering an injury each year, and 17 out of every 100 miners contract black lung disease. If the true cost of deep-mined coal were to be calculated, it would include at least the $1.50 for every $20 ton of coal that the government currently pays to miners incapacitated by black lung disease. . . . Coal burned in U.S. utilities currently accounts for about a sixth of all fine-particulate air pollution.

Nevertheless, as far back as the early postwar years, coal production began increasing again at a steady rate. Starting in 1963 the major oil companies began buying up coalfields and mines in Appalachia and the Midwest. A few years later they began to lease coal reserves on government territory and on Indian lands. Gulf purchased Pittsburgh and Midway Coal. Continental took over Consolidation Coal (the nation's largest independent) and became the second largest holder of coal leases on federal lands. Exxon, the leading holder of state, federal, and Indian leases in the West, acquired 11 billion tons. Standard Oil of Ohio took over Old Ben, and Occidental bought Island Creek. In all, seven of the fifteen largest coal producers are now oil companies. A quarter of all coal reserves are now in the hands of the petroleum industry.

By 1975 the bituminous coal industry had reached an all-time high. "America has more coal than the Middle East has oil. Let's dig it." So ran a familiar advertisement in the aftermath of the Energy Crisis. Coal fascinates U.S. Government energy planners as the "energy bridge to the future," as Exxon Corporation calls it in the ads. The reason why is that the U.S. literally sits on an enormous bed of coal. (Why coal fascinates Exxon is that they own a good piece of that bed through the Monterey Coal Company and the Carter Mining Company.) Anyone who dreams of making the U.S. "self-sufficient" in energy cannot help being enthusiastic about coal. The U.S. Geological Survey has identified over 1,700 billion tons of coal, all available at a depth of less than 3,000 feet. About 437 billion tons of it are available using present mining technology and assuming today's prices. President Carter's original proposals called for a 69 percent increase in coal use by 1985; at that point, coal would produce more than half of all the nation's electricity. The idea was that as oil imports were reduced, the coal would be substituted to meet industrial needs. Tax incentives would be used to persuade industry to convert to coal burners, and higher taxes would be imposed on those who chose to stay with oil or natural gas. Congress chopped away at the proposals, and the rush back to coal has been something less than a stampede. By the middle of 1977 coal accounted for only about one percent more of total energy consumption than it did five years earlier. About 44 percent of the electricity of the country is now produced with coal. The Office of Technology Assessment projects an increase in coal consumption for electric power generation between 50 and 90 percent by 1985. It all depends, of course, on total energy demand and what happens to nuclear power. Direct use by industry has been modest (62 million tons in 1975), but it is expected to double by 1985. Although "tripling of coal production and use by 2000 appears to be possible without either substantial regulatory relaxation or major technological innovations," according to a 1979 study of the Office of Technology Assessment, a coal-based energy system presents many problems.

One is money. According to Bankers Trust Company estimates, about $20 billion in new capital for mine development alone is needed in the next few years. This is a manageable sum for the big energy companies, but they are reluctant to commit it until the economics of coal become clearer. The cost of producing coal and hence the profits from mining it depend upon a variety of political choices: administration policy on western coal leases, subsidies, the permissiveness of the pollution controllers, the development of new transportation technology, and the enforcement of mine safety. Let us look at some of these choices.

How profitable it is for the energy companies to mine their newly acquired coal depends critically upon transportation costs. Railroads are antiquated, and massive shipments of coal in both raw and processed forms cause accidents. An alternative mode of transporting coal is to reduce it to slurry, a sort of carboniferous mud, which is then propelled through 48-inch pipelines to its final destination. In recent years, the Bechtel Corporation, the principal contractor for this new coal technology, has engaged in a continuing skirmish with the railroads to acquire right-of-ways for slurry pipelines. The railroads successfully blocked the acquisition as well as legislation that would have subsidized the system. But Bechtel, Fluor, and a consortium of associated companies outflanked the railroads by getting condemnation orders from state courts for land under the railroad crossings.

The fight between the railroads and the construction giants is a good example of a persistent problem in alternative energy planning. The choice of technology can mean the rise or fall of an industry. Slurry pipelines may be more convenient, more efficient, and safer than rail transportation of coal, but if national policy dictates rebuilding the railroads, as many believe, diverting the coal traffic, a traditional mainstay of the railraod business, does not make sense. Whether old technology like the railroads is developed or new technologies are introduced can determine the fate of millions of people, whether they will have jobs or find themselves in another ghost town.

The choice of where to mine coal can determine the fate of entire regions. Eighty percent of coal production is in the East, but the big increases in production are taking place in the West where 60 percent of the reserves are located. An estimated 80 billion tons of coal, 16 percent of total reserves, lies on Indian land. In the past, oil companies and their coal subsidiaries have succeeded in leasing vast acreage on reservations on terms reminiscent of those on which the Dutch settlers acquired Manhattan. The average royalty for a ton of coal in the early 1970s was twelve cents. The top holder of leases on Indian lands is Peabody Coal, which used to be a subsidiary of Kennecott Copper. When Kennecott was forced to divest, Peabody was picked up by a consortium of Bechtel, Boeing, Fluor, Newmont Mining, and the Equitable Life Assurance Society. In March 1973 the Northern Cheyenne tribe began a revolt against the one-sided leases and petitioned for their cancellation. Since that time twenty-five western Indian tribes have gotten together in a Council on Energy Resource Tribes and have developed new bargaining strategies that include lawsuits—in 1978 the Crow won a suit against Shell and AMAX to cancel an exploitive lease—special taxes of 25 percent on coal developers, injunctions against the toxic emissions of power plants, renegotiation of royalty rates, and invitations to the Japanese and OPEC nations to compete with the U.S. companies for the increasingly valuable coal leases.

There are disagreements among the tribes on how to proceed. The Northern Cheyenne, for example, believe that "progress means developing our timber and agricultural resources. These are our livelihood and the core of our values. If our air is degraded these things will be diminished." Thus they oppose all coal development of their land for the foreseeable future and have demanded federal protection under the Clean Air Act. The Crow Indians, who want to develop their coal, are concerned that protecting the pristine air of their neighbors will prevent development of their own reserves since the drift of coal dust might violate air quality standards. The Indians face the classic dilemma of underdeveloped countries: How much should you sacrifice traditional values and modes of living in the name of progress? For Indians who have a 50 percent unemployment rate, the highest suicide rate in the nation, and per capita income only 40 percent of the national average, progress is not an abstract concept. But the strategy for using the vast riches of Indian land to reverse the process of four centuries of destruction and degradation at the hands of the white man has not yet emerged.

Although Indian claims are a problem, there are great financial advantages for integrated energy companies in looking to the West rather than the East for coal. Take the case of a Cleveland utility that, like many power companies, owns both coal mines and transportation facilities. Let us assume that it needs 3 million tons of coal. The advantages lie in mining it in Wyoming instead of Ohio despite the transportation costs. Wyoming is open territory with relatively few entrenched political interests to oppose and virtually no bureaucratic web with which to become entangled. Government money will build the necessary roads, schools, etc., to take care of the new community that will be built around the 4,000 jobs that will be created. These workers will be nonunion. Environmental problems can be solved much more swiftly and at a lower cost than in the East. Best of all, the transportation costs can be added to the rates that

Clevelanders are charged for electricity, and the company can actually make a profit on the transportation. From the point of view of society it is irrational to waste energy and court accidents by importing distant coal. Ohio already has a developed coal industry that is running below capacity with growing unemployment. Mining the coal in the East, although costs to the company might be higher, would make economic and social sense from the standpoint of both consumers and workers in Ohio. Rather than intruding into virgin territory and creating new coal towns overnight without thought of what will happen after the coal is exhausted or what alternative uses of the land are forever thereby precluded, it would seem more reasonable to make use of coal facilities that already exist. This is one more example of the conflict between planning to maximize corporate profits and the development of a sound and sane national energy policy.

For the companies, there are attractions to scratching coal from the surface with huge bulldozers and power shovels in the West instead of employing increasingly angry miners in much larger numbers to dig for it in underground galleries in the East. The increase of wildcat strikes has made the coalfields the most tempestuous arena of labor-management relations in the country. One man can produce three times as much coal in an hour strip-mining as he can by digging for it. Thus the return on investment for strip-mined coal is almost double that of underground coal. The sociology of underground mining is completely different from that of strip mining. The traditional mining family in which one generation descended into the pits as the last one reached retirement is becoming a relic; subterranean life with all its hazards is losing its attractions for young people. Strip mining, on the other hand, attracts former construction workers and a host of other workers looking for relatively high wages.

The trouble with strip mining is that the bulldozers leave the twisted and churned earth looking like the surface of the moon. To reclaim land is expensive. Estimates range from $1,000 to $8,000 an acre, which makes the reclaimed land cost more than the best Corn Belt farmland. Proper reclamation, which in some areas is impossible because of lack of rainfall, would add about one dollar a ton to the cost of strip-mined coal, and it is a cost which the companies have stoutly and to a large extent successfully resisted. Industry pressure "watered down" the strip mine bill, as President Carter noted when he signed it. But an official in charge of regulating the industry told me he could "shut down 80 percent of the strip mining of the country" under the new legislation if the political power to do it existed. The industry is still permitted to cut the tops off the Appalachian mountains, and prosthetic peaks are still beyond the reach of modern technology.

All forms of mining involve health and environmental costs that under social pressure are translated into economic costs. Compensatory payments to miners whose lungs have been damaged by the ever present black lung disease are likely to reach $8 billion in 1980. New systems for controlling respirable dust, better lighting, and rescue systems for trapped miners using seismic detectors are being introduced as a result of increased pressure over the deplorable safety conditions in underground mines, but mining is still dangerous and burning coal is still toxic. According to a National Academy of Sciences study the sulphur dioxide emitted from one coal-fired plant causes about 25 fatalities, 60,000 cases of respiratory disease, and $12 million in property damage each year. Massive reliance on coal, the Academy study warned, could produce the "greenhouse effect," a global warming trend triggered by the release of carbon dioxide that could change the wind patterns and make the weather in vast areas too capricious for farming.

Coal burning produces dangerous carcinogens in the atmosphere which affect everybody. This has been suspected since 1775, when Percivall Pott published his report of the frequent occurrence of cancer of the scrotum among chimney sweeps. The incidence of skin cancer among the employees of a pilot coal conversion plant in West Virginia which operated in the 1950s was more than sixteen times higher than the incidence of similar cancers in the surrounding population. A recent study of the National Institutes of Health concluded that at least 20 percent of all cancers are caused by industrial pollution.

Under recent amendments to the Clean Air Act, utilities must install "scrubbers," devices to remove pollutants by rendering the sulphur dioxide harmless. Scrubbers, according to the Environmental Protection Agency, increase the cost of producing electricity anywhere from 6 to 15 percent. The devices are far from perfected; they carry only a ninety-day warranty. The ones now on the market do not purify nitrogen oxides, which cause lower-tract respiratory diseases, particularly in children. Under present plans to increase reliance on coal, nitrogen oxide levels would increase 18 percent by 1985, according to a Energy Research and Development Administration study.

Mining could be made substantially safer. Years of extra life for miners can be purchased by investing hundreds of millions in safer mines. This has been done in nationalized coal production systems in the Soviet Union, China, and Britain and in privately owned mines in Australia. Health care now takes about 8.5 percent of the gross national product, about as much as the military. Whether the United States can safely rely on coal for a major share of its energy needs depends upon our understanding the true environmental costs and devising a political strategy for sharing these costs in an equitable way. The relative market price of alternative fuels, as we have seen, is determined by a host of political and social factors, not by Adam Smith's invisible hand. The critical factor in determining the relative cost and safety of coal as compared, say, with nuclear energy is technology. How much safer, cheaper, and more transportable can new technology make an ancient geological deposit? How much will the new technology cost and who will pay for it?

Charles A. Berg, the former chief engineer of the Federal Power Commission, has traced the historical process by which coal replaced wood as the prime industrial fuel and concludes that "the advent of new and more effective processes, which happened to be designed about the use of coal, had at least as much to do with the industrial switch from wood to coal as did the relative prices of these two fuels." Such processes, beginning with the first coal gassification plant built in 1836 in Magdesprung, Germany, the Siemens iron-making furnace, the Bessemer steelmaking process a few years later, advanced techniques for glassmaking, and so on, seem "to have galvanized the scientific world and focused the world's talented minds on coal science. . . ." Thus patterns of innovation create a congenial culture within which to develop one energy source or another.

When coal was replaced by petroleum, coal science could no longer compete for the best innovative minds, and the state of technology in the industry declined. In the last few years, however, a great deal of attention and investment has gone to developing new processes for creating synthetic fuels from coal. The Department of Energy is sponsoring a number of pilot projects testing alternative processes for converting coal to gas. The first commercial plants are not expected to be ready until the mid-1980s. Conversion of coal to gas is still not cost competitive with oil, even at the high 1979 OPEC price. It also requires enormous quantities of water—from 30 to 200 gallons to produce a million BTU of coal-gas energy. Since the conversion plants are slated for location close to the western coal fields available for strip mining, an area of severe water shortage, this presents a serious problem for the development of coal gassification technology.

Major attention is turning to processes for turning coal into liquid fuel. During World War II the Germans produced synthetic petroleum from coal in commercial quantities by a process known as Fischer-Tropsch. South Africa, which has no domestic crude oil, has greatly improved the technology and is now dependent on it. The state-owned South African Coal and Gas Corporation supplies about 80 percent of the nation's energy needs from coal and coal-related fuels. For the United States, resorting to synthetic fuels involves great risks. The capital costs for building coal-based synthetic crude plants are estimated conservatively to be $150 billion. Some bankers privately believe these estimates should be doubled. Where all this money will come from is an obvious problem. The government cannot simply print it without fueling a crippling inflation. Nor can federal bureaucrats find it without cutting spending radically elsewhere more than they dare. Private bankers are likely to be reluctant to supply the capital on the scale needed, even with government guarantees, because the investment is risky. Whether expensive fuel alternatives are competitive depends upon the price of oil. Were OPEC to lower the price of a barrel of oil after major investments in synthetics were made, the consequences would be disastrous.

Exactly the same sorts of problems exist with respect to expensive processes for obtaining oil from shale and tar sands. Shale is a finely textured sedimentary rock that contains an organic material. A ton of shale heated to roughly 900 degrees F. can yield from 15 to 35 gallons of oil. Theoretically, shale oil is one of the most abundant energy sources in the U.S. Indeed, the Green River Formation oil shales of Colorado, Utah, and Wyoming make up the world's largest known hydrocarbon deposits. There are perhaps two trillion barrels of low-sulfur petroleum in the West, about 80 percent of which is on public lands.

There are two ways to extract shale. One is to mine it. That causes environmental damage and takes a good deal of water—as much as 250,000 acre-feet a year for a million barrels a day. This is no more than a coal liquefaction plant of the same size would take, but the water must come from the Colorado River, and there is not enough. Underground heating and thinning is an alternative process. Armand Hammer of Occidental Petroleum is investing in a pilot plant that he thinks can produce a barrel of oil at a cost competitive with OPEC oil. But the process is energy-intensive. Perhaps as much as half the energy is used to find, squeeze, thin, and transport the other half. Moreover, the industry has a long record of promising cost-efficient shale oil. Having leased federal shale lands at bargain prices over the years, oil companies have been unable to produce oil from shale at competitive prices and in sufficient quantities even in the face of the dramatic rise in the price of oil. Tar sands, which are another theoretically abundant source of oil, have the same high capital and water requirements and pose the same sort of environmental hazards as shale development.

Approximately 20,000 acres have been leased to Gulf, Standard of Indiana, Phillips, Sun, and Occidental for experimental operations. Gulf and Indiana Standard had originally planned to produce 75,000 barrels a day of shale by 1980, but because of unanticipated costs and environmental problems this will be delayed at least until 1985.

For these reasons the search is on for new coal technologies that could make it safer to transport, more efficient to burn, and less polluting. One promising technology is fluidized-bed combustion. Crushed coal is fed into a bed of inert ash mixed with limestone or similar material. The bed is "fluidized" or held in suspension by injecting air through the bottom of the bed at a controlled rate great enough to produce a boiling effect. The coal burns within the bed in such a way as to maintain high combustion efficiency, high heat transfer rates, and reduced emission of pollutants. A pilot plant will begin operation in 1980 at Woodbridge, New Jersey. The U.S. has joined Britain and Germany in building a test facility under the auspices of the International Energy Agency. Fluidized-bed devices are now being made in Sweden. According to the energy expert Amory Lovins, the technology can produce the same energy as a gassification plant using only two-fifths the coal and at half to two-thirds the cost.

The years in which the world discovered the oil shortage have been kind to the owners of coal. The price per ton jumped from $4.99 to $21.50 between 1969 and 1977, a bigger increase than for oil. In the mid-1970s profits jumped from 39 cents a ton to $3.25 a ton. Whether profits are "excessive" cannot be answered any better than in the case of oil. The energy companies defend their enormous profits and even their enormous profit increases (in the third quarter of 1979, as a consequence of the big OPEC price rise, Mobil increased its profits by 131 percent, Texaco by 211 percent) by noting that their return on investment since 1974 has averaged 12.5 percent, slightly less than the average return for all manufacturing companies. Jeffrey A. Nichols, president of a corporation doing economic research for oil companies, is not disturbed by his clients' profits, which, he says, are neither "excessive, abnormal or unfair." But this is not a judgment that can be made by comparing profit and loss statements. One would need to know how these figures were calculated and the extent to which monopoly, government subsidy, and illegal overcharging contribute to profits before making such a judgment. Concentration is crucial to profits in the coal industry. The top fifteen coal producers mine 41 percent of all the coal. But the industry is even more concentrated than this would suggest. Coal does not have a national market. It is sold regionally, and the regional markets are dominated by a single company. As the Office of Technology Assessment study puts it, "Consolidation is the key company among eastern-based producers, Peabody in the Midwest, and AMAX in the West." Four companies control 65 percent of the business in the Northern Plains and 64 percent in the Southwest. Interlocking directorates are commonplace. As the OTA study notes:

> Consolidation Coal—the Nation's second largest coal producer—is fairly typical of the ownership patterns among energy-owned coal pro-

ducers. Consol is a subsidiary of Continental Oil. Continental's board was tied to 12 coal-reserve holders or coal producers, 9 coal consumers, and 20 capital suppliers through at least one indirect director interlock as of 1976. Continental shared a director with Bankers Trust of New York, Continental Illinois, and Equitable Life Assurance. (Equitable is a major stockholder in Peabody Coal, the nation's biggest coal producer and fourth largest reserve holder.) Seven of the 20 capital suppliers were among the company's top 20 stockholders. Continental's biggest stockholder, Newmont Mining Company (3.29 percent) is also the principal stockholder in Peabody Coal (27.5 percent). Capital suppliers with whom Continental shares a director are major stockholders in other leading coal producers and reserve holders.

4.

There are three great issues surrounding nuclear energy. The most publicized battle is the clash of experts over safety. The second concerns the economics and efficiency of nuclear power. The third has to do with whether a plutonium economy and democracy are compatible.

The safety issue has aroused spontaneous citizens' movements in every industrial country outside the socialist world. The antinuclear movement is really a sort of people's international—large numbers of citizens in several different countries taking to the streets, roughly at the same time but quite independently, to express the same element of fear.* The movement sprang to life because people in every industrial country began to worry about contamination. Ironically, for more than thirty years the United States and the Soviet Union had been amassing nuclear weapons designed to produce radiation levels beyond anything the worst nuclear accident could produce and had been accumulating nuclear wastes from weapons production beyond anything the nuclear industry had created without eliciting a comparable public outcry.

Truth about the hazards of atomic fuel has been a casualty of the war between the nuclear industry and the antinuclear movement. The scientific process by which nuclear fission produces energy is clear enough. Barry Commoner describes it this way:

> The response of Uranium-235 is rare among natural atoms: When a neutron—moving sufficiently slowly—collides with it, there is a good possibility that the Uranium-235 nucleus will split. The fission products are two atomic fragments, each roughly one-half of the original atom,

* A few weeks after the Three Mile Island accident, nearly 100,000 people marched in protest in Washington, D.C.

plus some free but fast-moving neutrons. All of these fission products, in their sum, are slightly lighter than the Uranium-235 nucleus from which they were formed. This slight difference in mass is converted to energy, in accordance with the famous Einstein equation which states that the amount of energy (E) is equivalent to the mass (m) multiplied by the square of the speed of light (c). Since the speed of light is a very large number, its square is enormous, so that a truly tremendous amount of energy is given off when the very small mass "disappears" (that is, is converted into energy) as a uranium atom is split. . . .

If some of the free, fast neutrons produced when the Uranium-235 atoms split are slowed down and then collide with and split fresh Uranium-235 atoms, a chain reaction is set off which can quickly spread through a lump of uranium, releasing huge amounts of energy in a very short time.

There is no secret to the process for producing nuclear fuel, or for that matter nuclear weapons. The technology has been publicly available for years, and indeed a Princeton undergraduate with no special knowledge of physics was able to demonstrate that he could build a nuclear weapon with materials available from the local hardware store. But obtaining the facts about the safety record of nuclear reactors, the nature and extent of past accidents, the reliability of safety devices, the incidence of human error, the true nature of the threat of low-level radiation, and the problem of nuclear waste disposal are all much more difficult.

One reason why the nuclear establishment has a severe credibility problem is that the government and industry enthusiasts have a long record of making euphoric, misleading, or false public statements about safety and efficiency and of releasing unpleasant facts about the nuclear energy program only in response to lawsuits and other forms of pressure. When the Atoms for Peace program began in 1953, the proponents predicted that nuclear energy would be "too cheap to meter." More than twenty-five years later there are seventy-one reactors operating in the United States. None, as might be expected, provides free electricity. More to the point, the underlying assumption that nuclear energy is cheap and efficient relative to other fuels is coming increasingly under challenge.

There are three separate hazards that have been the focus of numerous investigative commissions, scientific reports, and lawsuits. The most catastrophic of course is the possibility of a "meltdown," such as was feared in the 1979 accident at Three Mile Island near Harrisburg, Pennsylvania. The radioactive core in a reactor becomes extremely hot, and elaborate water-circulating systems are employed to keep the reactor from overheating. Many nuclear scientists are worried that these complex cooling systems might fail and that the molten core could burn a hole through the bottom of the massive container that seals off the radioactive material from the outside world, thus allowing the deadly material to escape into the atmosphere. If that should happen, no one doubts that severe destruction would occur. A million-kilowatt nuclear power plant after a year of operation accumulates ten billion curies of radioactive material, more than enough, if properly distributed, to kill everyone in the U.S. Of course, there is enough water in the Mississippi River, if properly distributed, to accomplish the same end. The question, then, is how likely is a meltdown to occur, and if it does, how likely is a dangerous dispersal of radioactive poisons?

The Rasmussen Report, an assessment of accident risks published by the Nuclear Regulatory Commission in 1974, estimates the chances of a meltdown as one in 20,000 reactor-years (300 reactor-years have already elapsed without a catastrophic release of radioactivity). When it was released, the report was criticized by the Union of Concerned Scientists, a group organized by MIT Professor Henry Kendall, which since 1971 has been raising serious questions about the adequacy of the safety measures in the nuclear program. A group organized by the American Physical Society also questioned the report for adopting overly optimistic assumptions and thus arriving at overly complacent conclusions. In the "worst-case scenarios," according to the Rasmussen Report, 3,300 would die, 43,000 would become ill, and $14 billion of property damage would be incurred. In 1979 the Nuclear Regulatory Commission repudiated the study on the ground that the methodology for computing these figures was questionable. While nuclear critics celebrated the victory, other scientists who reviewed the report pointed out that the error might have in fact exaggerated the probability and the effects of a "meltdown." Critics of the report continue to point out that the casualty estimates assume something a good deal more improbable than a nuclear accident—that is, the successful evacuation of large cities in the vicinity of nuclear plants. Without evacuation, tens of thousands would die. The Union of Concerned Scientists believes that radioactive damage from a large reactor could be lethal at a range of 65 miles and cause fallout effects up to 400 miles.

No one, of course, knows the answer to the questions about catastrophic accident with scientific precision. What has alarmed those who worry about nuclear safety is a persistent pattern of concealing bad news. In 1957 Brookhaven National Laboratory carried out a study for the AEC which estimated that 3,400 people would be killed and 43,000 injured; six years later the laboratory updated the study to take into account the larger reactors then in use and estimated 45,000 fatalities and "an area of disaster . . . equal to that of the state of Pennsylvania." The revised study was kept secret and made available only after it was wrested from the AEC in a Freedom of Information suit.

The AEC has also suppressed internal criticism of safety standards. Whether a meltdown will happen and whether the radioactive materials can be contained if it does happen depend upon the reliability of emergency cooling systems that would be activated in the event the normal cooling system failed. Tests conducted by the AEC in 1971 showed that the systems did not behave in the way the computer programs had predicted. Scientists and engineers at AEC reactor safety research centers shared some of the misgivings of outside critics, but they were ordered not to speak out. The AEC official in charge of reactors admitted censoring research reports, and he was eventually removed from office.

The safety record of the nuclear submarine program, which is cited as reassuring evidence by nuclear proponents, is not available to the public. Indeed, the American Physical Society was denied access to it for its study of light water reactors. The Browns Ferry fire that occurred in 1975 knocked out five different elements of the emergency core cooling system and closed down two TVA reactors for more than a year. It is regarded by Carl Walske, president of the Atomic Industrial Forum, the industry trade association, as "a very annoying accident that didn't hurt anybody" just as Three Mile Island was an "unwelcome event." But for critics such as Allen Kneese, who points out that "we managed to incinerate three astronauts in an extremely high technology operation where the utmost precautions were allegedly being taken," such incidents confirm the vulnerability to human error of complex and dangerous systems. In the race between foolproof systems and fools, i.e., bored, careless, or overwrought people, the systems eventually lose. The Three Mile Island incident unveiled for a few days the world in which the managers of nuclear technology operate, and the glimpse was not reassuring: plants failing to meet specifications, inspectors failing to find the failures, politicians and technical advisors flailing about when the crisis arrived, unable to agree on the risk or whether evacuation was advisable.

Even after Three Mile Island, optimistic rhetoric continues from government and industry officials committed to nuclear power. In the end, it is asserted, no one was hurt. Being killed in a nuclear accident is as likely, former AEC Chairman Dixy Lee Ray used to say, as being bitten by a poisonous snake while crossing the street in Washington, D.C. Perhaps so, but no private insurance companies will insure against a nuclear accident, and Congress has taken the risk seriously enough to provide insurance of $560 million per accident, which the Supreme Court noted is a good "starting point" for calculating the costs of a reactor accident.

The risks of a catastrophic meltdown are no easier to calculate after

Three Mile Island than before. That is one of the strongest arguments against basing the economy on nuclear power. The costs and consequences of a catastrophic accident are literally incalculable. Proponents of nuclear power makes the telling point that life is dangerous, however one moves; coal dust kills, coal cars crash, mines explode, oil fields burn. The "greenhouse effect" from coal could theoretically ruin agriculture. No doubt the casualties to date from two hundred years of the fossil fuel economy exceed those of the nuclear economy. One government-sponsored study often cited by proponents of nuclear power estimates that from 2,000 to 20,000 deaths a year and as many as 50,000 injuries are traceable in one way or another to the use of fossil fuel for the generation of electric power. But the consequences of a single catastrophe in the plutonium economy, unlike the fossil fuel economy, can unleash a chain reaction of disasters that threaten the very life support systems themselves—water, air, and soil. The magnitude of a catastrophe flowing from the sort of human and technical errors that have already been made is potentially so enormous that society should choose less risky alternatives where they exist. The economist Hazel Henderson put it this way:

> In calculating probabilities [of a nuclear accident] for insurance purposes, equilibrium conditions are assumed, leading to the assumption that the greater the accident, the less likely its occurrence. In real life, we are now dealing with a disequilibrium economy that piles risk on risk. You could just as easily assume the greater the accident, the greater the probability of its occurrence. We don't know how to model probability under these conditions; the underlying logic of insurance breaks down and we merely socialize more and more risks. This in itself would be a good rationale for being very conservative about energy technologies— underwriting conservation and renewable energy where the risks are in the knowable range, rather than technologies where the multiplication of risks is totally unmodelable.

The catastrophic accident is the most dramatic battleground in the fight over nuclear power, but it is not the most urgent. Most critics rate the probability low—though not as low as the industry. Closer at hand are the deaths from low-level radiation that have already occurred and are now occuring. From 1946 to 1960, according to D. C. Johnson of the U.S. Public Health Service, 6,000 underground uranium miners were "significantly and needlessly exposed to radioactive gases present in the air of uranium mines," and he estimates that some 600 to 1,100 deaths from lung cancer will result. Better control of radiation levels in the mines was introduced in the 1960s, but the matter of "acceptable" radiation exposure for miners is still a matter of controversy. Workers in processing plants, particularly those who work with plutonium, also face hazards that are arousing increasing controversy. "26 plutonium workers who received serious lung doses in 1954 and another 25 who were exposed in 1965," according to a 1977 report in *Science,* had not yet developed symptoms of lung cancer. But a number of studies now suggest that the incidence of cancer deaths is 6 to 7 percent higher among workers in nuclear plants than among the general population. Dr. Thomas Mancuso conducted a ten-year study on the cause of death of 3,710 former atomic power workers and found that the radiation dose at which the likelihood of getting bone cancer or leukemia doubles is far smaller than previously estimated. According to the study of the Portsmouth, New Hampshire, shipyard workers by Thomas Najarian, the exposure to radiation produced an incidence of leukemia six times the national average.

Proponents of nuclear power attack the conclusions drawn from these studies as "going way beyond the data." The problem of course with all such studies is that the latency period for low level radiation-triggered cancer may be twenty years or more. The data may not be "complete" until a high percentage of the study population actually show cancer symptoms. In the history of science there are examples from time to time of alarmists who speak out on the dangerous social implications of scientific decisions on the basis of "incomplete" data and are usually deemed a bit irresponsible by their professional peers. (Occasionally, they are rehabilitated and honored for having made a nuisance of themselves. Linus Pauling, who was vilified in the late 1950s for condemning as fraudulent official levels of "safe" radiation then used to justify the continuation of atmospheric testing of nuclear weapons, later received the Nobel Peace Prize for his agitation. There is no agreement even today on what constitutes an "acceptable" dose of radiation.) An ordinary confused citizen cannot possibly follow the dispute over the methodology of radiation studies. One can reflect, however, that in every case of radiation exposure over the past thirty-five years—from the victims of Hiroshima (including U.S. soldiers who were sent in weeks after the explosion), to the natives of the Bikini atoll where bombs were tested, to exposed workers in the testing areas of Nevada, to X-rayed patients—the dangers of radiation and the persistence of these dangers have been significantly and in some cases, knowingly, underestimated by those in control of the technology.

The West Valley processing plant, which operated from 1966 to 1972, has been used as a case study of low-level radiation risk. According to the environmentalist Sheldon Novick, it released more radioactivity into the environment and exposed more workers to radiation than all the then-operating nuclear power plants taken together. Novick describes the casual recruitment process:

> Whenever a dirty clean-up job had to be done directly by hand or a repair job was needed in intensely radioactive surroundings, the company would recruit hundreds of unskilled workers. These men (apparently few or no women were employed) were given a few minutes of instruction, dressed in protective clothing and then sent to do their job —washing a wall, perhaps, or loosening a bolt on a highly radioactive bit of machinery. Within a few minutes, or perhaps a few hours, each worker received the maximum radiation exposure permitted, even if he had followed all of the safety procedures necessary in dressing and undressing; after the allotted time, therefore, each group of unskilled workers was pulled off the job and replaced with a fresh group. The pay was three dollars an hour, and a worker was paid for a minimum of four hours, even though he might be able to work only a few minutes in the radioactive setting. It was the possibility of receiving a half-day's pay for a few minutes work which attracted employees; it was popular work, and the company had no trouble recruiting temporary laborers, although there have been some accusations that some of the recruiting was done in bars and in the local skid row.

The radiological impact of West Valley on fish streams, plant life, and the human population have been examined in detail. In each of these areas the "safe" levels are controversial. Experts differ by factors of as much as 100,000 in their estimates of the cancer-causing effects of a given dose of plutonium. Nonetheless, specialists in various phases of the nuclear cycle are becoming increasingly conservative about what is an acceptable level of radiation. Government standards have in the past been found consistently too lax and in many cases have been tightened—but too late for perhaps thousands of individuals who have been doomed to cancer. Every tightening of standards and extra safety precaution involves extra costs. Since the matter of relative cost is a crucial issue that will decide what the energy base for the U.S. and much of the rest of the world is to be, the industry resists "unnecessary precautions" and tends to be complacent about what is necessary.

Waste disposal is a peculiar hazard that has evoked an intense sparring between the industry and environmental critics, and a number of bizarre suggestions for how to arrange our affairs in the age of plutonium. A typical billion-watt nuclear power plant produces about 2,500 tons of waste, enough to kill 100 times the population of the surrounding city if it were all released into the atmosphere. Some radioactive wastes have a half-life of a century or more, which means that some will persist thousands of years or more in a dangerous state. (Material with a half-life of one hundred years becomes half as radioactive after a century, the remainder a quarter as toxic after another century, and so on.)

About 80 million gallons of radioactive waste from the nation's military programs are stored in steel tanks in Hanford, Washington, and Aiken, South Carolina. Hundreds of thousands of gallons of radioactive waste have leaked from these underground tanks. Government inspectors believe the leakage poses no hazard, and no clear history of serious environmental damage or injuries to human beings has been established. Nevertheless, the vulnerability of metal tanks to corrosion and to the ceaseless bombardment of radioactive particles from the wastes has prompted a search for better solutions, none of them particularly reassuring. They include deep storage in salt, basalt, or shale; reprocessing the wastes into storable rocks, which are much less toxic; new reprocessing techniques that would reduce the danger period to a mere 300 years; digging storage facilities under the Antarctic ice cap; storing huge quantities in certain Kansas salt mines (a proposition that did not sell in Kansas); and—an idea once put forward by Energy Secretary James Schlesinger—shooting the wastes into outer space, where they would eventually be absorbed by the sun. The favored solution is now to store the wastes in huge glass containers underground. Some specialists on waste disposal, such as Rustum Roy of Pennsylvania State University, believe that new ceramic technology that will be available in a few years will provide much cheaper and more efficient means of disposal. But because the waste disposal issue has become the focus of antinuclear activity, neither the government nor the industry wish to wait. Roy's report for the National Academy of Science on new waste disposal technology was delayed at the urging of the Department of Energy.

The "breeder" reactor manufactures more fissionable fuel than it uses, and it has been pressed by the nuclear industry as the answer to the Energy Crisis. If the breeder reactor is built, the safety issues are likely to become more urgent. Its product is plutonium-239, a substance much more toxic than uranium, indeed the most poisonous substance known and certainly the most persistent. A substantial nuclear energy system would require large amounts of plutonium. Plutonium has a half-life of 24,000 years, which means in effect that dangerous poisons would remain on earth for eons. If even a little escaped into the atmosphere it could trigger perhaps as many as 600,000 additional cases of cancer a year in the U.S. according to former AEC scientist Dr. J. W. Gofman. If even one ten-millionth of the plutonium supply for a major breeder reactor program were stolen, the thief could construct a weapon capable of blowing up a medium-sized city.

Safety has been the most publicized battleground for attacking nuclear power. But the issue that has stopped the industry in its tracks, at least for the present, is not safety but economics. The nonrenewable mineral source of the nuclear fuel cycle is uranium. Since the early 1970s the price of uranium has soared from six dollars to over forty dollars a pound. The United States is self-sufficient in uranium and, according to a study by the Congressional Research Service, will continue to be so until 1990. Eighty-seven percent of world reserves that can be cheaply mined are located in four countries—the United States, Canada, Australia, and South Africa; the same countries have 70 percent of the additional reserves that could be exploited with more expensive technology. The U.S. Bureau of Mines estimates that total world resources are around 1,864,000 tons, about a third of which are located in North America. (Other countries that have significant reserves include Sweden, Niger, Gabon, France, and India. The oceans contain, according to U.S. government estimates, about 5 billion tons of uranium, but 5.5 million cubic feet of seawater must be processed to recover a single pound.

Orders for new reactors have fallen precipitously, from a high of forty-one ordered in 1973 to zero in 1977. The nuclear industry is in crisis not only because costs of nuclear plants and the price of uranium, but also the costs of waste disposal and environmental preservation have escalated wildly. (To preserve a stretch of seacliff threatened by the enlargement of the San Onofre nuclear power station near San Clemente, California, according to Southern California Edison officials, would cost $100 million.)

Whether these reserves are adequate depends upon the demand. In 1975 the United States, which had for many years banned imports of uranium to protect the domestic industry, started importing uranium. The demand for uranium in 1973 was 6,900 tons of ore, but the demand for the year 2000 is expected to be between 39,700 and 89,300 tons. Frank Baranowski, director of materials and production for the Atomic Energy Commission (now the Department of Energy), testified in 1974 that demand would race ahead of U.S. domestic supply by almost one million tons over the next twenty-five years. This is the reason why the House Committee on Government Operations in 1978 issued a report stating flatly that nuclear power "is no longer a cheap energy resource."

The oil companies have invested $2.4 billion in uranium exploration, mining, and processing since the 1960s. Five domestic oil producers, along with three other companies, control 80 percent of uranium reserves. Kerr-McGee and Gulf by themselves control over half. Gulf owns the deepest uranium mine in the country, located in New Mexico, and plans to invest about $800 million to develop it. Kerr-McGee also controls a quarter of the nation's uranium milling capacity. The familiar pattern of audacious acquisition and cautious development we noted with respect to coal and shale is also present in the nuclear fuel cycle. In the late 1960s oil companies had ambitions with respect to the nuclear power industry appropriate to their status. Exxon was planning to invest $4.5 billion in a uranium enrichment plant. In 1973 the nuclear industry secured orders for forty-one reactors, the all-time boom year for nuclear power. Four years later the industry, as *Nucleonics Week* put it, was "slowly, very slowly, bleeding to death."

Exxon abandoned its enrichment plant. Gulf, struggling to recover its respectability after bribery scandals had compelled the Mellon family to oust the chairman—a rare public rite in an economy supposedly run by managers—was too tied to nuclear power to disengage so easily. The most nuclear of the oil companies, Gulf has been in virtually all phases of the industry—mining, enriching, and reactor building, although it is getting out of the reactor business.

In 1972 a worldwide uranium cartel was formed to control the excess supplies in world commerce in the interests of "price stability." It succeeded handsomely. Within twenty months the price of uranium went from $6 to $26 a pound. Gulf participated in the cartel through its Canadian subsidiary, on orders of the Canadian Government, it claims, and for this misdemeanor was fined $40,000. But the discovery of the cartel, which all the participants say is now disbanded, set off a lawsuit boom. When the price rose, Westinghouse and other suppliers reneged on their contracts, and when the wickedness of the uranium owners was revealed, the legal justification for extrication from disastrous contracts was at hand. Westinghouse sued Gulf. Gulf sued Westinghouse. The uranium producers sued Gulf. Twenty-seven utilities sued Westinghouse. Gulf paid its lawyers $25 million in 1977, hoping thereby to recover $300 to $400 million from its countersuits and to avoid losing a roughly equivalent sum.

If the U.S. follows President Carter's original energy proposals and uses nuclear power to meet 23 percent of electric power production by 1985—it supplies about 13 percent of the nation's electricity today—and uranium is no more plentiful or cheap to produce than it appears to be, then the economic argument for breeder reactors becomes almost irresistible.

According to the Atomic Industrial Forum in 1976 it cost 1.5 cents to produce a kilowatt-hour of electricity with nuclear fuel, 1.8 cents with coal, and 3.5 cents with oil. As a 1975 study for the Department of Commerce by Richard J. Barber Associates points out, comparing costs of producing electricity by nuclear power or, say, by coal, is difficult. The government subsidizes the production process by making enrichment processing research and other facilities available to private industry at costs that do not reflect the huge capital outlays. Nuclear power plants otherwise prohibitively costly have been partially subsidized by plutonium sales to the U.S. Government for the weapons program. (In the 1950s the government was paying $50 a gram.) Thus the fuel may be relatively cheap to the consumer but only because the taxpayer is footing the bill.

There are hundreds of assumptions to take into account on fuel cost comparisons and studies to suit almost any argument or purpose. Nevertheless, the Barber Associates report concludes, "There is a distinct tendency in the nuclear energy literature to underestimate nuclear power costs." There has also been a distinct tendency to exaggerate nuclear power plant performance. The energy economist Charles Komanoff prepared a study in 1976 of the performance of nuclear power plants for the Council on Economic Priorities and found that commercial power plants were operating at an average of 59 percent of capacity, but actually they are cost efficient only when operating at 70 to 80 percent of capacity.

In the last two years, the capital costs to private industry have skyrocketed. A demonstration breeder that was supposed to have cost $2 billion when proposed a few years ago is now estimated to cost about $11 billion. Although the cost of uranium fuel has increased fivefold in the last few years, fuel has become a progressively less significant factor in the overall cost. The reason is that the costs of construction have risen even faster, mostly because of the heavy expense involved in redesigning reactors to meet new safety standards. The industry argues that the antinuclear activists themselves are responsible for delaying construction of nuclear power plants and for adding significantly to the cost. Environmentalists are blamed for pushing through unreasonable safety standards. (Why, industry spokesmen argue, should a reactor have to be fitted with a concrete covering sufficient to withstand the force of a crashing 747 jet?) But the report of the House Committee on Government Operations released in 1978 puts the blame for rising costs on industry mismanagement. The economic problems of the industry seem to be inherent in the nuclear fuel cycle itself. As society learns more of the hazards of nuclear energy, citizens demand more precautions, and these cost money, particularly in a time of high interest rates.

The health and safety risks of nuclear energy are serious but hard to evaluate; especially in the light of the competing risks of the obvious alternatives. Coal plants in large cities, Christian Hohenemser and associates report in *Science,* expose the surrounding population to more radioactivity than reactors of equivalent power. Power plants could become safer. Nuclear energy could, theoretically, become cheaper and even competitive. But there is a third issue, the least discussed but the most serious: A plutonium economy offers an unavoidable choice between nuclear anarchy and nuclear despotism.

The problem starts with the stubborn fact that nuclear power came into the world as a by-product of nuclear weapons. Public concern over nuclear power is in part, as the psychiatrist Robert Jay Lifton and others have suggested, displaced anxiety over nuclear war. A society in which nuclear materials are plentiful lives in danger, for the same fissionable materials that light cities can also explode atomic bombs. Diversion of fissionable materials and sabotage are not academic problems. Both have happened. According to a House subcommittee staff report, "more than 50 tons of nuclear material cannot be accounted for by the 34 uranium and plutonium processing plants in the country"—including 6,000 pounds of weapons-grade material. How much of this has been diverted we do not know. Declassified files of the Atomic Energy Commission reveal that the agency has been concerned that "uranium could theoretically have been diverted by a mechanism of overshipping and understating the true quantities on the transfer document." Official concern that weapons-grade material was diverted to China and Israel prompted a long but inconclusive investigation.

There have been threats of violence against nuclear facilities in the U.S.; sixty-four bombings of utilities in the U.S. took place in 1974 alone. In November 1972 three men with guns and grenades hijacked a Southern Airlines DC-9 and threatened to crash it into a reactor at the Oak Ridge National Laboratory if the desired ransom was not immediately forthcoming. Three years later, two French nuclear installations were bombed. An Illinois nuclear power plant had a series of accidents that strongly suggested inside sabotage.

Theft of about 20 pounds of fissionable material is enough to make a crude bomb. Former weapons maker Theodore Taylor estimates that a small bomb (about the size of the one dropped on Hiroshima) could kill a million people if exploded on Wall Street at lunch hour on a business day. At the American Nuclear Society Executive Conference on Safeguards held in 1977, industry executives said that the price for safeguarding nuclear material could run into the billions and even the most sophisticated security system, they concluded, could be outwitted or outgunned by terrorists.

In 1974 the AEC recommended the creation of a special federal police force to guard plutonium shipments; the National Regulatory Commission wants the Army to do the job. The Rosenbaum Report on nuclear plant security prepared in 1974 for the Atomic Energy Commission called for "an ongoing analysis of the people in the plant and of the community around the plant . . . electronic and other means of surveillance . . . [and] infiltration of [antinuclear] groups themselves.'' Police in several states, including Texas and New Hampshire, have collected dossiers on nuclear power opponents. The Virginia Electric Power Company a few years ago asked the legislature for the power to arrest suspicious persons around its nuclear plants and to search their homes.

The Karen Silkwood case has become the symbol of the civil liberties problem in a nuclear economy. On her way to meet a *New York Times* reporter to describe health hazards and the company's failure to take safety precautions at a Kerr-McGee nuclear fuel plant in Oklahoma, the young worker and union activist met with a mysterious fatal car accident. Though the state police concluded she had fallen asleep at the wheel, a private investigator reported that she had been forced off the road. A jury decided against Kerr-McGee and awarded $18 million in punitive damages for the willful disregard of her safety and for the harassment to which she was subjected when she tried to protect her fellow workers.

There is no way of avoiding what Alvin Weinberg, then director of the Energy Laboratory at Oak Ridge, called the ''Faustian bargain.'' An inexhaustible supply of energy is available but only at the price of a ''vigilance and a longevity of our social institutions that we are quite unaccustomed to.'' This is a gentle way of putting it. Society will be completely dependent on the ''nuclear people,'' as Weinberg calls the priests and guardians of the brave new world. The problem of nuclear power has involved Presidents in some form of public deception. President Eisenhower ordered a cover-up of the disastrous effects on soldiers at atomic weapons tests. President Carter gave the nuclear industry private support for the building of the breeder reactor while he was taking a public position against it. In the plutonium economy, there can be no hope of safety and peace of mind without making sure that the government has its eye on all potential terrorists and troublemakers. The result will be a degree of surveillance, centralization, and government intrusion that will cause us to remember America of the 1970s as a laissez-faire paradise.

5.

When a society buys an energy system, it is also buying a particular path of development. By choosing to burn up imported fossil fuels, to develop new coal technologies, to take the nuclear option, or to develop new alternatives—solar energy, fusion, harnessing of the ocean winds— leaders are also making decisions about how dependent society will be on scarce minerals, how much water it will use, how many jobs will be created, which cities and regions will rise and and which will fall, and who will hold political power. Some energy sources, such as solar or biomass conversion (burning of refuse and vegetable products), are well adapted to decentralized use, although they can also be used in centralized ways. Decentralized energy sources make more possible the self-reliance of local communities. If it has its own solar or wind-based energy sources, for example, the Northeast becomes less dependent upon the Southwest for natural gas. If local communities control their energy sources, they can determine the prices for their citizens instead of being dependent upon oil companies, the sheiks of Arabia, or the U.S. Government to decide how much of each dollar earned will go to drive the car or heat the house. The decisions of oil companies, electric utilities, and OPEC suppliers between 1973 and 1977 caused gas and electric rates to increase 99 percent in those years.

Thus energy choices are not technical choices. They directly determine who will feel the effect of inflation and who will pass those costs to others. (In 1978, according to one survey, one out of every five older Americans had to choose between buying groceries and paying the utility bill.) Energy choices involve the most basic decisions about values: What is efficiency and what do we sacrifice for it? Is interdependence good or bad? Is it avoidable? Is simplicity better than complexity? Is it important to protect individuals? Is democracy something worth preserving at the cost of rearranging the economy? Is the economy made for the people or are people servants of the economy? Which people?

How you answer these and other related questions ought to determine energy policy. In fact, energy choices are made explicitly on other grounds—comparative cost projections prepared on the basis of incomplete information, energy company plans and power, bureaucratic inertia, and the like—and the value questions are decided implicitly without public discussion or even public notice.

The crucial value questions about the goals of development are imbedded in three fundamental choices: How much energy is enough? What kind of energy technology is appropriate? and, Who should control it?

Until recently the first question was almost never asked. The prevailing assumption was that escalating energy demand is healthy, normal, indeed (except for cyclical recessions), inevitable. While "wasteful" consumption must be cut, growth is necessary and the quality and composition of growth are irrelevant. The problem is to find or to develop supplies that will keep pace with projected increase in demand. It is precisely on this point that the nuclear industry, despite its recent tribulations, confidently expects ultimate victory. If the choice is between blackouts and brownouts, which are now inevitable for the 1980s, and nuclear power, the public will take the latter along with all the risks. Polls taken a few days after the crisis at Three Mile Island which put that choice to the very people who days earlier had feared they would die in a nuclear accident support the industry prediction.

The power hierarchy in the world is indeed closely correlated with high energy consumption, but the British Thermal Units (BTUs) in which the world customarily measures energy consumption are not convertible into happiness units. There have been periods when energy consumption per capita remained constant, 1850 to 1900, for example, or 1920 to 1950. They were times of major technological development and, arguably, social progress. At any rate, these were not times of demonstrably greater unhappiness than the era of the great energy guzzle that began in the 1960s. Indeed, as Paul Lykoudis, head of the School of Nuclear Engineering at Purdue, points out, "there is an upper limit" to the energy a society should consume. Because high-energy societies eliminate the need for direct human contact "loneliness and alienation is a disease. . . ." Overuse is a direct cause of public unhappiness. In 1963 the United States used half as much electricity as in 1977. We now use 29 percent of our fossil fuels to produce electricity. By the year 2000, according to some projections, the use of electricity will double.

Do we really need to keep using this much? The President's Council on Environmental Quality in a 1979 report entitled *The Good News About Energy,* reviewing a number of recent studies, concludes that "the United States can do well, indeed prosper, on much less energy than has been commonly supposed." Automobile fuel costs can be reduced 50 percent or more. Energy productivity and efficiency can be greatly increased. The results, according to the council, would be a U.S. economy operating on 30 to 40 percent less energy than is used today.

Electric power stations produce more heat than is needed or can be used for the physical tasks they are supposed to perform. More than two-thirds of the cost of electric power in the U.S. goes to transport it from distant generators to homes and factories. Electric generators run well below capacity. Barry Commoner calculates that Chicago, the most nuclear-dependent city in the country, could close its nuclear power plants down if the nonnuclear plants operated at 57 percent of capacity instead of the present 37 percent. Industry could be much more efficient. West Germany uses only 68 percent as much energy as the U.S. to produce a ton of steel, 57 percent as much for a ton of paper.

In the United States, conservation is sold as a matter of individual moral virtue rather than as a political strategy. Thus, one President defined patriotism as turning down the thermostat of overheated homes, and another tried to make the cardigan sweater he wore while giving a sermon on energy-saving a symbol of good citizenship. But the market for virtue is always limited. Individual "sacrifice," if that is what it is, of three or four degrees of heat or fifteen miles of excessive speed on the highway promotes health, saves lives, and, possibly, gives rise to good feelings, but it does not begin to reduce energy consumption nearly enough. Real conservation requires refitting society and, above all, changing the way we think.

We can achieve a stable balance between energy supply and demand without destroying the environment, altering the climate, risking nuclear catastrophe, or invading Kuwait. A study of the American Institute of Architects concludes that "improved design of new buildings and modification of old ones could save a third of our current *total* U.S. energy use —and save money too." If Americans were as efficient as Swedes (who believe that they can improve their own efficiency) we would use about one-third less energy than we do. If we stopped harnessing mammoth energy systems to modest tasks, using a chainsaw to cut butter, as Amory Lovins puts it, and matched technology and end use in more appropriate fashion, it would be possible to bring U.S. consumption somewhat into line with the rest of the industrial world and thereby to avoid deepening conflicts within that world over access to energy.

But changing the consumption patterns of America is not so simple. The American Dream is built on the profligate use of space that must be heated and cooled, petroleum-based packaging and plastics, and, whenever possible, substitution of energy from prodigious quantities of minerals for human muscle power. Corporate profits are so dependent on selling energy-intensive antidotes to "drudgery," an advertising favorite that embraces a wide range of human activities, from peeling potatoes to walking around golf courses, that conservation is threatening. Theoretically, it is possible to cut consumption significantly without radical changes in how we live, but the nation has such a high investment in waste that the issue will not be resolved unless it is confronted head-on in the political arena.

The choices have been posed in terms of "hard" versus "soft" energy paths. "Hard" technologies are centralized, capital-intensive, and for the most part dependent upon depletable resources. "Soft" technologies, on the other hand, make use, to the greatest possible extent, of nondepletable resources like sun, wind, and vegetation. They emphasize diversification and dispersal of energy sources so as to avoid in the future the sort of dependence we now have upon fossil fuels. They are flexible, which means that recovery from the effects of wrong decisions is possible. (A wrong decision about nuclear wastes, in contrast, is irrevocable. Once they have been produced and it turns out that there is no safe way to get rid of them, the damage has been done.) Soft technologies employ easy-to-understand, adaptable processes that encourage the wide dispersion of skills, not the creation of a small energy priesthood. They are designed to flow with nature to the greatest possible extent, to emphasize decentralized delivery to the people who need energy, and to avoid creating huge centralized banks of energy which are inefficient and vulnerable. (A blackout of a generator serving a city is a different order of disaster from a power failure in a generator that serves a neighborhood.)

It is odd that these sensible criteria for developing an energy policy should be controversial, but, alas, the issue of "hard" versus "soft" technology has become an ideological divide. The owners and managers of high technology and the intellectuals who identify with them have rushed to condemn the new conservationists as Luddites, romantics, job destroyers, and enemies of progress. The new ideological battle lines that are forming on technology choices do not always coincide with old ideological divisions. Some of the biggest skeptics of "soft" technology are to be found in the Soviet Union and elsewhere in the socialist world. Nuclear reactors for profit are inherently unsafe; reactors run by a workers' state never have meltdowns, radiation hazards, or waste disposal problems.

The battle has been joined on the issue of jobs. The "soft" technology advocates agree that the historic trend toward replacing human labor with capital, energy, and materials has been overdone and that job creation in developed societies through aggregate growth is not happening and will not happen. The argument that energy guzzling is necessary for creating jobs is disputed by those like Bruce Hannon, of the University of Illinois Center for Advanced Computation, who calculates that each large power station destroys about 4,000 more jobs than it creates.

The Fortune 500, according to a study quoted by Senator Edward Kennedy at a Joint Economic Committee hearing, used 80 percent of the total tax credit and 50 percent of all industrially consumed energy and created 75,000 jobs over seven years. Six million small businesses, using far less energy, created 9 million new jobs in the same period.

No government agency has yet done a comprehensive analysis of the impact of alternative energy policy on employment. Individual case studies to date lend strong support to the "soft" technology faction. A 1978 survey of the Californian Public Policy Center estimates that if space and water heating needs in the 1980s were met by small-scale solar energy, the classic symbol of "soft" technology, some 376,000 jobs would be created, far more than the jobs that would be lost in fossil fuels. A better comparison is provided by a study of the comparative jobs impact on

Nassau and Suffolk counties of Long Island of a nuclear power plant and the introduction of certain energy conservation measures and solar energy technologies. The study, prepared by the Council on Economic Priorities, concluded that about four times as much employment in the Nassau/Suffolk County regional economy would be provided by conservation and solar energy as by the proposed nuclear power plant.

Technology choices arouse enormous passion because different answers lead to very different configurations of political power. While some resources lend themselves better than others to decentralized control, it is possible to pursue "soft" or "hard" systems with respect to virtually any energy source. Consider solar energy. In 1952 the Paley Commission report on the future of natural resources in the United States estimated that by 1975 technology for trapping the sun's rays could be supplying 10 percent of total energy needs. Thirteen million solar-heated homes, the report concluded, was a reasonable goal. Yet in 1978 only 30,000 homes had solar heating, and the Secretary of Energy, James Schlesinger, predicted that the 10 percent solar system would not arrive until the year 2000.

There is nothing new about using the sun for power. Of course, fossil fuels are merely trapped solar energy in concentrated form. "We think we heat our homes with oil, natural gas, or electricity," Dennis Hayes of the Worldwatch Institute told a House committee, "but 95 percent of their warmth comes from sunbeams. In a sunless world, our dwellings would be 400 degrees F. below zero when we turned on our furnaces." Solar technology has been around a long time. A solar still for producing fresh water from salt water was built in Chile in 1872, and a solar irrigation pump for the Nile was installed in 1913. A range of solar technologies are being developed. One of the most efficient is the redesign of buildings to enable them to take better advantage of the sun—in the jargon of the trade, "passive solar technology." In 1974 a study by the American Institute of Architects calculated that efficient design alone could save 12.5 million barrels of oil a day.

About 300 patents for solar heating have been issued since 1850. Before 1940 none went to the large companies. Since the midsixties, 30 of 47 patents have gone to Mobil, GE, GM, Dupont, Boeing, United Aircraft, and other giant corporations. Diversification into solar energy is a primary reason for the dramatic acquisition of copper mines by oil companies. Each solar collector for heating and cooling systems requires about a pound of copper, and oil companies now control almost 60 percent of domestic copper production in the U.S.

The U.S., according to government estimates, will have 2.5 million solar collectors installed by 1985. (The Japanese have already surpassed that figure. Niger already requires them for hospitals, hotels, schools, and government housing.) Recent legislation in the U.S. requires all new military installations to have solar heating and cooling units whenever the cost is competitive. The West Wing of the White House is being outfitted with solar heating devices.

Solar energy appears to be an obvious answer to the Energy Crisis. Every day enough sunlight falls on earth to meet energy needs for fifteen years. If solar energy reaching the earth were converted into electricity and sold at current prices, it would be worth more than a half-trillion dollars a day. Because it is spread diffusely across the earth, solar energy can be used for a variety of purposes by concentrating it to the extent needed to perform a particular task.

There is a wide variety of collectors for catching sunbeams. Simple flat plate collectors are now, according to a Mitre Corporation study, competitive with conventional electric heating everywhere in the U.S., and, according to the Department of Energy, the costs will soon be cut in half. For higher temperatures evacuated tube collectors developed by General Electric and Owens-Illinois are being tried by industry for various purposes. Anheuser-Busch uses this technology for beer pasteurization plants in Florida. A more complex system of solar collection uses reflectors to concentrate sunbeams which can develop temperatures up to 2,000 degrees F., high enough to generate electricity in turbine generators. Huge mirrors on a 735-foot "power tower" focus the sunlight on tanks of water spread over 400 acres. As many as 25,000 mirrors are needed. Power towers which work only in the Sun Belt of the Southwest pose serious environmental problems. Obviously, they require a great deal of land and, more importantly, huge quantities of water, in a region of the country with an acute water shortage.

Photovoltaic cells, which convert sunlight directly into electricity, originally developed by the Department of Defense and NASA to power satellites in orbit, are being developed by the energy companies. A square meter solar cell can theoretically power a 100-watt light bulb indefinitely. The technology is very expensive, although the costs have been reduced dramatically in recent years to a point where photovoltaic cells look like a promising commercial possibility. Oil companies hold six out of seven outstanding patents in these areas. They conduct their own research on solar cells, but they have also bought up most of the independent research firms. Thus Shell owns Solar Energy Systems, Exxon controls Solar Power, and Arco has Solar Tech.

The ultimate in "hard" solar technology is the solar power satellite, which is being developed by Grumman, Raytheon, and other aerospace companies. Photovoltaic cells in space, according to a study by Peter

Glaser of Arthur D. Little, would generate ten times the electricity such cells could produce if located on earth. All that would be necessary would be a 58,000-acre ground station, about $36.5 billion for each satellite and launch vehicle, and some way to keep the deadly microwaves produced in space away from the customers in their kitchens.

Thus solar energy lends itself to extremely simple technology. A simple solar cooker sells in India for $6.70. A space-heating system can be built in Oregon for $650 and save as much as $250 a year in electric bills. But solar energy can also be used in the most expensive and complex systems. Despite the unique advantages of decentralization, flexibility, and competition inherent in power through sunlight, government research favors big centralized technology. Ninety-five percent of all federal solar funds, according to a Citizens Energy Project report, go to large companies and universities for developing centralized delivery systems. Solar satellites are a way for energy and aerospace companies to meter the sun. Among the leading vendors of sunlight power are Alcoa, GE, GM, Grumman, Honeywell, and Reynolds Metal.

Until recently, the strategy of energy and high-technology companies was to disparage solar energy, stressing its high cost and uncertain operation. To make the point, Pacific Power and Light Company built a solar home for the Oregon Museum of Science and Industry and put a $150,000 price tag on the system. Worried at the prospect that every rooftop would become its own power plant, sensing that the cry for solar energy was a revolt against huge companies, utilities, and staggering electric bills, large corporations spent a share of their public relations budget on organized scoffing at the solar "messiahs." At the same time, they began buying up solar technology companies. President Carter's interest in solar energy, the tax incentives to encourage solar installation passed in 1978, and the growing public fascination with this most obvious and most available renewable energy source has caused the companies to change their tack. A big emphasis on solar energy would be a "a real mistake," says Roland W. Schmitt, vice president for corporate research and development of General Electric, but "if the nation decides it wants to go solar, we'll be ready to respond." Their role is a bit less passive than that. GE, along with Boeing, Lockheed, RCA, Martin Marietta, McDonnell Douglas, and others formed Sunsat to lobby for solar satellites. They want sixty of them by the year 2025 at a cost of $1 trillion.

The physical characteristics of the sun make decentralized small-scale technology efficient and cost competitive. So also with wind, which is another free resource that has been used for years by individuals on a small scale. In the nineteenth century, 6 million windmills were built in the U.S.; about 150,000 are still functioning. But research efforts are biased toward the development of big centralized turbines rather than small decentralized units.

6.

We began our look at the energy problem by asking three questions: Is there an Energy Crisis? Who is responsible? What is to be done? Here is where the complicated tale of oil depletion leaves me.

Oil is a finite resource, heading for exhaustion. Long before the last drop is squeezed out of the earth, industrial civilization will have had to find alternative sources or close down. The cost in dollars of finding it will become prohibitive and the cost in energy will exceed the return. Highly industrial countries are in serious trouble and will be in more serious trouble in the 1980s because demand is running ahead of available supply. But other countries on the road to industrialization, like China, Mexico, and Nigeria, and the Middle East have plenty of oil—for their needs, not the industrial world's needs. For poor countries, without oil, though they consume little, the oil shortage is a staggering blow.

Obviously, civilization cannot run for long, spending more energy than it produces. Engineers and businessmen seem able to understand this better than economists, who turn reality upside down and devoutly believe that making goods more expensive will make them less scarce. I have a friend, a successful entrepreneur, who thinks the scheme to make oil plentiful by raising the price is like saving air by charging a dollar a breath in a crowded room. The exponential growth of the cost of producing nonrenewable energy sources imposes long-term limits. There are renewable energy sources, but each requires using our present stock of nonrenewable energy for production. There are substitutes for almost everything, but not for energy.

The present petroleum-based economy is a planned system. Companies plot their future growth five to ten years ahead. Oil company executives are not paid to think about the nation's energy needs in the year 2000. They survive only if the company increases its profits during their administration. Glut is more of a problem than shortage. Oil-swapping arrangements, market sharing, and price conspiracies are the familiar planning mechanisms of the oil giants. Especially in a world headed for oil exhaustion, keeping control of the current supply is crucial to corporate profit strategies. The Energy Crisis of 1973–74 and its recurrence in 1979 was an unhappy mixture of fraud and blunder. More oil was being produced than was being delivered, and the distribution was arranged in such a way as to maximize the control of oil at the expense of ultimate consumers.

Deliveries were deliberately slowed, prices were deliberately raised, and oil was diverted to where it fetched the highest price rather than where it served the greatest need. Although a fraud, the Energy Crisis was a symptom of the real crisis that has yet to be faced.

The mechanism by which the United States and the U.S.-based oil companies plan energy policy is the heart of the Energy Crisis. Oil is heading for exhaustion, but there is no *necessary* scarcity of energy. The possibilities of solar, wind, and other renewable energy sources, which we have just summarized, are exciting and promising. Whether they are ''economic'' is totally dependent upon what government and business do. The tragedy is that the incentives for business are to delay the alternatives as long as higher profits are to be made depleting the rest of the oil.

An alternative energy source becomes profitable and worth developing only if the price is right. Whether the price is right depends critically on the price of oil. If oil continues to rise, at some point expensive technologies for unlocking alternative energy sources become practical. If the same companies control oil and the alternatives, the pace of development of the alternatives will depend upon what happens to oil. Planning for profit maximization calls for the development of everything potentially profitable—but each in its season. This means that as long as oil can be sold at high profits and there is still oil to sell, massive investment in alternatives should be postponed. From the point of view of prudent corporate managers it makes no sense to make alternative energy sources available for the market unless there is a market. And that depends upon many factors—the price of·oil, the willingness of Saudi Arabia to make oil available in the amounts needed at any price, and government regulation. The uncertainty of the market causes companies to delay.

It would be hard to imagine a more irrational arrangement for planning a national energy policy. Instead of saving oil and developing a transition strategy, the companies operate under a set of incentives that push them to speed up the production of oil, as price hikes guarantee ever higher profits. At the very same time, the dictates of profit call for delaying investment in the alternatives except where substantial government subsidies are available to guarantee a return that the market itself cannot assure. Indecision of government, pushed as it is in one direction or another by competing interest groups, compounds the problem of the energy companies.

Because government controls neither the oil supply nor alternative energy sources, it cannot develop a national energy policy. When it tries and fails, it reinforces the public impression that the scoundrels who run the oil companies are better bets for keeping the lights on and the stove working in the 1980s than the high-minded incompetents in the nation's capital. The triumph of the oil companies has been their ability to use the public frustration and confusion to discredit the idea of government at the very moment when planning in the public interest is so obviously needed for survival.

From the standpoint of public policy the question whether oil companies make too much money is much less important than whether high profits are providing the right incentives to companies to overcome the energy crisis. Profit maximization is the ultimate purpose of corporate planning. Unfortunately, these pressures are pushing energy companies toward policies that obstruct rather than facilitate the development of alternative energy sources. Having become multinational energy giants, the oil companies measure their performance by the global balance sheet. The goal is to maximize world profit. Each alternative energy source has a role to play in achieving that goal. Oil companies exhibit an impressive appetite for acquiring alternative energy reserves but considerable reticence in exploiting them.

The contours of a rational energy plan for the United States are clear. The nation must use significantly less oil. It is too late to produce enough domestic oil. Importing $50 billion or so a year is bleeding the country. It transfers economic and political power to the holders of dollars abroad, mortgages the U.S. productive system, and fuels a disastrous inflation. What can be done?

(1) To stop the outflow of dollars and the inflow of expensive oil our government should do what governments of some other countries do— take charge of the import process. The U.S.-based multinational oil companies are not American companies. Oil sufficiency for the U.S. is not their priority. Therefore, the country cannot afford to have them in charge of supplying the oil. The standby authority in present legislation for a government monopoly on oil imports should be made mandatory.

(2) The control of alternative energy sources by oil companies should be ended. The companies' timetable for development of the most promising alternatives is not the same as the nation's timetable. Without major government investment and direction the market will not make solar energy profitable enough for the companies to make it available fast enough. Since the alternative is escalating dependence upon oil, and a serious energy shortfall in the 1980s, at a minimum the oil giants should be required to divest themselves of control over alternative energy sources. Government policy should favor small entrepreneurial companies on the frontier of the most promising technologies for a renewable energy system instead of the established petrochemical, aerospace, and electronics giants, which are poor bets for the kinds of technologies most needed. A public corporation along the lines of the Tennessee Valley Authority

should be created as a vehicle for a crash program of government investment and research to make safe renewable energy systems economic and to provide competition in the energy industry. Perhaps 50 percent of remaining domestic oil is on federal lands. It should be developed by a federal corporation, as some senators have proposed. A "yardstick" industry under public control would help force better disclosure from the oil companies and discipline prices. A major role of government research would be to examine the social effects of alternative energy systems. Oil and the automobile carved the face of America by a Topsy-like process. We have a chance to exercise some choice over the shape of the postpetroleum civilization. That critical effort should be made through public discussion and public debate. Otherwise, a few big corporations will again be the landscapers of the nation.

(3) A national plan for a transition to an energy system based on a variety of renewable sources should be adopted after political debate. It should include a major effort to encourage through public financing the exploration of alternative energy sources in the Third World. The implementation of the plan should be highly decentralized because different energy sources are appropriate under different physical conditions. Solar collection is more efficient in the Sun Belt than in the Northeast. Biomass conversion, wind, photovoltaic cells, gasahol and other fuels should be fitted to their most appropriate end uses. Federal policy should be designed to enable local communities to make these choices, and tax revenues should be distributed in such a way as to encourage local energy development programs. A twenty-year strategy of transition relying on coal, natural gas, and, only to the extent necessary, existing nuclear plants, should be put into effect.

(4) Public control of the oil companies is essential. Whether this can be done simply by imposing stricter disclosure requirements, or by tying existing government subsidies to actual investment in exploration and to satisfactory performance in distributing oil is dubious. It may well be necessary to nationalize the companies, but how to establish effective public control is by no means clear. Any effort to exercise control involves a political battle. Therefore, the least radical remedies that would restore the public control needed to carry out the energy policy should be preferred. The practical choices for establishing national and regional public control ought to be a central issue for public debate.

(5) The national energy plan must include a serious conservation program. The U.S. cannot continue to use such a disproportionate share of the world's energy resources without sharpening conflict with the other industrial nations and increasing the risk of war with the producing nations. Conservation should include redesign of buildings, subsidies and

penalties to encourage less wasteful production processes in industry, and a change in the utilities rate structure to encourage maximum use of existing capacity. In addition, it should set as a national priority the development of nonenergy technologies that save energy. For example, millions of Americans have jobs that could be done as well at home as at the office with the help of sophisticated technology. Instead of consuming their daily share of gasoline or electricity to get to an overheated or air-cooled office they could stay home by the telephone, computer terminal, and the information-processing machine. The Energy Crisis offers an opportunity to rethink the way we organize our lives.

With the use of sophisticated computers public transportation could be tailored to the most efficient use. Impromptu schedules arranged on short notice would increase convenience and cut down on the relentless procession of empty airplanes and half-filled buses. Appropriate technology in the postpetroleum era can be either very simple or very complex. The real question is whether it is needed. If the U.S. cut down the squandering of energy to the levels of 1960 just before the great guzzle, the "sacrifice" would be marginal, and with any sensible planning, the quality of life for the majority of Americans would be considerably enhanced.

The trend toward capital-intensive, job-destroying technology all increasingly concentrated in the hands of a few huge companies will continue until there is a fundamental debate in the country on alternative paths of development. The absurdities of our industrial civilization ought to be challenged in the political arena—the peculiar dependence of the society on perpetual motion, the mania for plastic packaging, the addiction to industrial processes that require such extraordinary amounts of heat (and then extraordinary amounts of water for cooling), and the odd reluctance to take advantage of opportunities to use the by-products of one part of industrial and agricultural processes to fuel others. We should not delude ourselves that we can design our escape from the laws of nature. We will never overcome entropy. But we could imitate nature by seeking self-renewing systems.

Finally, we need to ask how much of our energy we ought to devote to something other than producing ever more goods. We could make a greater investment in improving the quality of life for people by cleaning rivers, streams and oceans, purifying air, breaking down the isolation of modern life—and probably save energy. Energy choices are the most crucial facing the nation. Who shall collect sunbeams? Who shall gather the wind? If we cannot develop a democratic planning system to touch these issues, historians will doubtless conclude that our experiment lasted barely two hundred years.

PART TWO

GUNS, BUTTER, AND OIL: THE CHANGING FACE OF POWER

CHAPTER V

Minerals: The Rocks of Civilization

1.

WHAT WE CALL PROGRESS is a mysterious marriage of creativity and plunder. Civilization has flowered when human beings have devised ingenious new ways to organize production and social life, but this has been done usually with stolen goods. The Greek city-state, the Roman Empire, and Elizabethan England come to mind. Undergirding their extraordinary achievements in art, philosophy, literature, and statecraft was military power and conquest. Rome lived off grain exacted as tribute from Sicily, Spain, North Africa, and Gaul. The civilization of modern Europe was built on the shiploads of gold and silver bullion extracted from the mines of the New World, the slaves, diamonds, copper, and vegetable oils of Africa, and the cotton, rubber, and spice of India and Malaysia—all taken at gunpoint.

The Industrial Revolution and modern imperialism, the latter an organizational system for selectively integrating non-European economies into an international capitalist order by force, fed on each other. Without the energy and power so swiftly generated in the industrializing economies, the military power to subjugate whole continents would not have developed. Without the cheap and easy access to raw materials in other continents the industrial expansion and the extraordinary enrichment of the beneficiaries of imperialism would not have taken place. Indeed, reaching for the resources of distant lands was indispensable for the triumph of the technology of terror which has marked the last five hundred years. The Spanish Armada depended heavily on oak from the Baltic, and the nineteenth-century European armies of steel were forged from chrome, columbite, and manganese extracted from the Dark Continent by exploited labor. The instrument for subduing spear-throwing or rifle-bearing tribes was a remarkable metallurgical achievement, the ma-

113

chine gun. Imperialism thus rested on an ingenious economy of terror by which the ancient tribal kingdoms supplied the raw materials for their own subjugation.

Energy has been central to the transformation of civilization, but the nonfuel minerals have been the conductors and facilitators of that transformation. There would be no railroad without iron; no steel without manganese, no modern airplanes without aluminum, no aluminum without bauxite, no electric plants without copper, no jet engines without nickel, and no atomic bomb without such esoteric minerals as beryllium and high-purity graphite. The key to the energy systems of the postpetroleum era are crucial elements embedded in the earth's crust.

The universe is 15 billion years old, and the geological underpinnings of the earth were formed long before the first sea creature slithered out of the slime. But it is only in the last 6,000 years or so that men have descended into mines to chop and scratch at the earth's crust. Human history is, as Carl Sagan has put it, the equivalent of a few seconds in the 15-billion-year life of the earth. What alarms those who keep track of the earth's crust is that since 1950 human beings have managed to consume more minerals than were mined in all previous history, a splurge of a millisecond in geologic time that cannot be long repeated without using up the finite riches of the earth.

The world supply of valuable minerals is of course finite. Minerals are not renewable resources. But the world supply of the most important industrial minerals seems almost inexhaustible. When or whether we will run out of any particular mineral no one knows. The radius of the planet is 4,000 miles; our deepest mines reach no more than five miles into the earth. We have literally just scratched the surface. The problem for the industrial nations is that they are becoming increasingly dependent upon imported nonfuel minerals; some of the most crucial ores are buried in the earth of their former colonies.

The minerals a society mines and uses set the pattern of its civilization in crucial ways. The resplendent kingdoms awash in gold—King Solomon's Israel, the Incas in Peru, the Nubians in Africa—remain vivid in historical memory long after their treasure was stolen by others. But minerals create more than a cultural tone; they are the sinews of political economy. Lewis Mumford points out in *Technics and Civilization* that modern civilization has developed through the successive uses of different materials. Each set of minerals is associated with a particular energy system. Interacting energy sources and material conductors lend themselves to their own distinctive forms of social and economic organization. Some are more compatible with centralized control, others with decentralization. Some systems fit better with private ownership than others.

Mixing iron and coal made the railroad possible and transformed rural America into a national market. Combining petroleum, copper, and aluminum in new ways produced the automobile, the jet airplane, and the global market. To be sure, technology does not in itself determine what society looks like. Saudi Arabia and Massachusetts may acquire the same technology, but no one would mistake one for the other even if Cape Cod turned into a desert. But the organization of materials provides the framework within which political economies evolve. New uses of energy sources and materials create new social relationships and even new social values. Among the plains Indians, for example, as the anthropologist Bernard Mishkin has shown, the energy revolution occasioned by the domestication of the horse changed the social values of hunting societies. On foot the ideal virtues were stoicism, patience, and diligence. Once the horse arrived, the bravado of the warrior and the skills of the horse thief became the survival values. As the capacity of a human being to do work has been progressively extended by finding ever new substitutes for arm, leg, and back muscles, civilization has evolved from low-energy societies into high-energy societies. Early and sophisticated use of new energy technologies established a hierarchy of power among nations and set the standard by which the modern world judges what is "developed" and what is "undeveloped."

2.

Conflicts over minerals arise from two facts of life. One is that ores already discovered are concentrated fortuitously in certain geographic areas. There is a great deal of iron in Minnesota and Brazil, considerable copper in Chile, most of the world's chromite in South Africa, much lead in Missouri, and so on. These geographic areas, to a greater or lesser extent, are independent political units. The second fact is that the consumption of materials in the world is grossly unequal. The average Chilean or inhabitant of Zaire makes a negligible demand on the world resource stores, because he is too poor. But every man, woman, and child living in the United States requires 40,000 pounds of minerals a year if one includes the individual's proper share of public roads, buildings, and the like, as well as the family car. (The U.S. auto industry consumes 20 percent of the steel and iron castings, 68 percent of the lead, 33 percent of the zinc, 9 percent of the copper and aluminum, 65 percent of the rubber, and 5 percent of the plastics used in the U.S.) Americans, who make up 5 percent of the world's population, have been consuming 27 percent of the world's production of materials in recent years. Back in

1940 they were gobbling 42 percent of the world's consumable resources annually, but the rise of reindustrialized postwar Europe, the Soviet Union, China, and the industrializing enclaves of the Third World are changing the world consumption pattern.

Endowed with huge reserves, more nearly self-sufficient than any other nation except South Africa, the Soviet Union, and possibly China, the United States is nonetheless critically dependent upon imported minerals. The nation mines 23 percent of the world's copper. It has one of the world's largest iron reserves. It is the largest producer of phosphates and has the second largest reserves of zinc. It is one of the four largest producers in the world of gold, vanadium, and molybdenum. But it imports 90 percent of its bauxite and virtually all its chromium, and 100 percent of its manganese, cobalt, mica, and colombium, which are equally indispensable in modern industry.

At regular intervals, there is a cry of panic that the United States is running out of critical minerals. Generally, people worry about mineral shortages in wartime. During the First World War 28 critical materials were found to be in short supply, and a planning office was set up in the War Department to keep track of them. By the next World War the economy had become much more dependent on minerals. Such alloys as nickel, vanadium, molybdenum, and zirconium were now in common use as well as nonmetallic industrial materials, such as mica, graphite, talc, and asbestos. During World War II 298 items were placed on the short supply list. In the midst of the Korean War the Paley Commission warned that the increasing rate of consumption of critical minerals was making the U.S. dangerously dependent on imported minerals. By that time, the enormous Mesabi Iron deposits in Minnesota were almost exhausted and U.S. industry was importing a considerable amount of copper. In John F. Kennedy's time, years before Americans gave a thought about the oil sheiks, Professor W. Y. Elliott of Harvard, Henry Kissinger's early mentor, warned in a study for the Office of Emergency Planning of possible mineral "blackmail" by developing nations.

The industrial world as a whole is even more dramatically dependent upon imported resources than is the United States. Japan must bring in from abroad more than 90 percent of its iron, copper, and tin, and 100 percent of its bauxite and nickel. Western Europe imports 96 percent of its tin, 93 percent of its copper, 75 percent of its lead, and 89 percent of its nickel (1972 figures). In the United States, annual consumption of metallic ores has multiplied six times since 1900. In 1900, 40 percent of the population still lived on the farm; by the mid-1950s, only 11 percent of the population were still farming, and they were increasing their consumption of industrial metals too.

The struggle for minerals is becoming more intense because fear of scarcity is growing. In his 1977 U.N. study, *The Future of the World Economy,* the Nobel Prize economist Wassily Leontief concluded that the world could run out of certain minerals such as lead and zinc by the year 2000 unless major new sources are found. He predicts the world will use, in the next thirty years, three to four times the total quantity of minerals used throughout human history. The most likely consequence, however, he concludes, is that the world will not run out but most regions outside the U.S. will remain net importers and will face critical shortages and steeply rising prices. In a Brookings Institution study John Tilton has calculated the life expectancy of current reserves of critical minerals. Assuming that production will grow at a rate roughly equal to what it was during the first generation following World War II, he estimates that world reserves of bauxite ore will run out in thirty-three years, iron in about forty years, mercury in nineteen years, zinc in fifteen years.

"At first blush," he says, "these findings are disconcerting." But, he argues, the news is not as bad as it appears. Like most mineral specialists, he emphasizes that reserves for important minerals are actually increasing at a faster rate than they are being depleted and that prices for the most part are actually declining. For almost every mineral, there are acceptable substitutes. New uses can be found for wood, a renewable resource. Materials can be used more efficiently through better processing and re-cycling. The useful life of material already in use can be extended; much of current steel production, for example, goes to replace steel already in use that has rusted or worn out.

When I hear geologists argue about whether the world is running out of minerals I find myself imagining the earth as an enormous tube of tooth-paste. The tube is of indeterminate length, but it is becoming progres-sively more difficult to squeeze out anything of value. The geologists Charles Park and Roy MacDiarmid define an ore as a mineral "that can be recovered at a profit." In 1700, typical copper ores contained 13 per-cent copper. By 1900 the superrich deposits had been exhausted but technology had improved to the point where deposits from 2.5 percent to 5 percent copper were profitable to exploit. Today copper is frequently extracted from 0.5 percent deposits. Where there are special circum-stances such as a captive market and cheap transportation, even lower-grade deposits become economically feasible. Thus a small mine in Cy-prus makes use of 0.24 percent copper for export to Spain, but a mine in Canada or the U.S. would have trouble making a profit from such a deposit. Sometimes the mining of poor-grade ores becomes profitable because a valuable by-product is recovered in the refining process.

In the case of oil, scarcity takes the form of physical depletion. There is not enough ready to deliver in time to meet rising demand. For most nonfuel minerals, scarcity is a matter of money. The industrial nations fear that they will lose control of prices. For most of the industrial era, however, minerals have been getting cheaper. A 1952 study of raw material prices for the years 1900–1950 by the Paley Commission appointed by President Truman found that except for timber "real costs of materials production have for some years been declining and this decline has helped our living standards to rise." In 1974, William D. Nordhaus studied prices of ten important minerals from 1900 to 1970 and found that the trend that the Paley Commission had noted more than twenty years earlier has continued. "There has been a continuous decline in resource prices for the entire century." According to Metals and Minerals Research Services, with certain dramatic exceptions such as uranium, gold, and platinum, the trend is expected to continue.

However, capital requirements for mineral exploitation are increasing enormously. Over the next decade they are predicted to be anywhere from $100 billion to one trillion dollars. Production costs are steadily rising because yields are declining. For example, it takes twice the ore to produce a pound of copper as it did in 1950. Construction costs for mine sites and processing plants in the U.S. have skyrocketed. To build a magnesium plant costs $75 million. A facility to produce 125,000 tons of aluminum, about half of what the three industry giants produced in 1977, costs $283 million. A steel plant to make 4 million tons costs $2.4 billion. Environmental problems are enormous. Copper smelters emit more than 1.5 million tons of sulphuric gases a year and huge amounts of solid wastes. The steel industry estimated in 1975 that it would spend 20 percent of its total capital expenditures, some $9 billion, just to bring its existing plants into compliance with environmental protection standards. About one-third of the costs of a new copper smelter goes for equipment to control fumes and wastes. One way or another, society must pay for this.

One of the reasons mineral prices were so cheap in the boom years of American industrialization is that true costs of producing and processing them were nowhere reflected. The nonquantifiable "quality of life" costs are obvious. But the true energy and water costs were not taken into account either. The heat requirements for removing impurities are significantly increasing as lower-grade ores are mined. To produce a ton of copper requires 112 million BTUs or the equivalent of 17.8 barrels of oil. The energy cost component of aluminum is twenty times higher. The economic costs of fouling air, ruining streams, and polluting soil often show up years after the damage is done and are paid for in a variety of indirect and confusing ways—hospital bills, loss of productivity, compensation to miners. The discovery in the 1960s of the dangerous effects of emissions from mineral-processing plants created a new tension between environmental protection and corporate growth.

The artificially low cost of domestically produced minerals in the past was also due to bargain lease arrangements that mining companies worked out with friendly public servants for digging up public lands and Indian territories, the same sort of alchemy that transformed so much of the national wealth in oil and coal into corporate assets. Since the late 1960s, however, a new consciousness in the West has made such exploitative arrangements more difficult. Five hundred million acres of federal lands which used to be available for mining—about 67 percent of all federal lands—are now off limits to miners for environmental reasons or because of the claims of Alaska natives and Indians.

3.

Another reason minerals are bound to become more expensive is the increasing role of the metals speculators. In dollar volume, commodity speculation is the world's biggest industry. *The Wall Street Journal* reported in January 1979 that $50 trillion in foreign exchange is traded around the world each year. This activity produces $5 billion in commissions. (In 1978, Citibank earned about one-third of its net profits from foreign exchange transactions.) The volume of dollars circulating in the world is perhaps twenty times the total volume of world trade, which means that dollars are being traded not as currency to buy goods and services but as commodities in themselves.

The same thing is happening with metals. While processing and mining is a concentrated industry, neither the mining companies nor the processors have the kind of global control over the flow of minerals that the Seven Sisters of oil still enjoy. Because the minerals market is subject to wild gyrations that invite speculation, it keeps thousands of commodity speculators busy. They magnify the cyclical effect of the market and ensure a succession of feasts and famines. Copper prices in 1978, for example, were less than half what they were in 1974. One reason was that four debt-ridden countries control 40 percent of the world supply outside the socialist bloc—Zambia, Zaire, Peru, and Chile. The governments own the mines in these countries, and copper is a principal source of foreign exchange. To pay their debts and to import their food, they put more and more copper on the market even when the price is falling. Because miners' wages are so depressed, Chile can make a profit even when prices are low. But the effect on U.S. copper producers is disastrous when, as in 1978, one million tons is stored in warehouses waiting for the price to rise. With continuing depression in the industry, the copper companies seek government aid, demanding tariffs and quotas on foreign copper and wheedling the government into purchasing great quantities of copper to add to the nation's $7.5 billion "strategic reserve." (In the humpty-dumpty world of mineral politics, commodities become "strategic" and candidates for national security stockpiling when they become too available and too cheap.)

Within the last ten years the trade in gold, silver, and platinum has exploded. In the late 1960s the price of gold was still being set by five men in the "gold ring" of London. Gold is now traded all over the world twenty-four hours a day, about $1 trillion worth a year. The annual sales of silver rose 5,000 percent in a decade to about $2 trillion a year. Until recently there were negligible futures markets for tin, lead, aluminum, or zinc. Now they are scattered across the globe, operating around the clock. Joseph Filner, the head of a metals trading company, estimates that the annual trade in metals is more than five times annual world production.

Speculators are buying large quantities of minerals when the price is low and are keeping them off the market. Because of the cyclical character of the market and the urgency of industrial needs, a 5 percent reduction of supply can lead to a 35 to 40 percent increase in price. In the 1970s the use of copper in industry expanded about 30 percent, but copper contracts on U.S. exchanges expanded tenfold. The price of platinum has gone in a short period from $95 an ounce to $450 an ounce. Perhaps $50 of this spread represents increased production costs. The rest is a consequence of commodity speculation, the hoarding of platinum as a hedge against inflation. Of course this fuels inflation and throws the consequences on those who cannot arrange to stockpile platinum. Leading multinational companies, especially the automobile companies, are heavily involved in trading pieces of paper that represent huge mineral stocks. The minerals themselves sit in warehouses in Rotterdam, Hong Kong, Singapore, and other easily accessible ports waiting for the merry-go-round to stop.

The rampant speculation in the minerals business is an outgrowth of a legitimate hedging function. In copper this activity was traditionally concentrated in the London Metal Exchange, which was set up in 1882 near the butcher shops of Leadenhill Market as a place where dealers, smelter operators, and the supporting cast of the international copper industry could hedge their bets. Here is how the *Economist* Intelligence Unit describes the Exchange:

Business in the morning session starts promptly at twelve o'clock when the Secretary of the Exchange rings his bell and draws the attention of those present by the traditional call "Copper, Gentlemen, copper." Dealings in copper proceed for five minutes, when they are closed abruptly by a further sounding of the bell and followed by similar periods devoted to tin, lead and zinc in succession. . . . Dealings in each metal are conducted by open bid and offer across the Ring, members stating the price at which they are prepared to buy or sell uniform lots on standardised contract terms either for spot or forward delivery. Any completed transaction may have been made for a variety of reasons. A forward sale of copper, for instance, may have been made by a producer's agent who has sold against metal either in warehouses or being shipped to the United Kingdom for eventual delivery to the market; the corresponding purchase could have been made by a broker acting on behalf of a manufacturer wishing to cover a commitment to supply manufactured copper in the future by buying for forward delivery. Alternatively, the forward sale may have been a hedging transaction made by a merchant wishing to protect the value of metal stocks which he did not contemplate delivering to the market, or made on behalf of a producer or smelter seeking to safeguard the value of ores or residues on a falling market. Finally, the forward sale could be a "bear" transaction on speculative account, made in anticipation that prices would fall in the near future and enable a small profit to be secured.

Speculation in the copper trade works against the poor producer countries because by and large they have less relevant information about world supplies, impending labor troubles, coming recessions, and other developments that cause copper prices to gyrate. It takes anywhere from three to five years to bring an ore body once discovered into production. The timing and pace of production has a crucial impact on world supply, and this information is in the hands of the companies. In Allende's Chile the bureaucrats who tried to run the nationalized mines were at a serious disadvantage because the surveys of the mines were in the company headquarters in New York. Geologists for the most part work for big companies whose bargaining power depends substantially on knowing more about what is under their earth than the governments with whom they are negotiating.

In recent years dramatic new technology has become available that may help solve the puzzle of where minerals are and how easy or hard it is to mine them. Earth satellites with remote sensing devices—using microwave, radar, thermal infrared and ultraviolet technology—now sweep across every country in the world every day. Photographs from space make it possible to assemble a global topographical map and a mineral profile of the earth's crust.

4.

National dependence on foreign minerals, like the nation's dependence on foreign oil, is a consequence of private corporate decisions. The U.S. Government influences private planning in various ways. It has a strategic stockpile and buys considerable quantities of certain metals at certain times. Its principal role in the metals economy has been to encourage, by tax, military and economic aid, pollution regulation, and other policies, the digging of the Third World. As a result, some of the most critical elements in the U.S. economy are no longer produced in the United States at all. In 1971 domestic production of cobalt ceased. Considerable amounts of it could be recovered as by-products of nickel, but because of the peculiar economics of the industry it is cheaper to import cobalt, and so domestic ores are simply wasted. The nation now imports about one-half its requirements from the province of Shaba in Zaire, making that country, from the point of view of U.S. dependence, the Saudi Arabia of metals.

In thinking about the true costs of critical minerals it is worth pondering the national investment in Zaire. Almost twenty years of covert operations and military aid have kept a corrupt but cooperative regime in power over the territory from which about 90 percent of the world's cobalt and 6 percent of the world's copper is extracted. The Mobutu regime was put in power in 1964 by a covert military intervention under cover of a Belgian humanitarian rescue mission. But the Central Intelligence Agency had been active in the Congo from at least four years before. The CIA, according to testimony of former agency officials before the Church Committee in 1975, prepared some poison for the nationalist leader, Patrice Lumumba, and Sid Gottlieb, chief of CIA "technical services," testified that he brought the deadly potion to Kinshasa. It turned out that the agent who was to perform the undercover execution had too finely developed moral sensitivities. He was prepared to "set up" the murder but not to do it personally. As a result, the actual circumstances of Lumumba's death are still in doubt. He was apparently beaten to death by a mysterious gang of Congolese, but one senior CIA official told his fellow CIA operative, John Stockwell, that he had Lumumba's body in the trunk of his car "trying to decide what to do with it." The details of the Lumumba murder are not trivial, because his death has become a symbol throughout the continent of the brutal efforts of the industrial powers to hold on.

In 1977, France airlifted Moroccan troops to Shaba province to secure the mineral-rich province from an incursion by the FNLC (National Front for the Liberation of the Congo). While the FNLC includes many who fought with Moise Tshombe in 1962 for an independent Shaba (Katanga, as it was called then), it is not a separatist movement. As the journal *West Africa* has put it, "their immediate demand is that Mobutu be toppled, not that Shaba Province secede." After the French thwarted the 1977 invasion about 150,000 refugees, fearing reprisals, fled to Angola to join the rebel forces. In 1978 they struck again, this time flooding some mines and driving away the white technicians. French, Belgian, and Moroccan troops flew in again to save Mobutu, and again the rebels withdrew to fight again. (France now has some 10,000 troops at four permanent bases in Africa. In addition to the Shaba operations, the French have launched military operations in recent years in Mauritania and Morocco to beat back Algerian-supported rebel attacks in the Western Sahara and in Chad against a local insurgency supported by Libya's Colonel Qaddafi.)

The economic motives of the NATO Allies in propping up Mobutu with military force are clear enough. Zaire has a huge external debt, much of it owed to private banks but guaranteed by official agencies such as the EximBank. But the problem of maintaining control by military and paramilitary means is much more complicated than is generally realized. In the early 1960s it was easy for the CIA to buy the "loyalty" of Congolese politicians by spreading bundles of cash (at one point the entire Congolese parliament was on the U.S. payroll). But that builds not only temporary enthusiasm for the American way of life but a culture of corruption. Twenty years later bribery and wholesale theft in Zaire are so pervasive that the country is at a standstill. Mobutu's uncle runs the food distribution system, selling food aid that is supposed to be given, and supplying various Zurich bank accounts with the proceeds. "Steal cleverly," was the admonition the President is reported to have delivered to his cabinet. The weaker a client regime is at home, the more aid it must receive and, paradoxically, the less a puppet it becomes. Dependence upon the United States becomes a weapon to use against the Americans, since, for a Great Power, undoing commitments is not such an easy matter, particularly when there are no obvious alternatives. There is a long tradition for U.S. diplomats to be bullied or ignored by the most-favored recipients of military largesse—Syngman Rhee in South Korea, Nguyen Van Thieu in Vietnam, the Shah in Iran, to name a few.

When Mobutu nationalized the copper mines formerly owned by Union Minière du Haut Katanga, the compensation agreements were exceedingly generous and Belgians were left in all the key managerial and technical positions. Eighty-five percent of Zaire's copper is shipped to Antwerp for processing. Twenty-five thousand Belgian jobs depend upon the present copper arrangements. A later effort at "Zairianization" of the copper enterprise by replacing Europeans with Zairians proved abortive, and the Belgians were welcomed back. Under the "Mobutu Plan" developed by the U.S., France, West Germany, Belgium, Britain, Japan, and others the International Monetary Fund, the World Bank, and the Common Market Commission have demanded the power to take over the collapsing economy and administration of the country. In return for another one billion dollars in loans the IMF now theoretically runs the Finance Ministry and the National Bank. These extraordinary measures may well moderate the traffic in valises stuffed with dollar bills that bank officials used to take out of the country with great regularity.

The military regime in Zaire, brought to power and maintained in power by outside force, exhibits an advanced case of a social and economic sickness rampant in a number of former colonial countries. According to a 1975 World Bank report, "about one third of the rural population suffer from deficiencies in caloric intake; and more seriously, a grave shortage of protein is characteristic of most of the population." Three-quarters of Zairians are subsistence farmers earning a per capita income of $25 to $50 a year. The fabulously rich Congo used to be a net food exporter. Zaire now spends $300 million a year to import food. A development model has been pursued which has served the interests of the mining companies and the Mobutu family, but it has been disastrous for the country. About 60 percent of Zaire's income is derived from copper. The steep decline in copper prices has been ruinous, but no effort has been made to reduce the country's dependence on the treacherous minerals market. To protect well over one billion dollars in U.S. investment the official impulse in Washington has been to back Mobutu up with military power—aid for his army and military intervention when necessary, by European and African powers. But a black minority government that flagrantly ignores the plight of three-quarters of the country and is totally dependent on outside intervention is only slightly more secure than a white minority government.

A region that geologists call "High Africa," stretching from Transvaal in South Africa to Shaba in Zaire and Angola, has the world's largest concentration of manganese and chrome (chromium). Manganese is absolutely essential for the production of iron and steel. The U.S. has no manganese reserves. South Africa has more than 2 billion tons and sells the U.S. about 10 percent of what it uses every year. The rest comes from Brazil, Gabon, and Australia. Chrome is almost equally critical. There is no known substitute for chrome in making steel, although for many common industrial uses, there are substitutes for steel. A generation ago Stalin asked, "How many divisions has the Pope?" Today the question that will decide the power balance on the continent of Africa is this: "How dependent is the industrial world on the manganese and chrome reserves of South Africa?"

Although chromite was discovered in Maryland in 1827 and the United States was briefly the principal world supplier, domestic production ceased in 1961. When the Bureau of Mines notes that chrome is "one of the Nation's most important strategic and critical materials," it is indulging in understatement. South Africa and Rhodesia have 97 percent of the known world's chrome reserves. The USSR is the next largest producer, but the extent of its reserves is secret.

Nature has been exceptionally bountiful in storing all sorts of resources under U.S. soil, but the world distribution of chrome is dramatic evidence of the limits of self-sufficiency. There is a certain irony in the fact that in a recent year the U.S. imported 31 percent of its requirements from its major antagonist, the Soviet Union; 27 percent from South Africa, the focus of what promises to be the major international political struggle of the 1980s; 18 percent from the Philippines, one of the most defiant violators of human rights; and 12 percent from Turkey, with which the U.S. has had strained relations since the Turks invaded Cyprus.

In its study *Contingency Plans for Chromium Utilization,* the National Research Council concluded that within twenty-five to seventy-five years South Africa and Rhodesia will have a monopoly on world chrome reserves. We should bear in mind, though, that *reserves* is a deceptive term. The size depends upon where and how hard one looks. If companies stopped looking in South Africa and turned their attention elsewhere, reserves would grow where the exploration was conducted and South Africa's would diminish. Recently, U.S. intelligence agencies have expressed concern that because of the boycott of Rhodesian chrome under a U.N. resolution, the Soviet Union has become America's major supplier. Thus the armor in one out of three new American tanks facing the Warsaw Pact forces on the Elbe River is probably fortified with Soviet chrome.

There are possible alternatives to the huge dependence on southern Africa—conservation measures, alternative technologies, increased exploration and mining elsewhere. But, as in the case of petroleum, the transition is the problem. It would take, according to the National Research Council, from five to ten years to adjust to a cutoff of chrome and manganese from southern Africa. The black African states lack a common minerals policy, as well as the technology and capital to develop their own reserves. They are dependent on South Africa to make their minerals industry work. Thus Zambia has had to use the South African transport system to ship its copper. Angola sells its diamonds through South Africa's Central Selling Organization, as indeed does the Soviet Union.

Minerals dependence on South Africa is real enough. In addition to possessing the indispensable steel-related minerals, chrome and manganese, South Africa has about one-third of the world's uranium supply (if you include Namibia). There is enormous interest in the U.S. and West Europe in the incredible riches of South Africa. For example, the British-based multinational corporation Rio Tinto-Zinc—in collaboration with a German company, Urangesellschaft, and a French government subsidiary, Total Compagnie Minière et Nucléaire—has been a partner with South Africa in developing the world's richest uranium mine at Rossing in Namibia. But there is also an ideology of minerals dependence that South Africa uses as a weapon. Just as oil companies have derived power from their exclusive knowledge of oil and natural gas reserves, warning of scarcity or celebrating abundance as their marketing strategies and public relations dictated, so these governments and some of the multinational corporations with investments in South Africa exaggerate the minerals dependence of the industrial world on South Africa.

"We now have a bargaining position equal to that of an Arab nation with a lot of oil," Louw Alberts, vice president of South Africa's Atomic Energy Board, boasts. In "Africa and Western Lifelines," a 1978 article published in the U.S. military journal *Strategic Review,* W. C. J. Van Rensburg, professor of energy economics at the Rand Afrikaans University, Johannesburg, argues that the West has no choice but to embrace South Africa, because it cannot do without her minerals. South Africa alone has, he reminds us, 86 percent of the platinum reserves, 83 percent of the chrome, 64 percent of the vanadium, 40 percent of the gold, and 48 percent of the manganese. (South Africa's mineral power is even greater because of its hold on the mineral economies of the surrounding black African states.) With the exception of the Soviet Union, South Africa is probably the most self-sufficient mineral producer in the world. The Soviet Union's increased interest in Africa of recent years is part of a plot, he suggests, to deny the West access to the minerals of southern Africa one way or another. Once the source of supply is cut off, the dependence of the U.S. and Europe on Soviet chrome and Soviet gold becomes nearly total. The South African analyst warns of the effects not only of "direct Soviet interference in the flow of strategic raw materials" but also of "economic strangulation," terrorism, or incursions by the neighboring black African states on the industrial order of the West. The message is clear: The industrial nations cannot afford to shun or to punish South Africa. Boycotts, blockades, and support for the forces of liberation and change—all will backfire. The beleaguered white regime is the international tar baby, as it was known in the Kissinger White House.

These views have dominated official NATO thinking for ten years.

Numerous examples of military collaboration between South Africa and NATO countries have come to light over the years despite rather elaborate efforts to keep them secret. The U.S., in what surely must be one of the most shortsighted decisions of recent years, supplied South Africa with about 100 pounds of highly enriched uranium—enough to produce at least five atomic bombs. Giving in to the feelings of the outraged but impotent black states of Africa, it is argued, would expose the West to mortal danger. Eighty percent of Europe's oil and 70 percent of its strategic minerals use the sea lanes around the Cape of Good Hope. The supertankers heading for America—one leaves every thirteen minutes—use the same water routes. A prolonged struggle to control that strategic real estate or the emergence in power of a more humane but less cooperative regime would mean endless trouble for the U.S. economy.

On the other hand, a recent study for the State Department by Robert Dean Consultants, of the mineral potential of countries neighboring South Africa, concludes that "the strategic dependence of the West on mineral supplies from South Africa can be lessened" by investing in the mineral economies of the black regimes despite the problems of inadequate transportation and lack of skilled workers. There is no comparison between the escalating investment that has been pouring into the minerals industry of Rhodesia and South Africa since the end of the last century and the trickle of funds to Mozambique, Zambia, Botswana, Lesotho, and Malawi.

How dependent the U.S. and Europe are on South Africa, how interested the Soviet Union is in denying these minerals to the West, and how significant is the mineral potential of the black states all depend on bits of politicized fact which serve as missiles in the information war. There is no "objective" answer to any of these questions, for each of these important issues depends upon the behavior of governments and corporations. If reducing U.S. dependence upon South Africa were a serious objective, the design of materials conservation policies and the massive investment in the development of alternative sources would also have to be a higher priority. It is ironic that the United States should have tied its economic health so closely to two of the most anachronistic regimes in the world, Saudi Arabia and South Africa. The more the U.S. identifies with the wrong side in South Africa—wrong morally and wrong politically because eventually the white minority will lose—the more it will cut itself off from the majority of nations and peoples on whom it must increasingly depend. If the rate of mineral consumption requires policies that compromise human rights standards and friendly relations with nonracist regimes, then prudence would dictate retooling our economy rather than fanning the flames of war in southern Africa.

5.

As the struggle for such industrial minerals as manganese and cobalt sharpens, interest in seabed mining grows. The sea contains all sorts of minerals. In 1924 a German expedition was dispatched on the *Meteor* to extract gold from seawater as a quick way of paying off the war debt, but the cost of mining the estimated 10 million tons of gold far surpassed its value, and the project was abandoned. Profitable sea mining of gold goes on off the Alaska coast, however. The waters off southwest Africa, the Marine Diamond Corporation estimated in 1964, contain 13 million carats of diamonds, and the De Beers Company has for some years been recovering gems from the sea, though not in great numbers. The Japanese have been extracting iron from gravel dredged up from the sea. For many years they have also been meeting about a quarter of their sand and gravel needs this way. So have the British. There are phosphates needed for fertilizer to be had off the coasts of California and Florida. The U.S. and Saudi Arabia are exploring a joint operation to mine the floor of the Red Sea for silver and zinc. One-third of the world's salt production comes from the sea, a process with a lineage reaching back to ancient Minoan civilization five thousand years ago.

But the mineral riches over which a major struggle is developing are the manganese deposits on the floor of the Pacific Ocean. Here in an area 1,500 kilometers long and 200 kilometers wide, known as the Pacific Quadrangle, are vast underwater beds of ferromanganese nodules shaped like small potatoes. These nodules also contain nickel, copper, and cobalt. Total resources are estimated to be as high as 1.7 trillion tons, of which anywhere from 10 billion to 500 billion, according to a 1978 report of the comptroller general of the U.S., are recoverable at a profit. As of now, no commercial mining has taken place, but the U.S., Japan, France, West Germany, and the Soviet Union have each been engaged in deep-ocean nodule exploration. In the U.S., Kennecott Copper Corporation, Deep Sea Ventures, Inc., Lockheed Missiles and Space Company, Ocean Management, Inc., and Global Marine Development, Inc., are among the firms that are pressing hard for a national commitment to deep-sea mineral exploitation. Subsidiaries of energy and steel companies, including U.S. Steel and Amoco, are also involved.

The struggle concerns the ownership of the ocean floor. In 1967, Arvid Pardo, the Maltese ambassador to the U.N., proposed an international authority to regulate the exploitation of the oceans as the "Common Heritage of Mankind." Since that time a long negotiation on the Law of the Sea has been underway in an attempt, so far unsuccessful, to reconcile the conflicting interests of the industrial countries and the Third World nations. Many of the issues are highly technical, but they come down to three principal points of contention. The Third World countries want an international authority, responsible to a majority of U.N. members, to have the power to decide who shall exploit the seabed and on which terms. They are pressing for an international agency with its own independent capacity to exploit the seabed directly. The U.S. companies (and the U.S. Government representing their interests) stoutly oppose this on the ground that it would foreclose private mining or would subject it to intolerable political control by the poor countries who make up a majority in the U.N. The U.S. is willing to accept some sort of international authority as long as it has no power to deny applications by private companies to sweep the ocean floor. The Group of 77, the caucus of the poor countries in the U.N. (there are now 110 of them), want regulation of deep-sea mining by an international body, and many of them prefer that most of the mining be done by a public international corporation rather than by private companies.

Behind all the legal maneuvering about decision making are two fundamental issues. The first is a matter of equity. Why, the poor countries ask, should the industrial countries grab the riches of the last frontier on the planet and thereby increase the gap between rich and poor? The high seas have always been international. Now that they turn out to be of great potential value, why should the strong and the rich take them over under the banner of free competiton? The Kennecott Group has informed the comptroller general that it will take an investment of $600 to $800 million to launch commercial operations in the Pacific Quadrangle by the early 1980s. Under the U.S. version of international control of the seabed, Mali and Honduras, each with a per capita income of about $200, are free to start scraping the ocean floor just as soon as they amass an equivalent amount of capital.

A majority of the poor countries have an interest in sharing in the riches that might be extracted from the seabed since they have few mineral resources themselves. A minority of poor countries, however, which do have minerals to export, have special interests in wishing to control deep-sea mining. Studies by the United Nations Conference on Trade and Development indicate that if mining companies were to extract nodules from the sea on the scale they have projected for the early 1980s, the price of nickel, copper, cobalt, and manganese would fall and certain key producers, such as Zaire, Zambia, Morocco, Cuba, and Gabon, might lose as much as 50 percent of their foreign exchange earnings. These countries especially have an interest in international regulation of deep-sea mining to protect land-based mining.

The Law of the Sea Conference has become a principal forum for dramatizing the fundamental economic conflicts between the rich nations and the poor. The industrialized countries (with the exception of Norway and to a lesser extent Sweden) by and large support the U.S. approach, and the Soviet Union's position is much closer to that of the U.S. than to that of the poor countries. Because the conference has been deadlocked, the mining companies and their lobby, the American Mining Congress, have been pressing hard for unilateral action by the U.S. The companies want the United States to guarantee specific seabed mining sites by issuing licenses to the companies. The major companies have each already spent over $100 million on exploration, and they do not wish to invest much more without being assured of specific rights to mine. In 1978 the Carter Administration endorsed legislation "to license and regulate the activities of the U.S.–based firms which are commercially recovering manganese nodules from the deep seabed."

The companies demand not only legal and military protection from the United States but also investment guarantees and other significant federal expenditures in the form of surveys and environmental impact studies. The latter are especially important because of the fear that scraping the seabed with a 50-foot-wide vacuum cleaner can upset delicate marine ecology by destroying the seafloor organisms in its path. (Unlike lawn mowing, however, underwater sweeping techniques provide for large gaps between the rows.) Pollution of the seabed by the sedimentary material stirred up by the mining device is another fear that has prompted environmentalists to oppose the whole idea of sea mining. Finally, the marine vacuum cleaner sucks up sediment and deep-sea water from the bottom and disgorges them at the ocean surface after the nodules have been removed. No one yet knows what damage these can do, although a federal agency is now conducting an environmental impact study of the effects of exploratory mining operations in order to find out. Future plans call for processing the nodules in floating refineries, and these ideas worry environmentalists most of all because of the problem of waste disposal.

Seabed mining is now projected as an important activity of U.S. companies for the last decade of the century. It will be expensive for the companies and, increasingly, for the U.S. Treasury. It will involve confrontation with a majority of poor countries that continue to insist that the oceans are the heritage of mankind rather than of Lockheed or U.S. Steel. The implacement of billions of dollars of U.S. property in vulnerable situations on the high seas will create new military "requirements" that must also be counted as part of the expense of extracting our minerals by vacuuming the ocean floor.

If seabed mining seems exotic, what is one to make of space mining?

The leading proponent is Professor Gerard K. O'Neill of Princeton, who testified before a House Committee in 1975 that it is now possible to "establish a highly industrialized self-maintaining human community in free space at a location along the orbit of the moon." Because of the absence of gravitational pull, it is possible to produce stronger alloys in space than on earth. Normally, when bronze is made, for example, the lighter tin atoms tend to rise and the heavier copper to sink, but in space the elements hug one another in a smooth, strong mixture. There are 400 or so other metallic combinations that will not mix at all on earth but will solidify in a weightless environment. Processing minerals in space could solve pollution problems on earth. "Lunar surface raw materials," Professor O'Neill claims, "are sources of metals, ceramics, glass, and oxygen. . . ." Asteroids can be mined for bauxite, iron, titanium, and silicon, and the technology to process them in space is at hand.

The issue is the cost not only in dollars but in energy. The first factory in space will be aboard the Space Shuttle scheduled to be put in orbit in 1981. The cost will be about $1.4 billion in 1979 alone, and this amount will increase greatly once the Shuttle is operational. Space mining and space materials processing offer a new identity for the space program, which ran out of new worlds to conquer once the U.S. defeated the Russians in the moon race. The materials that can be fashioned only in space are chiefly of interest to high-technology industry and the military —more perfect lasers, more perfect hydrogen isotopes for fusion research, more perfect crystals. Whether these are priority needs on earth is questionable.

Space mining fascinates us because it seems to offer a way out of dealing with the problems of finitude, limited resources, and the intractable problems of managing the ecology of the earth. Facing the unknown hardships of space is more glamorous than dealing with the known hardships of earth. Earth-bound skeptics can be dismissed as reincarnated savants from Columbus' day still warning of the dangers of falling off the earth. Escapist dreams in a time of mounting troubles on earth are powerful, and there is money to be made from them. Space mining also provides the Pentagon with a justification that has been lacking for supporting successive generations of military space technology.

6.

Lewis Mumford divides historical epochs according to the use societies have made of critical materials. In what he calls the "eotechnic age," roughly from A.D. 1000 to 1750, human beings learned to harness wind and water to achieve huge increases in productivity. By the fourteenth century the water mill was the foundation of the great industrial centers of the late Middle Ages—Bologna, Augsburg, and Ulm. It ground grain, pumped water, and furnished power for pulping rags into paper (as early as 1290 in Ravensburg), for spinning silk, tanning hides, and mining metals. A sophisticated system of canals in Venice, Amsterdam, and in the Baltic kingdoms brought about a revolution in transportation. By the sixteenth century, sixteen canal boats a day traveled between Delft and Rotterdam. Along with the harnessing of water came the mastery of wind. In 1105 the Abbot of Savigny was authorized to establish windmills in Normandy. Within 200 years the windmill and the wind turbine had become of such economic importance that the Bishop of Utrecht laid claim to all the winds that blew in his diocese. The crucial product of the eotechnic age was wood, the prime source of energy and the principal building material for houses, ships, carts, and plows. It was a time for the individual entrepreneur, the enterprising small farmer, and the explorer who could learn the art of mastering the wind by yielding to it.

By the middle of the eighteenth century the "paleotechnic era" had arrived. The energy source was coal, and the rock of the new civilization was iron. Mumford terms this era of "carboniferous capitalism" a radical new departure for humankind in which society was living "for the first time on an accumulation of potential energy, derived from the ferns of the carboniferous period instead of upon current income." The burning of coal made steam power possible and the exploitation of iron necessary. The new era was a mining civilization. The dominant color was black, the dominant value a "reckless, get-rich-quick, devil-take-the-hindmost attitude," the principal consequence a physical squalor and human degradation caught forever in the searing descriptions of Zola, Dickens, and Marx. Contemporary accounts of wild naked women pulling the coal carts deep in English mines testify to what Mumford calls the fever of exploitation.

The era of coal and iron led to a rapid concentration of economic power, for mining and smelting on a grand scale took considerable capital. Iron technology was, of course, not new. According to Fernand Braudel, the Chinese knew about cast iron and coal firing perhaps as early as the fifth century B.C. From medieval times to the eighteenth century, primitive forges and blast furnaces appeared all over Europe. But iron did not become the most important production material until the nineteenth century, when new furnace technology made possible the huge scale of the modern iron and steel industry. The ironmonger who measured his output in hundredweights had given way to the iron and steel complex that measured its product in the thousands of tons. The difference in scale in the metallurgical industry, Braudel suggests, divides two civilizations. One nineteenth-century writer called it "the event of events in the evolution of humanity."

The working day lengthened. In the fifteenth century, textile workers had a two-and-a-half-hour break in a fourteen- or fifteen-hour day. In the sixteenth century, German mines were run on three eight-hour shifts a day. But in the new iron age a sixteen-hour day with one hour off for dinner was the norm. The "iron horse" concentrated populations in valleys—it did not work well on anything over a 2 percent grade—and spread a blanket of soot over the new urban population. As Mumford puts it:

> Iron became the universal material. One went to sleep in an iron bed and washed one's face in the morning in an iron washbowl; one practiced gymnastics with the aid of iron dumb-bells or other iron weight-lifting apparatus; one played billiards on an iron billiard table, made by Mssrs. Sharp and Roberts; one sat behind an iron locomotive and drove to the city on iron rails, passing over an iron bridge and arriving at an iron-covered railroad station: in America, after 1847, the front of the office-building might even be made of cast iron. In the most typical of Victorian utopias, that of J. S. Buckingham, the ideal city is built almost entirely of iron.

By the mid-nineteenth century the Bessemer converter and the Siemens-Martin process had made possible the miraculous transformation of iron into steel and it ushered in the Steel Age, a time of suspension bridges, skyscrapers, the automobile, and the steadiest customer of all, the munitions industry.

The steel industry is undergoing a major process of restructuring. The everyday steels that have given the name to our age are being manufactured increasingly in Third World countries such as Korea and Brazil. Within the industrial world, there is increasing competition to manufacture and sell the advanced steels on which recent generations of high technology depend. All these take increasing amounts of the steel-transforming metals we have been discussing. It has been traditional for nations to boast of their steel output along with their missile arsenal. Indeed, one of the functions of the international potlatch that we call the arms race is to dramatize the conspicuous consumption of mineral resources that only the immensely powerful can afford to waste on such an extravagant scale.

The paleotechnic era persists. But for more than 100 years it has coexisted with the "neotechnic" era, which is based on an entirely different cluster of minerals. The end of the nineteenth century ushered in the age of electricity and gasoline. The key mineral facilitators, conductors, and converters of these new energy sources are copper and aluminum. Although the first modern treatise on electricity, John Gilbert's *De Magnete,* appeared in 1600, the theory of electric energy was not established until the time of Faraday at the beginning of the nineteenth century. By the second half of the nineteenth century, a stunning succession of inventions had occurred: an electric car that would travel on the roadbed of the Baltimore and Washington railroad at 19 miles an hour (1849); an electric lighthouse in Dungeness, England (1862); Siemens' dynamo (1866); Bell's electric telephone (1876); Coleman's compressed air refrigerator (1877); Tesla's alternator (1888); Edison's electric power station (1882); and hundreds of others including the elevator, television, phonograph, motion picture camera, adding machine—in short, most of the material amenities of modern life.

The electric current that breathed life into all these machines travels by wire. Copper, the crucial metal of the electric age, has been used by human beings for 6,000 years. (Mixed with tin, copper becomes bronze, and in such form it gave its name to an entire prehistoric civilization.) An extremely effective conductor of electricity, it has been used for 100 years, primarily in motors, dynamos, generators, and wiring. Most of the copper produced outside the socialist world is mined in the U.S., Chile, Canada, Zaire, and Zambia. The U.S. and Chile are by far the biggest producers.

In recent years, copper has been increasingly replaced by aluminum for high-voltage transmission of electricity. Copper is twice as good a conductor as aluminum, but aluminum, weighing half as much, has certain technical and economic advantages (as well as huge energy costs). Aluminum was first isolated by the Danish physicist Hans Christian Oersted in 1825, but Karl Bayer's process for producing aluminum from bauxite ore was not invented until 1888. Commercial production requires an enormous output of electricity—about ten to twelve kilowatt-hours for every pound of metal.

Aluminum has changed the face of modern industrial society as dramatically as iron and steel transformed earlier generations. The car, the airplane, and the sophisticated weapon, to name three growth industries of our time, all depend upon the light, tough metal with a thousand uses. It is the most plentiful metal in the earth's crust, but it appears as an ore, i.e., something to be extracted at a profit, in a red sand called bauxite. Between 40 and 50 percent of the aluminum now produced in the industrial countries comes from the soil of Jamaica, Surinam, Guyana, the Dominican Republic, and Haiti. The U.S. aluminum giants import more than 90 percent of their bauxite requirements. Almost half has come from Jamaica alone.

The use of aluminum has grown at a much faster rate than that of all other metals, and as the Bureau of Mines puts it, "measured whether in quantity or value, use of aluminum now exceeds that of any other metal except iron." Aluminum is used extensively in the construction industry for siding, roofing, windows, and bridges. In 1955 the average automobile used about 30 pounds of aluminum, but by 1976, as a result of government requirements for lighter, gas-saving vehicles, 85 pounds of the light metal were used per car.

If, as Mumford suggests, aluminum is the quintessential neotechnic metal, packaging is the quintessential neotechnic use. The crucial role of packaging in the U.S. economy is a consequence of two related revolutions in American capitalism—internationalization and concentration. The first is the galloping geographic spread of global markets. To service the newly integrated world market, not only jet aircraft and internal combustion engines are needed, but also light, secure, and attractive containers. Containerization, a process of loading goods into huge metal (usually aluminum) boxes and dropping them into the holds of ships by crane rather than employing stevedores, has become standard practice for lowering labor costs and speeding up deliveries. The second revolution, the concentration of major industry, has led to a ferocious competition among oligopolies for shares of the market, but the weapon is not the old-fashioned capitalist strategy of price cutting; it is space-age packaging. Customers are seduced by convenience, particularly convenience foods. About 15 percent of all the aluminum consumed in the U.S. goes for foils, caps, tabs, and closures, mostly for processed foods, and for the refrigerators and freezers in which to store them. One of the most enduring bits of aluminum packaging is the former headquarters of Alcoa. For many years the aluminum giant rented a floor in the Gulf building, a marble and bronze palace in Pittsburgh built in the Mellon era; on each floor save one are giant bronze doors fit for an imperial antechamber. On Alcoa's floor, they were replaced with shiny aluminum.

7.

Technology has transformed the minerals industry. The Gold Rush era of individual entrepreneurs, slippery fortunes, and nomadic prospecting gave way to the modern era of the metal oligopolies. Three generations ago the metals economy was dominated by individuals such as the Guggenheims who were Yukon gold and Colorado silver barons turned copper kings. Lead, an ancient metal once used as flooring for the hanging gardens of Babylon, now reincarnated as pipes, bearings, and storage batteries, was substantially in the hands of the Lewisohns.

The International Nickel Company was organized in 1902 by J. Pierpont Morgan "to consolidate and control the nickel production of the world." As late as 1956 it still provided 62 percent of all the nickel consumed outside the socialist countries. It now has about 40 percent of the world market, sharing it with Société Le Nickel, a Rothschild company; Falconbridge; AMAX; Western Mining Company of Australia, and a few others. It is a U.S. company whose assets are chiefly in Canada. Its claims go back to the 1880s, when a U.S. promoter, Samuel Ritchie, and a group of Ohio money people bought up the vast mineral-rich areas for one dollar an acre. Opposed by Canadian nationalists, the U.S.-financed nickel giant became "Canadian" in 1928 through reorganization.

Falconbridge was the creation of Thayer Lindsley, a Canadian Howard Hughes who parlayed $30,000 into a world mining empire and developed a remarkably global outlook. In 1943 he reported to the shareholders his delight that Falconbridge's refinery in Norway, then occupied by Hitler, "is safe so far and is being maintained . . . by your Norwegian staff under German control." His company was enormously assisted by the U.S. strategic stockpile program, which spent $789 million expanding the nickel supply in the 1950s. In those years Falconbridge stock rose more than six times. In 1967 it was taken over by Superior Oil Company.

Known as one of the "noble" metals (a step down from "precious"), nickel is playing an ever-increasing role in aerospace technology. A four-engine piston-driven plane takes about 125 pounds, a commercial four-engine jet 4,000 pounds, a 747 jumbo jet 11,000 pounds, and a supersonic transport 18,000 pounds. Forty-eight million pounds end up in the 12 million cars sold annually in the North American market. Originally developed as a material to strengthen armor plate for the U.S. Navy, nickel has always had an important role as a military metal, but it is becoming crucial in making strong, noncorrosive, heat-resistant steel.

The U.S. has almost no nickel reserves, and neither do the other industrial countries of the West. Most of the world's nickel has come from the Sudbury Basin in Canada. The role of the nickel economy in the development of Canada has been a matter of controversy for years. The Sudbury reserves are being exhausted, leaving a desolate and polluted company town. The companies blame the ravaged look of the area on the logging companies that cut down the trees to rebuild Chicago after the fire of 1871. But millions of tons of sulphur dioxide spew forth from INCO and Falconbridge smokestacks every year. According to former cabinet minister Eric Kierans, the exchange of pure air for taxes and jobs is a bad bargain. In his report *Natural Resources Policy in Manitoba,* he notes that the metals-mining industry had profits of $3.1 billion in the years 1965–69 and that they were taxed at an effective rate of 12 percent.

Kierans captures the growing nationalist feelings in Canada about minerals exploitation:

> If Canada cannot break out of its developing nation status, i.e. heavy reliance on staple exports, it is because our federal policy makers have so decided. They cling to the image of a Canada whose growth depends on the export of its wealth. They fail to see that their policies work against the real development that comes from the transformation of raw materials by human skills into final products.

In the early years of this century Henry Rogers of Standard Oil created American Smelting and Refining, a great smelting trust, which was eventually absorbed by the Guggenheims into the Kennecott Copper Company. Such entrepreneurs shamelessly fixed prices and made treaties with one another for dividing up mineral resources and markets to keep out meddling competitors. In Utah, the *Engineering and Mining Journal* reported at the turn of the century that "there is no competition and mines must comply with the conditions imposed by the smelters or go out of business." The West was represented in Washington by silver senators and copper congressmen: Simon Guggenheim himself arrived there in a private Pullman car to take his seat as senator from Colorado in January 1907.

New fortunes in the metals business depended upon outwitting the original prospectors or finding new ore outside already monopolized territory. Thus Marcus Daly, an Irish immigrant, launched Anaconda Copper Company on huge copper deposits found in 1882 in the Anaconda silver mine in Butte, Montana. The indispensable element in creating metals fortunes was an aptitude for preempting the right piece of the earth's crust at the right time. But to convert the fruits of individual good fortune into mammoth economic institutions took the very opposite of the gambler's instinct. It required the elimination of surprise through the judicious use of monopoly, the gathering of immense capital sums to exploit the advantage, and the development of technology. With his copper profits, Daly bought a smelter, a refinery, a railroad to carry the ore, timberlands to provide the material for the wooden mine supports, a sawmill to cut the wood, and a water company to supply the copper settlement of Butte. Then competitors and partners were bought out, copper-fabricating plants were begun, and by the 1920s, Anaconda had secured a huge share of the world copper market by controlling every phase of copper production "from mine to consumer."

Ores once worthless now represent billions of dollars, but the key to unlocking that fortune is immensely expensive equipment quite beyond the reach of the average man with a mule. The era of the modern metals conglomerates began when partnerships were forged between great financiers and enterprising engineers.

Herbert Hoover was the most famous of the small band of men with a nose for finding rich metal veins in far-off places for wealthy speculators. Starting off as a gold-mining engineer in Australia in 1897, he became an itinerant minerals consultant and investor in Russia, Burma, Turkestan, Korea, Egypt, Ceylon, and in the mountains of South and Central America.

The dean of mining engineers for a time was John Hays Hammond. Cecil Rhodes, the archtypical mineral imperialist, who dreamed, he said, of annexing the stars, hired Hammond for his South Africa mines. Among his duties was the plotting of an insurrection against the Boer government of South Africa in 1895 to take over the gold operation at Witwatersrand. But Sir Leander Jameson, the colonial administrator, staged a premature raid and botched the military operation that was supposed to deliver the gold into the hands of Consolidated Gold Fields, Ltd. Hammond was sentenced to be hanged. However, the U.S. Senate passed a resolution begging for mercy, and Rhodes rescued him by paying a $125,000 fine. Hammond then went to work for the Guggenheims at $1,250,000 a year (1902 dollars) and became a symbol to the mining men of the West that the mineral riches of the country had passed into the hands of eastern big money.

The marriage of high finance—Morgans, Rothschilds, Schiffs, Bernard Baruch—and the most successful mining entrepreneurs, principally the Guggenheims, in the early years of the century laid the foundation for the minerals oligopolies that control the world market today. The minerals industry lent itself naturally to concentration because of the huge capital requirements; it also lent itself to conglomeration because a variety of minerals are found in the earth together and each can support its own division of a mining empire. Thus the impurities detached from nuggets of gold and lodes of silver became the foundation of industrial minerals fortunes. Today the mining, processing, and distribution of each major metal is dominated by a handful of companies that represent the incorporated legacies of the mining entrepreneurs. There is a high degree of concentration in the industry, though less than in the era of the minerals trusts. The process of merger and takeover is escalating dramatically as environmental costs create the need to assemble ever larger amounts of capital. Kennecott, for example, acquired Carborundum, a pollution control company. It also tried unsuccessfully to acquire Peabody, the nation's largest steam-coal producer, then narrowly escaped being taken over itself.

Because they had the foresight and the luck to corner the two indispensable neotechnic metals, the copper-rich and the lords of aluminum have played a crucial political role. In 1977 four companies—Kennecott, Anaconda, Revere, and Phelps-Dodge—produced 58 percent of the copper produced in the U.S. About 40 percent of this came from five mines in Arizona. But the extraordinary growth of the copper companies has come from the control of rich foreign mines.

In 1890, Daniel Guggenheim had secured an extremely favorable concession from the Mexican dictator Porfirio Diaz. In 1910 he bought Chile's fabulous Chuquicamata mine for $25 million. (Ten years earlier he had had a chance to buy it for a tenth of that.) By 1920 all the important copper reserves of Chile and Mexico were in the hands of American companies. The British, French, and Belgians had preempted the copper of what is now Zambia and Zaire.

When the Guggenheims bought Chile's copper *The New York Times* predicted that the investment would be "vastly helpful" to the South American republic. But the copper bonanza has ended in tragedy. The companies invested $30 million in the years 1922 to 1968 and made $2 billion, almost two-thirds of which was taken out of the country. In the nineteenth century, Chile, which accounted for 40 percent of world production, had a flourishing copper export business firmly under the control of national capitalists. After 1870 the industry collapsed, and when it was revived in 1920 it was totally foreign-owned.

For years the Chilean state had welcomed foreign investors and left them alone. Until 1925 the tax on copper profits was 6 percent. The Chilean copper economy was totally tied to U.S. needs. In the 1930s Chilean copper was excluded to protect the depressed domestic industry. Norman Girvan, a Jamaican economist who has made a detailed study of the Chilean copper industry, points out that in World War II Chile was assigned the role of supplying large amounts of cheap copper for the war machine. The companies and the U.S. Government agreed to freeze the price at 12 cents a pound, and Chile lost as much as $500 million by these forced bargain sales. In the Korean War the U.S. needed copper again, and this time Chile was able to strike a better bargain. But when the bottom fell out of the copper market after the war, the stage was set for the return of laissez-faire, reduced taxes, and higher company profits.

By the 1960s, Chileans across the political spectrum were opposed to the foreign takeover of the nation's most valuable resource, because the once-prosperous country was now almost bankrupt. Annoyed by Kennedy Administration rhetoric about the need for land reform, even some of the old land-owning families demanded that something be done about the copper companies. In 1964 and 1970, Eduardo Frei, the Christian

Democrat, and Allende, the Socialist, differed only on whether the Chilean Government should nationalize a controlling interest in the mines or take them over altogether.

The slogan of the Unidad Popular, the coalition that brought Salvador Allende to power in the 1970 election, was *"Ahora, el cobre es Chileno."* But this challenge to the copper multinationals was a red flag that mobilized U.S. opposition to help bring Allende down in a bloody coup three years later. When Allende won and took over the mines without substantial compensation—he argued that the companies had already been handsomely paid in repatriated excess profits—Kennecott and Anaconda pressed the U.S. Government hard to squeeze the regime by denying credit, cutting aid, arranging for the withholding of crucial spare parts, and covertly supporting anti-Allende forces within the country. The companies shared Henry Kissinger's view: "I don't see why we need to stand by and watch a country go communist due to the irresponsibility of its own people." The showcase of Latin American democracy had become a problem. Cables between Washington and the U.S. embassy in Santiago which came to light in the Multinational Hearings in the Senate after the coup made it clear that the U.S. Government had followed a "destabilization" policy in Chile along the lines favored by the copper companies but on a somewhat more modest scale. CIA money poured in to support opposition newspapers and radio stations and a six-week-long truckers' strike. Nonmilitary aid fell to a trickle, but military aid, including supersonic jets, went to the Chilean military in a crucial show of support three months before the coup. As Girvan correctly notes, the nationalization of Kennecott and Anaconda properties in Chile was not the primary cause of U.S. intervention in Chile. No single company, however powerful, has that kind of hold on the U.S. Government. Rather, the expropriations were seen as a dominoes problem, much like the insurgency in Vietnam. If one small country could get away with taking back its mineral wealth, where would it end? I remember talking to a Guggenheim heir in the last days of Allende. It was not the Guggenheims, he told me, but "the little people like you" who were going to be hurt by all this disrespect for property. Once settled into the charred remains of the presidential palace, the *junta* lost little time in settling with the copper companies on favorable terms and announcing that Chile's copper was once again available for foreign investors. After five years of brutal despotism that became a model for Argentina, Uruguay, and other formerly democratic societies, rampant inflation, unemployment, the steady impoverishment of the middle class, and the abandonment of the poor, only Exxon and Arco had taken up the offer.

Bauxite, a term used universally for ores rich in aluminum dioxide, was first discovered in Les Baux, a town in the south of France built on chalk-white rock. Aluminum ore has become a battleground in the struggle for a new economic order second only to oil. "Over 40 percent of the world productive capacity for bauxite plus over half of the world alumina and aluminum capacity, is operated by six corporate groups, their subsidiaries, or affiliates," the U.S. Bureau of Mines reports in *Mineral Facts and Problems*. Three are U.S. companies—Alcoa, Reynolds, and Kaiser. A fourth, Alcan, is Canadian. Pechiney is French, and Alusuisse proclaims its national origin in its name. In 1977 the top three U.S. companies produced about 65 percent of all aluminum manufactured in the U.S.

Until the end of the Second World War, Alcoa and its Canadian sister, Alcan, had a total monopoly over the aluminum industry of North America on the basis first of patent rights to the electrolytic production process and then of control over all the bauxite in the U.S. Reynolds and Kaiser entered the industry after the Second World War with surplus alumina plants and smelters given them by the U.S. Government. In their quest for bauxite not yet owned by the monopoly—the bauxite soils of what are now Guyana and Surinam became Alcoa-Alcan assets in the 1912–25 period—the newcomers happened upon huge deposits in Jamaica. By the mid-1960s, Alcoa, Kaiser, Reynolds, Anaconda, Revere, and Alcan had acquired about 13 percent of the island, 225,000 acres of bauxite-rich land.

The Jamaican economist Norman Girvan, noting that unemployment in his country runs as high as 30 percent and weekly earnings average ten dollars, gives an account of the relationship between the companies and his country. It seethes with a sense of humiliation and outrage, but it is no less true for that.

> . . . the Caribbean bauxite industry is a classic case of economic imperialism. It is entirely owned and operated by a small number of vertically integrated North American transnational aluminum companies (except in Guyana, and then only since 1971). These companies also control the bulk of world production and reserves of bauxite and they dominate the world aluminum market. Capital and technology for the Caribbean bauxite industry come from the transnational aluminum companies. There is no "market" for its output other than the plants of the companies. Prices are fixed by the companies according to their convenience. Levels of production and the rates of investment and expansion are matters of company policy, determined by the global economics of the transnational firm. Only a part of the value of the industry's "sales" actually accrue to the Caribbean economies; and only an infinitesimal fraction of the value of the end products flows back to Caribbean people. . . . Bauxite valued at $50, say, yields aluminum products that can be sold for

anything up to $2,000. Evidently, the crucial activities in the generation of value and of industrial external economies are the processes of reducing aluminum from alumina and transforming the primary metal into semifabricated products used by manufacturers. But the Caribbean countries, in spite of their possession of some of the world's largest bauxite deposits, have been confined to the simple low-value activities, and particularly to the extraction of the bauxite ore and to that alone. . . . Thus, the Carribbean bauxite industry is entirely subject to the needs, policies, and authority of corporate monopoly capital based in North America.

In 1971, Guyana began nationalizing its bauxite deposits, and in March 1974, in the midst of the oil embargo, Jamaica took the lead in forming the International Bauxite Association, which included the major world suppliers, Australia, Guinea, Guyana, and Surinam. By then Jamaica had discovered transfer pricing. The aluminum monopolies did most of their buying and selling to themselves since they were fully integrated companies. By the alchemy of the accountant's art they could arrange to show virtually no profit at all on their Jamaican processing plant. Thus the prime minister of Jamaica reported in 1972 that 3.5 million tons of bauxite would net a tax of $1 million if processed in Jamaica and $9 million if exported without processing. The Government of Jamaica, headed by Michael Manley, raised its taxes on the U.S. aluminum companies, adopting a formula that tied the tax to the price of finished aluminum rather than to tons of bauxite mined. The effect was to undermine the exclusive power of the companies to decide what Jamaica should get for its own soil, and to raise the revenue for the Jamaican Government eightfold. Other bauxite producers, with the notable exception of Australia, followed suit. The Jamaican Government also acquired a majority interest in the local subsidiaries of the giant aluminum companies that control the world market.

The transformation of the bauxite industry had begun. Higher taxes throughout the Caribbean—an increase in Haiti from $1.88 to $11 a ton —increased participation of the state in production and processing, and increased government-to-government cooperation began to occur. In June 1974, Trinidad, Tobago, and Guyana announced plans for a jointly owned aluminum smelter complex. The International Bauxite Association did not, however, become an effective cartel for a number of reasons, chief among which was the fact that Australia and Brazil, both with larger reserves than the Caribbean producers, have close political ties with the U.S. and little interest in confronting the aluminum oligopolies. As the price of bauxite rises, the economics of producing aluminum from lower-quality clays becomes attractive. In 1974, Alcoa and Pechiney began construction of a clay-based aluminum plant in Marseilles. In the years since the bauxite takeover Jamaica has fallen on hard times. The companies have gone elsewhere. The world market price has declined. The country has been squeezed by private banks and the International Monetary Fund and has had to institute severe austerity measures to satisfy its creditors.

In 1974 and 1975 more than a dozen Third World countries nationalized copper, tin, bauxite, and iron mines. With the stroke of a pen the presidents of Venezuela and Peru took over from multinational corporations iron mines that supply ores equal to 30 percent of U.S. annual imports. But the Jamaican experience illustrates the limited power over the world minerals economy which individual Third World nations can exercise by nationalizing mines, and how difficult it is to recreate OPECs for other commodities. CIPEC, the Council of Copper Exporting Countries (Chile, Peru, Zambia, and Zaire), tried unsuccessfully to raise copper prices in the manner of OPEC by agreeing to cut world production 15 percent. The plan failed totally. In 1974, copper prices briefly rose to a historic high and then plummeted, falling from $1.51 a pound to 54 cents in eighteen months. In 1976, prices were slightly less than the average price for the preceding twenty years.

8.

There are two fundamental policy issues raised by the peculiarities of metals pricing. One has to do with assuring long-term supply. The situation is not so different from the history of oil. The oil companies bear great responsibility for the Energy Crisis, not only because of recent activities—withholding supplies, cutting refinery production, diverting oil from U.S. consumers to the "spot market"—but, more importantly, because of crucial decisions made a generation or more ago. The decision to exploit cheap Middle East oil instead of developing alternative energy sources in the United States was one of the most fateful policy choices of the century. It was made in private, but the consequences are public. So too with nonfuel minerals. It is now uneconomic to mine copper in most domestic mines. Environmental costs run 10 cents a pound, and together with labor and other production expenses the cost per pound for a while exceeded the world market price. Even if the price rises, as is predicted, it will not be enough to produce the kind of profits the copper companies expect. Companies have cut production. Because of long lead times and heavy capital requirements it is not so easy to start up again. Jack Thompson, president of Newmont Mining, predicts that "unless we get some help from the government, in the early eighties this excess of copper will turn into a great shortage, and this will put prices up.'' It is evident that the so-called free market cannot assure adequate supplies. The question, to which we will return, is not whether more explicit planning is needed to manage the flow of scarce resources, but who should do it and for whose benefit.

The other issue has to do with social justice. Mining is inevitably rapacious. In the name of progress the earth is assaulted and hidden treasure is carted away never to be replaced. The sharing of the fruits of progress is an issue to arouse strong political passions. People in the Third World feel more deeply about losing their mineral legacy to foreign control than about their bananas or their beaches. The human exploitation that goes with exploiting minerals is staggering. Miners are always being sacrificed for higher social purposes. Federal officials have determined that beryllium, a critical component in the aerospace and nuclear industries, exposes the 30,000 workers who mine and process it to increased risk of cancer. However, Energy Secretary James R. Schlesinger prevented the agency in charge of occupational health from enacting regulations to protect the workers because it would ''adversely affect national security.'' There are only two beryllium producers in the U.S., and they threaten to go out of production if the workers' exposure to the metal is reduced from two micrograms per cubic meter of air to one microgram.

Questions of social justice arise in connection with the distribution of rewards as well as risks. The aluminum industry grew to fantastic size in the U.S. with the aid of cheap federally subsidized power. The artificial cheapness of aluminum caused the electric and packaging industries to switch from copper and steel. These industries are now depressed, workers are laid off, and in one form or another taxpayers are footing the bill. Now the country is heavily dependent upon a metal that is a devourer of electricity, and power rates are no longer cheap. It is another momentous planning decision made by people we never knew.

Now a further planning decision with respect to aluminum is being implemented. Smelting and refining is shifting to Third World countries. ''The cheap power overseas will offset the cost of transporting the metal to the United States,'' John Stamper of the Bureau of Mines explains. The Export-Import Bank, a U.S. agency, has given preliminary approval of a large loan to finance an integrated aluminum industry in Zaire to be owned by Reynolds. The same company is negotiating for a smelter in Paraguay, and Martin Marietta hopes to develop an aluminum smelter in Costa Rica which will take 85 percent of the power produced by the Boruca Dam. The dam is being financed by the Inter-American Development Bank, an international aid agency. Kaiser owns a smelter in Ghana financed by EximBank and the Agency for International Development. The power comes from the Volta Dam, for which the Ghanian Government charges one of the lowest electrical rates in the world. The dam, financed by the World Bank and U.S. aid agencies, directs 70 percent of its capacity to the smelter. Ghana produces bauxite, but Kaiser and Reynolds import bauxite from the Caribbean. It is a huge capital-intensive project that employs seven-tenths of one percent of the labor force.

Underdeveloped countries have great needs for power. They are, as we have seen, more lavishly endowed with petroleum and hydroelectric reserves than the industrial world. There is a world petroleum shortage but no shortage in China, Mexico, Nigeria, and, of course, the Middle East. If these resources are preempted to keep extravagant civilizations consuming at exponential rates, a possibility for rescuing a billion or more people from the grip of hunger will be lost.

Until recently, almost no one we could hear questioned the right of developed countries to bend, burn, or melt as much of the earth's crust as they could take. It was the destiny of minerals lying within the borders of primitive peoples to supply the industrialization of the West. In return, a trickle of industrial goods and some enlightenment would flow to the darker regions of the earth. In such a division of labor which was established in the age of European exploration and colonization more than 300 years ago, rich and poor would grow rich together.

In the last 50 years or so a huge change in consciousness has occurred. Imperialism, proclaimed first as a divine right, then as a political achievement, is now an epithet. The demand for more equitable sharing of resources became increasingly insistent as colonial armies departed, white settlers fled, and collections of tribes and villages around the world set themselves up as nations. The "new nations," as they called themselves, became a majority in the United Nations. The call for a "new economic order" was put on the world agenda.

Third World statesmen now seek an end to the "bleeding and looting" of their natural resources. Nonrenewable resources are by definition things that can be lost forever. If they are taken without fair value, to that extent they have been stolen. But what is fair value? And who is to decide?

The prevailing view in the industrial nations is that the market dispenses justice. Supply and demand set prices. It is a comfortable belief because the market, as we have seen, has treated the minerals consumers well. But the market in the mineral resources world is a metaphysical construction. Market sharing, price fixing, speculation, monopolization, manipulation of credit, and, sometimes, military power determine the terms under which the Third World is relieved of its minerals. Visible hands with guns, money, and a tight hold on the world distribution system determine the minerals economy, while Adam Smith's invisible hand still provides the ideological music.

The north-south trade, in which minerals play a significant role, is producing a redistribution of wealth that favors the rich at the expense of the poor. According to Jan Tinbergen, the Dutch Nobel laureate, 10 percent of mankind consumes twenty-five times as much as the remaining 90 percent. Because manufactured goods are rising in price much faster than minerals (which in many cases are actually declining in real terms), the gap steadily widens. Julius Nyerere, president of Tanzania, illustrated the point with sisal, an agricultural product. "In 1965, I could buy a tractor by selling 17.25 tons of sisal. The price of the same model in 1972 needed 42 tons of sisal." The former ambassador to the United States from Sri Lanka, Neville Kanakaratne, makes the same point with respect to rubber. In 1960, 25 tons of rubber would buy six tractors; fifteen years later, only two. Identical calculations could be done for most minerals. For this reason, one demand of the Third World countries is "indexation"—some formula for tying the price of natural commodities to manufactured goods.

The response within the developed world varies in tone and degree. In general, Europeans have been somewhat more flexible than the U.S. in responding to the "new economic order" demands. The Lomé Convention between nine European Community members and a group of African, Carribbean, and Pacific states makes more concessions to the resource producers than the United States has yet been willing to make. But in comparison with what the poor countries are asking or with what would be needed to reverse the trends we have been discussing, the reforms of the international system are to date marginal indeed.

The demands of the Third World fall into three main categories. First, they would like some machinery for stabilizing the prices of minerals and other commodities, a "common fund" to support mineral prices when they fall. Second, they would like preferred access for their own manufactured goods to the markets of the developed countries. Third, they want financial aid, primarily in the form of debt relief and the extension of new credit on favorable terms. There is massive resistance within the industrial world to all three demands. Indeed, trends are moving in the opposite direction. The industrial countries facing tougher competition among themselves for their primary exports are in no mood to welcome great quantities of cheap goods from the Third World, even when they are manufactured there by their own multinational corporations. They are tightening, not loosening, the terms of credit. And as oil prices rise further, the industrial countries will more fiercely resist efforts to raise the prices of other minerals. Ironically, the pall of recession over the world economy tends to moderate militant Third World rhetoric and to discourage dramatic public confrontations even as it aggravates the systemic problems that gave rise to the demands in the first place. Julius Nyerere, a Christian and a moderate in the spectrum of Third World politics, puts the problem this way:

> The dominant philosophy of international exchange which we met at independence—and which still prevails—is that of a "free market." In theory this means unfettered competiton and bargaining between equals, with prices being the combined actions and wishes of sellers and buyers. . . . Unfortunately the theory bears little relation to fact. Equality between nations of the modern world is only a legal equality. It is not an economic reality. . . . Nor is it true that prices are determined by the operations of a free market, that is, by discussion and compromise between sellers and buyers. The price of manufactured goods is fixed by the producers; if any competition enters into the situation at all, it is between giant firms like Ford, General Motors, and Volkswagen. It is certainly no use the Tanzanian Motor Corporation trying to argue with any one of these firms about their prices: if it is not willing to pay what is asked, the vehicles will wait in stock and Tanzania will continue without transport.
>
> Conversely, the price of primary products is fixed by the purchasers. The producers put on the market whatever they have managed to grow or mine in that year; the goods are often perishable, and in any case the poor nations are desperate for foreign exchange and have no facilities for storage—known facts which further weaken their bargaining position! A small number of purchasers then decide how much they will buy, at what price. Only if natural disaster has made the year's supply unusually low will their competition push the price up. The primary producing countries which need to import manufactured goods are thus price-takers, not price-makers, both as seller and as buyer. We sell cheap and we buy dear, whether we like it or not. . . . The poor nations of the world remain poor because they are poor, and because they operate as if they were equals in a world dominated by the rich.

9.

What changes in the minerals system would make a difference? Nationalization by itself means very little. Ownership without control is an act of political symbolism but nothing more. Liberia has 51 percent of the shares of its iron mines but no vote. Zambia nationalized its copper mines with a flourish and then signed a contract with the old owners, Amax and Anglo-American, giving them the prerogatives of management. On stock markets around the world their stock went up at the news of the "take-over."

Developing countries ought to have a choice whether, when, and on what terms they wish to exploit their mineral resources. Because of decisions of foreigners made years in the past they have become dependent on a constant outflow of irreplaceable riches. The proceeds often go to keep the mineral sector working rather than to solve the food, employment, or other problems of development. Because the market is capricious and the sources are multiple any particular country can find itself without a place to sell its minerals.

The most important reforms of the mineral economy that would benefit Third World countries would be capital and technology transfers and a "common fund" to stabilize the market. These would make fairer control of the minerals economy possible, but such a gift or compensatory payment, depending on how you look at it, is not likely. Short of that, the most significant reform would be an international standard for calculating a fair return to the producing country. Mining companies typically calculate a 15 percent annual return over a ten-year life span for a mine. True, they sometimes miscalculate and lose money, but, by and large, mining has been enormously profitable and returns are frequently much higher. When the return on risk capital exceeds some agreed-upon figure, the profit should go to the producing country. Botswana has made an arrangement of this sort. An international agency should have sufficient access to company books to determine the profit realized on mineral ventures.

There is an argument based on self-interest for the rich countries to aid the poor by changing the terms under which they help themselves to the world's minerals. As John Sewell of the Overseas Development Council points out, there is a vast market for U.S. goods and potentially millions of jobs if the armies of $200-a-year peasants and slum dwellers in Asia, Africa, and Latin America can be lifted into the ranks of the international brotherhood of consumers. To think that they will not make their presence felt in the cities of North America, Europe, and Japan one way or another—either as customers, or, alternatively, as migrants, terrorists, and carriers of disease—is to hide from the future.

But the self-interest argument is complex. There is a trade-off of short-term loss for long-term gain, and that is never a popular bargain in the political arena. Nyerere says "the transfer of wealth from the rich to the poor is a matter of right." There is a strong moral foundation to the argument, if you accept the notion that one generation inherits from another not only privileges but responsibilities. There is a history of exploitation that is hidden in the West but that is etched into the consciousness of literate Third World people and felt by millions of others. Between

1503 and 1660 the Spanish shipped an estimated 16.8 million kilos of silver and 181,000 kilos of gold from Latin America while the population was reduced from 40 million to 12 million. The transfer of wealth from India to Britain is put at 500 million to one billion pounds. The booty Drake brought back on the *Golden Hind,* John Maynard Keynes concludes, "may fairly be considered the fountain and origin of British foreign investment" and the basis of 300 years of British prosperity and imperial rule. Between 1891 and 1911 perhaps as many as 10 million people died in the Congo as the Belgians pacified, relocated, and terrorized the population so that the mineral riches could be taken.

Punishing people for the bad luck of having made their home on valuable mineral sites is, unfortunately, not a thing of the past. The Amazon Basin in Brazil has been extensively surveyed from the air and is believed to have one of the richest "mineral profiles" in the world—large deposits of iron ore, manganese, tin, bauxite, coal, gold, diamonds, and uranium. U.S. Steel, Alcan, Rio Tinto Zinc, and other international mining companies have already invested billions in the region, which is the home of the Waimiri-Atroari and Yanomamo Indian tribes. The official Brazilian attitude toward the Indians was summarized in 1975 by General Fernando Ramos Pereira, the governor of Roraima: "I am of the opinion," he said, "that an area as rich as this—with gold, diamonds, and uranium—cannot afford the luxury of conserving a half a dozen Indian tribes who are holding back the development of Brazil." Technology has made it possible to replay ancient tragedies as farce. In recent years helicopters swooped down on Indian villages, dropping gifts of machetes, beads, and mirrors. But the strategy did not work. The Indians killed some of the agents who came to pacify and remove them, and the government resorted to harsher measures. For the Indians in the area, development has meant the loss of valuable timberland, cropland, and a network of roads crisscrossing their settlements. Most seriously, cutting away the jungle to make roads caused a huge rise in onchocerciasis, African river blindness, which has claimed the sight of a large proportion of the population in certain areas. The import of the white man's childhood diseases, notably measles, has also taken a big toll just as it has among many other primitive peoples. Despite some vague legislative promises, there is no reason to believe that the Indians will share in the riches with which they have been cursed.

What does past and present exploitation have to do with developing new ground rules for the economic relations between mineral producers and consumers? I would put it this way. Unless there is a shared sense of history that links the industrial and the underdeveloped world from which the impulse to make amends can spring, bloody confrontation over mineral resources is inevitable. The result will be a series of devastating shocks to the world industrial system—a loss for everybody. Guilt is personal and cannot be inherited. Responsibility is collective and cannot be avoided simply by opting out of history. The world needs some fundamental rethinking about how mineral resources should be shared. Neither the accident of having made one's home on top of them nor the luck of having turned minerals into capital in the past should decide who owns the earth. Because they are irreplaceable, all minerals are the common heritage of mankind.

CHAPTER VI

Food: Sowers, Reapers, Ranchers, and Eaters

1.

THE MORE ONE LOOKS at the five resource systems that undergird our civilization, the more one is struck by their mysterious connections. Energy is the currency with which we pay for the others. Agriculture is the world's largest solar energy system, a way of converting the sun's rays into animal energy. It is also the vehicle for introducing metals in infinitesimal amounts into the human body. Without such "trace elements" ingested in food, humans would wither and die. It has long been known that iron, magnesium, molybdenum, and copper atoms play a crucial role as activators of vital enzyme reactions in the human body. More recently, it has become clear that inadequate traces of zinc and other unappetizing-sounding metals cause stunted growth, sexual underdevelopment, and liver disease. To grow food takes truly astounding quantities of water. The food system stands squarely in the center of the resource chain that supports life and civilization. Throughout history there has never been enough.

Every day the world produces two pounds of grain for every man, woman and child on earth. That is sufficient to provide 3,000 calories a day for everyone, even without the enormous quantities of meat, fish, vegetables, and fruits that are produced each year. (Twenty-seven hundred calories, according to the Food and Nutrition Board of the National Research Council, is what a moderately active adult male should consume.) The fact that people are hungry is due less to insufficient food production than to maldistribution. Most people who stop eating do so not because there is insufficient food grown in the world but because they no longer grow it themselves and do not have the money to buy it.

What would a photograph taken from outer space of the food production and distribution system of the present world look like? On such a photograph would appear 462 million people actually starving, over half of them children under five. Sixty-seven million of these people live in Africa, 301 million in the Far East, 36 million in Latin America, 30 million in the Near East, and 28 million of them are scattered through what we call the "developed world." Of course the numbers change, depending upon what day you take the picture. These figures were put together by the Food and Agriculture Organization on the basis of pictures taken in the 1969–71 period. Since that time, acute starvation in sub-Saharan Africa has eased but has increased in war-ravaged Ethiopia, Cambodia, and parts of Latin America. About 1.3 billion persons are chronically undernourished.

When the picture is taken again in the year 1985 the situation will be much worse. Because of expected population increases, there may be a need for 44 percent more food in the world than in 1970. More than 70 percent of that additionally needed food will have to go to the poor in underdeveloped countries to avoid an escalation of mass starvation of unimaginable dimensions. According to the Office of Technology Assessment of the U.S. Congress, the developing countries will need to produce over the next twenty-five years "an additional 600 million tons of cereals over and above their current production of about 400 million tons." To do this would require annual production increases of 4 percent, but gains have averaged no more than 2.5 percent in recent years.

The goal is "out of reach under present conditions," the report concludes, and therefore developing countries will have to import somewhere between 94 million and 108 million metric tons. Two-thirds of the seriously food-deficient countries have annual per capita incomes of under $200 and lack the foreign exchange for these massive grain imports. To maintain the 1970 import level (18 million tons) many poor countries have already mortgaged themselves. Even oil-rich Mexico, according to a confidential estimate of the International Monetary Fund, will have to use its entire foreign exchange earnings from petroleum to pay for imported food. Only two Third World countries, Argentina and Thailand, are now net exporters of grain, although Brazil and Pakistan are expected to join that select company by 1985.

The latecomers to the hamburger and steak age—Japan and Western Europe—are devoting increasing amounts of grain to fatten beef. (It takes about 3 to 10 pounds of grain to produce one pound of meat.) The industrial countries are becoming more dependent on the international grain market. The grain deficit in the industrial world may double by 1985. Global grain reserves that provided something of a cushion in times of famine were largely wiped out as a result of the poor harvests of the early 1970s. By the end of the decade they were being built up again, but lean years follow fat years with such regularity that reserves offer no long-term security for food-importing countries

Increasingly, the world food system is becoming integrated into the international industrial economy. Agriculture is on the way to becoming a product line in the Global Factory. In quite specific ways this process is aggravating world hunger.

Modernization and development are the official goals of the elite in every poor country. As conventionally understood they are strategies for replicating the economic history of the industrial world by shifting local economies from agriculture to industry and commerce. More and more of the world's food is passing into international commerce, and fewer and fewer farmers are producing for ever larger numbers of eaters. Around the world food self-sufficiency is declining. People who used to grow food for themselves and their families no longer can. Because their land has acquired value for growing export crops, at least fifteen of the poorest countries in the world devote more acres to cash crops for export than for fruits and vegetables that could feed their own hungry people. Only 12 percent of the world's food is exported, but because of declining self-sufficiency in industrial and underdeveloped countries alike the international food distribution system now plays a critical role. This is a major new development of the postwar world.

The United States produces almost one-quarter of the world's grain. It exports 42 percent of all the wheat in international trade and 63 percent of all the corn. Canada, the next most important exporter, accounts for 12 percent of the world grain exports. While in good harvest years the Soviet Union, which produces about one-fifth of all the world's grain, and even India export grain, only the U.S., Canada, Argentina, Australia, and New Zealand regularly export more than they import. Canada, like the Soviet Union, has a short growing season and must make use of marginal land. The power of the United States over the world food distribution system is unrivaled by any other nation. The basis of U.S. food power is the extraordinary dependence of some of the poorest countries as well as the richest industrial countries in the world on agricultural imports to supply the proteins and calories needed by their populations.

In the mid-1960s the United Kingdom, Netherlands, Belgium, West Germany, and Norway were growing only between one-third and one-half of what their people ate, and Japan was importing 83 percent of its domestic food requirements. In the 1970s, Britain, West Germany, and Japan, along with Libya, Belgium, and Norway, spent more per person on imported food than any other countries. But for many poor countries such as Chile, Lebanon, or Trinidad, the dependence on imported food is a huge burden that exhausts meager foreign exchange reserves. For India and Bangladesh the degree of dependence is completely determined by the harvest. Neither rank on a world scale as a major importer of agricultural products, but in a bad year, emergency imports—which are badly distributed—mean the difference between life and death for hundreds of thousands of people.

As subsistence agriculture declines everywhere and more and more countries lose the ability to feed themselves, they become dependent upon the international grain traffic. For many years that traffic has been dominated by five family corporations. Four of them trace their origins to the early nineteenth century. Continental Grain Company is a legacy of Simon Fribourg's grain business that started in Arlon, Belgium, in 1813. Still run by the Fribourgs, it is believed to be one of the two largest privately held corporations in the U.S. Leopold Louis-Dreyfus, an Alsatian grain trader, founded the huge Paris-based firm that bears his name by taking over much of the Russian grain trade in the 1860s. The Bunge family established a trading monopoly over Argentine grain. Georges André from his headquarters in Nyon, Switzerland, began what is now a hundred years later a global grocery store and multinational bank. The fifth is Cargill, the biggest grain empire of them all, the creation of Will Cargill, a Wisconsin farm boy who in the middle of the nineteenth century bought up railroads, grain elevators, railroad depots, and coal mines of the Midwest.

In the Renaissance the grain trade was in the hands of Greek traders, Florentine merchant princes, and the grand dukes of Tuscany and Venice, but it was small. Until the beginning of the nineteenth century, internationally traded grain was a minute fraction of what was grown and consumed locally; even as late as the seventeenth century, only about 3 out of every 100 bushels of grain eaten in Europe were grown abroad. By 1800, however, dramatic changes were underway. Bread was now a staple for workers and was taking about half their salary. The concentration of population in the cities and the growing dependence on bread of the new urban population led to a huge expansion of the international grain trade. The bread riots of 1789 that marked the onset of the French Revolution taught a political lesson and made the import of Russian surplus wheat a requirement for domestic tranquility in West Europe. With a favorable climate and a sparse population the Russian Caucasus and Ukraine became for a few years "the breadbasket of Europe."

The international grain trade, as Dan Morgan of the Washington *Post* has shown in his pioneering study *Merchants of Grain,* is even more concentrated than the international oil business. Better known than the five families of grain, the Seven Sisters of oil do not exercise the same degree of control. Cargill's annual sales exceed those of Sears, Roebuck, and its profits in the bonanza years 1974 and 1975 exceeded those of Goodyear Tire and Rubber. In 1976, North Dakota's commissioner of agriculture described the power of the grain companies this way before the Senate Subcommittee on Multinational Corporations:

> The pyramid of power, as I see it, is 30,000 North Dakota farmers selling through about 500 grain elevators in North Dakota, farmer-owned but discreetly Minneapolis-run in my estimation, into one grain exchange which in turn sells mostly to six large exporters. So you know, the grain moves in that direction. And, the marketing power and marketing information really concentrates as it moves on up. You could say that we really have 2½ million farmers that feed into this thing and that power really becomes concentrated at the top.

Grain companies by and large do not grow grain. They buy it. The risk remains with the farmer. Because they are virtually the only customers for large international shipments, the five families of grain effectively set the prices. Like the oil companies, their power is derived from control over the entire process of growing, transporting, milling, and consuming grain. The large grain merchants are also millers. Continental has mills in Guadeloupe, Ecuador, and Puerto Rico and has a contract to run the state-owned flour mill of the Marxist regime in the Congo at Brazzaville. Cargill owns or leases several hundred grain elevators and runs 100-car shuttle trains to various parts of the U.S. According to Morgan, Cargill and Continental control "about half of all the grain storage space in the sixty-seven elevators at American ports. . . ."

Between 1955 and 1965, Cargill quadrupled its exports and tripled its assets. As the dollars accumulated abroad and the balance of payments worsened, the U.S. Government began to subsidize the grain trade so that U.S. wheat could be sold at a discount from world prices. The Department of Agriculture in cooperation with the companies became an aggressive pusher of soy and wheat. The P.L. 480 Food for Peace program, a scheme for distributing surplus grain to the needy, was the instrument. "Once we get into this market with our soybeans, no one can get us out," agricultural attaché for "market development" in Iran Charalambos Stephanides wrote his superiors at the Department of Agriculture. In the Congo another agricultural attaché was noting that bread was "winning against chilwanga at breakfast" because it was "the staple diet of the colonial masters and was adopted by the elite. Because of the effect of imitation, bread consumption is identified with progress and modernity for the masses." Thus it happened that the internationalization of the grain trade made possible the exercise of food power by companies and countries.

2.

Political power still comes out of guns, but the relationship between guns and power is shakier than it once was. In a time when oil producers who do not grow enough food to feed their populations can humble the most advanced industrial nations of the world, "No crude, no food" becomes an obvious battle cry. The United States has controlled about 35 percent of world wheat exports over the last generation. Only about 20 percent of world production is exported, but when "food deficits" are critical, the power represented by these wheat stocks becomes considerable.

How has this power been used? When OPEC imposed its embargo in 1973, U.S. officials immediately talked of "food power" as a response to the new "oil power." Secretary of Agriculture Earl Butz said publicly that the threat of food deprivation ought to be used as a "diplomatic weapon," and Henry Kissinger ordered a study of the vulnerabilities of various countries. The CIA published a study in August 1974 called "Potential Implications of Trends in World Population, Food Production and Climate." The world's increasing dependence upon American grain reserves, agency analysts noted, "portends an increase in U.S. power and influence, especially vis-a-vis the poor, food-deficit countries." It was quite possible that through food power "the United States might regain the primacy in world affairs it held in the immediate post-World War II era."

Increasing food dependency of many countries on a few countries is a reality of the contemporary world. Only the U.S., Canada, France, Argentina, and Australia have wheat surpluses year in and year out, and the U.S. has by far the most wheat to give or to withhold. Except for Brazil, which is increasing its export crop, all the soybeans for export come from the U.S. The U.S. dominates the rice trade and has the biggest corn surpluses. The U.S. thus has a role in the international food economy which dwarfs Saudi Arabia's role in the international oil economy. The U.S. supplies 5.5 million of the 7.6 million tons of corn Japan uses, virtually all of East Germany's corn, almost 80 percent of Venezuela's wheat, almost half of Brazil's, over half of Israel's, and virtually all of South Korea's.

The U.S. has used its food power as a diplomatic weapon on several occasions but without spectacular success. To date, companies are rather more successful than countries in wielding food power. In 1975, Henry Kissinger tried to use the threat of embargoing grain to the Soviet Union to persuade them to sell the U.S. oil at a 10 percent discount off the OPEC price, but the Russians regarded the proposal as extortion and said no. The embargo the Ford Administration imposed on grain sales to the USSR was supposed to set the stage for tough bargaining on the grain-for-oil deal, but it backfired because it alienated the farmers. In fact, the clumsy attempt to use food power might well have cost President Ford the 1976 election, for it is doubtful that he would have picked a mediocre Farm Belt senator as Vice Presidential candidate, a distinct liability in the rest of the country, if the farmers hadn't been so upset by the Administration's interference in the grain trade.

The U.S. imposed a trade boycott on China in 1949, but in the early 1960s, when the People's Republic needed to import grain, it was a time of world surplus and Canada and Australia were happy to supply several million tons. In 1962, President Kennedy proclaimed a total trade embargo on Cuba to overturn Castro's revolution, but the Canadians kept selling grain anyway. Perhaps the most successful application of food power was against the Allende Government in Chile because it was peculiarly dependent upon food imports. To implement Henry Kissinger's "destabilization" policy, U.S. food credits for Chile were cut off. Credit sales of U.S. wheat to Chile had been as high as 200,000 tons a year. The cutoff of credit from international organizations compounded the problem for Allende. Although domestic food production increased slightly in 1970–71, the stranglehold on wheat imports helped to generate the domestic crisis in Chile that led to Allende's downfall. Within a month of the military coup of September 11, 1973, which replaced the elected government with a murderous junta eligible for membership in the Free World, the food credits resumed and 600,000 tons of wheat flowed to Chile. Usually food power is used more subtly. The U.S. rapprochement with Egypt in 1974 was proclaimed with a 100,000-ton food aid pledge to President Sadat, for whom the domestic food crisis was threatening political survival. By 1978, Egypt was the largest recipient of P.L. 480 assistance, receiving more than one million tons of wheat a year at subsidized prices.

Rice too has been used as a diplomatic weapon. The embargo on food shipments to Cuba in the early 1960s hurt the Louisiana and Arkansas rice industry. The U.S. Government purchased large amounts of the crop for the P.L. 480 program and in 1971 exchanged $175 million in government surplus rice for a promise by South Korea to reduce its textile exports to the U.S. Thus P.L. 480 rice played a double role in Nixon's 1972 "southern strategy." It was used to subsidize the rice farmers of

Louisiana and to protect the dressmakers of South Carolina. By 1974 almost the entire P.L. 480 rice program was used to feed Vietnam and Cambodia, the last aid in support of the Indo-China war that Congress was prepared to cut off.

Since World War II, relief programs, Marshall Plan aid, and the Food for Peace program have financed a significant portion of U.S. agricultural exports. This was especially true in the early postwar period, when federal funds "financed more than 60 percent of total U.S. agricultural exports."* The P.L. 480 program was designed "to develop new markets for American farm products, to dispose of surplus U.S. agricultural commodities, to combat hunger and malnutrition, to encourage economic development in developing countries, and to promote the foreign policy of the United States."

Only countries that are heavily dependent on food aid from the U.S. are vulnerable to the threat of a cutoff. In 1966, for example, India, which had been receiving continuous food aid for years, was warned that such aid would be limited unless serious efforts to increase production and limit the population were introduced. "This use of food power," the Congressional Research Service study concludes, "appeared to convince the Indian leadership of the necessity to redirect the resources of that country toward activities leading to increased food production and improved storage."

The major political impact of food aid has been to create a long-range dependency. The introduction of cheap surplus American wheat has changed dietary habits around the world and created popular expectations that local governments must fulfill from the private grain market once the government surpluses are exhausted. (Diet creates dependency in curious ways. Thus French "soft" wheat dominates the market in their former colonies where the *mission civilisatrice* succeeded in leaving a legacy of croissants and brioches. U.S. grain and U.S.–owned flour mills control the market in countries now addicted to Wonder Bread or its local versions, such as Nigeria, Liberia, and Sierra Leone.) Food importation by Third World countries has grown dramatically in the last few years. A country such as Iran, which not so long ago was self-sufficient in agriculture, imported almost $800 million worth of food a year in the last years of the Shah. In 1965, Iran, an important recipient of P.L. 480 wheat, was a mere $15 million customer of the U.S. grain companies. By 1975 it was spending $325 million on U.S. wheat.

As Dan Morgan shows in *Merchants of Grain*, grain companies are able to use food power more effectively than governments. The reason the

---

* Congressional Research Service study, *Use of U.S. Food Resources for Diplomatic Purposes*, Jan. 1977.

U.S. Government has had scant success using food as a weapon is that it controls neither grain nor the grain companies. The reason the companies are more successful is that when they use wheat as bullets their targets are more modest than changing a foreign policy or government. Continental Grain opened a flour mill in Zaire in 1973 to import and process its own grain, only to find that because of severe foreign exchange problems President Mobutu was defaulting on his grain payments. Also disturbing was the news that the President's uncle was going into the grain business as an importer of European wheat. Morgan describes Continental's swift reaction:

> Its patience exhausted, the grain company took simple and direct action. It held back its monthly wheat shipment to its Zaire facility, and the mill at Matadi, on the Congo River downstream from Kinshasa, reduced its daily output of flour. As John Williams, the American agricultural attache in Kinshasa, explained Continental's action in a December 3 letter to the Department of Agriculture: "They diverted a shipload of wheat destined for Zaire to help the Government of Zaire realize just how important wheat is to their urban population."
>
> The realization was not long in coming. "The lines and hoarding that occurred at various bakeries were almost spontaneous. The mill did not shut off the flow of flour to bakers—they just merely slowed it down to put pressure on," Williams wrote home.
>
> Zairean officials hastily conferred with representatives of Continental and agreed to all the company's demands. It promised that the Central Bank would pay cash for all subsequent wheat shipments; that Zaire would start repaying its old debt at the rate of one million dollars a month; that only American hard wheat would be imported, except in some special circumstances; that Continental would have exclusive rights to mill flour in Zaire; and that the company would have the right to approve or disapprove all requests by others to import flour into Zaire. In other words, the company became Zaire's sole importer of wheat and sole manufacturer of flour, and it received authority to control imports of any competing flour almost as if it were a government agency.

3.

Malnutrition is the hidden holocaust of our day. It is avoidable, and because it is avoidable, it is as much an indictment of this generation of bystanders as Hitler's Holocaust stands as an indictment of the last. In his 1977 study *The Future of the World Economy*, commissioned by the U.N., Wassily Leontief concludes that hunger can be eliminated with a 5 percent increase in world food production. The "technological revolution" needed to feed the anticipated global population in the year 2000 is within our grasp, but "institutional, political, and social" obstacles stand in the way.

> The technological revolution depends to a large extent on land reform, and other social and institutional changes which are necessary to overcome non-technological barriers to increased land use and productivity. It also depends on creating, by special measures of agricultural policy, a favorable economic environment for agricultural development, including incentives directed towards eliminating inefficiencies in the use of land, labor and technology.

Well-fed people exhibit the same need to avert their eyes as did the good Germans. Occasionally, famine strikes the front pages, and a child's listless stare and bloated belly faces us at the breakfast table. The death rate in the north Indian state of Uttar Pradesh rose 25 percent in one year, 1971–72. Lester Brown of Worldwatch Institute calculates that the *rise* in the death rate alone due to more acute hunger than usual "claimed an estimated 829,000 lives" in just three states of India. In the Sahel famine, according to Michael Latham, a Cornell nutritionist, the lives lost from hunger ranged between 100,000 and 250,000. No one knows for sure. In mid-1978 the Ethiopian Government announced that one million persons in that country faced death from famine.

If the death toll reaches these levels, there may be forty-five seconds on the evening news of piled corpses, emaciated cattle crawling away to die, and spindley-legged toddlers too weak to move. But for the most part the nonstarving have taken effective measures to put the starving out of sight. Delhi, the capital of India, has been cleaned up and the hungry removed so as not to offend tourists and diplomats. In 1979 hungry beggars in Puebla, Mexico, were hustled off to jail for a few days during the Pope's visit so as not to depress either the Holy Father or the representatives of the world press. From April to November 1973 there was an international conspiracy of silence over the famine in Ethiopia. Perhaps as many as 500,000 eventually died. Starving nomads wandered across the border into Kenya, Sudan, Somalia, and elsewhere. The Emperor of Ethiopia denied there was a problem. Voluntary relief agencies and the U.S. Government were aware that a drastic relief program was necessary, but as Jack Shepherd has shown in *The Politics of Starvation,* they participated in a cover-up. The international community is not prepared to deal with famine, because the reforms needed to prevent it require the unseating of powerful interests.

People who think about starvation at all like to think of it as a natural disaster. Famine is one of the Four Horsemen of the Apocalypse; it visits every age. In 436 B.C. thousands of Romans hurled themselves into the Tiber to escape death from starvation. A million died in the Irish potato famine in 1845–46; 6 million died in 1943 in India and China. But such catastrophes in large part are the consequences of human decisions. They cannot be wholly blamed on the weather. According to the historian M. Ganzin, "the great French famines and food shortages of the Middle Ages occurred during periods when foodstuffs were not lacking; they were indeed produced in great quantity and exported. The social system and structure were largely responsible for these deficiencies." Similarly, after the 1943 famine in India the Royal Famine Commission concluded:

> Enormous profits were made out of this calamity, and in the circum-
> stances, profits for some meant death for others. A large part of the
> community lived in plenty while others starved, and there was much
> indifference in the face of suffering. Corruption was widespread through-
> out the province. . . .

The historian Michelet wrote that no one will understand the history of the nineteenth century until someone writes The History of Hunger. The point is even more apt in our own century. Deliberate starvation has been a recurring political weapon. In the early 1930s, Stalin confiscated the grain of several million previously prosperous peasants called "kulaks" and effectively starved an entire class. Seven weeks before the German invasion of Russia, the Nazis prepared a memorandum outlining the planned starvation of a whole population. "There is no doubt that as a result, many millions of persons will be starved to death, if we take out of the country the things necessary for us."

The hidden history of hunger affects our civilization more profoundly than these sporadic outbreaks of politically induced food terrorism. The pain of hunger has driven men to riot at critical moments in human history. The cry for bread launched the French Revolution; maggoty meat served aboard the *Potemkin* incited the famous mutiny that culminated in the Russian Revolution. But the usual social effect of hunger has not been revolution but passivity. The most serious energy crisis in the world is the depletion of human energy because the brain receives too few calories or too few proteins to think and the body too few to act. Damaged adults produce damaged children generation after generation. *The Inter-American Investigation of Mortality in Children,* a study of child health in Argentina, Bolivia, Brazil, Canada, Chile, El Salvador, Jamaica, Mexico, and California published by the Pan American Health Organization in 1975 concluded that nutritional deficiency was the most serious health problem of the hemisphere. For over half the children who died under the age of five, malnutrition was the principal cause. The effects of hunger resulted in a significant increase in infectious diseases and irreparable brain damage. Malnourished mothers give birth to small, underweight children who fall easy prey to disease. Those who survive a childhood seriously deficient in calories grow into listless adults unable to mobilize the energy to change the conditions that perpetuate their hunger. So the cycle repeats itself for another generation. Hungry people are a liability and a potential threat to governments. Passivity can give way suddenly to anger. Food riots have erupted in recent years in Egypt, Poland, and many other places. But more often inert masses of hungry humanity pose problems for leaders just by existing. There are too many of them. There is nothing for them to do. It takes only a small intellectual leap to conclude that the surplus population must be controlled or eliminated for the benefit of the productive citizens. Thus, hunger lies at the very heart of the global human rights problem.

4.

Most explanations of hunger prefer to emphasize nature rather than politics. Overgrazing of grasslands and impatient agriculture—overplowing, overplanting—is certainly a problem almost everywhere. The creeping desert claims 247,100 acres of range and cropland a year. The Sahara has been moving south at a rate of more than 10 kilometers a year, gobbling up the croplands and grazing areas in its wake. In the United States, according to the agricultural economist David Pimentel, each year more than 2,471,000 acres of arable cropland are lost to highways, urbanization, and other special uses. Iowa has lost half its topsoil in the last 100 years. So also in India, and in Egypt, where 64,246 acres of the best cropland along the Nile is now taken up by roads, factories, and military installations.

Overfishing has compounded the hunger problem. Between 1940 and 1970 the worldwide catch more than tripled, averaging almost 40 pounds a year for every person on earth. But in 1970 the growth stopped, and since then the catch has leveled off. The haddock catch in 1972 was only one-seventh of what it was in 1965. The halibut catch has declined 90 percent. The anchovy population off Peru has been shriveled permanently, so it seems. "The shrimp harvest in Galveston Bay in the Gulf of Mexico shrank by more than half between 1962 and 1966. The shad catch in Chesapeake Bay, estimated at fourteen million pounds in 1890, has averaged only three million pounds in recent years," Lester Brown reports. The dwindling stock of sea creatures is a legacy of industrial technology; oceans, lakes, and rivers suffocate in industrial wastes. The refrigerated fishing boat, floating processor, and fine-mesh nets have made the ancient cornucopian fantasies of fishermen real—for a while. It is no longer necessary to bring the catch home every night. Fishing continues around the clock for months on end. Eventually even the smallest anchovy will be caught.

Technology makes overfishing possible, but profits provide the incentive. The average American now eats two pounds more fish a year than ten years ago. Prices have jumped. Sixty percent of the fish consumed in the U.S. is imported from non-American waters. This means that the U.S., like many other nations, is becoming increasingly involved in disputes over fishing rights. A few years ago the fight between Iceland and Britain led to a small naval engagement. Tiny atolls in the Pacific in the world's richest tuna-fishing waters have declared their independence, proclaimed sovereignty over 200 miles of territorial waters, and laid exclusive claim to 6 million square miles of ocean. In the 1960s, until the catch fell off, the U.S. used to import protein-rich Peruvian fishmeal in huge quantities for broiler feed, enough, it has been calculated, to alleviate the severe protein deficiency in the diet of the average poor Peruvian.

As the returns from ocean fishing decline, the industry is turning to aquaculture. About 10 percent of the world's fish supply is raised artificially. Weyerhaeuser, Coca-Cola, Ralston Purina, Merck, Union Carbide, Arco, and other multinationals all have some sort of fish-farming enterprise. Ocean-ranching of salmon can be profitable if even 2 percent of the salmon are recaptured when they return to rivers and streams to spawn. Coca-Cola has a 50-acre shrimp farm off the Gulf of California in Mexico for growing the fat variety that ends up in shrimp cocktails.

However, the favorite explanation of world hunger is the population explosion. The exponential growth in births sets our time off, it is said, from all previous history. There are four times more people on earth right now than all the people who ever lived from creation to 1830. For the first 1,500 years of the Christian era, population was growing at 2 to 5 percent a *century,* but population in some countries now grows at a rate of 3 to 5 percent a *year.*

However, there were at least two previous occasions when humankind suddenly multiplied very rapidly. The first occurred one million years ago when the first of our species became hunters and toolmakers and began to survive in much greater numbers. The second took place about 10,000 years ago when the first hunters and food gatherers settled down to farm. There were, the historians Roland Oliver and J. D. Fage estimate, no more than 20,000 people in the Nile Valley at the end of the hunting and food-gathering era; two thousand years later the population of the Old Kingdom "has been variously estimated at from three to six millions." Humanity has been through a population explosion before and survived.

The population explosion of our time follows a certain consistent pattern. The introduction of public health measures dramatically reduces the death rate while the birth rate remains constant. Then the population rate begins to fall. Both parts of the process have already taken place in most of the developed world. East Germany, West Germany, Luxembourg, Austria, Belgium, and the U.K. all have stable or declining populations. By the late 1970s the growth rate for Western Europe as a whole was half what it was at the beginning of the decade. Between 1970 and 1975 the population growth rate in North America fell by almost one-third.

Many underdeveloped countries are still in the grip of the first part of the cycle—declining death rates and constant or increasing birth rates. But China has cut its birth rate from 32 (per 1,000 of total population) to 19. Sri Lanka, Singapore, and Taiwan have made substantial progress in cutting the birth rate, and Thailand, Indonesia, and the Philippines have made more modest gains. According to data collected at the Harvard Center for Population Studies, birth rates in the underdeveloped world as a whole dropped from 44 per 1,000 to 37 per 1,000 in the years 1970 to 1977.

There is a relationship between the level of prosperity of a country and its birth rate, provided that prosperity is decently distributed. The reason why illiterate, landless, or marginal farmers are likely to want more children than farmers with a more stable means of livelihood is not hard to figure out. For the world's poor, children are often the sole form of capital; they can work in the family fields or be hired out to big landowners. Ten children picking beans bring home twice the money of five little pairs of hands. Children are also a form of social security; in most cultures they are obligated to take care of their parents when they are old. No one else will. Ironically, the worse the health conditions and food supplies, the more incentive to reproduce. If half the children die before age five, a common situation in many poor countries, twice the number must be born to supply the family work force. Studies conducted in the state of Kerala in India in 1976 confirm what common sense suggests. Fertility rates fell when medical and public health facilities were improved. When the conditions for human development were present, people stopped wanting so many children. Then, and only then, did handing out contraceptives and "family planning" campaigns work. The World Bank has recently begun to recognize, as its President Robert McNamara puts it, "the apparent correlations between socioeconomic factors"—education, health, broadly distributed economic growth, urbanization and enhanced status for women—and the birth rate.

It is thus impossible to talk about the population explosion as a natural phenomenon, as is so often done. We do not know nearly enough about the relationship between social, economic, and cultural policies and human reproduction, but we know enough to recognize that birth rates respond much less to propaganda and bombardment by condoms than to equitable economic and social policies. The effect of cultural transformation is more important than generally realized. In a society in which there are neither jobs, income, nor dignity for masses of people, the only social function left may be the traditional role of carrying on the family, tribe, or the nation.

Other elements of the neo-Malthusian hypothesis are as questionable as the population explosion. There is much talk of increasingly scarce land, and indeed, as we have seen, deserts of sand are encroaching on African farmland, and asphalt equivalents are spreading throughout the developed world. But, according to the Panel on World Food Supply of the President's Science Advisory Committee, "the area of potentially arable land on earth is much larger than anyone has previously supposed, being 24 percent of the total ice-free area and considerably more than twice the land that has been cultivated at some time during the last few decades. It is more than three times the area actually harvested in any given year." The U.N. estimated in 1975 that farming area in the world could be increased by 50 percent in ten years by spending $90 billion, about two-thirds of the annual military expenditures of the U.S. A campaign to eliminate the tsetse fly in Africa could reclaim cropland and pasture in Africa comparable to that in the U.S. The U.S. Department of Agriculture estimates that there are 1,648 million hectares of agricultural land in the underdeveloped countries (excluding the socialist world); less than one-third of it is in use.

In the mid-1970s a number of climatologists argued that the climate on earth is becoming more changeable and much less hospitable to agriculture. The drought in the Sahel, floods in Pakistan, delay in the onset of the Indian monsoon, and apparent increase in the amount of snowcover and floating sea ice in the Northern Hemisphere—all of which took place in 1972—lend credence to the theory. The meterologist Reid Bryson thinks the Sahel drought was caused in large part by a cooling trend in the Northern Hemisphere triggered by dust from a "human volcano" of industrial activity. Jule Charney of the Massachusetts Institute of Technology theorizes that the drought is caused by an increase in the reflection of solar energy due to the removal of vegetation through overgrazing. This causes a radiation deficit that sucks warm monsoon air into the Sahel and leads to desertification. All such theories are controversial, but they do suggest, as Stephen H. Schneider of the National Center for Atmospheric Research in Boulder, Colorado, notes, that efforts to increase production have either negative or uncertain climatic effects and that uncertainty in the weather business "is not biased toward optimism."

A history of climatic changes in the past strongly suggests that the conditions in the Wheat Belt during fifteen years from the late 1950s to the early 1970s are not likely to be repeated. There is a cooling trend that disturbs a number of meteorologists. There is also a growing realization of the adverse effects of various forms of human intervention on the fragile ecosystem. The famine in the Sahel was aggravated by something as benign as digging wells in the desert. Because of the increased availability of water, the herds multiplied and ate and trampled the vegetation as they moved from well to well. The animals died because there was nothing more to eat. The loss of vegetation also apparently had an unfavorable effect on the weather.

Water itself, of course, is another limitation on increased productivity. Growing a pound of wheat in the United States takes about 1,500 pounds of water. A pound of rice can take as much as two tons of water. Many underdeveloped countries cannot hope to find water on such a scale. Consequently, they have much lower yields. In many parts of the world the lack of irrigation means that land is virtually useless. But the patterns of water distribution across the earth are also in large part a consequence of human practice, not nature's law. According to a Resources for the Future study: "Over two-thirds of the world's fresh water flows unused into the oceans, large groundwater stocks could be tapped for agriculture, and the technology exists to desalinate sea water." The most sobering thought, however, is that all the conventional proposals for increasing agricultural production, including irrigation, require enormous growth in energy and water consumption.

Estimates of land and water resources are much like estimates of mineral resources. Global supplies may be more than adequate, but two crucial problems intervene to prevent the supplies from being used by those who need them. The first is that the supply of arable land, like minerals, is unevenly distributed in the world. Eighty-three percent of the unutilized land is in South America and parts of Africa; only 9 percent is in Asia, where the hunger problem is the most severe. Since populations are by and large not transferable in times of famine—the great Irish immigration to the U.S. in the nineteenth century when the potato crop failed would not be tolerated in the age of scarcity—those parts of the underdeveloped world with little additional land to put into cultivation must raise their yields if they are to grow more food. They then encounter the second problem, cost. Irrigation, fertilizer, high-yielding seeds, all take energy and money. Recent history, it is true, does not confirm Ricardo's corollary of Malthus' law, that the cost of land and hence of food rises over time. In the U.S. at least, Barnett and Morse conclude in their study of scarcity, the unit cost of agricultural products in the U.S. declined by more than one-half between 1870 and the late 1950s. They prophesy that new technologies and new energy sources will permit this trend to continue. Despite increasingly bad news for shoppers at the supermarket checkout counter, the mythical average American was spending only 17.2 percent of his income on food in 1975, while in 1900 his grandfather had to spend 40 percent of his income to feed his family. Real-life Americans in the lower middle class were of course spending a considerably higher percentage of their income on food.

Costs are rising for agriculture in the areas of the world where food is in shortest supply. This has nothing to do with natural laws of scarcity but with specific economic and institutional arrangements in the operation of the global food system. There are ways to keep costs down. Agricultural technologies that require a low level of energy and minimize dependence upon imported seeds and petroleum-based products are available. The energy consumption in rural India, Harvard's Roger Revelle reports, is one-fiftieth what it is on U.S. farms because Indian farmers make use of human and animal dung, crop residues, and firewood. To increase productivity fourfold with a twofold increase in energy in such a setting requires a technology that is available, Revelle suggests, but one that is different from what agribusiness firms are generally promoting.

Moreover, there are promising sources of additional food which have not been developed. It appears possible to convert cassava, a low-protein staple grown throughout Africa, into a high-protein food through fermentation. Aquaculture, producing aquatic plants and animals, mostly oysters, shrimp, carp, catfish, plaice, mackerel, and pompano, in underwater farms, is a huge potential source of food. Chinese and Indonesian fish culturists can now produce 8,000 pounds of carp per acre; "under favorable conditions" notes John D. Bardach of the University of Michigan, "production of animal flesh from a unit volume of water far exceeds that attained from a unit surface of ground." Oil companies have run experiments showing that 1,000 pounds of bacteria in certain yeasts, if fermented with water, crude oil stock, nitrogen, and phosphate compounds, will multiply to 5,000 pounds in twenty-four hours, producing a 60 percent protein powder that could be used as livestock feed or as food for humans. The locusts on which John the Baptist fed may make a comeback in the modern diet. A Canadian scientist, T. J. Army, reported in the mid-1960s that an acre of land can yield more insect protein than beef protein.

All such unconventional food sources are in an early stage of development. None is a panacea; like emergency food relief, research for food to be eaten exclusively or primarily in poor countries is a voluntary transfer of resources from well-fed countries to countries on the edge of starvation. Whether the research produces anything more than intellectual excitement for the researchers depends upon conscience, good will, and subsidies of rich governments, because by definition, without money, there is no market for developing food for billions of hungry people. Thus, fewer than 20 out of a potential 350,000 vegetable products, according to a *Business Week* survey, have been developed as a source of food for humans. Corporate research concentrates on developing cheaper and more efficient animal feeds, for which there is a ready market, and on substitutes—such as synthetic sugar, coffee, and chocolate—for primary agricultural commodities to be consumed in the rich countries.

5.

More food is being produced than ever before. There have been dramatic increases in yields. A growing middle class around the world is eating better. But hunger is also increasing. Why should this be? Paper solutions to problems of underproduction and maldistribution abound. But they are not implemented. "Institutional, political, and social" obstacles are blamed. Let us now try to take a global look at the food system and see what some of the obstacles are.

The contemporary food system, a chain linking producers, distributors, and consumers, is set off from the rest of human history by two spectacular developments in food production which have culminated in our own generation—internationalization and industrialization.

The global migration of the poor from farm to city ghetto has cut off millions of people from their traditional source of food and left them scavengers in an urban world in which they have no productive role. The inexorable processes of agriculture—industrialization and internationalization—are probably responsible for more hungry people than either cruel and unusual whims of nature or acts of war. The cost of land, the cost of fertilizer, the mechanization of agriculture, and a credit system that encourages agribusiness and big farms at the expense of the small farmer are making a growing proportion of the world peasant population "marginal," a polite sociological term for those reduced to some form of peonage.

A survey by the Institute of Nutrition in Central America and Panama of eleven coffee-growing *fincas* in the Boca Costa region of Guatemala offers a glimpse of ordinary hunger. On the global scale of marginality the coffee workers are by no means the worst off. Adults are not falling down on the street and dying as in Calcutta. They are not nomads on an agonizing search for vegetation to support their collapsing herds. They live in some of the most fertile soil in the world. By law 10 percent of the *finca,* or plantation, must be planted with grain, but this is only enough to meet the needs of the workers and their families for about two months out of the year. Corn is sold to the workers at prices ranging from 40 cents a pound to $1.20 a pound. A family with three children earns $40 a month, with the exception of four months of harvest, when they may earn as much as $90 a month. With a maximum income of $680 a year the coffee workers, mostly Indians, cannot afford enough grain. This is especially true since some of the *fincas* charge the peasants as much as 6 cents a day to grind their corn in the plantation mill. There are variations in the prices charged the coffee workers from *finca* to *finca;* some plantation owners offer workers substantial food subsidies, but there are limitations on individual benevolence, for it is common for the surrounding plantation owners who are less disturbed by starvation to retaliate against, even murder, those they consider traitors to their class.

This in microcosm is how the political economy of starvation operates. The population of the eleven *fincas* studied showed exceptionally high birth rates, exceptionally small babies, exceptionally high incidence of disease, and a high infant death rate. An unusually large number of girl babies died in infancy. Indeed, it is characteristic for poor populations in underdeveloped countries to be disproportionately male, although in the world population, females at every age have better survival rates and predominate. The reason is that scarce food is distributed first to the adults, then to the male children, who are considered far more of an economic asset than females. Economics and culture conspire to make little girls expendable, and they account for a huge share of the statistics of hunger.

Increasingly, the worldwide food production and distribution system is coming under the control of a relatively small number of multinational corporations. Five grain companies, as we have seen, effectively control the world traffic in wheat, corn, barley, and soy. Two farm machinery companies control 60 percent of the farm machinery in the U.S. and also have a decisive role in the world market. A small number of grain and chemical companies now control the world seed market. As powerful and important as they are, multinational corporations are of course not the only factor in the world food system. Local landowners, local governments, peasants, and local consumers have their own interests, prejudices, and traditions, and these are important too in determining who eats and who does not.

The industrialization of agriculture is a process of substituting fossil fuels for human energy in the quest for mass production and high profits. Under the prevailing definition of efficiency petrochemical fertilizers are preferred because they are cheaper than hired hands and the social costs of coping with the ecological damage these fertilizers do is largely left out of account. For example, "wonder seeds" of the Green Revolution, which in some places have dramatically increased yields, require large amounts of chemical fertilizers. They have transformed agriculture of some of the poorest countries of the world. In Pakistan, for example, in less than ten years the area planted with the new seeds grew from 50,000 acres to more than 32 million.

The mechanization of agriculture has sharply reduced employment possibilities in the countryside. In the Punjab, for example, which has been a center of the Green Revolution, the amount of human labor needed in the fields has fallen by 50 percent. According to Donald K. Freebairn, "the introduction of mechanical harvesting will eventually result in an overall decrease of about 90 million man-days of employment in the Punjab, most of it for day laborers." According to K. C. Abercrombie's study, *Agricultural Employment in Latin America,* 2.5 million jobs in agriculture were lost in 1972 in that part of the world, and the trend is continuing.

At the production end of the chain, corporations have had several major effects. First, high-technology agriculture has led to increasing concentration of land, increasing dependence upon imported inputs such as seeds and fertilizers, and increasing use of cash crops to maintain the economies of underdeveloped countries. As land becomes more valuable, marginal farmers must sell and either work as sharecroppers or go to the city. In addition, mechanized agriculture requires increased credit. Obviously, wealthier farmers are preferred risks for loans with which to buy imported seeds and fertilizers. Thus the gap between the rich and poor increases within the country. Numerous studies in Mexico, Taiwan, China, and elsewhere show that where land is more equitably shared, production increases because the incentive to produce rises. Where the poor farmer is less able to control what he grows because these decisions are made by the moneylender or the owner of the land, he is less able to provide for himself and his family.

With the rise in agribusiness, cash cropping has increased dramatically. From the mid-1950s to the mid-1960s the principal cash crops—coffee, tea, bananas, cotton—grew more than twice as fast as the rest of the agricultural economy in underdeveloped countries. Coffee production in Africa has increased more than 400 percent in the last twenty years. Because export crops are much more profitable, they crowd out the non-commercial crops on which millions of poor people used to subsist. Land that was used for growing black beans, the staple of the poor in Brazil, has been converted to soybeans for cattle feed. Black beans then must be imported, and the price is prohibitive for the poor. There are similar examples from all over the Third World.

The high-technology–export-crop model distributes benefits unequally. Foreign sales of U.S. seed and fertilizer companies are highly profitable. Consumers of coffee, tea, bananas, and strawberries around the world benefit from increased production, and the plantation owners, usually foreigners, derive large profits. "Since the military coup in 1964," the agricultural economist Michael Perelman reports, "U.S. investors have purchased about 80 million acres of farm land in some seven or eight agricultural states of Brazil in chunks of about 1 million acres." Mechanization helps the richer peasants in India, K. N. Ray reports, to "get rid of tenants and to keep for themselves whatever portion of the harvest (a third to a half) used to fall due to the tenants."

There are several reasons why the high-technology–export-crop model increases hunger. Scarce land, credit, water, and technology are preempted for the export market. Most hungry people are not affected by the market at all. Theoretically, a country could make profit the test of what to grow but could invest the earnings in such a way as to keep people employed and eating. But that does not happen. The profits flow to corporations that have no interest in feeding hungry people without money. As callous as many Third World elites are about hunger in their midst, an executive of a multinational corporation running a local "profit center" is even less likely to worry about the starvation around him. That is not his job, and there is little he can do about it anyway. The problem is that his superiors in the corporate headquarters control the local agricultural economy and the distribution of its earnings. In their book *Food First* Lappé and Collins summarize a study of the strawberry industry in Mexico by a former official of the Food and Agriculture Organization:

> Officially, Mexican growers produce the berries and even own some of the processing facilities. The real control, however, remains with the American investors and food wholesalers. Using production contracts and credit facilities, these American firms make all the important decisions; the quantity, quality, types, and prices of inputs; how and when the crop will be cultivated; the marketing processes, including prices for the producers; the transportation and the distribution; and the returns on capital investments. U.S. marketing control is so powerful that despite efforts by the Mexican government to develop markets in Europe, all Mexican strawberries pass through American exporters even when ultimately retailed in a third country such as Canada or France.

Contract farmers attached to multinational export operations are now an exploited underclass in poor countries. In Guatemala, according to Ray Goldberg of the Harvard Business School, 70 percent of the cucumber pickers are children under fifteen. The "sorting and grading for export was done, in one operation, by twenty-seven women who were paid $.80 a day. . . ."

Rich and generally well-fed countries are now importing more and more of their food from countries with a high rate of malnutrition. Most of the food is nonessential—cocoa, coffee, tea, bananas, or sugar. Poor countries, on the other hand, as we have seen, import staples from the U.S. —chiefly wheat, corn, and rice. This division of labor and trade contributes directly to hunger in poor countries because the producers of the export crops are paid so little—the farmer in Ghana gets about 16 percent of the export price of his cocoa beans—that they cannot afford to pay the high price of imported wheat or rice.

Dependence upon exporting food makes poor countries extremely insecure, for they depend upon a world market they cannot control. While production has increased dramatically for tea, coffee, cocoa, sugar, and similar commodities, prices have fallen in real terms, and when compared with imported agricultural inputs and manufactured goods, disastrously so. Short-term price rises, as in sugar and coffee, bring on a strong reaction in the world market because there are many competitive sources of supply. The fluctuations in agricultural exports is a direct cause of hunger in poor countries dependent upon cash crops. Susan George describes some recent fluctuations:

> The value of Brazil's sugar exports to the U.S. drops from $100 million to zero. The Philippines, on the other hand, export over 800,000 pounds of sugar to the U.S. in 1975 and nearly three times that much in 1976. Guinea's cocoa exports to the U.S. fall from nearly two million to nothing; while Liberia and "other West Africa" make up part of the difference by jumping from zero to over four million pounds. Mexico's cotton exports to the U.S. are halved, while India's increase by 400% and Pakistan's drop by 90%. For long fibre cotton, Egyptian exports are multiplied by four and Sudan's by fourteen but Israel's are reduced ninefold. Peruvian cotton exports meanwhile move up from zero to nearly eight million pounds.

6.

The traditional distinctions between factory and farm are becoming blurred everywhere. Nowhere is this more true than in the United States.

The Jeffersonian utopia of a nation of small farmers has given way to agribusiness. Forty-five corporations own half of the farm land of California. One percent of the farms of the nation sell almost a quarter of the produce. To start a one-man farm in the early 1970s, according to a 1973 U.S. Department of Agriculture report, cost well over $250,000. It is much more today. In the world of corporate farming the most profitable product is land; in 1975 the value of farmland increased $51 billion while the net income for all the nation's farmers that year was $29 billion. The rise in land costs and the costs of petrochemical fertilizers and farm machinery has accelerated the disappearance of the family farm.

U.S. agriculture has become a planned system. Government policies and corporate strategies give American agriculture its distinctive cast. The implications for world hunger are considerable. From the days of the New Deal when little pigs were slaughtered to keep them off the market, a major task of the Department of Agriculture has been to keep food production down in order to keep farm prices up. In the present era government controls emphasize restrictions on acreage in production. Farmers who plant more than the government desires will hear from the Department of Agriculture. Satellites patrol the farm areas and provide instant detection of violations of the planting regulations. It is now possible to differentiate from outer space the particular crops being planted. According to Remote Sensing Engineering, Ltd., a company in the business of interpreting such data, corn "has an electro-magnetic signature distinct from that of rice or bananas."

The Department of Agriculture favors large farms. In 1971, price supports, which have since been substantially reduced, allowed the typical family farm to earn almost three times what it would have earned without them, but large farming operations earned nine times their normal income from supports. Credit policies favor the corporate farmer over the small farmer. The push to industrialize farming by government and private banks has encouraged resource conglomerates to add food departments. Tenneco, once known as Tennessee Gas Company, purchased 350,000 acres in Kern County, California, in 1967. Having bought J. I. Case, the farm machinery company, it could fuel its own tractors with its own gas and market the harvest through its own packaging division. Integration of food production "from seedling to supermarket" was defended by an assistant secretary of agriculture in 1973 as a way to "present a solid front to the consuming public." Tenneco later sold off much of its land. Like most agribusiness companies, it concluded that it was more profitable to run its operations in the U.S. much as in the Third World—by contracting food production and maintaining control of marketing and distribution.

Being for the family farm is one of the essential political pieties, but the planned obsolescence of the small agricultural producer continues at an accelerating pace. Some, like former Secretary of Agriculture Earl Butz, celebrate the rise of the integrated food factory; others are more wistful. The family farm is the backbone of the country, they say, but the industrialization of agriculture is efficient.

Nowhere does the concept of efficiency deserve greater scrutiny. Modern agriculture is phenomenally efficient in saving labor. One man using a modern feeding system for broilers can take care of 60,000 to 75,000 chickens or 5,000 head of cattle in a modern feedlot. But dependence on machines run by fossil fuels increased 146 percent between 1940 and 1970, and the use of pesticides jumped 700 percent. In 1950 the average farm was still largely self-sufficient; farmers purchased only 20 percent of what they used to keep the farm producing. By 1973, outside purchases had risen to 65 percent.

While large farms yield a larger gross income per acre than small farms, the latter show a better *net* return because their cost for expensive inputs, fertilizers and machines, is less. There is a considerable literature from underdeveloped countries which suggests that productivity per acre declines as farms become larger. To move food about the country cost more than $7 billion in 1974. Before the dramatic rise in energy prices, shipping costs for fresh fruits and vegetables averaged about 10 percent. They are more now and sometimes much more. Even in 1974 a carton of California lettuce selling on the West Coast at $1.25 had jumped to $2.25 after being trucked to the East.

Agriculture uses more energy than any other single industry. The food-processing industry is the fourth largest user of energy, according to Department of Commerce statistics. The industrialization of agriculture has multiplied the transportation requirements. About one-half of all trucks carry food and related items.

In the name of efficiency, American agriculture has substituted mineral energy for human energy. A calorie of human energy, according to Earl Cook, dean of the College of Geosciences at Texas A & M, writing a few months after the oil embargo of 1973, costs 400 times a calorie of fossil fuel. The agricultural system operates on the belief that prices signal scarcity. If fossil fuels are comparatively cheap, they must be abundant. One U.S. farm worker can now theoretically feed almost fifty people; thirty years ago only fifteen. But people are not being fed adequately, because the costs of production and distribution—in energy, and increasingly in money too—are higher than malnourished people can afford. To be sure, statistics on productivity are confused and misleading. But it should not be surprising that a family dependent upon a piece of land that represents their sole property and sole source of income would farm it better, provided they had the necessary equipment and access to a market, than exploited contract cultivators employed by a distant corporation.

The integration of agriculture into industry exacerbates the hunger problem because it wastes land and energy, the principal resource base for producing food. One-third of the topsoil in the United States is lost to erosion, according to the National Academy of Sciences. The size of the continent encouraged farmers to plant new land rather than care for the acres already in production. Thomas Jefferson thought it made no sense to fertilize on his plantation "because we can buy an acre of new land cheaper than we can manure an old acre." With industrialization the economic incentives to push land beyond its capacity increased.

7.

There are no such things as hungry countries. A detailed study of food consumption in northeast Brazil (one of the centers of poverty and hunger in Latin America) showed, reports Susan George, "that the poorest people were at the physiological starvation level with 1240 calories daily, while the richest were stuffing themselves with 4290!" The calorie intake in the state of Maharashtra, India, ranged from 3,150 to a starvation level of 940. Malnourished prime ministers (except from overeating) or hungry generals do not exist anywhere. Diplomats and food experts from the poorest countries can expect to eat well at hunger conferences. At the same time "at least 10 to 12 million Americans are starving or sick because they have too little to spend on food," according to a prerecession report of the U.S. Bureau of Census published in 1972. Hungry people exist in every country.

Nonetheless, it is possible to draw a rough map that shows who is eating what. Within countries, there is a direct connection between having a job and money and having enough food, and there are libraries of statistics which confirm this self-evident but often unstated point. There is, surprisingly, much less of an obvious relationship between producing food and eating. There is no necessary connection between being a farmer and eating well. Although the poor huddled in urban *barrios* are usually more malnourished than indigent farmers and their families, many of the hungriest people in the world are working to produce food eaten by others.

The world food map would reveal a hierarchy of diet that explains a good deal about the distribution of malnutrition. There are four distinct food cultures in the world. In each the staple edible products are different. To belong to one or another of these cultures determines to a considerable extent how long you will live and what you will be able to do with your life. Diet determines the international pecking order just as it is a badge of class distinction within every society. Two Americans may enter the same supermarket, one to buy a thick sirloin to prepare a Steak Diane, the other a can of dog food for his supper. (In recessions there is always a dog food boom but no noticeable dog boom.) Nations industrialize and become meat eaters, which is another way of saying that they have plenty of fossil fuels to burn to support an industry that converts grain calories into beef calories, and they have a rich and large enough internal market to be able to afford meat. When nations industrialize they also become more integrated into the international food system. The diet transcends the traditional staples and increasingly includes imported products and processed goods. Thus Japan, in addition to increasing its meat consumption, shifted from total reliance on rice to wheat. Since the war, the wheat component of the Japanese diet has tripled; the introduction of wheat products in school lunch programs supported by P.L. 480 surplus wheat shipments from the U.S. was an important factor in the change.

At the bottom of the food hierarchy is the root and coarse-grain culture. In West Africa the staples are yams, cassavas, and the coarse grains millet and sorghum, which in other food cultures are fed to animals. The foods of the root culture are deficient in vitamins and proteins, and the prolonged cooking, which is customary to render them palatable, makes them even less nutritious. Members of the root culture are closest to the prehistoric food gatherer. Much of what they eat may be wild. Indeed, the degree to which malnutrition is overcome depends upon luck in finding wild-growing fruits and vegetables to supplement the meager harvest of primitive farming. Groundnuts are a good source of protein, but increasingly these are being exported to extract the oil for making commercial soap. Okras, peppers, and marrows are also available, but these too are used as cash crops and not eaten much by the local population. In parts of Africa, maize supplements the root staples. Members of the root culture have traditionally consumed little that is not grown locally. Increasingly, however, the transistor radio, the automated missionary of "advanced" eating habits, paves the way for Coca-Cola and other processed foods for which even some of the poorest people in the world will spend the occasional pennies that come their way.

Many of the "food-deficit" countries are in the root culture. The food systems are vulnerable to drought. Yields are uncertain, and it is hard to increase them without more capital than poor people have. There is also, as Rene Dumont has put it, little incentive:

> The small farmer knows that if he makes an extra effort, most of the income obtained will go to the owners if he is a tenant; to the money-

lender if he is in debt; to the trader from whom he must buy dearly, before his next crop comes in, a part of what he had to sell cheaply from his preceding harvest—and if not to all these, then to the more or less corrupt civil-servant.

The process of integrating root culture farmers into the international food system by using better land for cash crops, and by increasing local dependency on imported fertilizers and capital equipment, has not helped them to eat better. One of the contributing factors to the Ethiopian famine of 1973 was the takeover by a foreign-owned sugar mill of thousands of acres of rich pastureland of the Awash Valley. The nomadic Afars had been using that land since the sixteenth century. The few that tried to continue grazing in the area reported that the mill had poisoned the local water supply and that their animals died.

Twenty-five to 30 percent of children in most developing countries die before their fifth birthday, and in some, more than half. The cause is frequently a disease of protein deficiency which overtakes young children. *Kwashiakor* is a West African word meaning "one two." Child number one is weaned to make room for child number two, and because he is deprived of milk, he falls prey immediately to protein deficiency. *Marasmus* is a medical designation for severe protein-calorie deprivation typical of emaciated concentration camp victims and others who do not have enough to eat. Official FAO statistics give a partial clue as to what has been happening in the root culture countries. Chad could supply 88 percent of its calorie needs in 1969; only 75 percent five years later. Guinea, Mali, and Zaire also precipitously declined in their ability to feed their population even at the low level of 1969. (These per capita figures of course understate the extent of famine for the bottom 40 percent of the population.)

The rice culture is concentrated in the Far East, although large quantities of rice are eaten throughout the world. But the billion people who subsist on rice live mostly in Asia. The demand for rice in the Far East in 1970 was four times the demand for the rest of the world together. China produces more than 36 percent of the world's rice, though the Chinese diet has become more varied. Wheat, soy products, and vegetables are consumed in great abundance. In certain parts of Latin America, too, rice is an important part of the diet, but it is supplemented with beans or potatoes, and in coastal regions, fish.

Fernand Braudel, the French historian, speaks of the tyranny of rice. The cultivation of rice which began around 2000 B.C. in central Asia has set the patterns of culture for billions of people as no other single food has done. The rice eaters are far more dependent on a single source of nourishment than members of the root culture, wheat eaters, or meat eaters. Rice exercises its tyranny by producing what Braudel calls "the miracle of the paddy fields." Aquatic rice, which came to China from India, produced yields even in the eighteenth century six times as great as the wheat crops grown in Europe. Intensive cultivation was the rule. "One sees neither hedges, ditches, nor almost any trees, so afraid are they of losing an inch of land," a Jesuit traveler to China observed in the early eighteenth century. Large-scale, centralized irrigation systems required a large managerial bureaucracy, a high degree of social discipline, and an authoritarian state. (Irrigation pumps worked by pedals are pictured in a Chinese drawing as early as 1210.) By producing enormous yields, the irrigated rice paddies encouraged a big population growth. Braudel notes:

> If southern China was dominant in about 1100, it was because of rice. As early as 1390 the population of the south was three times that of the north: 45 million to 15, according to official figures. And the real achievement of the rice fields was not their continuous use of the same cultivable area, nor their water technology designed to safeguard the yield, but the two or sometimes three harvests they produced every year.

The rice culture led to a concentration of population, the intensive use of a relatively small proportion of the arable land, and a rejection of alternative forms of agriculture such as forestry and animal raising, which became so important in, Europe. The fertilization of rice in the countryside was accomplished "with the refuse and human excreta from the towns and muck from their streets . . . ," and this symbiosis of town and country, as Braudel calls it, "imprisoned" both in its restrictions.

Rice, especially unmilled brown rice, is a nutritious food and can be the basis of a reasonably adequate diet if supplemented with even a small quantity of vegetables and fruits. The problem of the rice culture is that there is not enough rice for most people. In part this is due to the shortage of land. Asia is where most of the world's hungry people live, and it is also where arable land is in shortest supply. But the major reason why members of the rice culture starve is economic. A study of rice farmers in the Philippines in 1976 by F. T. Rivera reveals that the rice farmers in the richest farming areas are net purchasers of rice themselves. The majority of farmers sell their crop immediately to meet cash needs, usually being forced to sell what they had stored for family consumption. More than 63 percent of the rice farmers admit to food scarcity for their families. They spend between two-thirds and three-fourths of their income on food. They work harder, expend more calories, need more proteins than truck drivers and shoemakers, who were also studied, but they have a much lower intake of both calories and proteins. The fantasies of Filipino rice farmers give perhaps a better clue of their deprivation than statistics do: They dream of meat—fried chicken, roasted pig, barbecued dog.

The Chinese have been able to grow food for over 800 million people on 11 percent of their total available land. While wheat, corn, soybeans, and coarse grains such as sorghum and millet are widely consumed, the staple remains rice. Over 110 million tons are produced a year. Productivity is high, G. F. Sprague, a University of Illinois agronomist who visited China in 1974, concludes, because the country "has probably the world's most efficient system for the utilization of human and animal wastes and of crop residues." The agriculture is highly labor-intensive. Saving time at the expense of labor to permit long growing seasons and the planting of successive crops on the same land is a key strategy. Decentralized "backyard" fertilizer plants for supplementing organic wastes with nitrogen is also an important part of their farming. Since the death of Mao, the Chinese leaders have admitted to some difficulties in agriculture. There may be more hunger than previously thought. But the eradication of hunger has been a priority, and most Chinese, it seems, have the means either to grow or to purchase what is needed.

To move from the rice culture to the wheat culture is to join the global middle class. Obviously, not everyone who eats wheat is well off; extremely poor people subsist substantially on bread. Wheat is not more nutritious than rice. Wheat eating is, however, associated with richer and more varied diets than rice eating. The wheat eaters of Pakistan are taller, better nourished, and live longer than the rice eaters who live in a different region of the same country. The relative prosperity of wheat eaters, taken globally, exists because wheat grows in temperate climates, and it is these regions that form the belt of developed societies. To be a wheat eater means that you probably belong to the privileged economies of the Northern Hemisphere, that there is ample petroleum to expend on modern energy-intensive methods for the production of wheat, and that you are something of a meat eater too.

Wheat was probably grown first in the Middle East as early as 7000 B.C. and came to Europe in the fourth millenium B.C. It was always a minor product in the Orient. The Chinese were not much given to bread making, producing what one seventeenth-century Western traveler called "a very heavy dough that lay like stone on the stomach." (By the same token, rice, which was imported from the East to Europe and grown in the Balkans, Italy, and Spain, was, except for the Turkish-dominated parts of southern Europe, considered food for the poor, to be distributed to hospitals, ships, and military barracks.) Cereal yields in Europe were on the whole low; therefore, wheat farmers supplemented their harvest by raising livestock. (Thus wheat eaters tend to be more carnivorous than rice eaters.) Only in the eighteenth century did wheat take first place over other cereals such as barley, rye, and oats. Coarse grains such as millet and chestnut flour were also used, and in times of famine acorns and roots were ground and baked as bread. As yields declined in certain parts of Europe a grain trade flourished, and with it the ports and waterways of Europe on which it depended. In the wake of famine, grain traders would make a killing—the Portuguese firm Ximenes made profits of 300 to 400 percent moving northern grain to the Mediterranean in 1590—but until the eighteenth century, grain trade was considered a risky business and attracted only a few bold entrepreneurs.

Historians have tried to reconstruct calorie levels of the grain-eating civilization of Europe. Just before the French Revolution, average daily consumption in Paris was about 2,000 calories, one-half of it bread. The princes of Pavia at the beginning of the seventeenth century, on the other hand, according to the historian F. Spooner, who has examined their menus, thought nothing of putting away 7,000 calories a day. In Berlin at the beginning of the nineteenth century 75 percent of the family budget went for food, considerably more than half of that for bread. The quality of bread varied enormously and depended considerably on the fluctuating price of wheat. In fourteenth-century Poitiers, Braudel tells us, there were three grades of bread when prices were low and seven when flour became expensive. The grade of bread one ate was a badge of social class. Below a certain level there was no bread at all, just coarse soups and gruels. White bread was for the very rich; not until the mid-eighteenth century did it become commonplace in Europe. The revolution in white bread was given its primary push in France, where a National School of Bakery was organized in 1780. The new product spread through Europe in the knapsacks of Napoleon's soldiers.

In 1970 the world consumed 332 million tons of wheat, 70 million of it in the form of animal feed. Almost two-thirds of it was consumed in the developed world—North America, Europe, Australia, and the Soviet Union. The projected increase in the demand for wheat for human consumption in the 1980s is roughly half the projected increase in the demand for rice, a reflection of the fact that the wheat-eating population is more or less stable (the big projected increase in wheat consumption is for animal feed) while the rice eaters are growing at a rapid rate. Wheat may be the staple, but, characteristically, the climate permits the cultivation of a wide range of vegetables and fruits, and the level of development makes it possible to import much of the produce grown in the root and rice cultures. Wheat eaters tend to be healthier and better nourished and to live longer than members of the rice and root cultures. The history of imperialism is the story of the domination of the rice and root cultures by wheat-eating carnivors from the North.

In recent years, however, this pattern has changed. Underdeveloped countries, as we have seen, have been importing more and more wheat. The U.S. Department of Agriculture expects that the richer "food-deficit" countries of North Africa, the Middle East, and east Asia will almost double their wheat imports by 1985. The Food for Peace program was abruptly curtailed in 1972 when the world prices shot up. Wheat had become a basic food in the ordinary diet in such South American countries as Bolivia, Ecuador, Colombia, and Peru as a result of 20 years of subsidized imports, and some of the governments continued them. Peru, although on the edge of bankruptcy, subsidized U.S. imports at a cost of $5 million a month in order to cut 40 percent off the price of flour for the consumer. At the same time, local production of wheat has declined sharply. Wheat production in Ecuador in 1976 was about half of what it was in 1969. In Peru it is down about one-fifth. Most of the land formerly used for wheat is now pastureland for beef cattle for export to the rich countries. Dependence on a temporary subsidy from the U.S. created new members of the wheat-eating culture but under conditions that discouraged local production and exacerbated the financial crisis of the wheat-importing countries.

At the top of the diet hierarchy are the meat eaters. This has for a long time been so. The ancient Chinese ideograph for provincial administrator was literally "meat eater." His subjects ate rice. In medieval Europe, however, meat was plentiful even for the lower classes. Consumption, according to the following description by Braudel, was extraordinarily high:

> Meat abounded in butchers' shops and eating houses: beef, mutton, pork, poultry, pigeon, goat and lamb. As for game, a treatise on cooking, possibly dating from 1306, gave a fairly long list available in France; wild boar was so common in Sicily in the fifteenth century that it cost less than butcher's meat; Rabelais' list of feathered game is interminable: herons, egrets, wild swans, bitterns, cranes, partridges, francolins, quails, wood pigeons, turtledoves, pheasants, blackbirds, larks, flamingoes, water fowl, divers, etc. Except for large items (boar, stag, roe deer) the long price list for the Orleans market (from 1391 to 1560) indicates regular and abundant supplies of game: hare, rabbit, heron, partridge, woodcook, lark, plover, teal. The description of the Venice markets in the sixteenth century is equally rich.

Meat eating declined sharply at the end of the sixteenth century owing, most likely, to the population rise. It was then that fresh meat became a luxury food; the poor, when they could get it, subsisted on salt beef and salt pork. According to the German scholar H. J. Teuteberg, per capita meat consumption in Germany tripled during the nineteenth century, but the average German was eating only about half the meat consumed by his medieval ancestors even as late as 1914.

Europe was a carnivorous island in a largely vegetarian world. True, Chinese mandarins in the seventeenth century would "nibble a few mouthfuls of pork or chicken"; black slaves on Brazilian plantations would eat *carne do sol* (sun-dried meat). In the seraglio there was plenty of mutton served. Africans feasted from time to time on young monkey. But most of the world, as today, tasted little of animal protein or dairy products.

Meat eaters run the world, but not because meat eating is virtuous. Indeed it is now commonplace to scold meat eaters for luxurious and wasteful eating habits. Eating too much meat causes heart attacks and strokes, many medical authorities believe. The middle-aged male collapsing over a steak has become a symbol of the achieving society. Studies of the lethal effects of overindulging in animal fats have supported successful advertising campaigns for margarine and vegetable oil. In 1975 meat consumption in the U.S. peaked and it has been down a little ever since. The explanation is more likely butcher-shop prices than cholesterol.

North Americans derive almost three-quarters of their proteins from animals, far more than anyone else. Canada and the U.S. use over 1,800 pounds of grain per person a year, all but 100 pounds of it to feed milk-producing cows, chickens, and above all beef cattle; Iran, Morocco, Pakistan, Thailand, and India consume about 400 pounds per person, almost all of it directly in the form of bread and cereal products. The Soviet Union has had a dietary transformation. When a Soviet citizen sat down to dinner in 1950, 70 percent of what was on his plate was bread and potatoes. Now because of greatly increased consumption of meat, fats and oils, vegetables, and dairy products, the starch component is no more than 50 percent. Thus the per capita grain consumption in the USSR has reached 1,600 pounds, most of which goes into meat and dairy products. This dietary change has had profound political consequences. It has created expectations that can be satisfied only by massive imports when the Russian harvest fails, as it periodically does. In the Stalin days the official solution was to allow those designated as "class enemies" to starve. By the early 1960s, however, the terror was over and Khrushchev was importing grain for bread. Ten years later his successors were importing grain for beef. The dependency on the outside world to maintain internal stability had increased enormously and with it a strong motivation for detente.

In the Far East, with the exception of Japan, 14 percent of the protein diet comes from animals. The increase in meat eating in the U.S. in the last two generations has been phenomenal. The average American ate about 49 pounds of beef a year in 1930, almost 120 pounds forty-five years later. Americans today eat much less veal, lamb, and pork than did their grandparents. But consumption of poultry in the era of the chicken speedup has tripled. It used to take fourteen weeks to fatten a 3-pound broiler. Now, owing to the use of chemicals, only eight weeks—on half the feed. The U.S. is the world's most voracious consumer of beef. About 40 percent of all the beef traded in the world ends up in the U.S. Costa Rica is a major source. The small Central American country shipped 60 million pounds of beef to the U.S. in 1975, but its own per capita meat consumption fell. Why U.S. ranchers prefer Costa Rica is clear. The land and labor costs to raise a cow in Montana are ninety-five dollars, in Costa Rica, twenty-five dollars.

The beef industry, like the grain industry, is becoming increasingly internationalized. The great meat-packers about whom Upton Sinclair wrote in *The Jungle* are now owned by such conglomerates as Greyhound, L.T.V., Beatrice Foods, and United Brands. Even Volkswagen is in the beef business. "You get a lot more for a pound of sirloin than a pound of beetle in Tokyo," a company executive noted. To make room for export beef, farmers in Costa Rica, Honduras, and other countries with cheap grazing land are turning away from dairy cattle. As a result, milk prices have become prohibitive for poor families.

The international poultry industry is also changing dietary habits. Ralston Purina has created a thriving broiler and egg industry in Colombia by financing local farmers to grow feed grains such as sorghum on land once devoted to beans and corn. As Robert J. Ledogar put it in his study *Hungry for Profits,* "The displacement of cropland from pulses and beans to feed crops did not simply replace a cheap source of protein with an expensive one. It also reduced the total availability of protein in the country." Planting an acre of soybeans will produce sixteen times more protein than an acre planted in feed to produce eggs. But for more than a quarter of the Columbian population a dozen eggs cost more than a week's wages. As Lappé and Collins point out, the figures showing an impressive per capita increase in egg, chicken, and beef consumption in such poor countries mask the fact that much of it is going to the local "El Big Mac," the tourist hotels and restaurants, and the mayonnaise factory. Little of it is reaching that part of the population for which the protein gap is widening every year.

The Global Ranch, as Lappé and Collins call it, is expanding throughout Latin America and soon, if the plans of several European corporations and the World Bank materialize, in Kenya and Sudan, too. The ultimate consumers are located in the rich countries or in the gradually expanding enclaves of affluence in poor countries. There are more than one billion sheep in the world and more than one-half billion goats. More sheep are raised in Australia, USSR, China, New Zealand, Argentina, Iran, South Africa, and Brazil than in the U.S. There are 667 million hogs in the world, less than a tenth in the U.S. Much of this livestock is raised on big farms and ranches across the world, including the Soviet collective farms. But a significant portion belong to a nomadic economy that survives from another age. In various parts of the world, in the Sahel, in Tanzania, in Kurdistan, Afghanistan, and elsewhere, the population follows the herds. A major political struggle has been waged in Tanzania to induce the nomads to take up permanent settlements.

A world food map would not be complete without at least mentioning two other products that also play an important role in the global diet. One is corn, which is widely consumed in Latin America, where the plant originated. Excavations near Mexico City have come upon fossilized grains of corn estimated to be between seven and eight thousand years old. Without corn, Braudel observes, "the giant Mayan or Aztec pyramids, the cyclopean walls of Cuzco or the wonders of Machu Picchu would have been impossible. They were achieved because maize virtually produces itself."

Corn is the largest single commercial agricultural product in the U.S. In 1976 almost three times as much corn as wheat was produced in the U.S. Almost a third of it went for exports. Except for the tortilla eaters of Latin America, and partakers of such delicacies as Italian *polenta* and New England corn on the cob, most of the human consumption of corn is in processed form—oils, margarines, and a host of other commercial products, edible and otherwise. Most of it goes to animals. Commercial corn farming in the U.S. produces incredibly high yields; it is one of the leading U.S. exports and the mainstay of the rapidly growing worldwide beef culture.

The other product is the soybean. It originated in China and is an important supplementary food in the rice culture, especially in China, Japan, and Indonesia. It grows poorly in Europe. The Soviet Far East has had only moderate success with it. But it has become the bonanza crop for the United States. In 1930 only about a million acres in the U.S. were planted in soybeans, producing about 14 million bushels. Forty-five years later the U.S. crop was approaching 2 billion bushels, and the soybean had become the number one agricultural export, accounting for about 10 percent of all U.S. foreign exchange earnings. The U.S. grows about three-fourths of all the soybeans produced and is by far the largest exporter. The major competitor is Brazil, which converted vast former black-bean-growing areas into soy. As a result the country now imports black beans, the traditional staple of the poor, and the price has risen 275 percent, thus putting it beyond the reach of the poorest.

Soybeans are high in protein and fat. About a fifth of the soybean oil produced in the U.S. goes to make margarine, which is now consumed in twice the quantity of butter. (In 1940, before the age of the soybean bonanza, seven pounds of butter were sold for every pound of sickly pale, uncolored margarine.) Over two-thirds of U.S. beef feedstocks are soybean; thus the world's cheapest source of protein is converted into the most expensive. But, the U.S. Department of Agriculture estimates, "textured vegetable protein," meat extenders made of soy-protein concentrate, will be used to replace about 20 percent of ground meat in such processed foods as chili, hot dogs, and bologna by the 1980s.

8.

Food has always been a badge of status; in every culture there are certain foods and certain ways of preparing them that are appropriate for serving guests and others that are not. Some foods are associated with great social, economic, or technological changes. As the compass brought the spices of India to the tables of Europe, so in our day the petroleum-based plastic wrapper has brought Ritz crackers to Brazil. Coffee was introduced to the West in the early seventeenth century from Turkey as a luxury brew to accompany interminable after-dinner conversations, but it became a necessity of modern factory life. In the nineteenth century the coffee break was used to "kill time" in the midst of a twelve-hour workday. Today the industrial and office consumption of coffee supports a considerable service industry, and the coffee break is a subject of collective bargaining. When coffee arrived in Western Europe it was trumpeted as a cure for scrofula and a strengthener of livers, but its principal pharmaceutical effect has been to keep successive generations of workers sufficiently awake to do their job.

Take the case of sugar. The extraordinary role of sweets in the U.S. diet—about twice the average consumption in France, for example—must have a psychological as well as an economic explanation. The sugar trade was of course an early source of American wealth. According to Braudel, sugar was a luxury and not in widespread use until the beginning of the nineteenth century. Why did it become so popular in the New World? One anthropologist argues that sugar was systematically introduced into workers' diets to maximize human energy at the lowest cost. In recent years billions of little jars of sweetened baby food and boxes of sugared breakfast cereals have conditioned new generations of Americans to expect food to be sweet. Whatever the explanation, our very language testifies to our sugar love—"sweeteners" to make a deal more enticing, "sweet" technology, etc.

Changing taste and consumption patterns often have more to do with fashion (a process aided considerably by advertising), collective fantasies and taboos, and the intrusion of social organization than with economics. The monopolization of time in the nineteenth century by the assembly line and the office preempted the spare minutes and the energy to prepare decent meals. Thus August Bebel's vision of socialism included huge community kitchens that would relieve housewives of the burden of meal preparation.

Rushed meals open the way to commercially prepared foods. The first vacuum cooker invented by Denis Papin in 1681 had the unappetizing name of Papin's digester. The man who is credited with inventing the technology of canning was Nicolas-François Appert, the French cook of a German duke, who received a prize for his feat from Napoleon in 1801. By 1830 the forerunner of the bouillon cube had arrived, and before long commercially prepared products of all sorts were available. Another important consequence of the merciless working day of the nineteenth century was of course alcoholism. As H. J. Teuteberg puts it, "cheap liquor had to make up for inadequate food."

Convenience food continues to alter the culture of advanced countries in our own day. Within the last generation and a half the corner grocery store where the proprietor jostled boxes of cereal from a high shelf with a long pole and figured the bill on the back of an envelope has largely disappeared. It has been replaced by the suburban supermarket, the TV dinner and its myriad foil-wrapped cousins, and a chain of fast food restaurants in which Americans and Europeans are spending an increasing share of the family food budget. Three consequences flow from this. The unit cost of food increases substantially as consumers pay for processing they formerly did themselves. Second, the food system has become much more energy-intensive, not only because of the gallons of gasoline and oil that go into making fertilizer and pesticides and driving enormous tractors, but also because of the millions of truck miles driven each year to transport food products across the country—the average American broiler, someone has calculated, travels 1,200 miles from the automated barnyard to the microwave oven—and the millions of station wagon miles required to transport billions of brown bags from the checkout counter to the kitchen counter. Third, convenience is the enemy of conviviality; it is too much to blame McDonald's and frozen pizzas for the contemporary assault on family togetherness, but the decline of the ceremonial function of the family meal and the simultaneous rise of a "gourmet food" industry is a sign that something important has happened in our culture.

In underdeveloped countries tradition continues to play a crucial role in diet. There are more cows congregated in India than in any other country, a puzzling fact since most Indians are Hindus, who are forbidden to eat them. That the country with the most starving people chooses to support such a large number of sacred nuisances has caused several generations of Western tongues to cluck. And cows in India do appear to be nuisances. An economist at the University of Pennsylvania has pronounced thirty million of them "unproductive." The government maintains old age homes for cows, a service that is not available for people. The police station in Madras maintains a grazing area for stray cattle. It is a common sight to see them wander about almost everywhere. The differing view of the cow that divides Hindu and Moslem has erupted in periodic massacres. The Indian constitution contains a bill of rights for cows, but it is not enough to satisfy the most ardent cow lovers. In 1966, 120,000 of them demonstrated in front of parliament, and eight persons were killed in the riot that followed.

The Columbia University anthropologist Marvin Harris offers an intriguing explanation of cow love. He suggests that a taboo on slaughtering cattle is not as uneconomic as one might think. India depends upon animals for plowing, mostly oxen and water buffaloes. The economic function of the zebu cow is to breed male traction animals and to deposit 700 million tons of recoverable manure for fertilizer. Because the temptation to slaughter is so strong in a starvation economy, the taboo must be even stronger. Massive slaughter of cattle would destroy the ecology of Indian agriculture, for both plow and fertilizer would be gone. The utter profanity of cow-eating has its roots, Harris suggests, "in the excruciating contradiction between immediate needs and long-run conditions of survival." It is a neat theory, although it leaves a good deal unexplained. There are other people in the world facing starvation who do not put their cows on pedestals. Nonetheless, developed societies in the grip of the same contradiction between short-run and long-run needs are hardly more fortunate because they lack taboos that would keep them from making catastrophic choices.

Economics and culture also conspire to produce differing attitudes toward pigs. There are pig lovers in New Guinea who have such a craving for swine flesh that their principal festival is a prolonged orgy of roast pork in which they kill almost all their pigs. It is a form of ancestor worship held every twelve years or so, a way of mobilizing the society to produce proteins, and a way of showing strength to the rival tribes. Instead of accumulating missiles, they accumulate pigs, eat them with abandon, and show their toughness and resiliency by starting the pig cycle all over again. Jewish and Muslim cultures, on the other hand, are rooted in pig hatred. Pigs appear throughout the Old and New Testaments at critical moments as a creature to be loathed. A great mutiny of Muslim soldiers in India was sparked by the rumor that bullets were greased with pig fat. Marvin Harris has an economic explanation for the Jewish and Muslim taboos against pork, too.

Contrary to popular understanding, pigs do not sweat much. Below 84 degrees they take pains to keep clean, but above that temperature they will cool themselves off with their own excrement. Since meat is a luxury anyway, there is more survival value in raising other animals that are more adaptive to the climate and can produce milk, cheese, and wool for human use. The repulsive habits of overheated pigs, he argues, thus provided a convenient pretext for imposing a code of survival for desert tribes.

Whatever the power of local culture and custom in determining eating habits, it is under assault everywhere. The world has entered the era of the global food market. Increasingly, production and marketing of food are passing from local control to international control by multinational conglomerates. The key to creating a global food market, according to Lee S. Bickmore, former chairman of National Biscuit Company, is to encourage "the tendency for people all over the world to adopt the same tastes and consumption habits." The globalization of taste is perhaps best symbolized by China's surrender to Coke and Russia's to Pepsi a mere twenty years after the American soft drinks were the targets of ideological campaigns against "coca colonization" throughout the socialist world.

9.

What would a serious attack on the hidden holocaust of hunger look like? What can be done?

(1) Any serious effort to feed hungry people ought to begin by recognizing that starvation and malnutrition are symptoms of social pathology. People do not eat enough because they are poor. The malnourished lack the wherewithal to grow food or to buy it. Extreme poverty is a product of maldistribution of wealth. Any intervention to correct gross economic inequalities, whether in energy policies, employment policies, water policy, has a beneficial impact on the food system.

(2) The United States should take the lead in promoting food security as a human right. The United Nations Covenants on Human Rights drafted at the end of World War II and signed by the President of the United States explicitly promise access to food. Nutrition is the most

basic human right. Without it, all other rights, individual and social, lose their meaning. The rhetoric of human rights ought to be made real. The place to start is an examination of existing policies—governmental and corporate—to determine the extent to which they keep the present world food system from feeding the hungry.

(3) The hungry will eat to the extent that they are able to feed themselves. The goal for the world food system should be maximum feasible self-reliance of nations and regions. The injunction to feed the hungry cannot be accomplished with food aid, the modern missionary basket, or with the ethic of the zoo in which "basic needs" are periodically dumped into the cage.

(4) To increase agricultural self-reliance in poor countries, the terms of trade for the producers of primary products must be improved. To end poverty in poor countries, the rich countries must be prepared to pay higher prices for imported sugar, beef, cocoa, and other products. Other New International Economic Order proposals such as reduction of tariff barriers, reserve programs, buffer stocks, and a common fund for commodity supports should become the basis for a reordered world food system. Unless producing countries receive a better share of the proceeds, they will not be able to cover their production costs and will not pay decent wages.

(5) International pressure on poor countries should change direction. The "austerity" programs of the International Monetary Fund now increase malnutrition and hunger because they require countries to impose wage controls, higher food prices, and the elimination of social services that benefit the poor. International loans and limited food aid should instead be conditioned on structural reforms within poor countries which promise an end to hunger. Land reform that would give poor people the incentive and the opportunity to produce for local needs is the key. Political reforms that encourage the active participation of farmers in the developing of new food systems are a necessity. Elimination of corruption that siphons off the proceeds of the food system to Swiss banks and Mediterranean villas is another critical internal change needed to make the food system work to eliminate hunger. A "planetary bargain" between the rich and the poor should consist of the following exchange: From the industrial countries concessions on terms of trade, financing, and transfer of technology. From the developing countries explicit commitments to redistribution and development: austerity programs for the rich, an end to bureaucratic plunder, programs to favor the landless and the poor farmer, enforcement of minimum wage, reversal of policies that drive poor people off the land. A primary need is an international standard on what constitutes minimum development. Governments that do not qualify ought not to receive the concessions available to those that do.

Some Third World leaders will denounce such a bargain as "intervention" and "paternalism." But if the development goals are clear—building local self-reliance, strengthening the agricultural economy, redistribution to enable everyone to eat—an international consensus for a human rights policy on food could be developed.

(6) The industrial world lacks the political and moral power to induce such structural changes in the Third World unless necessary structural changes take place within the rich nations as well. Within U.S. agriculture, too, local and regional self-reliance should be promoted. Federal policy should favor the consumption of food to the greatest possible extent in the regions where it is grown. If Americans are to pay more to the farmers of the Third World countries for primary products to keep them from starving, then we must eliminate unnecessary costs that are added to food products on the way to the shelf. Food prices are higher than they need to be because of concentration in the industry. The energy costs in the food system—transportation, petrochemical fertilizers, petrochemical packaging—need to be radically reduced. This would mean changing the present system of incentives under which the U.S. food system operates—specifically, changing federal policies that favor corporate farming at the expense of the smaller farm and encourage wasteful soil management and marketing practices. Until it becomes more profitable to conserve energy and to produce moderately priced nutritious food than to market expensive processed food, the food system will continue to be biased against the consumer and the small farmer.

(7) The national commitment to agribusiness should be reexamined. The concentration of the food industry into a highly capital-intensive, energy-guzzling system is producing declining returns for those who actually produce food, and skyrocketing prices for those who eat it. A fundamental look at what has happened to American agriculture and a systematic look at the incentives now operating in the food system are crucial for developing a long-term alternative policy. In order to promote food self-reliance in poor countries, the overwhelming dependence of American agriculture on food exports must be reduced. This can be done only by cutting energy imports and by promoting long-term structural reform in the U.S. food system. Federal policy should encourage smaller farms because they are more saving of both soil and energy and should discourage the takeover of strategic farmland by out-of-state or foreign corporations, particularly those primarily in other businesses. Land tilled by local people who make the basic decisions about it and are rewarded for it serves the interest of consumers better than land that functions primarily as a corporate asset.

Chapter VII

Water: The Springs of Life

1.

THE MOST ESSENTIAL resource of all for sustaining life is water. In large areas of the world human beings can get by with primitive shelter and little or no clothes. A strong adult can survive weeks without food. But without water the metabolism of the body is thrown off balance and death comes in a matter of days. A fifth of a gallon a day, about half a common household pailful, is all one needs, but that need is basic in the most literal sense. Beyond the minimum needed for drinking, much larger amounts are needed to grow food, to mine metals, to produce energy, and to manufacture anything. It takes thousands of gallons to produce a pound of beef for the table and more than 100,000 gallons to make an automobile.

Water is the sculptor of the earth's crust, the force that moves mountains, deposits and removes soil, creates and abandons rivers and streams, and distributes swamps, cliffs, and deserts. Taming rivers and subjecting them to human will is an ancient practice. There is even a suggestion of irrigation in the second chapter of Genesis: "And a river went out of Eden to water the garden; and from thence it was parted and became unto four heads."

So obviously crucial is water that historians have constructed elaborate theories in which access to springs, rivers, and the sea, and the utilization of hydraulic technology, become the essential variables to explain the march of civilization. Thus the "fertile crescent" that lay between the valleys of the Tigris and the Euphrates became the cradle of civilization. The great rivers of India and China, the Indus, the Ganges, and the Yangtze, supported the ancient settlements of Asia. The Rhine, the Danube, the Seine, the Po, the Thames, and the Volga shaped the face of Europe, and in the New World a variety of Indian civilizations flourished by the banks of the Mississippi, the Colorado, and the Amazon.

191

Civilizations rise and fall with the water table. The ancient Sumerians had an intricate network of canals and sewers, and their civilization literally dried up when these life-support systems fell into disrepair. The Chinese ruler Yü, in about 2300 B.C., mastered the art of flood control, inspired a high culture sustained by irrigated agriculture, and established a dynasty that lasted eight hundred years. In 700 B.C., we know from archeological discoveries of almost fifty years ago, King Sennacherib of Nineveh brought fresh water to the city from 60 miles away by means of a stone canal and an arched stone aqueduct 900 feet long and 25 feet high. Almost a thousand years earlier Joseph's well, near Cairo, was sunk 295 feet through solid rock.

Herodotus describes a canal begun by King Darius of Persia linking the Nile to the Arabian Gulf. Its length was "four days journey by boat" and its width enough "for two triremes to be rowed side by side." (The original Suez Canal was built much earlier, in 1500 B.C.) The sophisticated water systems of the Romans are well known thanks in large measure to Sextus Frontinus, writer and soldier of the first century A.D., who became Rome's water commissioner and left a book, *The Aqueducts of Rome*.

Irrigation and flood control, the historian Karl Wittfogel argued, gives rise to the absolutist state. Organizing the massive amounts of human energy to tame water and to put it to the service of agriculture required various forms of what he calls "oriental despotism." "The bulkiness of all except the smallest sources of water supply creates a technical task which is solved either by mass labor or not at all," and the political task of organizing such labor could be accomplished only by "hydraulic" despots. Thus, elaborate systems of flood control, irrigation, and water distribution led to a degree of centralization and authoritarianism not known in feudal Europe, where the management of water was less of a problem because the sources were more widely distributed and, hence, political power was more diffuse. The power of the feudal lords of Europe could not be compared with that of the hydraulic rulers of the Orient or other water-scarce areas such as pre-Colombian America (Inca and Mayan civilizations), Hawaii, and East and North Africa. In all these hydraulic civilizations, Wittfogel argues, the state dominated the society because it was the chief landowner and the monopolizer of the technology needed for massive water projects. This technology was in turn transferred to other massive labor-intensive projects such as the Great Wall of China or the pyramids of Egypt, which gave the despotic civilizations their peculiar tyranny and grandeur.

Wittfogel's theory has all the problems of single-cause explanations of complex phenomena complicated by a large dose of contemporary bias. (His purpose in expounding the theory in 1957 was to show the Russian and Chinese Communist leaders as throwbacks to the water tyrants of the past.) Nonetheless, water provides as good a place as any to begin a serious look at the interconnection between man's physical needs and the political struggles to meet them.

If we survey the contemporary world and its water needs, the irony of Coleridge's famous "water, water everywhere" line is striking. The earth is about two-thirds water, but only 2.7 percent of the world's total water supply is fresh water. Theoretically, that is more than enough. The Yangtze River alone with a mean annual flow of 150 cubic miles has enough to provide every person in the world with 150 gallons a day. The problem, obviously, is a double one. Much of the world's fresh water is undrinkable, and this, unfortunately, includes a considerable amount designated as drinking water. The second problem is one of distribution. In many areas of the world the problem, of course, is too much water. In the U.S., for example, it is traditional for parts of the Northeast to drown periodically while the Southwest thirsts, although in recent years easterners have experienced both floods and water shortage. Floods take more lives in an average year than drought.

The global maldistribution of water is even more pronounced than the maldistribution of energy or food. The average resident of Pheonix, Arizona, in a relatively water-scarce area of the United States, uses, conservatively, 160 gallons a day; an inhabitant of the semi-arid regions of Africa uses 0.8 gallons a day. The escalation in water use in the advanced countries has been enormous. In 1900 the U.S. consumed 40 billion gallons a day. Today the consumption is almost 400 billion. Most water for households is reused, but because of contamination, inefficient industrial and agricultural use, and leakage in transportation, the U.S. loses 110 billion gallons a day.

In part, the increase in population explains the heavy demand on water resources. But the most important reason for this demand is that new uses for water have been found which are the hallmarks of modern civilization—advanced plumbing, large-scale agricultural irrigation, and industrial cooling.

A 1962 study of water use in Akron, Ohio, by a typical family of five illustrates what has been happening in the American home. The Akron family used a little more than 160 gallons a day, 113 of which went to flush the family toilet; 14 gallons were drunk in various ways; and 16.5 went for cooking and washing dishes, 11 for laundry, 3 for washing the car, and 8 for watering the lawn. Typical Akron families in those days did not have swimming pools, but that is now an increasingly popular way to use considerable amounts of water. In the last twenty years water has become even more of an amenity—dishwashers, washing machines, more vigorous toilets, the lawns of suburbia—so that the above figures are extremely conservative; in 1978 in many parts of the country, 200 gallons per person is a reasonable average, and such a figure does not include the family share of the thousands of gallons expended to keep the local golf course green.

Plumbing, which for many people is the sole reason why they would not trade the crime, pollution, alienation, and nuclear threat of this century for any of the quieter but less fastidious ages of the past, is a devourer of water. About 70 percent of household water use is for toilets, baths, and showers. (The technology exists to cut this in half.) In 1900, fewer than one million Americans were connected to municipal sewer systems. By the mid-1970s, 170 million were.

But the biggest user of water of all is agriculture. More than 80 percent of the nation's water supply goes to irrigation. The replacement of small subsistence farms with the highly mechanized, large food-producing factories called agribusiness depends heavily on massive watering efforts. The dramatic increase in yields in various parts of the world are directly related to dramatic increases in water use. A 1976 U.N. study estimates that increases in agricultural production necessary to avoid widespread famine will almost double the world's demand for water by the end of the century.

Industrial use is also increasing significantly. Water use in factories has doubled since 1954, although more than 90 percent of the 60 billion gallons used a day are recycled. By the year 2000 water use, it is projected, will be about ten times what it was in 1954, although because of improvements in recycling technology, the amount of water available for reuse in industry will increase. Many modern processes require complex cooling operations. Nuclear power plants are of course an important example. A crucial element in a series of political setbacks for nuclear power plants in California was the opposition of farmers, who objected to the enormous drain on the state's scarce water supply.

As mining becomes more difficult, the consumption of water to produce energy and nonfuel minerals rises. The U.S. Water Resources Council projects that by the year 2000 there will be a 61 percent increase in water "withdrawals" for mining, 11 billion gallons a day, most of which will return to the water supply, over a period of hundreds of years but of course will not be available for other purposes while it is being used for mining. Hence the growing fights among mine operators, farmers, and environmentalists in the West. More than 95 billion gallons a day are used to produce energy. The Water Council projects that water consumption will increase roughly ten times by the end of the century.

The deposit of wastes into rivers and streams is a form of consumption since it renders the water useless for other purposes. The death of Lake Erie and other horror stories of industrial pollution that began to appear in the early 1960s led to an unending series of struggles over who has the right to pollute water, who has the obligation to clean it up, what is the best way to do it, and who is going to pay for it. There is a vast literature on the subject and we will not go into it further here.

2.

Water famine, as House Majority Leader Jim Wright called it in a book that appeared shortly after the drought of 1965, is not hyperbole. There is in various parts of the world an acute water shortage which increasingly is becoming a source of conflict across the planet. Like the other scarcities, it is most acute in the Third World. By Western hygienic standards, the lack of clean drinking water is catastrophic; by local standards, still serious but less urgent. The World Bank estimates that well over a billion human beings are without adequate water. Martin Beyer, UNICEF drinking-water advisor, puts the figure at 2 billion. The majority of people without sanitary drinking water live in Asia, and most of them are farmers. A 1970 survey by the World Health Organization concluded that only 15 percent of the rural population had access to decent water; in the cities about 70 percent of the population was reasonably well served. The WHO maintains that "provision of a safe and convenient water supply is the single most important activity that could be undertaken to improve the health of people living in rural areas."

Where there is no safe well in the village, the typical situation throughout parts of the Third World, someone must walk for water. The fetchers of water are for the most part women and children. It is not uncommon, according to Martin Beyer, for mothers of young children to walk fifteen miles a day to the nearest water source. He describes a young woman whom he met on the road in Sudan carrying a four-gallon tin of water on her head. Eight hours a day, she explained, were taken up with water fetching. The water system imposes its own serfdom. For many women, these are hours away from their children, from work in the fields, or from the chance to learn new skills. True, for some even a long walk to the well fills a social need—a chance to stop hoeing or picking, to meet neighbors and to talk.

But the fact remains that the water system in poor countries determines who will live and who will die, who will eat and who will go hungry, and how men and women—women mostly—will spend their day. The worst killers of children are the waterborne and water-related diseases that abound almost everywhere in the Third World—diarrhea, malaria, and schistosomiasis, an enervating, parasitic disease that affects more than 200 million people, mostly children. Live guinea worms sticking out of the bodies of children, babies blinded by onchocerciasis, indolent boys and girls with the sleeping sickness transmitted by the tsetse fly, are part of the landscape in many Third World countries. The source of all of them is bad water. The traditional aftermath of the floods of India is the cholera epidemic.

Compounding the public health problem is the promotion of baby formula by the multinationals in poor countries where the formula is mixed with contaminated water and causes diarrhea in infants, facts that by now are well known to the companies and have generated charges against Nestle that they are "baby killers." Yet despite the publicity, the lawsuits involving such formula producers, and a campaign by the National Council of Churches to stop high-powered and misleading promotion of infant formula, the practice continues. "Milk nurses" hired by infant-formula producers visit maternity wards in the Third World countries and leave samples of formula bearing such messages as "Sustains the baby like mother's milk," and "a superior food for the infant." Unsuitable commercial advertising, says Dr. Paulo Luis R. Sousa, pediatrician at Brazil's Universidade Católica de Pelotas, "is partly responsible for high rates of infant morbidity and mortality." The dependence of infants on the local water supply in such regions has increased dramatically. By 1974 only 12 percent of Brazilian babies were breast-fed. In the previous generation more than two-thirds were on mother's milk for the first six months of life.

Children who play by open drains or stagnant pools, or adults who drink contaminated water, or splash in polluted streams, or fish in infested ponds, are doomed in the same way as victims of poisoned air. The life-supporting elements turn lethal. Sometimes the capriciousness of nature is at fault. A river spontaneously changes course and abandons those who depend upon it. Or it stops raining. But usually it is the foolishness of men who either are tricked by nature into congregating in areas without adequate or decent water or are determined to improve on nature in ways that won't work. Bangladesh is an example of the former. Once immensely fertile because of the monsoon that floods the paddies for four months a year, Bangladesh became overpopulated with rice farmers. The logic of Malthus dictates that sewage deposits increase at a geometric rate, and the result is contaminated water, typhoid, dysentery, and the more exotic diseases just mentioned—and months of drought. Human intervention into the water system often makes things worse from a health standpoint. Great dams, including the famous Aswan High Dam, create stagnant pools and a huge increase in schistosomiasis. World Bank water consultant Herbert Bernstein has noted numerous water projects that neglect the human consequences of engineering—the physical and psychological effects on farmers relocated from land taken for dams, the social effects of introducing water meters for what used to be a free good, and the cultural and economic impact of a water bureaucracy suddenly thrown up in the midst of a traditional society.

Although few Americans must walk miles to fill the family pail, there is also a serious water shortage in the United States. In parts of the country water is still free. Only recently did New York City begin to charge consumers. It is underpriced almost everywhere. But there is not enough water to go around. From time to time nature dramatizes that reality. There have been periodic droughts in the U.S. The human suffering wrought by the dust bowl of the 1930s was caught in Steinbeck's *Grapes of Wrath.* (In those days, the county agent for the Department of Agriculture in the parched range land of Wyoming was empowered to pay farmers eight dollars for every cow he shot.) In the 1950s there were several severe widespread droughts requiring water rationing. Livestock was again killed to save feed. In the midst of one drought President Eisenhower appointed a commission on the national water problem, but it stopped meeting when the rains came. In 1965 drought struck the East. New York City started fining restaurants that served glasses of water without being asked. The West, almost always short of water, experienced two successive years of severe drought caused by the unusually dry winters of 1975–76 and 1976–77. Two or three years of above-average rainfall, according to the U.S. Water Resources Council, could relieve the shortage. That has happened in the past, but there is increasing concern among weather experts that the U.S. may be headed for an extended dry spell and the end of the era of cheap water.

There are, as we have seen, Cassandras and Panglosses among the long-range weather prognosticators, but both are guessing. J. Murray Mitchell, Jr., a climatologist with the Environmental Data Service of the National Oceanic and Atmospheric Administration, predicts that in the next ten years the Long Range Prediction Group will develop thirty-day and ninety-day forecasts that will have more than "the marginal value" they now have, but that it probably will be decades before it will be possible to forecast weather several years ahead. Unfortunately, in the absence of such long-range information on future rainfall, prudent planning requires the assumption that unusually heavy rains will not solve America's water problem.

The water problem is in large measure a consequence of our peculiar system of accounting. Because water, like air, is "free," that is, no one owns it, or else the state owns it, it is used liberally in the manufacture of commodities that would be more expensive if water use were less profligate. If we ever decided that a unit of water was more valuable than a unit of money, then we would presumably arrange our affairs very differently. For example, a mature steer consumes 25 to 35 pounds of alfalfa a day and drinks about 12 gallons of water. Alfalfa has a "transpiration ratio" of 800, that is, it takes 800 pounds of water circulating through the alfalfa plant into the air to bring one pound of alfalfa to maturity. Thus, to feed the steer takes, conservatively, 1,262 gallons a day. Dean Charles C. Bradley of Montana State University calculated in 1962 that the water cost of the typical beef-rich American diet was 2,500 gallons per day per person. So if we reconsider our typical Akron family of five and see them not as casual faucet turners and toilet flushers but as participants in an integrated system of water use, the consumption rate is enormous. If we rationed each person's water use in accordance with the water consumed to produce his automobile, his synthetic shirt, or his tennis racket, or for that matter to print this book, we might get more insight into the gravity of the impending water famine. But here again prices do not accurately reflect supply and demand. Theoretically, factories pass on to the consumer what they pay for water. That is still frequently nothing, but even where municipal water charges must be paid, the costs do not reflect the precious nature of the commodity nor its scant supply.

3.

Water supply in the U.S. is a serious problem, but the problem of water quality is more serious. Ten years ago the geographer Gilbert F. White dismissed predictions "that the community pulse of Los Angeles will ebb slowly to a halt or that New Yorkers will fall gasping of thirst on their grimy pavement through lack of water," but he warned that the likelihood "that the quality of life will be impaired by misuse and degradation of the quality of available water is much greater."

Impure water, a huge global problem, as we have seen, has in recent years become a visible public issue in the United States. Ironically, this has happened despite the phenomenal success in eradicating such waterborne killers as typhoid fever. (George Washington, though he would scarcely be tempted today, took sick and almost died after taking a drink from the Potomac. John Wilkes Booth's father, the great actor Junius Brutus Booth, died of typhoid fever days after quenching his thirst from the Mississippi River.)

Tampering with the water supply evokes a peculiar horror. In the Middle Ages the greatest opprobrium was reserved for the crime of well poisoning. (So much fear and loathing did the crime arouse that it became a stock anti-Semitic charge to foment pogroms.) In the 1950s the John Birch Society, an ultraconservative group, built its membership on its campaign against fluoridization of the public water supply. The purveyors of fluoride were part of a Communist conspiracy to weaken the American will and to deprive citizens of their freedom to choose tooth decay. Actually, as medieval as the Birchers sounded, the use of the city water system to promote public health purposes raises profound ideological questions. In Chile some nutrition experts have favored enriching the water supply with nutrients as an alternative to subsidizing food and improving incomes, as the Allende Government tried to do, on the theory that the only way to make sure people received their nutritional requirements was to bypass individual choice.

In the last few years the evidence has been accumulating that we have been systematically tampering with our own water supply. In 1974, a little over a month after the Environmental Defense Fund released its study showing a link between cancer deaths and the chloroform found in New Orleans water, Congress passed the Safe Drinking Water Act, which legislates how much pesticide, chloroform, chromium, lead, silver, cadmium, mercury, nitrate, fluoride, and arsenic it is safe for us to drink along with our water. Traces of asbestos fiber, which is known to cause cancer when breathed, have been found in the Duluth, Minnesota, water supply, and lead has been found in substantial quantities in some New England cities and towns. Carbon tetrachloride, which is no longer permitted for dry cleaning because it has been found to cause cancer in animals, has been found in significant amounts in certain rivers that provide the drinking water for 1,800,000 people. A recent study of the National Academy of Science finds that about 3 percent of the water systems surveyed contain high levels of nitrate from fertilized fields. Such traces can cause anemia in infants. The Academy exonerated fluoride, which causes, many charges to the contrary nothwithstanding, neither cancer nor mongolism. Indeed, its only discernible effect, besides the discoloration of tooth enamel, is to increase bone density, which is quite possibly an advantage. The Environmental Protection Agency surveyed eighty cities and found traces of chloroform in all of them. Ironically, the cause appears to be chlorine, which is put into the water as a disinfectant but which reacts with certain natural substances to produce chloroform. "We are far behind the Europeans in treatment processes to remove chemicals as well as bacteria," says Lewis D. Walker, assistant director of the U.S. Water Resources Council, the agency that is supposed to coordinate federal water programs. As supplies decrease, quality also deteriorates because cities are pressed to use water from streams that have not been flushed with proper rainfall.

4.

There are several strategies for increasing and improving water supplies —building dams, restructuring rivers, collecting and storing rainwater, desalination of seawater, and harvesting icebergs. Each method for increasing the water supply of one city, region, or nation diverts water that could potentially be used by others; hence the water wars of Asia and the Middle East and the political struggles over water in this country which we shall consider shortly.

In surveying water augmentation strategies, let us start with the most outlandish—towing Antarctic icebergs to coastal deserts. The idea, circulating in oceanographic circles since the mid-1960s, was developed in a scientific paper published in 1973 by Wilford F. Weeks of the U.S. Army Cold Regions Research and Engineering Laboratory and W. J. Campbell of the U.S. Geological Survey's Ice Dynamic Project. Four years later it received considerable publicity at the First International Conference on Iceberg Utilization held at Iowa State University, an undertaking backed by Prince Mohammed al-Faisal of Saudi Arabia. The Prince had been working with Paul-Emile Victor, the head of the French Polar Expedition, on plans to tow a 100-million-ton iceberg to Saudi Arabia, using five powerful tugs. (The iceberg, according to the technical studies, would travel at one knot and arrive in a year. The cost of the water once it arrived would be fifty cents per cubic meter as compared with the present cost of desalinated water of eighty cents.)

Actually, the idea of transporting icebergs is not new. In 1773, Captain James Cook, sailing south of the Antarctic Circle, noted in his journal that he filled three small boats with loose pieces of iceberg that yielded about 15 tons of fresh water and loaded them on ship. "The melting of the ice is a little tedious, otherwise this is the most expeditious way of watering I ever met with." Between 1800 and 1900 small icebergs were towed from the tip of Chile to the port of Valparaiso and even to Peru, a distance of 3,900 kilometers.

To be an important factor in solving the severe water problem of the Middle East, however, huge icebergs would have to be used. This would require enormously complex technology—satellites to locate the icebergs and possibly such exotic devices as specially designed nuclear submarines to carry the iceberg on their back, paddle wheels attached to the iceberg (an idea offered by the Prince at the Iowa Conference), or propulsion units inserted into the iceberg. Solving the water problem with the dramatic application of high technology is almost as exciting a challenge to engineers as space exploration. The technical difficulties involved in wrapping, slicing, and eventually melting the iceberg are staggering.

Iceberg harvesting could give rise to another new set of "military requirements." In 1978, Colonel Roy L. Thompson of the U.S. Air Force speculated in *Strategic Review* on the "potential for conflict" attached to the harvesting operation. "If two or more countries should be involved in harvesting within the same general area in the Antarctic, how would claims to specific icebergs be exercised and competing claims resolved?" Since 77 percent of all the world's fresh water is in the form of ice caps and glaciers—only 0.5 percent is to be found in lakes and rivers—and 90 percent of this aquatic store is at the South Pole, iceberg harvesting is an enticing technical solution. Whether it makes sense as a strategy for increasing the water supply given the alternatives is as yet unclear, but it is plausible enough to be a potential source of political conflict.

Desalination has been promoted as a panacea ever since 1952 when, as Gilbert F. White puts it in his *Strategies of American Water Management,* it received "sudden, almost hysterical endorsement by administrators and scientists in the U.S." Every President from Truman to Johnson delivered ringing speeches on the impending breakthrough in desalination research. For John F. Kennedy the prospect of developing technology to make the deserts surrounding the Mediterranean and the Indian Ocean bloom would be "the prime accomplishment of science in improving the life of people in the long history of the world." By 1966 about one-fifth of all funds for water resources research was going to the Office of Saline Water. Desalination research was fashionable and grew at a much faster rate than the more important research on recycling and decontamination of fresh water. While desalination plants are important in the Middle East, where alternative sources are scarce—as of 1974 there were 153 desalination plants in the Middle East and 104 in Africa—the costs of desalination are too high to make it a major solution to the water problem in the U.S. In the irrigation areas, water costs one to seven cents per thousand gallons. The lowest costs of desalinated water are estimated to be between fifteen and thirty cents, and this assumes that desalting operations, according to White, would be "linked with very large nuclear energy plants. . . ." Thus, while there are more than 300 desalination plants in the U.S., producing about 100 million gallons a day, this is only one-tenth of one percent of the water in use.

White thinks the preoccupation with desalination "is an example of the way in which belief in a single scientific advance may run away with those who espouse it . . . a sobering caution for those who would engage in environmental modification on a grand scale, a caution against promising too much too soon, becoming bemused with one answer, against making a public commitment for which there then becomes a political necessity to build support by continuing heavy investment in research which does not fulfill high hopes.''

If desalination is controversial, huge concrete structures for managing the storage and flow of water are much more so. Public water projects—dams, reservoirs, irrigation pipelines, schemes for rerouting streams, and a host of other feats of engineering—are viewed by proponents—usually the U.S. Army Corps of Engineers who build them, politicians looking for federal money, and large agribusiness interests and power companies, which directly benefit from them—as modern wonders of the world. Opponents—environmentalists, Indian tribes whose land is taken or ruined, and cost-conscious politicians and bureaucrats (who usually live elsewhere)—denounce the implantation of huge concrete waterworks in the midst of America's wilderness and the accompanying hydraulic technology as the worst examples of pork barrel politics and extravagant waste.

Arthur E. Morgan, who designed a flood control project in Ohio after the 1913 Dayton flood, became the first head of the Tennessee Valley Authority, and worked with water problems all his life, at the age of ninety-three wrote a stinging denunciation of the Army Corps of Engineers which he called *Dams and Other Disasters*. The book is a recital of one hundred years of environmental insensitivity, waste, mismanagement, boondoggling, and the exercise of irresponsible power. Yet it was not only avarice and the lust for bureaucratic power that sparked the mighty effort to make the western deserts bloom. There was some of the same nobility of spirit that transformed the deserts of Palestine. But the era of the great water projects peaked in the 1950s and is now over. A generation ago almost one-third of the employees in the Department of the Interior were in the water business. There is relatively less federal money for such projects today. Moreover, there is a growing constituency of dam haters. "If you are against a dam, you are for a river,"says David Brower, former head of the Sierra Club who has succeeded in his career in blocking a number of high dams.

Shortly after taking office, President Carter approved what was quickly termed a "hit list" of eighteen "questionable" water projects. These included draining the Cache River basin in Arkansas, the wintering spot of the largest congregation of Mallard duck in North America; the Central Arizona Project, a scheme to pipe Colorado River water 200 miles and store it behind a dam at the confluence of the Salt and Verde rivers (where it would flood the land of the Yavapai Indians); and the Richard B. Russell dam, which, according to the conservationist publication *Outdoor Life,* "would destroy a sizable bloc of forest and wildlife land in Georgia and South Carolina." President Carter declared after three weeks in office that "I personally don't believe that any of the projects ought to be built," but under intense political pressure the President backed down. He allowed half the projects to continue but successfully vetoed a bill to revive the other half.

Water is the most intensely local public issue of all. Proprietary feelings about "my water" make it difficult to develop federal policy or regional planning. Only when Washington bureaucrats came with large checks could they influence local citizens in managing their water supply. It is possible to view federal bureaucrats with funds to dispense as having statesmanlike impulses, but bureaucrats who come with regulations, advice, and empty pockets rank in local esteem somewhere between welfare recipients and proprietors of adult book shops.

The constituencies in support of large water projects are strong and visible. A formidable federal bureaucracy and one of the oldest, the U.S. Army Corps of Engineers, has the same sort of interest in stockpiling dams as the Air Force and the Navy have in stockpiling missiles. Like the weapons accumulators, the dam builders are able to tap the American collective unconscious. As weapons satisfy the yearning for safety, so dams feed the dreams of riches and growth. Mark Twain and Charles Warner caught the spirit in *The Gilded Age*. A young engineer takes the visitor to a local stream long known as Goose Run but just renamed the Columbus River. "The Columbus River," he says proudly, "if deepened, and widened, and straightened, and made a little longer, would be one of the greatest rivers in our western country."

The great concrete dams—Hoover Dam on the Colorado, Grand Coulee on the Columbia—is the American version of the Gothic cathedral, a "magnificent, mysterious, monolithically faceless incredibility," as the Colorado writer George Sibley puts it, like the pyramids of Egypt and Central America, the Great Wall of China, the temples of Angkor, Stonehenge, or the heads of Easter Island. Hoover Dam, the quintessential New Deal project begun ten years before by Herbert Hoover, the Great Engineer (who would not have his name attached to it until his successor was in his grave), contains according to the official tour guides, "enough concrete to pave a standard highway sixteen feet wide from San Francisco to New York." It was, as Floyd E. Dominy, former United States Commissioner of Reclamation, puts it, the "first major river plug in the world. As Joseph in Egypt had learned to store food against famine, "we in the West had learned to store water." The technological euphoria of dam building spilled over into the Soviet Union at an early date—American engineers helped build the great Dnieper dam in the 1930s—and Soviet managers from time to time put their energy into massive plastic surgery operations on their rivers. (They once talked of using the atomic bomb to make the Volga flow backward.)

The great dams of the Colorado have transformed Southern California and with it American agriculture. (Eighty percent of all water used in Southern California comes from the Lower Colorado.) In the drought of 1977 the Imperial Valley, which had crop losses of $10 million in the drought of 1934, had a normal harvest, thanks to the miracle of irrigation. Hoover Dam also prevented the flood of 1952 from becoming a major disaster. The extraordinary growth of California would have been impossible without the grand schemes for draining, pumping, and storing Colorado River water. Nonetheless, the reality remains that the richest agricultural land and some of the fastest-growing population centers in the United States that resulted are located in a desert. Armies of engineers and acres of concrete may not be enough to sustain them.

In 1978, Cecil D. Andrus, the Secretary of the Interior, reported that 21 of the country's 106 water subregions were in a state of "severe water shortages" and that by the year 2000 the number would almost double. In the drought of 1977 Florida, Georgia, and Alabama suffered more than $1 billion in agricultural losses, and California about the same. The water table in parts of California is falling at the rate of six feet a month. (In one year 8,000 new wells were dug in the state.) Seventy thousand wells around Lubbock, Texas, an area that produces about 25 percent of the nation's cotton, went dry. The water shortage is mostly concentrated in the West. The Colorado River evaporates under the hot sun at a rate of about six feet a year. Even in nondrought years there is never enough rain. West of the hundredth meridian—a line approximately bisecting the Dakotas and extending to Laredo, Texas—Sibley points out, nearly all the land below 8,000 feet is too dry for unirrigated agriculture. West of the Rockies it becomes desert.

All this was known over one hundred years ago. In 1877 the river explorer John Wesley Powell wrote his *Report on the Lands of the Arid Region of the United States,* in which he emphasized that water availability was the limiting factor in the development of the West and made the sensible but ignored recommendation that water rights should be sold along with land rights. People would be discouraged from settling on the mere faith that they would find water; they would have to figure out where they were going to find it. Any nine persons could draw up plans for decentralized irrigation "commonwealths" and get government help if their plans for water development kept pace with land development. "I say to the Government: Hands Off: Furnish the people with institutions of justice, and let them do the work for themselves."

A very different approach was tried, a combination of witchcraft, fancy engineering, and big money. More than $90 billion of water development money has been spent by the Federal Government in this century. The witchcraft has consisted of a bizarre succession of wishes, misrepresented as science. As Sibley recounts it:

> Rain would follow the plow (because of the increased evaporation from worked soil); rain would follow the train (because of smoke particles for drops to form around); rain would follow the telegraph (because of electricity in the air). Soldiers had a saying "Rain follows a battle," so experiments were conducted in Texas with explosives and cannons. There were even those who came right out and said what everyone else was more or less hinting at: rain will follow settlement for no reason other than the presence of good people with a destiny to fulfill. On the basis of these myths, in the face of all evidence and good sense, the Homestead Act of 1862 was passed.

On the faith of the nineteenth-century rain prognosticators, the rush to the West took off. Water was another resource on which to make a private killing. Entrepreneurs moved in with pumps, ditches, and headgates and proceeded to sell "water shares" to farmers. On the faith of the twentieth-century engineers and massive federal funds, the rush became a torrent. When the West Coast aerospace and agribusiness boom was launched at the beginning of World War II twenty years of water importation had paved the way. The process had begun with the Colorado River Compact of 1922, under which California agreed to share the water of the Colorado with six other states. Despite statutory limitations on water use, California still uses almost a million acre-feet a year of water it will eventually have to relinquish under its agreements. The Metropolitan Water District that supplies well over half the domestic and industrial use of water in a 4,900-square-mile area of Southern California negotiated arrangements with the Federal Government and the other states that made it possible for Los Angeles and San Diego to grow on water credit and live beyond their means. While California in recent years has developed its own water projects in an effort to reduce the use of borrowed water, in the 1977 drought it was pumping a billion gallons a day from the Colorado at a huge cost in energy.

The production of energy, as we have seen, requires huge amounts of water, but the process of finding and transporting water itself involves a heavy energy drain. Oil, gas, and coal are consumed in great quantities in order to direct and tame the flow of water. Indeed, one of the absurdities of energy policy in California is that more energy is expended in moving water from northern California to the south—in the operation of pumping plants, canals, and irrigation networks—than is generated by the dams that store the water.

In the first four years of its operation Hoover Dam supplied Los Angeles with 98 percent of its power. The great concern was whether there would be a market for all the water that was being collected. (Lake Mead, part of the huge project for redoing the Colorado River, had facilities for storing more than three years' flow of the river.) But the Hoover Dam is a multiple-purpose dam. It supplies both power and water. Water used for one purpose is not available for others. Thus when the irrigation needs became enormous, dam generators were cut back and now run at about 40 percent capacity. (Most of Southern California's power comes from natural gas-fired plants in Redondo and El Segundo, and the Navaho Generating Station on Lake Powell.)

Technological achievements gave rise to unforeseen technological problems. The stored water from the elaborately plugged river evaporates, and the evaporation process increases the salt concentration in the water that remains, making the water unsuitable for irrigation. "Salinity Control" is the bureaucratic answer, but desalination is an expensive, energy-intensive process. Recounting all these incredible problems of bringing water to the West, Sibley terms it an "act of naive faith" to turn on a faucet in Los Angeles.

The declining water tables across the country—a 1977 White House study reveals a significant drop in water levels in Minnesota, Wisconsin, and Michigan's Upper Peninsula, as well as in the West—are a dramatic illustration of the laws of entropy. More and more energy, expense, and human effort produces a diminishing return. Every technological solution however ingenious incurs its own debts, which usually involve new technological problems and new energy costs. Since energy costs also involve water costs, there is no way to short-circuit the circular resource chain in which we are caught. Everything is connected to everything else in the natural order. It is easy to speculate about those connections but very difficult to take them into account in the day-to-day planning of policy.

Our language, our orderly intellectual habits (one thing at a time), our bureaucratic organization in which specialization is used as a franchise to build baronies—all conspire to keep us from integrating, comprehending, and fitting with the natural order. Developers have no responsibility for water policy. They see themselves as controllers or consumers of water. Energy planners do not think in terms of water costs. The water "augmentors" operate with much the same mentality as other sorts of government financiers. Increase the debt. Borrow against the future. Someday the ship will come in and we can pay ourselves back. They even use the term "water overdraft." Even among the heirs of the New Deal there are intimations that printing money and adding a zero or two every few years to something called the national debt has real consequences that are not always pleasant. But borrowing water and betting on rescue from the skies is more hazardous still. We can't print rain, although we could probably entrap more. (Less than 10 percent of the rainfall over the entire U.S. is used.)

Seeding of winter clouds with silver iodide, frozen carbon dioxide, and other chemicals has been effective in increasing the snowpack on the mountains of the West and has accounted for a total increase in precipitation in these areas from 5 to 25 percent. But summer clouds present much more of a problem, and a number of experiments with seeding summer cumulus clouds have succeeded in decreasing rainfall. (In Florida after various seeding operations the results ranged from an increase of 18 percent to a decrease of 6 percent.) In all, cloud doctoring is an uncertain business.

Water use in the U.S. is very uneven. By the year 2000 the per capita daily withdrawal rate in the upper Colorado region, because of the concentration of mining and agriculture, will be 100 times greater than the rates in the Northeast. Thus, there may not be enough water where it is needed to support the desert-rescued civilization we have already built. There is a long list of proud cities that drank up their surrounding water and expired. Babylon, Persepolis, Gomorrah, and in thirteenth-century America a collection of Pueblo settlements (after what appears to have been a twenty-three-year drought). There are those who believe that Phoenix, Los Angeles, and San Diego must inevitably join them.

5.

Because water is so obviously a finite and scarce resource and because there are always competing drinkers, irrigators, and industrial users for the same water, conflict is inevitable. In the international arena water disputes erupt periodically in bitter charges and countercharges, and sometimes war. After the 1947 partition of the subcontinent, India and Pakistan began to squabble about water. The headwaters of three rivers that feed the rich Punjab region of Pakistan—Ravi, Beas, and Sutlej—lie in India; and waters of the Indus, Chenab, and Jhelum, of great importance to India, are in Pakistan. As in many other areas of the world where puckish nature mocks the mapmakers, the location of these rivers spelled trouble. In 1948 Pakistan accused India of diverting water by stopping the flow of water to Pakistan in the canals under Indian control. The skirmishes over Kashmir were further embittered by the fight over water.

Eventually, with the mediation of the World Bank, the two countries signed the Indus Waters Treaty, which more or less settled the problem.

Israel and Syria have come to blows over rival plans to divert water from the Jordan River, and the Iraqis and the Syrians have been in bitter dispute over rights to the waters of the Euphrates. Deploying tanks and infantry units on the Syrian border in April 1975, the Iraqis demanded that Syria release more water. The Syrians made some military counter-moves, and eventually the dispute was mediated by the Saudis. South Africa justified its intervention in Angola in 1975 on the ground that it was protecting the Cunene Dam which provided hydroelectric power for its protectorate, Namibia. In retaliation for the Bay of Pigs invasion in 1961, Castro cut off the water supply to the U.S. Naval base at Guantanamo, but U.S. technology prevailed. Desalination facilities were brought in, and the base remains to this day.

Of the 200 largest river basins in the world 148 are shared by two countries, and 52 by three to ten countries. The "incentives for coercive manipulation of water resources are likely to grow," Colonel Roy L. Thompson argues, "as inter-basin transfer systems expand." The growing demand for water reinforced by a growing interdependence of reluctant partners in shared water systems is increasing the conflict among nations over the most precious resource of all.

The United States and Mexico have a chronic dispute over Colorado River water. As the river water flows toward the border it naturally becomes saltier because it picks up mineral sediments. But the diversion of considerable quantities of water for making electricity and the increased pollution of the remaining water has caused a sharp rise in the salt levels by the time it reaches Mexico. Beginning in 1961, drainage operations of the U.S. Bureau of Reclamation dumped large saline deposits close to the Mexican border and severely damaged croplands in the Mexicali Valley. When the Mexicans protested, the U.S. agreed after more than ten years of negotiation to desalinate the water flowing to Mexico, but the promise is becoming increasingly difficult to implement. The Colorado River, as Francisco Tomargo and Robert Young point out in the *Journal of Natural Resources*, is "water short"—indeed, more so than any other river basin in the U.S. It already serves 15 million people, and because it is "one of the largest storehouses of energy resources in the U.S.—including coal, oil, natural gas, uranium, tar sands and oil shale deposits," it is sure to be drained at an ever faster rate and to spread increasing amount of salt on Mexican farmland.

Precisely the same sort of conflict exists within the territory of the United States; several of the fifty sovereign states that make up the union have disputes with one another over water. In 1964 the Attorney General of Nebraska filed a brief in the Supreme Court of the United States containing language reminiscent of the sort France and Germany used to employ just before they went to war. "The aggressive policies of the State of Iowa have caused great consternation to the State of Nebraska and its citizens, and have threatened to result in armed conflict on the part of landowners of the State of Iowa and its representatives." At issue were contesting claims to some islands in the Missouri River, a boundary dispute occasioned by a Corps of Engineers water project. After the engineers had finished altering the river course, 15,000 acres of Nebraska land now lay in Iowa. In 1959 the Supreme Court declared that New York is "on a collision course with Philadelphia" over water. Water battles have erupted from time to time between New York and New Jersey. Regional planning has increased in response to the water wars between the states, but local feelings run so high that water compacts are difficult to implement.

Water, Blackstone noted, "is a moveable, wandering thing, and must of necessity continue common by the law of nature, so that I can have only a temporary, transient, usufructuary property therein." A reasonable principle, but difficult to implement in practice. Water law has become enormously complex because rivers are no respecters of boundaries, because they are fickle and change course or dry up. One community, by drawing only its "needs" from a common water supply, can condemn another downstream to thirst and even death.

Conflict, understandably, is most intense in the Southwest. Like most water-short areas, the law of "prior appropriation" is in force: First come, first serve. This principle encourages extravagant use since rights can be lost if the water is not appropriately used. The Federal Government has tried to encourage changes in local law to provide incentives to conserve rather than waste water, but reforms can be imposed by Washington only by attaching them as conditions to hydraulic bribes.

The court reports of the West give some of the flavor of local water battles. In May 1975, Pete Naranjo was flooding his alfalfa field outside Espanola, New Mexico, from the Santo Nino irrigation ditch when the majordomo, the elected overseer of the ditch, told him he had used enough. A fight ensued, and the majordomo bit off the farmer's right ear. The overseer claimed in court that he had a privilege that came with his office to bite ears if necessary to enforce the water regulations. The court agreed with him and dismissed the farmer's lawsuit.

The Spanish introduced ditch irrigation, a notion they borrowed from the Moors, throughout the Southwest. In some places, including Arizona, the Indians had a ditch irrigation system in operation when the Spanish arrived. The system for distributing water to villages has been working pretty much as it worked in the seventeenth century, but recently three dams built at the headwaters of the Santa Fe River have diverted water from the ancient villages. "We used to get a small stream of water, more than enough to irrigate," says Ignacio Moya, the majordomo of the "mother ditch" that feeds Sante Fe, "but they took that last little bit of water." The New Mexico Public Service Commission's new filtering plant is so efficient at gathering in what used to be spare water, that it no longer percolates into the surrounding soil. The result is withered orchards, parched gardens, and a lot of law suits.

The rivers of the Southwest—the Pecos, the Chama, the Vermejo Creek—are all seriously "overappropriated." Rights to the water have been sold to competing users which exceed the water supply. Some years are so dry that the irrigation ditches are closed. A Colorado mining company claims water to which New Mexico's Natural Resources Conservation Commission also has rights. Indian claims are senior to all others under the first come, first served rule—if they are recognized. "It creates a tap," Richard Simms, chief legal counsel to the New Mexico state engineer, declared, "by which Indians or the Federal government can just suck all the water they want out from under people with historic expectations."

The convergence of a variety of political struggles encourages contradictory expectations. Nowhere is this clearer than in California. Overshadowing hundreds of local fights over water are two unpublicized but fierce battles: a struggle between northern California, which has water and relatively few people, and Southern California, which has a huge population and no water; and a struggle between agribusiness and a much weakened historic movement to preserve the family farm. On all sides of these struggles, people have made plans on the assumption that they would have water. But there is not enough to go around.

Take the matter of the "north-south dialog" within the state of California. There are large amounts of water stored in the reservoirs of northern California which are contracted for use in the populous Los Angeles–San Diego region. A prolonged fight has developed over plans to shoot the water south by means of a complex network of projects and waterways slated to cost about $7 billion. The project has been delayed because it would divert water from the delta north of San Francisco which otherwise would flow into the sea. At first blush that would seem to be a good water conservation measure even if a little expensive. The trouble is that the freshwater flow around the delta is necessary to maintain the delicate balance between land and sea. If the fresh water did not flow out at a certain rate, salt water would flow in and ruin the land around the delta.

How such struggles come out will depend upon what sort of strange new political coalitions can be built around water issues. The cost in money and in energy of moving massive amounts of water is, increasingly, becoming a public concern. The environmental damage caused by rerouting rivers, squeezing streams, and building dams is becoming apparent to groups with diverse interests. The Auburn Dam to be built on the American River in California would destroy archeological sites in the heart of the historic Gold Rush area; the Central Arizona Project would threaten hawks and bald eagles; the Meremac Park Dam in Missouri would flood caves; the Dickey-Lincoln Project in northern Maine would inundate timberland, and so on.

Who is to decide whether the alleged power needs of, say, the citizens of Boston justify the destruction of recreation and fishing areas belonging to the citizens of Maine? The answer up to now has been political muscle, theoretically a democratic solution to tough resource allocation problems but in reality a capitulation to large corporate interests. A few major water issues have become matters for wide political debate. It is now easier to stop dams. A coalition of environmental groups has succeeded in killing or delaying more than fifty water projects in a decade.

But there is no adequate democratic machinery for positive planning of resource allocation. In the absence of a coalition dedicated to designing, explaining, and carrying forward alternative programs for supplying water and energy, the victories of the environmentalists and the antinuclear coalitions will be short-lived. Like such military phoenixes as the advanced bomber or the nuclear aircraft carrier, which keep reappearing after being periodically strangled by vote of Congress, high-technology water projects have excellent prospects for resurrection. The only weapon that could, perhaps, keep them in their grave is the political imagination to design a civilization that does not keep borrowing water.

Fights over dams are really struggles between regions and communities —how much water one place can take from another or how much environmental damage should be sustained by one community in order to supply water or energy for another. Fights over water rights, on the other hand, are struggles over competing models of development. The classic contestants in these struggles are the entrepreneurs versus small farmers and consumers.

In California, the tension between equitable public policy and historic practice has been evident since the days of the Gold Rush. In settling the West the intent of Congress was to encourage homesteading and family farming and to make the vast new territories available for anyone with courage, stamina, and entrepreneurial spirit. But the reality was that those who were specially endowed with these admirable qualities along with inordinate amounts of greed and cunning ended up owning huge tracts of public land and the water rights that went with them. While the Jeffersonian model of a nation of small farmers was promoted in congressional oratory, the lawmakers proceeded to pass a number of giveaway measures that promoted the land and water monopoly scandals of the West. Thus Henry Miller arriving penniless in California in the last century managed to take advantage of the Swamp Lands Act of 1850, which gave free land to anyone who would drain it, to end up at his death with 14 million acres. Two other land grabbers, Haggin and Tevis, amassed enormous holdings in the southern part of the Central Valley which came to be known as the Kern County Land Company. Purchased in 1967 by Tenneco, it is still one of the largest ranches in the state.

In 1902, at the urging of President Theodore Roosevelt, the Reclamation Act was passed that provided that "no right to the use of water for land in private ownership shall be sold for a tract exceeding 160 acres to any one landowner . . . and no such sale shall be made to any landowner unless he be an actual bona fide resident on such land. . . ." The purpose was to prevent further gobbling up of public lands by monopolies. Through the years the stated objective of the Congress in amending the law and the Bureau of Reclamation in administering it has been to spread the benefits of land reclamation and to encourage home ownership and family farms. But in fact the owners of excess acreage have because of lax enforcement always been able to get the water they have needed. According to Professor Joseph Sax, a water law expert at the University of Michigan Law School:

> The basic reasons for failure were these: first, the arrangement used for controlling the sale price did not prevent sales to middlemen who were free to resell without restriction; second, and perhaps even more important, sales of excess lands were required only after the issuance of public notice, which was often delayed indefinitely, and the law was interpreted to permit the delivery of water to excess lands prior to their sale. Excess-land owners were thus able to receive project water for their excess lands for very long periods—precisely the result the reclamation was designed to prevent; and when they did sell, they were able to reap as speculative profit the capitalized value of the federal subsidy.

In his investigation of land sales in the Westlands Water District, David Weiman of Agricultural Resources found elaborately fraudulent sales carried out to escape the 160-acre limitation, including one to a New York corporation organized to sell false teeth by mail. An audit of the Central Valley Project by the Department of the Interior confirmed that California has a bumper crop of paper farmers and that the water charges by the Bureau of Reclamation for supplying the water district are so low as to amount to a substantial subsidy to large landowners. This particular water district has had a unique amount of public scrutiny. The same sort of water grab could be traced in many other places. Water theft under color of law is a major industry.

Exactly what is "theft" of natural resources and what is "partnership" is now a matter of political struggle all over the world. The former colonial countries of Asia, Africa, and Latin America whose rich mineral deposits have been exploited by the dominant white civilizations for centuries are seeking to exercise greater "control" over their own natural resources while they continue to sell them on the international market with the help of corporate partners. There is a worldwide search for new ground rules that will take both the history of colonial plunder and the realities of contemporary power distribution into account. Precisely the same issues are at stake in the matter of Indian claims within the United States.

"We declare that as nations of Indian people," the Second International Indian Treaty Conference declared in June 1976, "we have exclusive control of our natural resources. We will use these resources to provide food and livelihood for our people, for trade and economic development in non-capitalist, non-exploitative and non-ecologically destructive methods pursuant to our traditional values. The United States through its Federal Power Commission and contrary to tribal desires licenses tribal lands for flooding and other ecological destruction to support power projects." Garrison Dam in North Dakota, to take one example, built in the late 1940s and 1950s, flooded hundreds of acres used for centuries by the Fort Berthold Indians as grazing and crop lands. Under the Treaty of Fort Laramie of 1851 the Indians had been granted 12.5 million acres, which was whittled down to 643,368 acres by Acts of Congress without the consent of the tribe. For a payment of $5 million the Indians lost all mineral, grazing, and fishing rights. Their requests for irrigation rights and 20,000 kwh of electricity a year at cost were denied. At the signing of the contract of sale in the office of the Secretary of the Interior in 1948, the leader of the tribe wept openly.

The International Indian Treaty Council, it will be recalled, claims that 30 percent of the nation's coal, 30 percent of the petroleum, 20 percent of the natural gas, and 90 percent of the uranium are on Indian reservations and "much higher percentages are on our treaty land" (land granted in treaties but subsequently taken away). The exploitation of these minerals raises not only the question of Indian rights to the proceeds and the right to decide whether they should be mined and at what pace, but also the matter of water use and water pollution. The disposal of uranium wastes at the bottom of strip mines owned by Peabody Coal, a number of which are located over the water tables that supply the Navaho and Hopi tribes, is, as Winona La Duke Westigard of the Indian Treaty Council, puts it, turning her people into "forced caretakers of the U.S. government's nuclear garbage."

Indian water claims may turn out to be as important as mineral claims. In 1908 the U.S. Supreme Court declared in the so-called "Winters Doctrine" that Indians had the beneficial use of water that is adjacent to, or rises on, or flows through the reservations. But it did not define whether it meant the sort of use that was common in 1908 or whether Indians ought to be able to use water for growth and development like anyone else. The Fort Peck Indians, through whose reservation the Missouri runs, have laid claim to all the water of the Missouri they can use, and they say that is a lot. As many as 5,000 white Montanans are caught in a web of litigation because of Indian claims. Utah, which has a right under the Colorado River Compact to 23 percent of the water allocated to the Upper Basin States, does not know how much of that 23 percent belongs to the Uinta-Ouray reservation.

Coming to terms with history is expensive. Genocide is a fair term to describe the white man's 400-year strategy for dealing with the "Indian problem" on the North American continent. As a consequence, of the great tribes that roamed the West, there are, according to the Department of Commerce, only 37,526 Indians left in all five Rocky Mountain states. But these survivors, through a quirk of the white man's conscience and the idiosyncrasy of his law, have rights to the nation's most precious resource. The unwitting banishment of Indian survivors to the reservoirs and mineral preserves of the nation built on the destruction of Indian civilization is an irony to test American conscience and American law. Whether either is strong enough to bear the costs of doing justice is by no means clear.

Developing a rational water policy for the whole United States is not easy, because water is such an intensely local concern. There are two major necessities. One is conservation. While there is something faintly obscene about the extravagant use of water in the American home, given the worldwide distribution of thirst, the places where the most significant amounts of water can be saved are factories and farms. Some water specialists have calculated that water use could be cut 30 percent by installing more efficient irrigation systems. But this would take considerable capital. Many processes that waste energy in order to produce great heat also require considerable water for cooling. A federal commitment to the design and financing of a major industrial conversion program is a necessity for saving both energy and water.

The other necessity is regional planning. The Federal Government has tried unsuccessfully to promote it. The Tennessee Valley Authority was a noble experiment that miscarried. Some of the original ideas behind it are still valid. But there is no effective public control over this powerful anomaly in the American system. There are regional planning organizations with impressive paper powers across the country, but they do not exercise their considerable powers, because competing local interests make it impossible.

For me, the most persuasive students of water politics are those who urge the return to local communities of the responsibility for providing a safe and ample water supply. The Federal Government cannot make local communities act in their own self-interest. Present policy rewards those communities that have acted most irresponsibly in water matters. If Washington gets out of the way, communities may well find they have no alternative but to take three essential steps. One is to raise the price of water so that it more nearly reflects its precious nature. A second is to take public control of crucial water supplies; private ownership of the rainfall is too much. A third is for communities to get together and to resolve water conflicts themselves. There is a better chance that such regional planning can emerge from the bottom up than by an elaborate mechanism of ukases and bribes from Washington. We could do worse than take a hard look at John Wesley Powell's ideas for ''irrigation commonwealths'' put forward one hundred years ago.

CHAPTER VIII

Scarce Resources and the New International Military Order

1.

THE VINDICATION OF HELEN'S VIRTUE was, as Euripides suggests, the cover story for the Greek assault on the treasures of Troy. Taking gold, ivory, and slaves by force was part of the ordinary operations of running a thriving state. Until the rise of capitalism, plunder was its own reward, something to be consumed and enjoyed. With the coming of the Industrial Revolution, resources, including human resources, acquired their principal value from their power to create much greater wealth. In the age of imperialism the great powers built their booming economies on imported oil, copper, and iron, and they prepared for war and went to war to protect their access to these crucial materials. The carve-up of Africa was an attempt by the European imperial powers to regulate their competition for the riches of the continent.

Considerable effort has been made to develop a theory to explain the wave of imperialism that swept over Africa and Asia in the late nineteenth century and subsided only after the First World War. J. A. Hobson and V. I. Lenin developed the notion that once a certain stage of capitalist development had been achieved, colonies to provide new outlets for investment, new markets, and new sources of raw materials became essential. Hobson thought rational domestic economic policies aimed at building up the domestic market could break the link between capitalism and imperialism. Lenin, on the other hand, thought imperialism was a necessary stage of capitalism, not a policy but a condition. Non-Marxist historians and economists have advanced a variety of noneconomic explanations for imperialism, arguing that geopolitical and strategic thinking on the part of governments, ideological fervor, and popular enthusiasm

216

rather than greed of merchants or the inexorable laws of capital accumulation explain the phenomenon. There is a huge literature on the subject, and the historical evidence is rather confusing. For our purposes the "true" explanation of imperialism is less important than the ideological myths that developed to justify it; for these myths, which still persist, are the backdrop to contemporary policy with regard to access to resources.

With the rising dependence of industrial economies on foreign trade, markets, and resources, a variety of ideologies of expansionism developed. For the British, imperialism was the White Man's Burden; for the French, it was a *mission civilisatrice*. At the turn of the century geopoliticians such as Mackinder, Mahan, and Haushofer developed the theoretical framework that still guides official thinking on the relationship between access to natural resources and national power.

Geopolitik, according to Karl Haushofer, the German philosopher who developed "the doctrine of earth relations of political developments" (*Erdgebundenheit der Politik*) is "the geographical conscience of the state." An understanding of space and resources gives leaders the key to their destiny, which, for Japan and Germany, the nations that interested him primarily, meant expansionism of all sorts. The geopolitical ideologies of the German school were the incubators of the crude notion of *Lebensraum,* the living space that restless and energetic people needed and whose destiny it was to take. These expansionist theories, which served as the official justification of German ambitions in two world wars, grew out of a solid scientific tradition of the early nineteenth century which tried to analyze the relationship between climate and geography to politics. The dominant ideology of the age of Darwinism offered the respectability of science to any policy designed to assure "the survival of the fittest." In such a climate geopolitical analysis rapidly degenerated into apologetics for official theft. The U.S. brand name for it was *manifest destiny*.

"Vigorous vital states with limited space," the Swedish geopolitical scholar Rudolph Kjellen put it, "obey the categorical political imperative of expanding their space by colonization, amalgamation, or conquest." The idea still lies at the heart of most thinking on international relations. Space itself is not so important, perhaps, as it was. Being crowded seems inevitable in many parts of the world. But the use of space for resources, whether as land for agriculture or as the site for the exploitation of minerals, is as important as ever, and the notion still strongly prevails that historic political units are not prisoners of geography. If they are not endowed with natural resources, they must then find ways to take them from their more fortunate neighbors. Since the end of colonialism, the ethos of the bazaar rather than the law of the jungle has usually governed.

Minerals have been extracted at favorable prices because of the superior bargaining power of the industrial states. Military power lurks in the background. Occasionally it is used in the traditional manner of the last century; more often in new and more sophisticated ways. In this chapter we shall look at the role of military power in the world resource systems we have been describing, how it is changing, and how new forms of power are being created.

The search for neat, efficient causes for an enterprise as vast and as irrational as a world war offers intriguing but essentially futile employment for historians. Nations go to war for all sorts of reasons—gold, oil, boredom, frustration, revenge, and more. Yet at two crucial moments in the history of World War II the pressures to obtain vital raw materials were responsible for fateful decisions that ultimately decided the war. One was Germany's curious decision to invade Russia at a moment when Britain was reeling. The lure of the oil of Rumania and the wheat of the Ukraine proved irresistible and ultimately disastrous. Six months later Japan's equally ruinous decision to bomb Pearl Harbor and to occupy Southeast Asia was a military spasm prompted by the oil squeeze. Japan's military machine and imperial ambition could not be fed on the sparse resources of the home islands.

When the United States entered the war it concentrated on destroying Nazism and Japanese imperialism, but it conducted, on the side, a lively competition with Britain concerning the shape of the postwar world. By wooing the Saudis and others in the Middle East and the Mediterranean, the Roosevelt Administration made it clear that such former British preserves now must follow the logic of what Henry Luce called the American Century. Under the Truman Doctrine enunciated at the time of the Greek Civil War in 1947, the United States replaced Britain as the power with the commitment, energy, and resources to police the region. When Britain informed the United States on February 21, 1947, that she could no longer maintain her forces in Greece nor continue economic support of that beleaguered nation, the American Responsibility was born. Joseph Jones, a State Department official of the time who worked on the Truman Doctrine message, reflected the euphoria of the moment: "Great Britain had within the hour handed the job of world leadership, with all its burdens and all its glory, to the United States."

The concern over access to raw materials surfaces periodically in state papers. Some officials, like Secretary of the Navy James Forrestal, judging by his diaries, thought a good deal all during the Second World War about where the U.S. was going to get its oil and other raw materials. Others thought in vaguer geopolitical terms, using such phrases as "power vacuum" and "strategic access." Either there must be a U.S.

economic and military presence in strategic areas of the world, or Russian power would inexorably sweep over them, and their resources would be lost forever to the West. Minerals panic is a product of war. In peacetime, most essential materials are available. If there is scarcity at all, it is a function of price. But in wartime, access may actually be cut off, as happened in the case of rubber during World War II. U.S. military thinkers have been influenced considerably by the thinking of the British geopolitician H. J. Mackinder, whose famous dictum still provides the geopolitical foundation for a policy of "containment" of the Soviet Union: "Who controls eastern Europe rules the Heartland [Eurasian land mass]; who rules the Heartland rules the World Island [essentially everything else]; and who rules the World Island rules the World." The dictum expresses the strategic interests of Britain and the United States in not having the Eurasian land mass dominated by a single power, the principal geopolitical explanation for going to war against Germany twice in a lifetime.

At the time of the Korean War, official U.S. interest in preserving access to raw materials was articulated with special clarity. In November 1950 a Presidential commission headed by Gordon Gray declared that "it is vital not to lose the sources of these needed raw materials to the forces of Communist aggression." In the same period Averell Harriman testified before a Senate committee: "I do not believe this country can survive if the sources of the raw materials are in the hands of unfriendly people who are determined to destroy us." In a memo to Truman of January 1952, Harriman noted that raw materials supply justified U.S. involvement in the entire Third World. The Materials Policy Commission was nearing completion of its work under the chairmanship of William S. Paley, chairman of Columbia Broadcasting System. We have to be "more mindful than ever before," he said at a closed meeting of the commission in December 1951, "of creating either climate or mechanisms of one kind or another which would make it easier for us to get these materials from foreign sources at lowest prices possible under circumstances which are most advantageous to us." The commission recommended in its final report seven months later that government aid and government loans to private business be employed to open up raw materials sources in the countries emerging from colonization.

Between 1945 and 1976, 133 wars were waged on the territory of more than seventy such countries, according to Frank Barnaby, director of the Swedish Peace Research Institute. Istvan Kende of the Karl Marx University of Economies in Budapest calculates that, as a consequence, approximately 25 million people died. In a number of these wars, the United States participated. For much of this period the United States was employing its military or paramilitary (CIA) forces on an average of once every eighteen months either to bring down an unfriendly government (Mosaddeq's in Iran, 1953; Arbenz's in Guatemala, 1954; Castro's in Cuba, 1961; etc.) or to shore up a friendly one faced with insurrection (Greece, 1948; Lebanon, 1958; Vietnam, 1950–75).

How much of this military activity had to do with access to resources? U.S. military operations in the Middle East are obviously related to an overriding national interest in the oil of the region. The copper companies were in a position to encourage Henry Kissinger's campaign to bring down the Allende government; getting rid of the *Unidad Popular* would secure corporate profits and national control over a strategic metal at one stroke. The long military and paramilitary involvement of the United States in Zaire is a reflection of the fact that the U.S. is far more interested in what is happening under the earth of the Congo than what is happening on it. But other cases are much less clear. At the height of the Vietnam War many in the antiwar movement were convinced that oil was the reason the United States was so determined to keep sinking in the famous quagmire. Only a few observers of the time were astute enough to predict that once the revolutionaries emerged from the jungle they would summon the international oil companies to develop their resources. President Eisenhower once provided ammunition for the exponents of the theory of raw materials determinism as applied to Indo-China by mentioning at a press conference all the important resources the region had. He got a few wrong, but that did not matter. The reality, I concluded in *Intervention and Revolution,* after studying the U.S. interventions from 1947 to 1970, was that bureaucratic momentum, the enthusiasm of anticommunism, and vague geopolitical terrors usually played a far more important role than worry over specific minerals. Indeed, sometimes minerals seem to be mentioned to give a rational veneer to policies whose roots are deeply irrational.

In an age of scarcity, however, resource-grabbing is becoming a much more powerful rationale for military intervention. Whatever the role securing access to minerals might have had in military planning a generation ago, there is no doubt that increased access did follow the commitment of military power. In the Caribbean, in Africa, in the Middle East, and in Asia there has been a dramatic increase in drilling and mining by American firms in the era of the American Responsibility. Thus the increasing dependence of the United States on critical minerals of the Third World has gone hand in hand with increasing military presence in those areas of the world, increased military aid programs, government purchases for the strategic stockpile, and other forms of official intervention on behalf of U.S. firms engaged in extracting, refining, and shipping the foreign minerals on which U.S. prosperity increasingly depends.

In the mid-1960s three historic events occurred that would change the distribution of world power. One was an explosion of foreign investment as the multinational corporations became truly global and assumed domination of a huge share of world production. As a consequence every national economy became to a greater or lesser extent a branch of the integrated world economy. Another was a growing consciousness in the industrial world of a new vulnerability of developed societies because of their increasing dependence on imported minerals and food. Even before the oil shocks of 1973–74 the accelerating demand for energy and the growing dependence of meat-eating societies on imported grain to feed their cattle had made officials in the U.S., Japan, and Western Europe acutely aware of the potential power of other nations to withhold vital resources. Japan's strategy for reducing her extreme vulnerability was to send her businessmen forth to make supply contracts, enter into joint ventures, and build processing plants in far corners of the globe. Instead of the Greater East Asian Co-Prosperity Sphere, which she attempted to create by force in World War II—in the early 1970s only negligible amounts of her imported coal, iron, and copper came from Asia—Japan had followed the strategy of building a complex set of global market arrangements. The U.S. strategy, in contrast, was to develop and to project military power to maintain "stable" regional powers, a diplomatic code word for regimes that welcomed foreign investment and made their natural resources easily available and were prepared to crush internal rebellion and to resist Soviet influence.

The third development was the meteoric rise in world military expenditures. By 1979 the global investment in military systems was approaching $400 billion a year. About a third of this huge sum, which is roughly twice the global investment in public health, is spent in the Third World; the militarization of the underdeveloped countries is proceeding at a faster pace than in the industrialized countries. The United States is by far the world's largest supplier of arms. The Soviet Union is next.

These three developments—increasing integration of the world economy, increasing consciousness of resource scarcity and resource dependence, and increasingly sophisticated use of military systems for maintaining control over resources—produced a new military order for the world. The new order is in some ways a legacy of the old colonial military order, but it is new in striking and important ways. In the colonial system the imperial powers maintained control over the resources of Asia and Africa by stationing their own troops and naval forces in the area. In the new military order, the development of which was accelerated in response to the failure of counterinsurgency warfare in Indo-China, the emphasis is on building up "indigenous forces" with the help of massive amounts of sophisticated military equipment supplied by outside powers.

When President Nixon enunciated his "Nixon Doctrine" in 1969 and called for "Vietnamization" of the Indo-China war, he was accelerating a process already underway. By the mid-1960s it had become clear in the White House that the U.S. could not field a global army big enough to match its global commitments. The involvement of drafted middle-class Americans in foreign wars produced a revulsion against foreign entanglements which U.S. officials feared would revive the isolationism of the 1930s. The solution was to transfer "peacekeeping responsibilities" to regional powers whose task it was to "stabilize" their regions and to support them with arms and advisors. The deputy peacekeeper in South America was Brazil; in Asia, Korea, the Philippines, and Indonesia; in the crucial Persian Gulf, Israel, Iran, and Saudi Arabia; and in Africa, Nigeria. In the Kissinger era South Africa was also seen as a bastion of stability and deserving of discreet support, including some covert military assistance. The Carter Administration did not believe that the white minority governments in southern Africa were good long-term risks, but it felt trapped because South Africa exerts great power by virtue of its control of resources. It has the most advanced technology for making synthetic oil from coal. Certain black African countries depend on it for wheat. South Africa's control of minerals, such as chromite and vanadium becomes more important as the worldwide competitive demand increases.

In the geopolitical world view of the Pentagon, the maintenance of strong local military would yield a number of advantages for the United States. It would produce local military elites who would be loyal to the United States, for the U.S. would provide the arms by which they could maintain themselves in power. The military regimes could be counted on to repress nationalist or radical movements that might be pro-Soviet or might have troublesome ideas about what to do with their resources or what prices to charge for them. Once having ordered billions of dollars worth of hardware, recipients such as Iran would be beholden to the U.S. indefinitely for servicing, technical advice, and modernization. As a bonus, multibillion dollar arms sales to the Persian Gulf would help alleviate the balance of payments crisis caused by the sharp rise of oil imports and oil prices, and provide a steady market for the aerospace industry which from time to time is in delicate health. For the Department of Defense, increasing dependence upon imported resources offered a splendid rationale for an ever-expanding military budget. Here is the statement of the chairman of the Joint Chiefs of Staff, General George Brown, in defense of his 1977 budget:

Africa: Any large scale breach of the peace could destroy capital investment of American firms and interrupt U.S. access to important raw materials such as aluminum, chromium, oil, manganese, tin, tungsten, copper, iron and lead. The rising Black African demand for U.S. military equipment and training offers the United States both political and economic opportunities that should be evaluated as they arise. . . .

Asia: U.S. security interests in this area continue to place a premium on stable, independent governments favorably disposed toward the U.S. from the standpoint of naval operations, trade, access to raw materials, ports and military facilities; and of passage for maritime and airborne commerce, and the denial of political, economic and military advantages to major outside Communist powers.

Latin America: The nations of Latin America are of significant importance to the United States. Their raw materials and industrial potential . . . could become critical for U.S. defense. The importance of Latin America as a market place for U.S. products should not be overlooked. In addition to imports of substantial quantities for raw materials from the United States, such as wheat and coal, the increasing industrialization drive in Latin America is creating new and enlarged opportunities for capital goods. . . .

From such an analysis has sprung the new international military order, a phenomenon as rapid as the rise of the global corporation and, perhaps, equally transforming. Seventy-five Third World countries, most of them very poor, import sophisticated weapons. The U.S. accounts for about 50 percent of this trade and the Soviets about 30 percent. Britain and France each supply between 3 and 5 percent, and China, Canada, Czechoslovakia, and West Germany sell a steady but much smaller supply of lethal technology. The political and psychological dependence on imported weapons in the Third World is truly extraordinary. In 1974, after the price of oil rose and the non-oil-producers suffered a foreign exchange crisis so severe that they had to cut food imports, the poor countries stepped up their orders of military hardware at a faster rate than even the oil-rich countries. Between 1946 and 1975 the United States delivered $40 billion of military aid, most of it for hardware (4,400 fighter planes, 22,000 tanks, hundreds of thousands of jeeps, rifles, and smaller weapons).

The course of the international arms economy has followed that of the nonmilitary economy. The explosion of the weapons trade has been followed by the internationalization of military production. Like cars, shirts, and televisions, tanks, missiles, and aircraft are being manufactured all over the Third World. The 1960s was the decade that established the Global Factory; the 1970s was the decade of the Global Arsenal. The Department of Defense has more than forty coproduction projects under which it assists other nations to become weapons producers in their own right. Private U.S. firms have another seventy-five such projects. Such nations as Argentina, Brazil, Colombia, Egypt, India, Pakistan, Peru, Philippines, Singapore, South Africa, Taiwan, and Venezuela, most of them only a few years ago supplicants for cast-off weapons from the United States, now are significant producers of sophisticated battlefield weapons and some are even exporters.

"When you buy an airplane," as William D. Penreault, a Lockheed official, once put it, "you also buy a supplier and a supply line—in other words, you buy a political partner." Weapons systems are social systems, and the transfer of military technology transforms politics by creating an international military brotherhood. To put it simply, the brotherhood is an uneasy alliance of weapons producers in the developed countries, their home governments, and local military elites in Third World countries. The alliance, as we shall see, is inherently unstable because while the interests of each member appear to be complementary, there are deep contradictions within the brotherhood.

It is not surprising that the international arms economy should resemble the world economy dominated by the global corporations, for the same corporations also control the arms trade and the technology for creating the emerging global arsenal. Of the twenty-five top Pentagon contractors in 1971, thirteen were multinational corporations. Since then the role of multinationals in the arms business has increased. The electronics, aerospace, and, increasingly, the automobile industry are heavily dependent upon foreign and military sales. The internationalization of the industry is well advanced. Boeing owns about 15 percent of the West German firm MBB. United Aircraft and Northrop each own at least a fifth of the West German–Dutch joint enture VFW-Fokker. Lockheed has a fifth of the Italian company Aeronautica Macchi Spa, and Raytheon has 24 percent of another Italian firm. Volkswagen is the largest private shareholder in EMBRAER, Brazil's largest aircraft manufacturer. There has been an explosion of joint ventures for the coproduction of specific weapons systems. Fiat, Alfa-Romeo, and the British Aircraft Corporation have jointly produced military aircraft.

The new international military order is having some profound effects upon the relationship between multinational corporations and their home governments. In essence it is feeding two important trends in which the industrial nations are caught up. One is concentration. Sixteen firms in 1974–75 supplied 75 percent of all U.S. arms exports. (On the list in addition to the aerospace companies were GM, Chrysler, American Motors, and General Electric. The fourth largest arms shipper was Food Machinery Corporation, an example of the contemporary predilection for beating plowshares into swords.) The second trend is the growing symbiosis of large corporations and government. With the decline of government aid, the first thing to be cut in austere times, the role of private corporations in the international arms traffic increases. Governments stop distributing gifts and assume the role of financier to the arms industry. Military sales are heavily regulated and subsidized by the Department of Defense. Contracts for major weapons sales are concluded between the manufacturer and the Pentagon, which negotiates with the purchasing country and functions as bill collector. Since national security issues presumably arise in connection with weapons transfers, there is a strong rationale for tight government control. But since the government acts as guarantor and financier of the weapons sales, it provides substantial assistance to the arms manufacturers. Thus when Iran, after deposing the Shah, canceled some $12 billion worth of undelivered arms purchases, the taxpayer had to compensate the companies for their losses with several hundred millions in termination payments. The Pentagon's interest in landing bigger arms budgets and in keeping its principal suppliers prosperous during the hiatus between major new U.S. weapons programs neatly dovetails with the companies' interest in selling as many weapons as they can to anyone who will buy them.

But there are some basic conflicts. The Department of Defense is interested in diffusing weapons but in holding on to military secrets. The companies under intensifying competition see future profits in the increasing internationalization of the weapons market. Thus forty-six countries are producing advanced weapons systems under licenses granted by multinational corporations. The rationale is economic. Just as shirts can be made cheaper in Korea than in Massachusetts, Northrop F-5 fighters can be made cheaper in Spain than in Connecticut. The drive to make standardized "world" weapons that can be sold globally with the cheapest available labor reflects the intense competition among the aerospace and electronics oligopolies. But the diffusion of weapons technology creates new national security problems. Up to a certain point weapons transfers create conditions of dependency; beyond that point they create independent power and introduce new military actors into the world. Thus Argentina and Chile, armed with weapons from the U.S., have been on the brink of war with each other. There have been more than 100 military coups in the Third World since 1945, most of them in the last fifteen years. Arms sales have fed arms races between Kenya and Uganda, India and Pakistan, and Egypt and Somalia. In Vietnam and in Iran billions of dollars of U.S. military equipment passed into the hands of regimes distinctly less friendly to the U.S. than the one that ordered the weapons.

The international military brotherhood has been an important and often effective instrument for maintaining U.S. influence over societies with vital resources, but increasingly, military investments are yielding diminishing returns. Promoting militarism in the Third World produces side effects that destroy the prospects for balanced development and long-term stability. For a generation or more the U.S. has operated on the fundamental premise that political and military control over foreign societies is essential to obtain access to minerals at favorable prices. Despite their official capitalist ideology the national security managers have deeply distrusted the free market to provide the resources they needed or thought they needed.

2.

Besides creating the international military brotherhood, the United States has used or considered using military power in two other ways to preserve access to resources. One important rationale for the maintenance of "superiority" in nuclear weapons over the Soviet Union for many years and for new missile systems now being planned to match the recent Soviet buildup is that maintaining a world power balance will keep the Soviets from exercising influence in Third World areas of interest to the United States. The vaunted "overkill" capacity of the United States is not designed to make the "rubble bounce," as Churchill put it, but to make the Soviets "behave." Here, too, military power seems to be a wasting asset. Soviet leaders are still cautious in projecting military power far from the continental empire they control, but as the arms race developed they too began to amass naval power, supply proxy armies, and to provide military aid. The U.S. arms buildup has not encouraged Soviet restraint but rather Soviet imitation. Nonetheless, as the following 1978 report of the General Accounting Office makes clear, both direct military aid to resource-producing countries and continued military confrontation with the Soviets to counter their influence remain cornerstones of U.S. policy:

> U.S. interests in Africa, in addition to balancing Soviet influence, are varied. Africa is a continent of vast resources and provides the U.S. with cobalt, manganese, oil, platinum, and other materials. U.S. investment in subSahara Africa in the past two decades has more than quadrupled to 1.5 billion and trade has grown at an even faster rate. . . . The U.S. views the FMS (Foreign Military Sales) program as an important way to further its political and military interests, and FMS will continue to be an important tool in U.S. foreign policy. The U.S. sells to African nations because these nations perceive military threats and because of the U.S. desire to balance growing Soviet influence and to maintain specific

interests, as exemplified in the 5 countries we reviewed. U.S. military
sales to African nations will probably continue, and perhaps increase.

The third and most direct way the military power of one country can
affect the resource policies of another is traditional gunboat diplomacy.
At the height of the 1974 oil crisis Secretary of Defense James R. Schles-
inger hinted that U.S. public opinion might force the government to invade the Middle East and take the oil it needed, and Secretary of State
Henry Kissinger reinforced the threat a year later in an interview with
Business Week. An upbeat feasibility study of a possible armed takeover
of the oil fields of Arabia and the Gulf States arrived on the desks of key
Saudi and Kuwaiti officials. In the intervening years the dependence upon
Middle East oil has become much greater. The U.S. military presence in
the region, particularly the naval base at Diego Garcia, has expanded.
However, the shutdown in 1978 of the Iranian oil flow, on which Israel,
South Africa, and other nonsocialist nations depend, dramatized the reality that politically inspired interruptions in the oil supply can happen and
that the direct use of force, despite the reiteration of the threat by Secretary of Defense Harold Brown, has a marginal role at best in securing
access to oil.

The Shah's massive purchases of military hardware lay idle while the
mobs rioted against him. Neither the tanks nor planes nor the Sixth Fleet
could keep the oil flowing. Indeed, the military hardware became the
hated symbol of foreign intervention that triggered revolutionary passion.
A year earlier in a study entitled "Foreign Energy Sources and Military
Power," two army officers who had worked in the White House, Major
Daniel W. Christman and Major Wesley K. Clark, concluded that "the
use of force was not a feasible alternative to diplomacy [in the 1973
embargo] and will not be directly useful in similar confrontations in the
future." Since 80 percent of Aramco workers are Arabs, the "threat of
sabotage would require a continued presence by sizable American
forces." Christman and Clark correctly observe that "even the support
of the U.S. oil companies affected was highly problematical. U.S. intervention in one area would have left company assets in another area as
hostage." Company interests are in long-term profitability. Since that
interest is better served by siding with the local regimes than with a
temporary force of occupying Marines, the political foundations for successful gunboat diplomacy are missing. "U.S. military force," they conclude, "will be ineffective in coercing petroleum-producing states to
respond to America's wishes." A Congressional Research Service study
by a distinguished retired colonel came to the same general conclusions.

The use of paramilitary force to maintain control over resource-rich regions of the Third World continues, and the results are mixed. In Angola in 1975 the CIA stepped up its covert operations against MPLA, a Marxist guerrilla movement, by funneling increased amounts of money and arms to two rival guerrilla movements, UNITA and FNLA. Angola is rich in oil, diamonds, and other resources, and the MPLA was perceived in Washington as a likely instrument of Soviet expansion. The covert operations failed not only because Congress resisted sending the funds Kissinger wanted, but also because once again the interests of a multinational corporation and the interests of the U.S. Government did not entirely coincide. Since 1968, Gulf Oil Company had been pumping 150,000 barrels a day from offshore wells in the Cabinda region of Angola and paying $500 million a year in royalties. When the MPLA took control of Cabinda they guaranteed the safety of Gulf employees, promised no nationalization, and urged Gulf to keep pumping and to keep making payments. At the height of the covert operation, as John Stockwell, former chief of the Angola Task Force, relates it, Gulf was about to make another payment of $200 million to the MPLA while the CIA working group charged with destroying the MPLA had a total budget of only $31.7 million. At the same time, Boeing wished to deliver two 737s to the Angola national airline, for which it had been paid $30 million, to sell some air buses, and to install a radar system in Luanda, the capital. While the U.S. Government temporarily delayed both transactions, the companies eventually established commercial relations with the revolutionary government. The president of Boeing was recruited to deliver a secret message to the MPLA containing a clumsy threat to use technology as an American weapon:

> The MPLA would do well to heed our advice that no government can plan the reconstruction in postwar Angola without United States and Western help. No government can obtain the technical and financial resources to stimulate economic development without American consent. In fact, the United States would be quite responsive and helpful to a coalition government that was not dependent on the Soviet Union.
>
> The United States Government is prepared to think further about the supply of Boeing Aircraft to Angola and is willing to undertake further discussions depending on the courses of events in Angola.

The MPLA never responded. They were quite aware that corporations control American technology and that their guiding star is not geopolitics but profits. The shady regime in Luanda is still trying to govern despite continuing low-level covert operations conducted against it, and Cuban troops are still guarding the installations of Gulf Oil at Cabinda.

Modern complex societies are not very good at thinking about what they are actually paying for their resources. We have noted this problem in connection with "net energy" deficits, which are becoming increasingly commonplace, i.e., situations where it takes one or more units of energy to produce a unit of energy. A similar paradox presents itself with respect to the use of a complex, internationalized military machine to maintain access to "cheap" foreign resources. Helge Hveem of the International Peace Research Institute in Oslo has looked into the mineral consumption by the U.S. military. While the assessment is difficult, he says, because the information is hard to come by, some reasonably accurate and revealing calculations have been made:

> In terms of *energy consumption,* one source estimates the direct energy consumption of the U.S. military system worldwide to be 2460 trillion Btu's in 1971. In that same year, the "military-related" consumption, that is the energy consumed by those industries which supply the military system with goods and services, was 1870 trillion Btu's (Mow and Ives, 1974). This means that between 4 and 7 percent of the total U.S. consumption of energy by industry and by utilities producing energy, is consumed by the military-related sector. By comparision, the U.S. direct military consumption of petroleum equalled ⅔ of all of Africa's total consumption in 1974. If private and governmental consumption of energy is included in the total, the direct military consumption of energy accounts for some 3 percent of total energy consumption in the United States (early 70s) or 7 percent of total consumption of oil (Westing, 1977). If "direct military" and "military-related" consumption of energy are added, they then would probably account for some *7–8 percent of total energy use in the United States.* For particular end uses, the percentage is much higher. One third of all jet fuel consumed in the United States is reportedly consumed by the military (Sivard, 1974).
>
> As far as *non-fuel minerals and other raw materials* are concerned the military is a particularly important consumer of cobalt and bismuth; it accounts for 13 percent of national U.S. consumption of these minerals. . . . Almost equally high shares have mica sheet (12) and thorium (11 percent) (1973 data). The military-related consumption of some of the economically less important minerals is even higher; thus 42 percent of thallium and 28 percent of germanium consumption in the United States in 1972 was military-related (Hughes et al., 1974).

If one calculated the economic cost and the cost in the very materials the military is supposed to secure, it is quite possible that production of, say, cobalt from stingy domestic deposits would actually be cheaper than Zairian cobalt.

The international economic order dominated by the global corporations has been dependent upon military power, we have seen, to serve many purposes. Military aid and a military presence have been used to secure access to resources. Military sales have been used to balance the domestic economies of the industrial nations and to keep their rates of unemployment down. Perhaps the most important function of military power has been to facilitate a dynamic expansion of economic growth and capital accumulation in certain key Third World countries that have been thoroughly integrated into the international economy—Brazil, South Korea, Philippines, Indonesia, Bolivia, and others. All these countries follow in varying degrees what might be called the Brazilian model—attractive terms for foreign private investment, heavy commitment to high-technology industry and to the "infrastructure" of industrialization (roads, highways, dams, etc.), and, most important, tight control of wages and brutal discipline for the labor force. The model produces high growth rates, highly unequal distribution, and, inevitably, repression. It is not possible to bias the economic system so decisively against workers and those without any economic role at all without substituting systems of terror to perform the function assigned in democratic capitalist societies to the economic lottery—the chance to be rich through hard work and ingenuity. Where there are no economic incentives for a majority of the population, the knout, the truncheon, the electric shocker, and the death squad are the means of assuring social peace.

The United States Government and corporations were quite willing to accept this reality if it were the price for effectively integrating these countries into a global economy. Indeed, U.S.–based corporations in the Philippines and elsewhere have strongly endorsed the most repressive regimes and given them legitimacy and economic support. But when, as we saw in the last chapter, these same regimes launch their own multinational corporations on the world scene, making tractors instead of shirt pockets with the same skilled, underpaid workers, the concern for human rights in boardrooms in New York and Chicago rises. It is beginning to look as if the continued militarization of the Third World could be good for neither General Motors nor America.

Yet the reflex in the business world as elsewhere is to reach for the gun and, when it is not there, to worry. The decline of American power, defined as the capacity to bend other governments to the American will, has hurt business, weakened the dollar, and emboldened the competition. Spokesmen of multinational corporations and banks usually favor the reassertion of U.S. military power; yet, as Edwin van den Bark, senior vice president of Phillips Petroleum, put it, "If we tried to rule the world with an iron fist, I think it would probably hurt business more than it would help." The dilemma is that while the "erosion of American power" is bad for business, increasing the military budget has negative economic effects. Maintaining a big force overseas hurts the U.S. balance of payments, further weakens the dollar, and fuels inflation at home.

3.

The withholding of commodities for political ends works better on paper than in practice. The main reason is that, oil aside, global resource systems are now so complex and so integrated that a truly global consensus is a precondition for exerting commodity power. The closest approximation of such a universal consensus was aroused in the case of Rhodesia. A white minority rebel government repeatedly condemned in the U.N., the former British colony had the misfortune to be less strategic and more vulnerable and hence even more isolated than South Africa. Yet United Nations trade sanctions, which were designed particularly to cut off the country's oil supplies, were systematically violated by multinational oil companies. According to the Center for Social Action of the United Church of Christ, which got hold of incriminating company documents, Mobil Oil's subsidiary in South Africa and in Rhodesia have "helped to plan a decade-long campaign to provide Rhodesia's oil needs." One Mobil document described with the company's customary thoroughness its covert operations for revoking the boycott:

> When orders for lubricants and solvents are placed on our South African associates [i.e., Mobil (South Africa)], a carefully planned "paper chase" is used to disguise the final destination of these products. This is necessary to make sure that there is no link between MOSA [Mobil (South Africa)] and MOSR's [Mobil (Rhodesia)'s] supplies. . . . This "paper-chase" which costs very little to administer, is done primarily to hide the fact that MOSA is in fact supplying MOSR with products in contravention of U.S. Sanctions Regulations. . . .

Thus whether the target of a boycott is Rhodesia or Cuba, the companies that control the strategic resources of the world, being more interested in profits than politics, regularly sabotage the best-laid plans for conducting economic warfare.

If rich countries cannot effectively withhold their resources because minerals and grains are already under the de facto international control of the global corporations, poor countries face a different but more serious problem. Nations that depend upon selling their natural resources for revenue or to pay off debts are in the same weak bargaining position as the workman described by Friedrich Engels. "The Capitalist, if he cannot agree with the Laborer, can afford to wait, and live upon his capital. The workman cannot. He has but wages to live upon, and must therefore take work when, where, and at what terms he can get it. The workman has no fair start. He is fearfully handicapped by hunger." Few countries have the capital reserves to resist selling their products at world market prices. Thus even where spectacular temporary successes for the commodity producers have been achieved, as in the fourfold increase in Moroccan phosphates or Jamaica's new deal in bauxite, the realities of the market have largely wiped out the victory.

What Mahbub ul Haq of the World Bank has called "the emerging trade union of the poor nations" has been able to exercise only marginal power—again oil is an exception—for several reasons. Most of the world's proven mineral reserves are in the rich nations. Poor nations that sit on strategic reserves are vulnerable to a variety of pressures from the rich because they have not figured out how to process and sell their minerals without becoming dependent upon the capital, technology, shipping, and marketing systems of the industrial nations. Buyers have many more options than sellers. Usually there are several alternative sources for strategic minerals. Substitutes, stockpiling, and recycling strategies are available. In most countries governments lack sufficient information about their own resources to control them. Few have the techniques of control even when mines are nominally nationalized, because effective control is in the hands of the suppliers of technology, the multinational companies. Marginal gains in bargaining have been achieved almost everywhere in the last ten years, but taken all together they do not appear to have even slowed the trend toward the further impoverishment of the Third World.

One commodity that has seemed to offer power to those nations with access to ores and the technology to process them is uranium. For some time the United States has been developing an export market for nuclear reactors. The primary incentive in recent years for pushing nuclear reactors in Third World countries has been the rescue of the collapsing U.S. nuclear industry, which can no longer manage to sell reactors in the United States. Four U.S. multinationals—General Electric, Westinghouse, Babcock & Wilcox, and Combustion Engineering—control more than 70 percent of total world orders for nuclear reactors. A powerful argument made in support of the nuclear export program, however, is that since the United States Government has a 95 percent monopoly on uranium enrichment processing, fuel supply could be used as an instrument to keep the new nuclear nations in line. Tied to the United States for the fuel on which their economies would become increasingly dependent, they would not dare to develop their own nuclear weapons capability.

Translating nuclear power into political power for the U.S. has proved a good deal harder than it was once believed. For one thing, the U.S. share of the nuclear export market dropped precipitously in the mid-1970s. Canada, West Germany, and France have been willing to export reactors that are more adaptable to weapons-making than the U.S. light water reactors.

The most avid customers for nuclear reactors outside the industrial world have turned out to be military dictatorships with historic ambitions or historic enemies or both: Brazil, Argentina, Iran, Pakistan, India, Philippines, South Korea. All these countries have plausible reasons for making bombs. India did make a bomb with the aid of the CANDU reactor supplied by Canada, which produces weapons-grade plutonium as a waste product. The Canadian companies are subsidiaries of U.S. companies, and one Canadian authority estimates that 20 to 30 percent of the proceeds of the sale of CANDU reactors goes directly to the U.S. parent companies, but this does not give the U.S. Government power to control proliferation of nuclear weapons. The Shah's nuclear program supplied largely by U.S. companies did not give the U.S. Government much leverage over domestic politics in Iran either.

The export sales are, however, a substantial subsidy to the nuclear industry. By 1976 the U.S. Export-Import Bank had financed fifty out of the sixty nuclear reactor exports with $4.8 billion in direct loans and guarantees at rates about 25 percent lower than commercial terms. The Bank agreed to finance a $1.1 billion Westinghouse reactor in the Philippines by putting up $644 million in loans and guarantees. The case stirred considerable controversy because the proposed reactor is to be located in an area with a long history of earthquakes and tidal waves which is ten miles from an active volcano and twelve miles from a huge ammunitions store at the U.S. Naval Base at Subic Bay.

Of greater long-term consequence to a country such as the Philippines than even a nuclear catastrophe are the development choices associated with nuclear energy. The real political power associated with peaceful nuclear energy is ideological. Lenin once defined the two ingredients of communism as soviets (councils) and electrification. The dream of electrification is one of the most powerful ideologies of the century. Born of the dream was the American all-electric kitchen. So high have utility bills become that increasing numbers of wage earners find themselves working extra hours to support their automatic ovens and freezers. Rural electrification was a New Deal dream and a considerable achievement. Transplanted to the Third World, the image of a million darkened villages suddenly bursting into light like a giant Christmas tree was an inspiration for social reformers and corporate salesmen. The logic was irresistible. Poor countries are poor because of an "energy deficit." They are literally in the dark. Nuclear energy can create enormous flows of electricity overnight. *Ergo,* the atom is the hope of the Third World.

The trouble was of course that neither the economic costs nor the social consequences of creating energy in this particular way were given much thought. Until people began to worry about being irradiated by reactors, no one had any incentive to do anything but celebrate the technological rite of passage through which the advanced nations of the Third World were about to pass. "Agriculture, manufacturing, schools and hospitals as well as every other sector of the economy and all levels of society depend on electric power," Louis Nisenzo of the State Department testified at a 1978 hearing on the Philippine reactor, "and there can be no significant development without it." But as J. Nicanor Perlas III, former consultant on environmental planning to the Philippine Government, points out, the Marcos Government is planning to spend about 37 percent of its entire public investment on electrification, and most of it is to be consumed by industrial exporters of copper, paper, chemicals, and steel. According to Perlas, "only 2.3 percent of total electricity consumption" goes for agriculture, fishing, and forestry, although these employ 54 percent of the work force. Rural electrification has been brought to 20,000 out of 3.5 million hectares of rice land. Despite major emphasis on electrification, only 7 percent of the rural dwellings have electricity. The maldistribution of electric energy and the dependence upon imported technology for electrification reflect political choices.

Like many other Third World countries caught by the ideology of instant electrification through nuclear energy, the Philippines has become an exporter of electricity. In every pound of copper in a Ford car that leaves Manila, there is a significant component of spent electrical energy. Thus the regime is planning to spend $9 billion of mostly borrowed money in the next ten years to develop energy sources the end users of which are affluent consumers in the industrial world and the local rich. If the dream were really to light up every hut—40-watt bulbs could revolutionize village life, and small pumps for irrigation and drinking water could mean years of life and health for billions of people—then the technology choices would be totally different. The emphasis would be on indigenous energy sources. For example, the Philippines have considerable potential in geothermal power, which costs consumers much less than electricity created through imported technology. According to the Philippine National Economic Development Authority, hydroelectric power "is the cheapest and most important source of power in the country." But the financial support for these alternatives, from U.S. aid funds, the Exim-Bank, the World Bank, and the Philippine Government itself, has been modest. The interests of the ailing nuclear industry in the U.S. and the ruling elite in the Philippines coincide. Developmentalism, the ideology of Third World military dictatorships around the world, is a model for the electrification of export platforms and affluent suburbs. Whether the sinews of imported technology are strong enough to tie poor nations to the rich ones in the face of mounting misery and domestic disorder is by no means clear.

Is control over scarce resources the new foundation of political power? Is there a global shift as a result of new patterns of resource discovery and resource use? The answers will emerge over the next two decades. Certain issues have become clearer since the 1973 Energy Crisis. Being endowed with oil is a way of acquiring prestige, the shadow of power if not power itself. Mexico, Nigeria, Saudi Arabia, and Iran have become by virtue of oil and gas alone "regional influentials," as Brzezinski calls them, and recipients of attention and courtesies from the industrial nations not traditionally accorded to the nonwhite and the underdeveloped. Possessing oil affects national style and international perceptions. The vulnerability of the U.S. to oil producers such as Iran and Mexico is leading to what Otto Schoeppler, chairman of Chase Manhattan, Ltd., of London, calls "a parallel decline in standing and prestige of U.S. companies in international markets." Nothing epitomizes "the erosion of American power" more, says S. A. Constance, another American banker in London, "than the spectacle of a Mexican President lecturing the President of the U.S.," as happened when Jimmy Carter visited López Portillo. The accidental distribution of resources opens up the possibilities of radically new alliances and axes in the world—a Western Hemisphere axis based on the mineral wealth of Canada, the oil of Latin America, and the industrial base of the U.S., or a Eurafrican axis based on Europe's technology and Africa's treasure. North-South alliances could fundamentally change the distribution of power on a global scale.

But the ability of individual countries to use their control of commodities to exert power beyond their borders, whether to influence world prices or specific political developments in other countries, is limited; control over individual resources is not easily translatable into political power. The key to power is control over the global systems of distribution through which resources flow. These systems have been integrated into the Global Factory.

PART THREE

THE GLOBAL FACTORY: THE PLANNING OF SCARCITY

CHAPTER IX

Multinational Corporations and the World Employment Crisis

1.

INCREASINGLY, GLOBAL RESOURCE SYSTEMS are being managed by multinational corporations. The mining, melting, refining, and mixing of animal, vegetable, mineral, and human resources into products for sale is an integrated operation on a planetary scale. Viewed from space, the Global Factory suggests a human organism. The brain is housed in steel-and-glass slabs located in or near a few crowded cities—New York, London, Frankfort, Zurich, and Tokyo. The blood is capital, and it is pumped through the system by global banks assisted by a few governments. The financial centers New York, London, Frankfort, and Tokyo, and their fictional extensions in such tax havens as Panama and the Bahamas, function as the heart. The hands are steadily moving to the outer rim of civilization. More and more goods are now made in the poor countries of the southern periphery under direction from the headquarters in the North, and most are destined to be consumed in the industrial heartland with the new postindustrial look.

If the United States and its European competitors have not yet become "nations of hamburger stands," as some labor leaders have charged, there is no doubt that they are producing less of the world product and doing it with relatively fewer hands than even ten years ago. A new division of labor is taking place across the planet, and as a consequence the smoke, sweat, and tears that have always accompanied the process of industrialization are shifting to the new production centers of Asia, Africa, and Latin America.

In this chapter we will look at the new division of labor and its consequences for the control of the resource systems we have been describing.

In the last few years sharply increasing competition among U.S., European, and Japanese multinational corporations has changed the appearance of the Global Factory and as a consequence a process of fundamental recontruction of the world economy is underway. In 1968, Jean-Jacques Servan-Schreiber wrote *The American Challenge,* which warned that U.S.–based corporations in Europe were emerging as the third greatest economic power on earth and that they would dominate the industrial world altogether if something was not done about it.

Something was. As a consequence, ten years later the dominant note in the U.S. business press was "the ebbing of the multinational tide," as *Fortune* put it, or the "Decline of U.S. Power," a *Business Week* designation for the loss of U.S. foreign policy initiative and with it the loss of the competitive edge enjoyed by the U.S. multinationals. What happened was predictable and indeed had been predicted by many students of the multinational phenomenon. First, the European states took counter action once they had perceived the American Challenge. Government-inspired mergers changed the industrial landscape of Europe. In Britain the Industrial Reorganization Corporation blocked merger attempts by General Foods and SKF, a ball-bearing giant originating in Sweden, and created two giants, British Leyland Motor Company and International Computers, Ltd. France concentrated its steel, electronic, chemical, and computer industries as preparation for the counteroffensive of the 1970s. Germany, Italy, and Austria followed suit. In each the ties between government and big corporations grew closer. More recently, the French Government has taken steps to concentrate the textile industry and to restructure further the steel industry. By blessing and financing increased concentration in aging sectors of the economy, French planners hoped to make them more competitive. In the French steel industry the cost of streamlining is 23,000 jobs. In Japan nominally private and nominally public institutions have become so intertwined that only the most sophisticated would even attempt to unravel them. Japan, Inc., as the competitors call it, is now "rationalizing" its steel, aluminum, and shipbuilding industries, which means closing less-efficient plants and facilities and putting thousands of workers out of a job and hundreds of suppliers out of business.

The extraordinary recovery and enviable prosperity of the war-ravaged economies of Western Europe and Japan in the late 1950s and 1960s was built on a massive outflow of exports. Relatively low wage-rates in Europe and especially in Japan and an overvalued dollar made their goods competitive with those of the U.S. in foreign markets, including the huge U.S. market. In the last twenty years the share of the world market held by U.S.–based multinational companies has significantly declined in im-

portant industries. In 1959 an American company was the largest in the
world in 11 out of 13 major industries—aerospace, automotive, chemicals, electrical equipment, food products, general machinery, iron and
steel, metal products, paper, petroleum, pharmaceuticals, textiles, and
commercial banking. These industries make up all but an insignificant
share of the world product that is commercially traded across national
borders, and they are the end users of virtually all the natural resources
we have been discussing.

By 1976 the U.S. companies were dominating only 7 out of the 13. In
each industry the number of U.S. companies appearing among the
world's top 12 corporations declined except in aerospace. Lawrence G.
Franko, formerly of the Harvard Project on Multinational Enterprise, has
additional statistics that confirm what was predicted in our earlier study,
Global Reach: the peculiar worldwide dominance of U.S. corporations in
the first postwar generation would give way to an era in which oligopolies
would carry many flags. Thus of the 156 companies that dominate the 13
industrial groups mentioned, the U.S. controlled only 68 of them in 1976
as compared with 111 in 1959. In chemicals, automotive, primary metals,
metal products, commercial banking, and general machinery, Franko reports, "the number of continental Europe and Japanese companies on the
list of the world's top 12 in each industry equaled or exceeded the number
of U.S. companies in 1976."

Why did it happen? There are a number of plausible explanations. In
Global Reach the phases of the Product Life Cycle were described. Put
briefly, latecomers in marketing products always have a certain advantage
over the pioneers because they do not have to duplicate their development costs. The technology is available to be copied, licensed, or
adapted. In their start-up phases the latecomers have lower wages and
better productivity rates.

Ironically, the nations defeated in World War II had the advantage of
having their old industrial base substantially smashed and of ending up in
the older industries with more modern plants and equipment than the
victors. Then, too, there are special circumstances stemming from national style and tradition which help to explain why the U.S. companies
are losing their lead. Because of the enormous demand of the military and
space industry in the U.S. there has been, according to a recent U.S.
National Science Foundation report, a significant decline since the mid-
1960s in the proportion of the U.S. gross national product invested in
civilian research and development. Privately funded research and development in West Germany, Japan, Switzerland, and Holland take a bigger
share of the national wealth than in the U.S. The rate of innovation for
the civilian market has declined sharply in the U.S. in large part because

so much of our intellectual energy and research money is going into the military. The Europeans and Japanese with economies that are much less energy-intensive can produce resource-saving items more efficiently than can U.S. companies, which have built their global empires with energy-guzzling strategies. In an oil shortage Japanese energy-efficient locomotives or the French-German airbuses become attractive to U.S. customers. Pechiney is gaining a bigger share of the U.S. market because its process for smelting aluminum saves electricity.

Finally, there is the matter of government support. "Our multinationals get no Brownie points from the State Department for getting a piece of the action for the U.S.," says Walter E. Hoadley, executive vice president of Bank of America. Expressing the growing demand of U.S. firms for less "interference" and more "support" from government, he argues that the other industrial countries are developing a concerted strategy with their home-based multinationals for challenging U.S. leadership in world markets. The U.S. Government, on the other hand, does little to help; instead it enacts restrictive legislation—antibribery laws, laws to prevent compliance with Arab boycotts, and trade restrictions to achieve human rights in the Soviet Union—which ties company hands and delivers business to pushier and less high-minded competitors.

There are several things to be said about the matter of government support. When the U.S. was an unchallenged giant, government support was continually exerted in behalf of U.S. firms; American prestige was a blanket. The military might and the banker's role assured proper treatment in most cases for U.S. firms. When that treatment was not accorded, the U.S. Government did act, as in Cuba. But the overriding interest of the U.S. in the first postwar generation was to advance the cause of U.S. business in general, not to help particular firms grab a larger share of the market. (Although, here too, there were huge exceptions. The story of how U.S. foreign aid policies helped to create a European market for the oil companies and a global market for the grain companies has been told.) When the competition from Europe and Japan became more intense, the business-getting, door-opening, company-supporting activities of the Commerce, State, and Defense departments became more obvious. But there is no doubt that the relationship between government and business in the U.S. and elsewhere in the industrial world is different. The competitors are not entangled in that awesome contradiction by which U.S. firms simultaneously condemn government meddling and demand government support. Several of the European multinationals in fact are government corporations. In France, for example, 5 of the 21 top nonbanking companies are owned entirely or in part by government. The European and Japanese tradition of government intervention in economic life, of willingness to experiment with national planning, and of healthy skepticism about letting "rugged individuals" run with the economy—all create a different culture within which the non-American multinationals operate. The competition is posing a direct challenge to basic American myths about what is public and what is private.

As dramatic as the European challenge and Japanese challenge may be, they do not portend either the dethroning of U.S. multinationals or "the ebbing of the multinational tide." U.S. foreign investment continues to grow at 10 to 12 percent a year and by 1977 exceeded $150 billion. Thus, in a decade, according to Commerce Department figures, the investment has doubled, the income from foreign investment has tripled, and the rate of return on capital from abroad is up more than 50 percent. There has been, to be sure, a pruning of U.S. multinationals. Between 1971 and 1975, according to a study by Brent Wilson of the University of Virginia, U.S. multinationals sold off 1,359 overseas subsidiaries, about 10 percent of the total. Most of them had been engaged in low-technology, competitive industries such as textiles, leather goods, and tires. Many of these operations were ill conceived from the start and reflected what James Greene, executive vice president of American Express International Banking Corporation, calls the "aura of phony glamour" of the sixties. "It was immensely flattering for U.S. executives to be courted and dined by the ministers of finance of many developing nations. As a result, some executives were cajoled into making investments that they subsequently had cause to regret."

The high-technology industries where the oligopoly power of the U.S. firms was especially strong did very little divesting in the 1970s but continually added to their international holdings. U.S. foreign investment has thus become increasingly concentrated in the giant companies that can most effectively plan on a global scale and most successfully integrate local operations into a worldwide enterprise. The bigger the company, the greater advantages it can derive. Around the world, GM set out to challenge Ford, which had pioneered the non–U.S. market with a new compact "world car." It could beat out its rivals in adapting to new energy-saving technologies because of its size, power, and access to capital.

One change that is occurring in the operation of U.S. multinationals is a greater willingness to share control over subsidiaries with local investors. U.S. companies used to reject diluting their ownership of local corporations by saying they were not prepared "to take in lodgers." The biggest companies still feel the same way. IBM and Coca-Cola left India rather than accept Indian partners. General Electric refuses to share control of high-technology products such as diesel locomotives and generators, but it will now share control of the technology of toasters. Firms without a special technological lead are increasingly forced to take in local partners, particularly since European and Japanese firms have been much more forthcoming about sharing control. One of the important consequences of the increasing competition among multinationals is that U.S. firms are being forced to adopt some of the approaches which the Japanese and Europeans have used so successfully—strategies of adapting more to local markets and of planning for long-term relationships instead of quick profits.

A good indication of what is happening in the Global Factory is the transformation of the automobile industry. Henry Ford began selling the Model A in Europe in 1903, and GM created an export operation in 1911. But the world market has been invaded by smaller, energy-saving cars and trucks from Europe and Japan. Indeed, in 1977, 18.3 percent of the U.S. market was in the hands of foreign competition. The reaction of the car makers of Detroit has been to spend an estimated $70 billion to equip their factories to compete with the Toyotas, Volkswagens, and Fiats. The object is to produce millions of small standardized vehicles for a global market to recapture for U.S. manufacturers the allegiance of domestic customers and to challenge the European and Japanese compacts in the growing markets of the Third World. The world car will have, according to Donald E. Petersen, vice president of Ford's International Automotive Operations, "common engineering" in its various national guises with minor modifications for local markets. Every other vehicle manufacturer appears to be trying to market a global car too.

The U.S. market is not expected to grow much over the next decade, but U.S. companies are counting on the market in Asia and Latin America to double and the African market to triple. The thirteen European manufacturers and the Japanese are fighting for this potential 15 million car market, which is roughly equal to what the U.S. car market is also expected to be in 1990. To compete more effectively, the Europeans are merging. Peugeot-Citroen took over Chrysler's European operation. Renault, Peugeot, and Volvo have a joint venture to build engines in northern France. Chrysler and Ford are buying aluminum engine parts from Fiat. Ford gets axles from Toyota, Chrysler diesels from Mitsubishi, and GM is arranging to procure transmissions from Japanese partners. Consortiums and mergers are inevitable, according to Lee Iacocca, president of Chrysler. "You're driven into trying to get the economies of scale. . . ."

The more global the market, the more the giants prevail. GM captured 60 percent of the domestic car market in the U.S. because it could beat out its competitors in making the massive investments needed to retool for small, efficient cars. Chrysler is tottering, and there is suspicion in the industry that GM, always reticent about pushing the number three auto-maker too far for fear of antitrust consequences, may be throwing caution to the wind. In a time of fierce global competition the niceties of free enterprise ideology may well be sacrificed to what is perceived as the national interest: consolidating the car business into a giant export machine.

2.

The new division of labor in the Global Factory is made possible by two sorts of technology. The first is the technology for conquering distance—containerized shipping, jet air-cargo carriers, telecommunications systems, etc. The second is the technology for fragmenting the productive process into a variety of component operations that can be performed across the planet at different production sites and then reintegrated into a global product. Breaking the production process down into small components and performing each in far-flung places to take advantage of unique features of different countries is commonplace. The "wafer," which is the heart of the semiconductor, is typically made in the U.S. and then flown to, say, Singapore, where gold threads are soldered to the terminal. The finished semiconductor is then flown back to the U.S. Quantities of leather covers, yarn, thread, and cement made in the U.S. are shipped to Haiti, where local women, at wage rates as low as any in the hemisphere, assemble them into baseballs. The second type of technology embraces new methods of routinizing production through advanced data-processing machines and improved techniques of communications. The purpose of the remarkable geographic spread of production facilities to the underdeveloped countries is to take advantage of an inexhaustible supply of cheap labor. The shift in production is already so advanced that it is now a matter of necessity, not choice, for companies to control labor costs. They can do it either by staying home and automating production or by moving to cheaper labor markets. The usual strategy for large integrated multinational corporations is to do both. The intensified competition among multinationals for shares of the world market is creating ever new incentives to keep labor costs down.

The shift of productive facilities to the Third World appears at first to restore one's faith in the capacity of the market to dispense justice. After all, the historic complaint of poor countries has been that they have been the hewers of wood, carriers of water, and the sellers of bananas while the rich countries have cornered production, which is the real source of wealth in the modern world. If most of the unemployed are in the Third

World, why does it not make sense to locate production there? If the process can be adapted so that those with the simplest skills can be employed, is that not the very definition of humane progress?

To answer the question, one must look at the Global Factory as it is and as it is becoming, not at economic models. The most thorough investigation of production for export facilities in developing countries has been done by the Max Planck Institute in Germany on the basis of information from 103 countries—33 in Asia, 44 in Africa, and 26 in Latin America. It is worth pondering the findings of the investigation. Production in developing countries takes place for the most part in "free production zones." These are enclaves designed to attract foreign capital by offering a range of commercial and financial incentives—exemption from duties and taxes on machinery and raw materials, a five- to ten-year income tax "holiday," freedom from foreign exchange controls, preferential financing, preferential tariffs, furnishing by the local government of factory and office buildings, and a variety of supporting services. In Masan Free Export Zone in South Korea the foreign firm is "treated on the same footing as public utilities in relation to the handling of labor disputes," which is a lawyerly way of saying that there is no right to strike. Mauritius offers a twenty-year tax holiday and advertises that its "wage rates are relatively low for both men and women." The Zona Franca Industrial y Comercial in Palmaseca in Colombia advertises:

> The essential aim of free zones is to make available factory space and other facilities to export manufacturers at a low cost and with a minimum of controls and red tape, so that they will be induced to take advantage of the ample supply of low-cost labor. . . . An ample supply is available, with wages ranging from U.S. $0.13 to U.S. $0.24 per hour actually worked (including legal benefits for unskilled workers). This compares favorably with rates in most Free Zones throughout the world. . . .

The Max Planck Institute study shows a rapid increase in free zones throughout the underdeveloped world as well as in the poor fringe of Europe—Greece, Malta, Yugoslavia, and Ireland. The numbers of employees in the export platforms are considerable, although no one knows how many there are altogether. William Tyler has estimated the number of workers employed in manufacturing for export in Brazil at 412,000, and in 1971 the Trade Development Council put the number of workers in Hong Kong at 677,000.

The crucial and controversial questions raised by the growing reliance of Third World countries on exports to support their economies have to do with the long-term impact of this strategy on their social structure, their chances for development, and the world employment problem. The only requirement imposed by the host country on a firm taking advantage of a free production zone is that it export what it makes there. The attractions are considerable. In addition to providing the tax holidays, some countries, such as South Korea, offer the possibility of a sixty-hour work week, and Chile even offers to subsidize the payment of wages. (In South Korea a seven-day work week is considered a "patriotic act.")

From the point of view of the host country the export platform is a way to export its most plentiful product, labor. To take advantage of it, the electronics companies pioneered the rush to the Far East. Fairchild set up semiconductor assembly plants in Hong Kong in 1962, in Korea in 1966, in Singapore in 1969, and in Okinawa in 1969. In Malaysia, where the pay is less than $2 a day, National Semiconductor, a U.S. company; Teledyne; Siemens; Toshiba; and Plessey of Britain have put up plants. In the Philippines, assembly line workers at Bataan receive $1.50 a day including cost of living allowance. For the same work, according to an American electronics executive quoted in *Far Eastern Economic Review,* the U.S. cost would be $7 an hour.

The product that the export platform countries are selling is not merely cheap labor, but highly productive labor. In Singapore, to which more than 500 companies flocked in the late 1960s, McGraw-Hill produces in one year an encyclopedia that takes five years to produce in the U.S. According to the Max Planck world survey, export platform manufacturing is heavily concentrated in textiles, garments, electronics, metal products, optical equipment, and toys. The world market labor force is largely unskilled or semiskilled, and little opportunity for advancement through training is possible. The U.S. Tariff Commission says that "the productivity of workers in world market factories of U.S. companies in general approximated that of workers of the same job classifications in the U.S." For electronics, the Commission notes, "foreign labor in world market factories required 8 percent more man-hours than the hours required by U.S. workers to assemble such articles as radios, phonographs, television receivers and sub-assemblies and semi-conductors"; but for baseballs, toys, footwear, gloves, photographic equipment, and scientific instruments, foreign labor required 3 percent fewer man-hours than U.S. labor. Donald Baerresen, who has studied the assembly plants on the Mexican border, finds that Mexican metal workers are 40 percent more productive than U.S. workers, electronics workers 10 to 25 percent more productive, and seamstresses complete 30 percent more sewing per hour than their U.S. counterparts. He quotes American managers who told him that the productivity of the Korean workers was 20 to 40 percent higher than the

Mexican workers'. Richard W. Moxon in his study *Offshore Production in the Less Developed Countries* concludes that productivity for the electronics industry in underdeveloped countries is generally higher than in the U.S.

The work force in the free export zones is predominantly young and female. A Japanese textile factory in Malaysia employs 1,900 workers, 80 percent of them women. Women predominate to the same extent in the Korean textile industry. The microcomputer industry, for which the market has exploded in recent years—pocket calculators, video games, automated record-keeping, and advanced weapons circuitry—employs mostly women between the ages of sixteen and twenty-five. Export platforms are selling facile fingers—women are by and large more agile than men—docile dispositions, and perfect eyesight. (20/15 vision is a job requirement in some South Korean factories). The hands become ever more skilled. The dispositions are soothed with continuous rock music, as in National Semiconductor's plant in Penang, Malaysia, and with beauty classes and beauty contests. However, spending the day attaching wires one-tenth of an inch long to tiny chips of silicon takes its toll on eyes. One study in South Korea revealed that after a year 88 percent of the women had chronic conjunctivitis and 44 percent had become nearsighted.

In the textile industry in South Korea there are 300,000 workers, four-fifths of them women. The government-controlled Federation of Korea Trade Unions set up "action squads" in 1978 to settle labor disputes. In one factory the "action squad" accomplished its objective by smearing human excrement on militant workers and arranging for the removal of the local union leadership. Forty-four percent of textile workers in the union earn less than $62 a month. According to *Korea Communique*, there has been a 24.3 percent decline in the real wages of textile workers in the past five years despite the boom in exports. South Korea has received $390 million worth of subsidized cotton under the Food for Peace program most of which ends up in U.S. textile corporations. Vladimir Pregelj, a Library of Congress economist, says that the bargain-price cotton allows for bigger markups than on U.S.–made apparel but does "not result in any price benefits to the consumer."

According to the government-controlled union in South Korea, the minimum wage to lift a single person above the poverty line is $94 a month. Forty-two percent of textile workers in the National Textile Union earn one-third less than the minimum subsistence wage. But wages are rising enough to make less developed countries more attractive export platforms. An unskilled worker in the Bombay free production zone gets $25 a month, fringe benefits and all. In Bataan, the site of the infamous "death march" in World War II, workers in the export processing zone were earning $36 a month in 1975. The Banco Central de Nicaragua advertised its semiskilled workers, who will assemble electronic components for 27 cents an hour. In the La Romana free zone of the Dominican Republic controlled by the U.S. conglomerate Gulf & Western the wage in 1978 was 45 centavos an hour (34 cents at the free market rate). In Mauritius in 1975, unskilled female workers were paid 70 cents per *day*.

Besides low wages, there is freedom from militant unions. AFL–CIO officials have charged that the La Romana zone had the air of a "modern slave-labor camp" with barbed wire, high chain-linked fence, and shotgun-carrying police guards. Officials of the Dominican labor ministry told organizers that they would not be permitted to form a union in the zone despite guarantees in the republic's law. According to Michael Flannery of the Chicago *Sun Times,* who visited the zone in 1978, this is what happened when they tried:

- Many workers sympathetic to the union were fired by a Gulf & Western subsidiary and were immediately jailed by local police.

- Key organizers also were arrested and deported from the province.

- A scheduled union rally twice was foiled, the second time by troops in full combat gear armed with submachine guns who surrounded a theater where it was to be held.

- Members of a G & W–supported motorcycle club, led by a G & W employe, followed union sympathizers through town and identified them to police and plant supervisors. The bikers also threatened to storm a union meeting to break it up.

Not all investment in the free production zones is labor-intensive. In Bataan, Ford built a $39 million body stamping plant that employs only 300 workers. But most of the investment in the free production zones and other export enclaves is designed to employ larger numbers. Not only do they advertise their "attractive" wage rates, but governments also market their cultural traditions. Thus, the Office of the Board of Investment of Thailand notes in its *15 Powerful Reasons Why You Should Invest in Thailand* that "the Thai people are naturally clever with their hands" and that the relationship between employer and employee resembles that of "guardian and ward."

A booming free zone is the Mexican border. More than 450 assembly plants have been located along the 2,000-mile frontier. General Electric, RCA, Rockwell, Samsonite, and many others operate twin factories on each side of the border. Complex operations are performed on the U.S. side. The components are then shipped across the river for final assembly by Mexican workers, who receive a fifth to a third of the U.S. wage rate.

The assembled electrical appliances, calculators, suits, luggage, musical instruments, and furniture are then reshipped to the U.S. for distribution. The only duty to be paid is on the value of the labor added in Mexico. About 83,000 Mexicans are employed in the border operations; 98 percent are under the direction of a U.S. manager.

Chamberlain Manufacturing Co. used to assemble its electronic garage doors in Chicago but it opened a subassembly plant in Nogales and a twin plant in Rio Rico, Arizona, and closed its Chicago factory. The average wage in Mexico is $5 a day and the productivity is higher than it was in Chicago. Samsonite sends its products assembled in Nogales to Denver. The cheaper transportation costs make production in Mexico more attractive than the Far East and the proximity allows for better supervision. "Without the Nogales plant," Lawrence Pugh, president of Samsonite, told *Dun's Review* "we wouldn't be as viable a competitor against foreign goods as we are now."

The rise of the export platform has also given birth to the Third World multinational. Thirty-four of the *Fortune* "overseas 500" companies have their headquarters in underdeveloped countries. Some, like Ford do Brasil, 89 percent of which is in the hands of the Ford Motor Company, are really transplanted U.S. operations. But the Taiwanese steel company building mills in Nigeria, the Filipino beer monopoly that operates breweries in Spain and New Guinea, and the Korean construction companies in the Middle East with more than $4 billion in contracts are primarily the creatures of local capitalists and Third World governments. It is a new development that reflects the absorption of transferred technologies and the unique opportunities companies from small countries have to take markets away from the giants. "We favor investors from small places like Hong Kong," says the trade minister of Sri Lanka, "because nobody can talk about a sell-out to imperialism in the case of a country that is as small or smaller than we are."

There is a certain irony to the new prominence of Third World businessmen on the world scene. When the Hong Kong–based watchmaking firm Stelex bought 29 percent of the Bulova Watch Company, C. P. Wong took over as Bulova's chairman for eighteen months to save the company once run by the war hero General Omar Bradley. Hong Kong and Shanghai Bank bought a controlling interest in Marine Midland Bank. South Korean shipbuilders are taking business away from the Japanese and causing unemployment in Japan. Ghaith R. Pharaon of Saudi Arabia became the President's banker by buying the National Bank of Georgia from Bert Lance. A Chilean company has two subsidiaries in Puerto Rico, and a Bangladesh mattress company is operating in Georgia. The Lucky Group, a South Korean petroleum and electronics conglomerate with the slogan "transforming dreams into reality," did almost $2.5 billion worth of business in 1978. It advertises: "Sorry. We didn't have enough room for "Made in Korea, Japan, USA, Germany, Canada, UK, Switzerland, etc. etc." "In the developing country," says Nam Duck Woo, South Korea's economic planning minister, "government initiative plays the leading role." The model of the aggressive new Third World multinationals is the Japanese trading company, which is seen as a happy blend of public guidance and private enrichment.

3.

There is another way for poor countries to sell labor: they can export workers as migrants. In 1977 the remittances of Indian construction workers from the Middle East was the major factor in improving India's balance of payments. The Shah of Iran's five-year plan called for the importation of 600,000 skilled and semiskilled workers. Out of an estimated 4.5 million population of Saudi Arabia more than a million are migrant workers from North and South Yemen. North Yemen is probably the world's biggest exporter of migrant labor, about 19 percent of the whole population. (Each of the 1,234,000 North Yemeni workers sends home an average of a dollar a day.)

Human beings have always migrated. Until the idea of agriculture and animal husbandry occurred to primitive men about 12,000 years ago, the economy depended upon continuous migration. Hunters, slash and burn cultivators, and nomadic herdsmen moved from one forest and field to another. For much of human history slavery played the crucial role in organizing work, and where it did not exist, various forms of indentured servitude determined the productive life. After slavery was abolished in the nineteenth century the modern form of migrant labor developed. The British and Dutch brought workers from densely populated areas of China, Java, and India to the plantations of Malaya, Sumatra, Burma, Ceylon, and Fiji. The typical contract of indenture called for a three- to five-year contract and a guaranteed return fare, but the migrants were often induced to stay through reinlistment bonuses. There were other resemblances to military service as well, including forms of conscription. In the latter half of the nineteenth century, the population expert Kingsley Davis tells us, "the practice of kidnapping Melanesians to work in Queensland and Fiji was notorious under the name of 'blackbirding,' and the impressment of Chinese coolies for naval duty gave rise to the verb 'shanghai.' " Professor Davis calculates that 16.8 million Indians left India in the nineteenth century as migrant labor, and of them, 4.4 million stayed away permanently. Several millions more Chinese emigrated in the same period.

The United States, as John Kennedy liked to say, is a nation of immigrants. From 1840 to 1930, 52 million Europeans migrated, mostly to North America. They were a crucial form of capital. They were the beneficiaries of high-energy societies; they had been given education and a relatively decent level of nutrition. The waves of immigrants had profited from centuries of development, and it was all a free gift to the new world.

The postwar labor migrations are much closer to the indentured migrations of Asians than to the free migration of Europeans in the last century. For the Europeans in America, there was the prospect of social mobility. (There was also, it should be noted, substantial reemigration. At the turn of the century 30 percent of the Polish immigrants to the U.S., mostly peasants, returned to their village. Some authorities estimate the total of reemigrants from the U.S. to Europe between 1897 and 1918 as high as 47 percent). Each successive wave of immigrants created a new underclass to serve as a floor from which the previous wave could rise. Besides, there was a slave or recently freed black population to do the lowest menial tasks of the society. The postwar migrants for the most part return to their own country, much like most of the nineteenth-century Asians. In the last century few migrants from poor countries who stayed in the countries to which they emigrated—except a small proportion of Chinese merchants and entrepreneurs—ever rose out of the lowest reaches of the service economy. The same appears true with respect to the principal waves of postwar migrant labor—the guest workers in Europe and the Latin Americans in the U.S.

Since the late 1950s about 15 million men and women have migrated to Western Europe as laborers. Most come from the southern fringes of Europe—Turkey, Greece, Portugal, Yugoslavia (the only socialist country that admits unemployment and exports workers), and Algeria. In 1974 there were more than three-quarters of a million Turkish immigrants in West Europe. (The population of Turkey was about 38 million.) More than two-thirds of the migrants are men. At the height of the "guest labor" era one out of every seven manual laborers in Germany and Britain was a migrant, one out of four in France, Switzerland, and Belgium. In East Europe, too, Czechoslovakia has imported Polish migrants because of a scarcity of unskilled labor.

The advantages of inviting guest workers seemed compelling to the governments and employers of West Europe in the late 1950s. The European economy was booming. Native Frenchmen, Germans, English, and Swedes did not flock to the menial, dirty jobs in the sewers, tunnels, abattoirs, factory maintenance crews, kitchens, and road gangs of Europe. The migrants were eager to work overtime, the faster to amass the nest egg with which they could return to their families in the village. From the point of view of the state, migrants were cheap. They paid taxes and social security contributions but would leave before they could collect the benefits. Nothing had been spent on their education. From the point of view of employers they were also a bargain. The wages for legal immigrants were the lowest allowable; for the hundreds of thousands of illegal immigrants any pittance would do, for the alternative was deportation. Most workers fresh from villages were hard-working, politically unsophisticated (unlike French, German, and Italian workers), and driven by a single-minded goal—return to their native land with money in their pocket. The occasional troublemaker could be easily expelled. The presence of millions of low-wage workers on the Continent would, as the German Institute for Economic Research puts it, reduce "the pressure of wages in the Federal Republic . . . due to increased competition by employers for the domestic labor potential." Should the economy stop booming and native workers have no choice but to take the dirty jobs, the guests, it was widely believed, would be shown the door.

But it did not turn out to be quite so easy. With the recession the West European governments decided to stem the tide of guest workers and a million or so were sent home. But perhaps as many as 7 or 8 million remain, and more than 10 percent of them are without documents. So eager is the French Government to reduce the pool of guest workers in a time of rising unemployment that it is offering $5,000 to every migrant, legal or illegal, who agrees to go home. (Only about 7,000 have accepted.) In Germany an employer of illegals can be fined as much as $20,000. The presence of millions of underpaid, illiterate, and diseased workers, many of whom have tuberculosis, is creating ugly social tensions.

In a recession, a study of the International Labor Organization finds, foreign workers are more employable than natives because they are prepared to take the jobs that Germans, French, and Belgians find beneath them. Thus, of 6 million unemployed in the nine countries studied by the ILO only 300,000, or 5 percent, were foreign workers. In response to the oversupply of foreign workers parts of West Berlin have been declared off limits for all foreigners except Americans and citizens of the EEC countries of Western Europe. In Britain, political appeals to racism under the battle cry of ending immigration are splitting the country. Like slavery, forms of indentured servitude leave their traces long after the system has ceased to work.

The flow of human resources is organized as an international business just like the other resource systems. There are recruiters who travel to villages with train tickets and promises of enrichment beyond the dreams of peasants. There are agencies in Istanbul, Athens, and Zagreb which prepare the indenture contracts, recruitment centers with production lines for administering simple tests and medical examinations, and smugglers who for $350 a body will procure Portuguese workers for service in France. (In the early 1970s about 80 percent of migrant workers were illegal and had no papers, although the government favored their presence and usually looked the other way.) Once having arrived at his new workplace the guest may be met by a company representative and taken to his bed in the company barracks. More than half of all migrant workers, according to John Berger and Jean Mohr's moving pictorial study *A Seventh Man,* live in cramped conditions in company housing a few yards from their work. The alternative for many is to patronize other entrepreneurs who work the migrant labor economy, the so-called *marchands de sommeil,* from whom it is possible to rent what Berger calls a nineteenth-century maid's room in which nine men sleep in three beds by working different shifts and each for this convenience parts with about one-tenth of his salary. There are enterprising middlemen who will get an illegal immigrant a job by simply reading the want ads, which the immigrant cannot do—in return for two weeks' wages.

Two principal humanitarian arguments are usually made to justify this modern variant of an ancient practice. One is that emigration reduces unemployment in poor countries, and the other is that commerce in temporary labor is a form of technology transfer. When the workers return they take some of the skills of developed societies with them. The evidence supports neither proposition. Unemployment in the labor-selling countries (with the exception of Yugoslavia) worsened in the years of booming emigration. It is about 23 percent in Turkey. As Berger points out, the migrants are usually the most enterprising, strongest, and most skilled of their generation. The countries that export them have "invested" perhaps $4,000, the cumulative costs of producing a healthy eighteen-year-old in a poor country. To produce a healthy eighteen-year-old in a rich country can cost anywhere from $16,000 to $35,000. Thus, some argue, migrant labor is another form of subsidization of rich countries by poor ones.

As to the technology transfer, what seems to get transferred is not the skills so much as the fantasies of developed societies. A study by Madelaine Trebous for the OECD Development Centre a few years ago of the Algerian returnees suggests that "the vocational training offered to migrants is very limited and the knowledge they acquire is often of little use to them in Algeria." There is not much other empirical evidence to go on, but the widespread impression of observers of labor migration is that returning migrants, because of what has happened to them, are by and large less able to adjust to village life than they once were and have little new to offer. In many cases, of course, the village is gone because without the men who left there was not enough human energy to keep it together. Migrant workers are, without doubt, however, an impressive source of money for the home country. In 1972 the remittances of migrant workers in Germany totaled at least $3 billion.

The U.S. equivalent of the guest worker is the Latin migrant. Most of them come from Mexico, but now increasingly men and women from South and Central America and the Caribbean are pouring across the border in search of jobs. A typical example is a dishwasher at Dominique's, a fancy Washington, D.C., restaurant, who was interviewed in 1978 by the Washington *Post.* He could not support his wife and ten children on the $2 a day he earned in the cotton fields in El Salvador, he explained, so he saved up enough to pay a "coyote" (smuggler) who arranged his passage to Washington. He now earns $460 a month and meals and is able to send $300 a month home to El Salvador. (All told, illegal immigrants, it is estimated, repatriate about $2.5 billion from the U.S. a year.)

A generation ago Mexican migrants stayed near the border. Now they are in Massachusetts, New Hampshire, Kansas, and Washington, D.C. The Commissioner of Immigration and Naturalization predicts that in about fifteen years the Latin population will outnumber the blacks who now make up about 70 percent of the population of the nation's capital. In the 1940s most of the Latins were hired as seasonal agricultural workers in the South; now they are imported with the help of the Texas Labor Commission for work in the mushroom sheds of Pennsylvania and the asparagus fields of New Jersey. No one knows how many of the migrants are "illegals," i.e., without proper papers. It is at least 7 million. Secretary of Labor F. Ray Marshall estimates that between 500,000 and one million "illegals" enter each year.

Federal authorities have on the whole been lenient with employers who make use of this ready supply of cheap labor. "The illegals will do the unpleasant work, the dull work," Harold M. Sherr, president of a San Antonio suit factory explains. But the presence of 7 million of them in a time of chronic unemployment has created political problems because they are competing for jobs and costing cities money for welfare and social services. New York City officials claim that they were short-changed $20 million a year in revenue-sharing funds because they under-estimated their population of illegals by 750,000.

On the other hand, despite these pressures, the reasons why the illegals were welcomed in the first place still hold. Black workers stopped playing their traditional role as a result of changing self-image, increased opportunities for better jobs in the 1960s, and easier access to welfare checks. The aging industries like shoes, textiles, and tanning were looking for cheap and motivated workers as an alternative to going to Taiwan or as a stopgap. (A worker subject to instant deportation is likely to be very accommodating.) Some New York and New Jersey employers, according to William De Chessi, executive vice president of the Amalgamated Clothing and Textile Workers Union, require their illegals to work an extra two hours a day after punching out their time cards. Some California employers, a state official told *Business Week,* eventually turn in their employees anyway just "to avoid paying wages."

In most countries women represent a pool of internal migrant labor. They are habitually used as temporary workers in times of boom and laid off in recession. In the recession of the late 1970s in Europe women were by far the hardest hit. There are 8 million women working in France out of a labor force of 23 million, but women account for more than half of the 1.2 million unemployed. The recent influx of women into the labor market all across the world has been spurred by the development of the technology of mass production. On the assembly line, dexterity and quickness are now more important than brute strength, and thus women, who are almost invariably hired for less, are a more economical form of human energy than men. Since they have less protection from unions— indeed, organized labor in many parts of the world is bent on protecting their male members at the expense of women—they, like all migrants, are the first to be laid off.

Traditionally, women were self-employed, and most still are. But, as the anthropologist June Nash points out, in both developed and underdeveloped societies, the term *self-employed* is somewhat misleading since they could be literally dismissed by their husbands and have no control over income nor much choice with respect to their hours of work. However, in the traditional self-employment role in agriculture, women had more control over family consumption than they do in the money economy. It is now commonplace in underdeveloped countries for families to sell food that they have raised and for the husband to take a disproportionate amount of money to buy cheap consumer goods—a bicycle or a transistor—instead of food needed for the children.

Due to the pressure of men the entry of women into the job market in such places as Mexico, Puerto Rico, and Brazil has been slowed. Indeed, in Puerto Rico the unions, June Nash reports, succeeded in getting the government to offer special incentives to companies that gave at least two-thirds of their jobs to men. In 1875, women constituted 45.5 percent of the labor force in Brazil; by 1970 it was down to 21 percent. Women played a much bigger role in the tin mines of Bolivia up until the 1940s, but a good deal of female labor has been eliminated in the name of progress. Ironically, liberal maternity leaves—in Peru 36 days before delivery and 36 days after the child is born is typical—negotiated by unions hurt the competitive position of women in the job market. The big increase in female employment worldwide appears to be in the clothing industry. Much of the work is done at home on a contract basis. Most modern labor legislation for the protection of employees does not apply. In developed countries the entry into the job market of women who used to stay home has swelled the unemployment statistics. With inflation one family paycheck will no longer do.

Another significant form of labor migration is the "brain drain," a global process by which members of the tiny professional elites in poor countries have been attracted to the life of rich ones. They move from one to the other because they prefer the money, security, culture, climate, and professional challenge that come with living in New York or Paris to the frustrations, hard work, physical insecurity, insects, and shortages in their native land. But often they were the only doctor or accountant for miles around and the consequences are serious. In 1972 the U.S. imported 7,143 physicians, mostly from Third World countries. Filipino doctors have become a politically effective interest group inside the U.S. medical profession. Foreign doctors play a traditional migrant laborer's role, working the county, municipal, and rural hospitals that the graduates of U.S. medical schools avoid.

The dynamics of the brain drain are familiar. Poor countries lack the educational facilities to educate their own professional class. They travel to America or to England and develop new habits and a new consciousness. They do not wish to return to work as salaried employees in the state bureaucracy, particularly since the governments are under a certain pressure to keep the salaries of the elites down to avoid increasing the inequality between the top and bottom in the society. Another stimulus for the export of intelligence from poor countries is the lack of job opportunities for the educated. The growing ranks of unemployed lawyers, managers, and other professional mainstays of business civilization in countries where little of it has yet arrived pose a severe challenge to political stability. Exporting frustrated brains is a good way to relieve some of the pressure.

When a revolution occurs, as in Cuba, or a process of radical reform as in Allende's Chile or, to a lesser degree, in Manley's Jamaica, an accelerated brain drain usually takes place. Doctors, lawyers, accountants, and engineers tend, as a rule, to be immune to revolutionary enthusiasm and protective of their property, i.e., their marketable skills. A few months after Castro took over, only a handful of doctors remained in the country. The outflow of talent is crippling to a country that is trying to mobilize itself for change. In 1952, Marshal Tito traveled through Europe persuading professionals to return to Yugoslavia, promising even to restore their homes and art collections.

4.

There is looming a world employment crisis of horrendous proportions. According to the International Labor Organization every year between now and the year 2000, 36 million people will enter the labor force—a huge increase. Between 1950 and 1975 only 22 million people a year were looking for jobs. About 85 percent of the people seeking employment at the dawn of the new century will be in the Third World—well over one billion men and women. To employ them the Global Factory, the remaining farms, and the growing service economy will have to come up with 120,000 new jobs a day. In order for the Third World countries to provide their share of the 120,000 new jobs a day, the market for what they produce will have to grow dramatically. Third World markets now absorb 30 percent of the manufactured goods of the developed world. Thus, while the poor countries have been gearing up to sell to the rich, the industrial world has been dominating the markets in the poor countries. One out of every six jobs in the U.S. and one out of every three acres are devoted one way or another to exports to poor countries. But the market for most goods is limited. Only a sliver of the population can afford cars, and a slightly larger number are able to buy refrigerators and TVs. In absolute numbers the ranks of the international consumption community have swelled in the last generation. In the "miracle" countries, despite the widening gap between rich and poor, the consuming middle class has mushroomed. But the politics of austerity means that consuming classes in poor countries are growing slowly. Indeed, in Chile under the *junta* the very rich are doing very well indeed, but more people are leaving the middle class than are entering it. The market for consumer goods in the Third World is sure to increase, but without more money in the hands of many more people the market will not be big enough to support a significant addition to the work force. The domestic market will be inadequate to create enough jobs.

The process of industrialization in the Third World is taking place almost automatically. The pace differs greatly from country to country, but the basic social effects are much the same. The subsistence economy in which money was rarely used—small peasants bartered their cotton for a little wheat or some rice for the rare luxury of a pair of shoes from the village cobbler—is being sucked into the international money economy.

By the magic of modern fertilizer, miserable grazing land suddenly becomes valuable. The local landlord takes over the land, either dismissing tenants he no longer needs or simply appropriating the land, to which the poor self-employed farmer may have only a tenuous legal claim, despite having farmed it for years. The migration to the cities and into the modern economy begins. U.N. studies project that such cities as Mexico City, Rio, and São Paulo will double in population by the end of the century. Between 1963 and 1970, just to give one example of a worldwide trend, 750,000 South Koreans (out of an average population in those years of 28 million) left the farm and went to the city, most of them to Seoul. But only a relatively few complete the long march from farm to factory. The Yale economist Gustav Ranis estimates that the rapidly growing industrial sector of the Philippines absorbs less than 10 percent of the total working force.

But statistics tell a less-compelling story of what is happening to the world's work force than do the glimpses of village life and what is happening to it buried in reports of international agencies or in the anecdotes of travelers. I began to understand the process of the disappearing peasant when a friend told me of his conversation with one former shepherd from Pakistan. Bereft of his suddenly valuable land, the man went to Lahore with nothing but the clothes on his back and a hammer in his hand and, as the economists grandly put it, "entered the labor market." What he did in fact was to stand around construction sites and offer to crush bricks with his hammer. When someone took him up on his offer, he received the relatively handsome wage of 11 rupees a day, a little over a dollar, enough to feed himself but not a family. There are millions of stories of this sort all over the Third World. Ten percent of the population of Seoul live in shacks; two-thirds of them, it is estimated, used to be rice farmers. The Women's Unit of the European Commission for Africa reports that as a consequence of similar migrations in Africa there are no longer men to work the fields in some agricultural communities. The traditional division of labor in the family, the traditional integration of work and leisure, and the traditional connections between the family and the larger economy have all been disrupted.

The industrialization of the Third World has destroyed jobs in the countryside without creating anything approaching equivalent opportunities inside the factory. The reason is that modern technology of production is job-displacing. For example, in the Venezuelan oil industry, Norman Girvan has calculated, the labor force was reduced by 33 percent between 1950 and 1966, and in the Dutch Antilles by 70 percent. Dramatic job displacement has taken place in the petrochemicals industry. The labor component, Charles Levinson calculates, is now under 10 percent of total cost. The capital requirements for creating a job in high-technology industry in Colombia more than doubled in the years 1957–66. A smaller percentage of the Latin American work force was employed in the manufacturing sector in 1970 than in 1925 despite the burst of industrialization that had occurred in the intervening years.

Although the problems caused by capital-intensive technology have been widely publicized in recent years and talk of "appropriate technology" has become fashionable, little has been accomplished within the Global Factory to retard these job-destroying trends. Louis Wells of Harvard, on the basis of research conducted in Indonesia, believes that in certain industries labor-intensive technology can provide "more than ten times as many jobs as the capital-intensive plants for the same output." Why then is the basic trend toward capital-intensive industrialization of the Third World continuing?

There are several plausible explanations for what appears on the surface to be a highly irrational policy of relying on scarce capital instead of abundant labor. One is that cost cutting through the employment of cheap labor may not be the primary goal. There is a difference in the behavior of the giant oligopolies that depend upon marketing brand names and that of the smaller firms that make shoes, textiles, etc. The latter compete on price and hence feel a strong pressure to reduce labor costs. Increasingly this is done by combining low-wage labor and automation. In the textile industries employment in the developed countries fell 1.3 percent a year in the 1962–74 period as jobs shifted to low-wage areas. "In Formosa a single female operative on roller skates" can adequately look after 150 looms "producing high quality poplin for the North American market," one textile company reported to its stockholders.

Oligopolies, on the other hand, do not compete on price. They have easier access to credit on the most favorable terms and can pass the increased costs of credit on to the consumer because the consumer has no cheaper source for such needs of modern civilization as oil, packaged food, drugs, household appliances, etc. The oligopolies that are steadily increasing their hold over the Global Factory are primarily interested in control and stability. Expensive machines can make standardized products more reliably than cheap labor, which inevitably poses some serious problems for management. One is that it doesn't always stay cheap. Wage rates in export platform countries have risen in the last few years.

Another is that employing a native labor force involves the uncertainties and complications of human relationships, which well-oiled machines, science fiction to the contrary, rarely present. Thus it may be commonplace for members of a family to share a job, a most untidy practice bound to be disconcerting for modern managers. A corporation can find itself drawn into the net of complex family social arrangements. Since traditional family obligations have not been totally destroyed, corporations are finding themselves subject to essentially feudal demands. If the paycheck goes to support an array of unemployed cousins and uncles and some catastrophe strikes one or more of them, the corporation may be presented with the choice of extending charity or confirming the popular view that, being too foreign, too antiseptic, and too singleminded, it is even more exploitative than the old local landlord. Neither is an enviable situation for managers whose own job depends upon producing a consistent and tidy profit. Therefore, despite the competitive need to keep labor costs down in the short run by increasing payrolls in the Third World, many firms prefer a long-term strategy of increasing reliance on machines with their more predictable cost and more predictable life.

Thus capital-intensive technology is chosen over more appropriate alternatives for what Professor John W. Thomas calls "organizational requirements." Both government bureaucrats and corporate bureaucrats who arrange "technology transfers" are interested more in minimizing risks and uncertainties than in maximizing employment or cutting costs. The corporation has a negative interest in substantially reducing unemployment, because doing so would dissolve the reserve army of jobless who by simply waiting hungrily at the factory door keep wage rates down. The rewards of government bureaucracies are such that a piece of splashy technology such as a big dam is more likely to enhance the career of bureacrats who buy it than a shipment of small pumps. To be on the frontier of technology is a principal source of bureaucratic pride in Jakarta and São Paulo just as it is in the Pentagon or the Bell Laboratories.

But the main reason why labor-intensive policies have not caught on is political. As John Friedman and Flora Sullivan have shown in their study "The Absorption of Labor in the Urban Economy," the labor-intensive sectors of the urban economy include the unemployed, the "street economy" (hawkers, beggars, pickpockets, spies, peddlers, prostitutes) and the family enterprise—small workshops and service establishments that require no formal schooling and little capital. (In Nairobi, an ILO study estimates, the start-up costs for one of these average sixteen dollars.) Government policies, such as access to credit, social legislation, and subsidization choices favor the 3 percent of the population who are managers, owners, and privileged employees in the corporate sector. Professional and managerial personnel, they point out, "are the principal beneficiaries of continued economic growth." The lower two-thirds who are in the labor-intensive economy become progressively poorer because most of the productivity gains are in the corporate sector, and the swelling numbers within the labor-intensive economy insure that any gains for the class as a whole are spread so thin that the average individual member actually loses ground.

A study of the politics of Kenya by Warren F. Ilchman and Norman T.

Uphoff makes it clear why the institution of labor-favoring policies is not taking place. To move in such a direction would, they argue, bankrupt the regime politically. Subsidies would have to go to the labor-intensive sector rather than to the capital-intensive one; worker benefits would have to be extended; taxes would have to be raised; land would have to be redistributed. Neither landlords nor factory owners nor bureaucrats in or out of military uniform have an interest in promoting such policies. Even unions who represent the labor aristocracy are not interested in extending protection to the workers at the bottom, because they fear that their own privileged position might suffer and that incorporating millions of unprotected workers into the labor movement might actually force wages down. "As a general rule, in Kenya and elsewhere, we find that the holders of capital, whether indigenous or foreign, are too well entrenched with the ruling coalition and too linked with a variety of policies to be successfully countervailed."

E. F. Schumacher summed up the prevailing attitudes that keep people in the Third World jobless and hungry in the following true story:

> I was in a developing country not so long ago and was shown around a textile factory—the manager was a European, a very courteous man, and he said he was proud to show me this factory because it was one of the most modern in the world. I said, "Before you go on, can you tell me what's happening outside, because as I came through here there were armed guards there, and you are beleaguered by hundreds and hundreds of Africans." "Oh," he said, "take no notice of that. These are unemployed chaps and they hope that I might sack somebody and give them the job." I said, "Well, as you were saying, you have one of the most modern factories in the world." "Oh, yes," he said, "you couldn't find anything better." "How many people do you employ?" "Five hundred. But it's not running perfectly yet; I am going to get it down to three hundred and fifty." I said, "So there's no hope for those chaps outside?" He replied, "The people demand perfect products and these machines don't make mistakes. My job is to eliminate the human factor." I then asked, "If you make such a perfect product, why are you here in this wretched provincial town and not in the capital city?" He said, "It was that stupid government that forced me to come here." I said, "I wonder why?" He replied, "Because of the unemployment in the provinces."

5.

Can the Global Factory, which is devouring more and more of the world's resources, solve the world employment problem? Many people think so. Economists see the migration of factories to exotic places with

fast-breeding populations and the migration of workers to the construction sites of the Middle East and the laundries of Europe and California
as further proof of the miracle of the marketplace. The orderly processes
of human acquisitiveness operate to smooth out the destabilizing dispari-
ties in wealth on the planet. Eventually the world market will bring a new
global economic balance arising from a reordered global division of labor.
Governments evidently think so too. There is acute competition in Third
World countries to attract foreign investment for local branches of the
Global Factory which will provide not only jobs for the idle population
but also foreign exchange from a steady stream of exported radios, baseballs, wigs, strawberries, steel, ships, and cars. Communities in the U.S.
also vie for the privilege of becoming bases for multinationals. Now
China, once fanatically autarchic, is preparing to welcome a gathering
throng of multinationals, which will help "modernize" the country by
turning parts of it into export platforms.

In the city-states of Singapore and Hong Kong, which do not have a
vast rural population pressing in on them, the free production zones and
the world market factories have played a significant role in reducing unemployment. In the late 1960s, 30 percent of Singapore's labor force was
employed by foreign-owned multinationals. In the early 1970s the share
of the South Korean labor market working for multinationals jumped
from 3 percent to 11 percent. But the worldwide prospects for reducing
unemployment via the Global Factory are not encouraging. As the United
Nations report *Transnational Corporations in World Development* issued
in May 1978 put it, the number of people employed in foreign affiliates of
multinationals is "relatively small." In Asia and Latin America, industrial
growth has not meant a surge in employment; rather, as the new industrial
countries develop, each unit produced requires progressively less labor.

The Max Planck Institute study suggests some reasons why even a
large increase in Third World production sites will not do much for the
employment problems of most poor countries. It cites the "exceptionally
unbalanced employment structure in the free production zones and world
market factories. . . ." and concludes that this sort of employment cannot significantly reduce unemployment among the male population or for
older men and women. A second problem is that employment is not
steady but responds dramatically to shifts in the world economy and to
changes in company strategy. Thus, in the 1974–75 recession 17,000
workers were dismissed from world market factories in Mexico, the Hong
Kong work force dropped 15 percent, and the Singapore work force in
the electronics industry alone was cut by almost 20,000 workers. The
Max Planck study reports that when "the specifically selected labor force
has been used up, production is extended at other industrial sites or is

shifted to other sites where this specific labor force is still available." In other words, employment opportunities at any given site may be temporary either because the firm is prepared to shift production to even cheaper labor areas as wage rates rise or, as in the electronics industry, certain processes once assigned to export platform factories now, because of automation, become more profitable to perform at home.

Another problem is what the Max Planck Institute study calls "inland labor migrations." In a country with high unemployment—about 40 percent of the Filipinos and 55 percent of the Indonesians live in what the World Bank calls "absolute poverty"—the announcement that a factory is opening draws thousands to the vicinity. Here is an example of what typically happens, taken from Mexico, which has an unemployment rate, government officials privately admit, as high as 50 percent. A manager of a certain plant in Ciudad Juarez put an ad in the newspaper for three days. On the first day 2,000 applicants appeared from which 300 were selected for "dexterity tests." Two hundred and eighty scored over 20 on the test—the average score among U.S. workers is between 14 and 16— and from this group the manager hired the 90 workers he needed. But unemployment in the area might have actually increased because the factory attracted from the countryside multitudes it could not begin to employ.

Many Third World economists object to the export platform model of development because the benefits do not spread to the country as a whole. There is very little transfer of technology since control is firmly locked in the firms and they are willing to license it to Third World countries only on terms much less favorable than those that prevail in the industrial world. Multinationals determine the prices they charge in the local market, and they are often exorbitant. By the subterfuge of accounting the firms can repatriate profits even where local law forbids it. The technology is likely to be inappropriate. An example is the U.S. drug industry, which is notorious for shipping drugs outlawed in the U.S. to Third World countries. A development model that encouraged local industry would result in better control over such products and could better tailor what is produced in the country to its particular needs. India, for example, has had a drug industry since 1901, but sixty foreign firms accounted for 70 percent of the market in 1973–74. According to a survey in *Far Eastern Economic Review* they sold tetracycline, which went in the U.S. for $24 to $30 a kilogram, to Indians for $100 to $270 and vitamin C at about four times the price in Britain.

There are discernible reasons why the export platform model of development allows certain poor countries to accumulate industrial power but condemns millions of their people to "absolute poverty." In the year

2000 despite steady economic growth in the Third World, there will be well over one billion people living in such conditions. The reason is that the process of industrialization, as we have seen, destroys self-provisioning agriculture and leaves millions of former small farmers with neither land nor job. The job opportunities in the growing industrial sector cannot keep pace with the rise in population.

There is a third factor. The export platform model of development requires poor countries to go heavily into debt. The external financing requirements for all developing countries in 1985 will be $276 billion in current prices, four times what it was in 1975. Half of it is simply to service past debt and cannot be used to invest in productive facilities that create jobs. The high level of debt and the need to keep "rolling over" the debt as bills become due means that austerity is the rule everywhere. Good bankers, public and private, exact solemn oaths of frugality from debtor governments and sometimes enforce them by moving into their finance ministries to put their affairs in order. Presidents and generals preach austerity when they are told they must, but by and large only poor people have to practice it. Generally, austerity means cutting all social services that can be designated as frills, and that includes a good many public health, education, and nutrition programs as well as public service employment projects. Austerity also requires keeping a lid on wages. Since the high debt fuels inflation, the banker-imposed wage controls mean that the bottom 40 to 60 percent of the population continually lose ground as prices rise. To a greater or lesser extent this pattern is evident in most of the export platform countries.

There is a curious irony in what is happening in the developing countries which was perhaps summed up best by the offhand remark of the former president of Brazil: "Brazil is doing well but the people are not." The growth rate of developing countries as a whole now exceeds that of industrial countries. By the mid-1980s, 64 percent of Third World exports will be manufactured products, up from only 25 percent in 1975. That will mean that the developing countries will account for 13 percent of world exports of manufactured goods. It was about 9 percent in 1978. But the prevailing development model has had perverse effects on income distribution everywhere. Some countries such as Taiwan and South Korea have for peculiar historical reasons had some success with land reform, and, according to World Bank economist Parvez Hasan, the latter has emphasized "extremely employment-intensive growth," with the result that income distribution is somewhat better than in most other nonsocialist Third World countries. Yet even in these dubious showcases of "growth with equity" the share of the lowest 40 percent has declined and, Parvan suggests, is likely to decline even more sharply. Elsewhere, the export platforms with the most impressive growth—Brazil, Mexico, Iran—have exhibited highly inequitable income distribution as the richest 5 percent cream off the dividends of development.

The argument is frequently made that the widening gap between rich and poor in such countries ought not to be a matter of great concern, because in absolute terms the poor are doing better. But it is not so clear. The situation varies greatly. Some extremely poor people huddled in urban slums would not trade places with their rural parents, but some clearly would. They are eating fewer calories and fewer proteins. Where people have exchanged a life of ordered drudgery amid familiar surroundings and community support, for the uncertain existence of a city street hawker, begger, or maid, it is not obvious that they are better off or happier though twice as much money may jangle in their pockets as their grandparents ever saw. In a traditional society where nothing changes, most people accept their place with a certain grace. That the landlord should live in luxury and the tenant farmer in a hovel was as natural as the sunrise. But when the principle of mobility is introduced into a society and envy is stimulated to induce people to work harder and to consume more, the pain of deprivation becomes more intense and gaps begin to matter. In an industrializing world in which the principal activity is getting and spending, more and more people are becoming irrelevant to the productive process, either as producers or consumers. Almost a billion people cannot find enough work at wages adequate to provide food for their families. Every sign suggests that the number will increase dramatically. It is the monumental social problem of the planet, the cause of mass starvation, repression, and crime, petty and cosmic.

CHAPTER X

The Internationalization of Labor: Jobs and the New Economic Order

1.

To UNDERSTAND HOW THE WORLD employment crisis has developed within the Global Factory we need to look at some peculiar characteristics of the industrial process itself. The modern industrial machine operates by means of the purchase and sale of labor as a commodity. Although Aristotle talks of "service for hire" and the purchase and sale of labor has occurred since earliest times, the first substantial class of wage workers did not appear until the fourteenth century in Europe, and the selling of free labor did not become the dominant relationship for the organization of human energy until the development of industrial capitalism at the end of the eighteenth century. Ancient civilizations were largely slave economies. In the age of Pericles, Athens had between 75,000 and 150,000 slaves, about 25 to 35 percent of the population. (Twenty thousand of them worked the silver mines at Laureion.) One of the primary purposes of warfare was to capture slaves. The old Sumerian ideograph for slave, the historian William Linn Westermann tells us, was "male of foreign land." The Romans captured as many as 50,000 of them in a single campaign, and by imperial times, Tenny Frank calculated from inscriptions, at least 80 percent of the Roman population was of slave extraction. Between 1451 and 1870, when slavery was finally abolished in the Western Hemisphere—it took Brazil seven years after Lincoln's Emancipation Proclamation to follow suit—9.6 million slaves had been imported into the slave-using areas of the New World, most of them from Africa. The population specialist Kingsley Davis notes that the figure is probably closer to 11 million, since 10 to 25 percent regularly died during the voyage. The import of captive labor into the Americas, he notes, "transcended any other slave migration in history."

With the coming of industrial capitalism, work, a word used in economics and physics to mean the expenditure of energy, ceased to be organized as servitude and became employment. But it was not only the descendants of slaves and indentured servants who became employees. The independent, self-employed laborers, artisans, and farmers who in the early nineteenth century made up four-fifths of the population, also became employees. By 1870 the "self-employed" constituted a third of the U.S. population; a hundred years later, one-tenth.

Industrial capitalism, which gave birth to mass production, high consumption, and increasingly automated societies, became possible only by organizing human energy in new ways. In his remarkable study of work in the twentieth century, *Labor and Monopoly Capital,* Harry Braverman notes that capitalists cannot buy a given amount of labor as they might, say, buy a given quantity of nails. They buy only labor power, renting time, as it were. How much work hirelings do depends upon many factors. Thus the control of the work process becomes crucial for the control of costs, for the stability of the firm, and for the making of profit. The drive to control the work process has, increasingly, led to an ever greater division of labor, automation, and hierarchical management. All three have phenomenally increased the outpouring of goods and services; all three are responsible for the increasing irrelevance of the world's poor majority to the productive process.

Division of labor is a confusing term because it is often used to describe quite different things. It is common to talk of the organization of global production as a division of labor. Thus manufacturing is mostly concentrated in the Northern Hemisphere but is shifting to the south. The Third World provides a good share of the world's raw materials and so on. Within communities it is obvious that different people do different things and that specialization to some degree is characteristic of all human society. Emile Durkheim rhapsodized about the division of labor in his treatise on the subject, asserting that "the ideal of human fraternity can be realized only in proportion to the progress of the division of labor." But division of labor in factories and offices he called "abnormal forms." Yet it is precisely specialization at the plant level that gives the modern organization of work its distinctive character.

Primitive societies practice a division of labor into crafts, but only modern industrial society divides work within crafts into separate tasks and assigns the tasks to different workers. In 1832, Charles Babbage analyzed the way in which division of labor in the factory could lead to increased productivity and profits.

That the master manufacturer, by dividing the work to be executed into different processes, each requiring different degrees of skill or of force, can purchase exactly that precise quantity of both which is necessary for each process; whereas, if the whole work were executed by one workman, that person must possess sufficient skill to perform the most difficult, and sufficient strength to execute the most laborious, of the operations into which the art is divided.

J. R. Commons, the great Wisconsin economist of two generations ago, gives an example from the meatpacking industry, in which, he says, division of labor has been "ingeniously and microscopically worked out."

The animal has been surveyed and laid off like a map; and the men have been classified in over thirty specialties and twenty rates of pay, from 16 cents to 50 cents an hour. The 50-cent man is restricted to using the knife on the most delicate parts of the hide (floorman) or to using the ax in splitting the backbone (splitter); and wherever a less-skilled man can be slipped in at 18 cents, 18½ cents, 20 cents, 21 cents, 22½ cents, 24 cents, 25 cents, and so on, a place is made for him, and an occupation mapped out. In working on the hide alone there are nine positions, at eight different rates of pay. A 20-cent man pulls off the tail, a 22½-cent man pounds off another part where good leather is not found, and the knife of the 40-cent man cuts a different texture and has a different "feel" from that of the 50-cent man.

In the Global Factory is is now possible to arrange production so that the contemporary equivalent of the "50-cent man" may actually be located 10,000 miles away from the "22-cent man." Technology has made it possible to assign simple tasks such as assembly to low-wage workers in underdeveloped societies while more complex tasks are assigned to relatively skilled workers.

As the production process becomes more complex, the technology of scientific control assumes ever greater importance. Frederick Winslow Taylor, the founder of scientific management, introduced the idea of measuring tasks to determine how long they should take and hence what "a fair day's work" from a worker would be. His famous time and motion studies, while not in good repute in the era of "human engineering," "job enrichment," and other efforts to change the dehumanizing aspects of modern work, have nevertheless been adapted not only to the modern factory but to the automated office. The Systems and Procedures Association of America Guide to Office Clerical Time Standards, which is based on data supplied by some leading corporations and universities, illustrates the minute control over use of time and bodily movement inherent in the modern labor relationship:

Open and close	*Minutes*
File drawer, open and close, no selection	.040
Folder, open or close flaps	.040
Desk drawer, open side drawer of standard desk	.014
Open center drawer	.026
Close side	.015
Close center	.027

Chair activity	
Get up from chair	.033
Sit down in chair	.033
Turn in swivel chair	.009
Move in chair to adjoining desk or file (4 ft. maximum)	.050

Scientific management, according to Taylor, involves "the burden of gathering together all the traditional knowledge which in the past has been possessed by the workmen and then of classifying, tabulating, and reducing this knowledge to rules, laws, and formulae." As Braverman puts it, the labor process is to be rendered independent of craft, tradition, and workers' knowledge. The dehumanization of work on a global scale is a direct consequence of management's monopolization of the conceptual function—"All possible brain work should be removed from the shop and centered in the planning or laying-out department" was the way Taylor put it. The process of control means that the work relationship is reduced to the purchase of muscular twitches.

Contrary to the hopes of forty years ago, mechanization has not increased the skill level of the world labor force as a whole. The skill requirements of managers, engineers, and supervisors have no doubt increased, but the mass of workers across the world have by no means been "upgraded." Through the magic of census statistics the number of "unskilled workers" in the U.S. dropped by almost two-thirds between 1900 and 1970, but the number of "semiskilled" workers has increased dramatically. The U.S. Department of Labor's "Occupational Outlook Handbook" makes it clear that the shift is mostly a matter of nomenclature.

> Semiskilled workers ordinarily receive only brief on-the-job training. Usually they are told exactly what to do and how to do it, and their work is supervised closely. They often repeat the same motions or the same jobs throughout the working day.

> Semiskilled workers do not need to invest many years in learning their jobs. The simplest repetitive and routine semiskilled jobs can be learned in a day and mastered in a few weeks. . . .
>
> . . . New employees starting out in semiskilled jobs are not expected to be highly proficient.

A manpower survey of the New York State Department of Labor, Charles Silberman reports in *Fortune,* reveals "that approximately two-thirds of all the jobs in existence in that state involved such simple skills that they can be—and are—learned in a few days, weeks, or at most months of on-the-job training."

The rationalization process that removes the requirement of skill from workers as well as the opportunity to acquire skill has the effect of enormously expanding the labor market. If it is true, as Braverman concludes, that "even pick and shovel work takes more learning before it can be done to required standards than many assembly or machine-feeding jobs," then the barrier to entry into the job market has been lowered for hundreds of millions of people across the planet. Workers no longer need "capital," i.e., skills, training, long apprenticeship to become eligible for a job in the Global Factory, and they no longer have the chance to acquire them. Workers in Third World countries with an experienced and disciplined work force frequently achieve rates of productivity that exceed that of the U.S. laborers. Workers are thus becoming increasingly interchangeable. One can replace another. That so many offer their labor power to a limited number of employers means that it is a buyer's market. That the buyer can pick and choose the cheapest and most cooperative workers from anywhere in the global labor market means that workers in the U.S. are now in direct competiton with workers in Hong Kong and Singapore.

The Energy Crisis was the time bomb of the 1970s; the world employment crisis is likely to be the time bomb of the 1980s. Unemployment figures are, it should be noted, the world's slipperiest statistics. If oil companies have incentives to understate petroleum reserves, governments have even stronger reason to understate the true extent of what Marx called the reserve army of the unemployed. To say that 40 percent or 50 percent of the population is seeking work for a livable wage and cannot find it is an admission few governments can make for very long. Such an admission would amount to a self-indictment with revolutionary implications, and, understandably, prime ministers, mayors, and industrialists prefer to handle the problem in more traditional ways. One is to understate it by manipulating the definition of unemployment. Thus the hawkers of Kleenex, flowers, and chewing gum that are to be found on the streets of every Third World metropolis are members of the "underemployed," a class that by and large cannot earn enough to buy sufficient calories to support themselves and their families. They do not, however, swell the "unemployment" statistics. So called "seasonal adjustments," the snapshot approach—if you are working at any instant during the period under consideration you are counted as working, no matter how quickly you lose your job—and, most important, the failure to count a few million here and there as members of the work force give the world employment figures, as bad as they look, a rosier glow than they deserve. U.S. labor statistics can be criticized for certain built-in biases, but statistics in most countries of the world are so crude that they amount to no more than official guesses for public consumption. (There are no incentives to exaggerate.)

The employment problem in Third World countries is completely different from that in industrial countries. In the former the average "unemployment" rate, according to the ILO, is 5 percent, lower than in the U.S. The reason it is so low is that only middle-class members of the work force can afford to be unemployed. If you are poor and stop earning *any* income in a poor country, you probably will not survive long enough to be counted. There is no state unemployment insurance, no welfare, only help from your family if you are lucky. Thirty-six percent of workers in the underdeveloped countries fall into the category of "underemployed," which is defined by the ILO as either having a job of "less than normal duration," being of a mind to "accept additional work," or—and this is by far the largest category—having "a job yielding inadequate income."

In industrial countries the causes of unemployment are somewhat different. The population explosion is cyclical, not steady. The effects of the wartime baby boom are receding, and there is now a labor shortage in parts of the industrial world, particularly in certain skills and in certain industries. Industrial countries do not have the huge influx of former farmers looking for jobs in the city, because the farming economy was transformed generations ago. The principal causes of unemployment are structural. It becomes uneconomic to produce certain goods in certain places. Factories move, and the workers are left without jobs. The mobility of capital and the relatively immobility of native labor in industrial societies is a crucial part of the problem because every industrial society is slow to find new jobs for displaced workers. There are sharp differences within the industrial world on what a tolerable unemployment rate is, but, increasingly, the specter of inflation is cooling enthusiasm for traditional expansionary economic policies to create full employment.

Beyond a certain point unemployment constitutes a serious political problem. Statistics that cannot be fudged are interpreted away. Certain numbers have the status of Holy Writ in contemporary society. They tell us whether we are on the road to heaven or to hell. Thus the gross national product must grow and the unemployment rate must not. If each behaves contrary to our optimistic expectations, then either a radical cure or a new diagnosis is called for. Obviously the latter is easier to arrange than the former. And so it is that new theories have been developed to explain why "unemployment numbers have simply looked too high in the 1970's," as *The Wall Street Journal* put it. Essentially, these theories suggest that the big increase in unemployment in the industrial world—Germany's unemployment rate quadrupled in the years 1973–76, France's and Australia's more than doubled, and Japan's almost doubled—have to do less with structural problems of the economy than with the habits and preferences of workers. Laziness subsidized by unemployment insurance, the frivolous entry into the job market of women and teenagers, the welfare program, which discourages work but requires recipients to seek it, are among the explanations for the disturbingly high rates of joblessness of our time widely believed by those with regular paychecks. Theories of unemployment that look anywhere but to the productive process itself are, as James S. Henry of Harvard notes, perennially popular. (In 1936 the *Quarterly Journal of Economics* was putting its money on W. Stanley Jevon's discovery from the 1870s that business cycles are caused by sunspots.)

The profile of the U.S. labor market is almost exactly the reverse of the typical pattern in the Third World. There, the population is disproportionately young. In the U.S., on the other hand, as Richard B. Freeman of the Harvard Institute of Economic Research notes, because of the stable birth rate, there is a predicted "shortage of youth" and an "enormous increase in the number of prime-age workers" left over from the postwar baby boom. Officially, unemployment in the U.S. still hovers at around 6 percent. In certain communities it is much higher. For young blacks it is three to four times the national average, the consequence of racism and its effects, bad education and isolation. Of the 96 million persons in the U.S. work force in 1976 only 15 percent had traditional factory jobs. Almost 50 percent of the work force is female.

The unemployment problem in the U.S. is in large measure a consequence of the restructuring of world industry. The steel industry, for example, has been transformed by the competition from low-wage countries. In 1947 the U.S. produced 60 percent of the world's steel; in 1975, 16 percent. Imported steel has captured 20 percent of the U.S. market. Japan accounts for about one-half of these steel imports, but about 10 percent comes from underdeveloped countries. The eight U.S. firms that produce 95 percent of American steel—the top two, U.S. Steel and Bethlehem, have 40 percent of the output—are in trouble. The companies argue that foreign firms with the connivance of their governments are dumping cheap steel on the American market and that the U.S. Government with its expensive antipollution requirements and U.S. unions with their incessant demands for ever higher wages are killing the industry. But studies by Chase Econometrics Associates indicate that Japanese costs are from $78 to $133 a ton less than U.S. costs. Efficiency, good fortune to develop the industry at the right time, and lower labor costs give Japan the competitive edge, not government subsidies, which amount to about 46 cents a ton, according to a 1977 study by the Federal Trade Commission.

The U.S. steel companies have lagged badly in technological innovation. To derive maximum profit from capital already invested, they delayed such important new approaches as basic oxygen furnaces and continuous casting. The latter process is a way of pouring molten steel directly into slabs. It eliminates half the steps of the hot rolling mills where steel is shaped, saving about 10 to 15 percent of labor power. About 10 percent of the steel produced in the U.S. is made by the new process; in Japan it is more than 35 percent.

The technological backwardness of the U.S. steel industry has opened the door to a major shift of world steel production. Underdeveloped countries have quadrupled their output of steel since 1960, and by the year 2000, it is expected, they will produce 25 percent of the world's capacity and consume about the same proportion. Brazil, with what are probably the largest iron ore reserves in the world, is now the world's eighth largest steel producer. It is a huge consumer of steel, and its production jumped almost 22 percent between 1976 and 1977. Although there is substantial Japanese investment in the Brazilian steel industry, almost 80 percent of steel capacity is under the control of a public company called SIDER-BRAS. Brazil lacks coal for coking furnaces and has been importing a good deal from the U.S., but because of worries over labor unrest and instability in the U.S., the Brazilians are looking to what they regard as more secure long-term sources—South Africa, Poland, and Australia.

The steel industry in poor countries has been financed with foreign investment. Since World War II about $4.5 billion of U.S. foreign aid has gone to develop steel in forty-six countries. According to Congressman Clarence Long, who considers it misplaced generosity, the EximBank is responsible for developing 37 million tons in steelmaking capacity, which competes directly with U.S. producers. Some of these producers are hedging their bets by investing directly in Third World steel companies. Thus, U.S. Steel has interests in Spain, Italy, Nicaragua, and Guatemala, and there are Armco subsidiaries in Brazil, Argentina, Chile, Peru, Mexico, and Venezuela. But investment by U.S. steel companies has been modest in comparison with the Japanese efforts to diversify its supplies and to control its pollution by shifting production abroad. The Japanese Government, one diplomat is quoted in *Latin America Economic Report,* is encouraging "the long-term trend toward developing countries increasingly doing the 'dirty work' of producing semi-finished products from iron ore, which countries like Japan would then import for rerolling."

U.S. companies are fleeing older industrial communities for export platforms or are changing what they make, and the legacy is chronic unemployment in the industrial belt of the Northeast and Midwest. At the same time, other regions are desperate for skilled workers, but labor is not as mobile as capital. One reason why industry is leaving the U.S. is declining productivity. High wages, environmental concerns, taxes for social services, and a number of other factors have produced the entropic growth that seems to be characteristic of mature industrial societies: More and more resources go in and relatively less product comes out. For example, the U.S. now imports more machine tools than it exports, because U.S. industry can no longer compete in Cincinnati and Milwaukee factories. A radial drill that sells for $40,000 if made in the U.S. can be sold from a Taiwan factory for $19,500. So Carleton Machine Tool Company has moved to Taiwan. "It's either that or get out of business," according to Barry Savage, the director of sales and marketing.

Yet because of the devaluation of the dollar and the declining power of U.S. unions, U.S. labor costs are becoming more competitive and foreign firms are increasingly making use of the U.S. labor market. Volkswagen, Michelin, Volvo, and other European giants have been building plants in the U.S. The head of European operations for General Telephone and Electronic says that labor costs at its Huntsville and Albuquerque plants are about the same as at its Milan factory and the productivity of U.S. workers is higher. Foreign firms do not normally locate, however, in the older industrial centers from which U.S. firms have fled.

The modern measure of prosperity is productivity—more output for the same or less input. The United States in a recent year made a poorer record of increased productivity than any other industrial country except Britain and Italy. The reasons vary with the ideological preferences of the analysts—the decline of the work ethic, too many women, too many blacks in the labor force, too much governmental regulation, too much military spending, dehumanizing conditions of the modern factory, too high prices for energy, industrial mismanagement.

Governments of mature capitalist societies face a Hobson's choice. They can expand public payrolls, encourage "disguised unemployment," and adopt protectionist policies to keep unemployment down. Japan, for example, has had a system of lifetime employment that guaranteed about 30 to 40 percent of the population with a job until age fifty-five. In slack periods surplus production-line workers were employed as door to door salesmen for company products or as landscape gardeners in factory beautification campaigns. In other industrial countries with powerful unions, government policy has encouraged industry to keep more people on payrolls than are needed. Had this not been done there would have been many more than 13 million people still out of work in the seven largest capitalist economies in 1978. But the consequence is a loss of productivity and competitive edge in pushing exports, and in recessions "redundant" workers, as they are called, are fired. The Chinese, who created an employment-intensive economy, now also feel pushed in the direction of more "efficient" use of labor. Officials in charge of that billion-person economy say that they have a labor shortage because for many jobs it takes five people to do what one could do in the West and they are interested in modernizing through mass production.

Throughout the industrial world the unemployment problem is being managed in two ways. One is for communities to engage in what amounts to an auction for jobs. A city, region, or country will try to outdo its competitors in crafting an enticing package for any company with jobs to offer. Ford intends to locate a new plant in Europe to produce 750 cars a day. It will cost $450 million, but the company is asking for a cash subsidy to cover 35 percent of that amount plus subsidies for training and other infrastructure costs and relief from duties and local taxes. Belgium, Britain, France, and West Germany all responded, and Austria, eager to capture the 20,000 jobs that the plant and its suppliers might produce, dangled an even bigger package. A 1979 advertisement in *Business Week* for an industrial plant in the north of France promises a "$6,000 grant per job created." Britain recently bribed Hoffman–La Roche into building a vitamin plant with a $140 million subsidy and promised Ford 40 percent of the cost of an engine plant in Wales. Industrial recruiting by local chambers of commerce or similar groups in the U.S. makes use of tax holidays and other concessions. Recruiting has been particularly aggressive in the U.S. South. Ironically, "there are literally scores of companies that have been turned away from southern towns because of their wage rates or union policies," according to an executive of Fantus Company, a Dun & Bradstreet subsidiary that acts as travel agent for corporations on the move. The reason is that the companies' wage rates were too high for local industry long used to paying the bare minimum.

The other way the unemployment problem is being solved in the U.S. is by applying the Doctrine of the Superfluous Worker. When the Employment Act of 1946 was passed, the definition of "full employment" in the U.S. was 3 percent unemployed. Current folklore has it that unless 6 percent of the work force is unemployed the economy will "heat," since the 7 million men and women looking for work and unable to get it are not needed. They have no productive role to play in the economy. They are a welfare problem. In 1973 the federal unemployment insurance system cost taxpayers $4.5 billion. Two years later with the recession the cost had reached $16.8 billion. Well-organized unions have exacted supplemental unemployment benefits for laid-off workers, and these plans now cover about 10 percent of workers in the private sector.

It is fashionable in conservative circles to argue that unemployment benefits reward idleness and so cushion workers from the effects of hunger that they do not diligently search for a job. Even liberal politicians such as former Massachusetts governor Michael Dukakis recommend taxing unemployment benefits to save the state money and to make hunger a little more real for those who have grown accustomed to the weekly unemployment check. A great deal of research has been done on the motivations of workers whom society has designated as temporarily or chronically superfluous. Those with a high investment in a particular job tend to wait to be recalled since they do not wish to lose their seniority rights even though they might find a job elsewhere. The jobs that go begging everywhere—laundry work, dishwashing, short-order cooking —do not attract members of the work force with higher expectations and pleasanter experience. It is true that almost anyone who wants to can get one of those jobs, but the price of introducing the Doctrine of the Superfluous Worker is the decline of the work ethic. Social peace is purchased with unemployment insurance, and because so many receive it, joining the Monday morning line is in no sense felt as a greater disgrace than washing dishes in McDonald's. Quite the opposite.

Thus the U.S. labor market is full of contradictions. It is sometimes suggested that unemployment can be explained by the huge increase in working women who made up 28 percent of the work force in 1947 and 47 percent in 1976. But the economic reasons for women working are at least as important a cause as the women's liberation movement. With inflation and the enormous escalation in consumer expectations on which the economy depends, a double income is necessary for those who aspire to middle-class living. For the lower middle class it is often a matter of family survival. Thus the competition for desirable jobs intensifies.

Because of the footloose character of industry, there may be temporary shortages of good jobs in certain areas. The dramatic shift of industry to the Sun Belt, according to the Labor Department, has produced critical shortages of engineers, welders, and machinists in places such as Birmingham, Huntsville, and Fort Worth. In Sioux Falls, South Dakota, where Litton opened a microwave oven factory, the company had almost 10,000 applicants for 600 assembly line openings, but it could not fill the technical and management jobs from the local community. The U.S. is fated, it seems, to live with a growing labor shortage and growing unemployment simultaneously. The same is true of Japan, where perhaps 750,000 skilled jobs are unfilled and there are perhaps as many as 5 million disguised unemployed. Skilled jobs in regions that attract new industry or revive old industry and "dirty" jobs everywhere are becoming harder to fill throughout the developed world.

In the U.S. the working-age competitors for the manufacturing, managerial, and higher-level service jobs are finding it increasingly difficult to find their niche in the productive economy, because it is changing in ways that are making many of them superfluous. The educational system that provided so many of these jobs in the 1960s is not growing, because the baby boom is over and there are more schoolrooms, campuses, teachers, and deans than students to make use of them. Those who make the enormous investment in graduate education increasingly find that they have prepared themselves for careers that do not exist. The explosion in the helping professions that also occurred in the 1960s—social workers, counselors, medical aids, therapists, etc.—is also leveling off in a time of austerity, for these are services that for the most part are directed to the poor and the "nonproductive." The retooling of the economy to reduce energy requirements could theoretically create many more jobs, as we have seen. But if the strategy depends heavily upon high technology instead of employment-intensive technology, the consequence will be a net loss of jobs. Thus a major attack on energy waste in the U.S. could well involve a reduction in work-related travel. The automobile industry, according to the Motor Vehicle Manufacturers Association, accounts for 26 percent of all retail sales and provides one out of every six jobs in the economy. Thousands of hands that facilitate the daily trip to the office and satisfy the national passion for roaming the highways may no longer be needed.

The Panglosses in the employment business count on technology to come to the rescue. Automation eventually creates more jobs, they say, than it destroys. The passing of the buggy whip and carriage industry opened the way for a much larger automobile industry. Something similar is bound to turn up. But the signs point in the opposite direction. The population explosion has far outstripped the capacity of the Global Factory and its extensions in the service economy to provide enough jobs. Since the U.S. labor market is merely a division of the world labor market, the effects of global oversupply are felt here. The explosion will not stop, mounting evidence suggests, until there are much greater opportunities in the Third World for people to take part in the productive process and to receive a decent wage for doing so.

Moreover, the new technological developments are particularly threatening from an employment standpoint. In the past two generations new technologies displaced workers in agriculture and industry, but at the same time they created a new service economy. Now, however, with factory production lines already heavily automated, the microprocessor threatens to revolutionize the service economy as well. This new technology is eliminating not only thousands of clerks, secretaries, and paper pushers but also highly skilled office positions. A French Government report predicts that microprocessors could cut employment in banking and insurance by 30 percent. A German electronics firm estimates that 40 percent of all office work now done by human beings will be performed by machines in about ten years. Where is the new sector to absorb these superfluous heads and hands? Workers in Britain are attempting to organize against the companies that make the machines in distant export platforms which will eliminate the service bureaucracies at home. But without a political commitment to shaping an economy the very purpose of which is to enable each person to make a creative contribution, it is a losing battle. The "technological imperative" is not a law of nature but it is a law of economics in a market economy, and it can be deflected only by a more powerful political vision.

2.

One approach to the employment crisis everywhere is the government payroll. It is fashionable in the business world to decry this, but there is a close relationship between the rise of the Global Factory and the padding of government payrolls. Increasingly, the state has become the largest employer all over the world. In the United States one out of every six working Americans is employed by local, state, or federal government; when the New Deal took over in 1933 it was about one out of ten. Public sector employment in the U.S. has grown faster than any other, and wages have risen faster—so fast, indeed, that the pay of garbagemen, policemen, and teachers has become one of the big issues of the "taxpayer revolt." If one includes in public sector employment men and women in defense industries, then the figures are even higher. More significantly, the crucial role of public sector employment in controlling the unemployment problem can be seen. The decline in the unemployment rate in the first two years of the Carter Administration was helped considerably by increasing the number of defense-related jobs by 240,000 and launching a new public service job program that picked up 750,000 persons hitherto unemployable in the private sector.

In the United States the public sector operates social service programs, police, military, and the burgeoning regulatory bureaucracies. From time to time it finances or bails out failing private enterprises. The $250 million Lockheed loan guarantee in 1971 is just one celebrated example, the federal effort to rescue Chrysler is another. But except for a few isolated experiments—the TVA is the best known—the Federal Government has shied away from acquiring profitable enterprises. Lemon socialism, as it is called, is the only socialism consistent with rugged individualism; failures can be rescued when it is in the national interest, but profitable enterprises, with a little help in tax subsidies, must stand on their own two feet. At the state level, profitable public enterprise in the United States is more acceptable. There is a state bank in North Dakota. There are a number of municipal power companies that do well. These, too, swell the ranks of the public employees.

In the rest of the world the public sector is even bigger. In socialist states that have abolished private capitalism everybody in some sense is a state employee. In the social democracies of Western Europe the state-controlled sectors of the economy are large and expanding. The Italian economy is 40 percent publicly owned or publicly controlled; in France about one-third is public. In other countries, such as Egypt, which call themselves socialist but encourage private capitalism, the role of the state has increased enormously. In the early 1960s in Egypt in its radical nationalist phase, now mostly passed, the number of bureaucrats jumped 61 percent over four years; their pay increased 215 per cent in the same period. The same trend has taken place in Latin America, not only in Peru, where the military regime for a while talked a socialist rhetoric, but also in Brazil and Argentina, which are avowedly hostile to socialism. In Brazil, Petrobras, the energy monopoly, and other dynamic sectors of the economy are in the hands of the state, and they employ immense bureaucracies, which constitute an important but not well understood social force in the country.

The curious phenomenon that the most stalwart apostles of free enterprise, such as Brazil, Iran under the Shah, and Indonesia, are putting more and more of their economies into the hands of state bureaucrats is actually not hard to explain. Different considerations may be at work in different places. In Egypt, the rise of Nasser-brand socialism with its mushrooming state bureaucracy was the result of failures to attract foreign investment. Brazil, on the other hand, which produced its "miracle" by turning itself into a welcome mat for multinational corporations, has built up its state bureaucracy in reaction to foreign investment. Exactly because foreign corporations play such a dominant role in key sectors of the economy, the state has moved in to take control of others, particularly those of strategic importance, such as energy. In addition, the increasingly successful effort in the more advanced underdeveloped countries to make better deals with the multinationals than in the buccaneer phase of international capitalism now drawing to a close, keeps a considerable number of government bookkeepers, accountants, inspectors, lawyers, letter writers, paper pushers, regulators, and facilitators busy—or, if not busy, at least employed. Selling a disciplined labor force to foreign firms supports another bureaucracy of police, military, and administrators.

For most of the recently freed former colonial lands, state capitalism is the only kind of capitalism there is. Neither a local entrepreneurial class nor a pool of entrepreneurial skills exists. In the process of "nation-building," as it used to be called, the class that identifies with the nation are the state employees. Rich landowners may tolerate the new state if it does not interfere with their holdings; otherwise their heart will follow their treasure into numbered accounts in Zurich banks. (In the more dynamic state capitalist regimes, increasing state control over land is an important part of their strategy.) Most of the population in villages and tribes are barely aware that the new nation exists. Their primary loyalty is to family, tribe, or village. Their only contact with the fatherland may be an occasional visiting expert from the Department of Agriculture or more likely the tax collector. Thus the state bureaucracy and the new entrepreneurs who work for or service the multinationals, take charge of the nation. In most of the Third World the most active and sophisticated pool of bureaucrats are the military. They also have guns, which can be remarkably persuasive in bureaucratic infighting.

What does it mean that the state is becoming the boss all over the world? For one thing, without the rising opportunities for petty bureaucrats in the Third World, there would be more people sleeping on the street than there now are. But the expansion of the bureaucracy, which is inefficient and low in productivity, fuels the cycle of strangulating debt and inflation. This creates pressures to hold wages down, which in turn elicit government repression. In much of the Third World, independent labor unions have disappeared. Brazil, Argentina, and Thailand, just to give a few examples, used to have powerful organizations representing workers. Militant organizing is banned now, as in the Philippines, South Korea, and many other places.

Most governments believe with Calvin Coolidge that there is no right to strike against the public safety, anytime, anywhere, and since they decide when the public safety is involved, they reserve the right to treat labor disputes as insurrections. In the history of the U.S. labor movement, the power of the state was frequently invoked by the owners of capital to keep obstreperous workers in line, but now the state is becoming in most places of the world, and increasingly in the U.S. too, not just arbiter and policeman but principal party in interest. Miners in Rumania, Soviet Union, and Peru and workers in many other places have been periodically persuaded to go back to work by bursts of rifle fire.

State bureaucrats may in a classic Marxist sense have the same class interests as workers in factories or peasants on mechanized farms. They own very little. They have little control over their lives. They are likely to spend more of their day being terrorized by superiors than in exerting power over the long lines of supplicants who come their way. (The pictures of the great state bureaucracies of Tsarist Russia developed so brilliantly in the works of Gogol, Dostoevsky, and Tolstoy shed more light on what is happening to government in the Third World today than most of contemporary political science literature.) But, subjectively, state bureaucrats do not ordinarily identify with workers. In Thailand, for example, the bureaucrats are eager for foreign investment. A private entrepreneurial boom will not only make life in the capital more splendid and more comfortable, but it will increase their power. There will be more to regulate, to inspect, and to service and hence more jobs, more perquisites, and more authority. High wages for workers would reduce all this. The foreign firms would go elsewhere. Hence the bureaucrats oppose workers' demands and support the restriction of unions and the prohibition of strikes, pointing out that the whole idea violates the natural harmony Buddha preached.

3.

The cheapening and growing obsolescence of human labor appears inevitable as the global work force multiplies and the opportunities for employment tighten owing to automation, environmental constraints, and a general slowing of the economy. One factor that could change this is the workers themselves. If they refused to play their assigned role in the Global Factory, that would upset a good many assumptions about where the world is heading.

"Why don't they revolt?" It is a common question asked by visitors from the West when they come face to face with the degradation and slow death of Asian poverty or the brutal realities of life on sugar plantations in Latin America or the tropical infernos in which the assembly of the world's watches, transistors, and calculators increasingly takes place. For the poorest and hungriest the answer seems clear. Those with the greatest reason to become revolutionaries lack the energy and strength to do so. Generations of malnutrition have taken their toll. But what about the better-off wage workers who are not on the edge of starvation? Why has the internationalization of the world economy not given birth to a global proletariat ready to shake off its chains? The political inertness of the urban proletariat in poor countries and the accommodating or even conservative role of the labor movement in rich ones represent ideological setbacks for Marxist theory. The Third World revolutions, notably China's and Vietnam's, were peasant revolutions. The working class in Western Europe and America has been a force for reform but hardly revolution. To argue, as some Marxist writers do, that urban workers in the Third World are revolutionary is to sacrifice reality to theory.

In general, workers in the Third World make up a much less homogeneous class than workers in advanced countries. In part this is true because of differences of language, tradition, and race, but perhaps, even more important, because the typical Third World society in transition to industrialization exhibits more complex relationships. The worker may well see himself as a temporary employee, waiting to amass enough money to go back to his village. There is no single identifiable enemy against which to struggle. Typically, feudal elites remain, but they share power with the so-called "modernizing elites," military officers, bureaucrats, some of whom may appear to workers as allies, not antagonists. As Peter Waterman, formerly of the World Federation of Trade Unions, notes, workers in the modern sector have demands that "may divide them from their unemployed brothers, their peasant fathers, or their petty trader wives."

Personal relationships of dependence and obligation, the legacy of a feudal culture that still persists, conflict with the sort of "working class consciousness" needed for militancy in bargaining or for making revolutionary demands. In Peru, for example, workers are more likely to join regional clubs than labor unions, and in West Africa, village improvement unions are more popular than labor organizations. These societies help migrants, provide loans, give information and fellowship, but do not foster class solidarity, since the organizations may typically include traders, unemployed, civil servants, and even some members of the dominant elites. Then, too, labor unions have split over ideological issues. Membership is low—in Latin America it ranges from generally about 2.7 percent of workers to 34.6 percent. In some places less than 0.4 percent of the total labor force are in unions. Also, as Waterman points out, the commitment among members is much lower than, say, among nineteenth-century British workers, who often gave 5 to 10 percent of their income to the union. (Indian workers in the 1960s were giving one percent.) Nonetheless, the trade union movement in South Yemen, Chile, Cuba, Bolivia, and China have played a significant role in the revolutions that have taken place in these countries since World War II. The oil workers in Iran were a critical force in deposing the Shah.

However, in most of the Third World such unions as do exist are organized or orchestrated by the government. Spies and provocateurs abound and have an understandably dampening effect on labor militancy. Strikes are outlawed by a long list of countries, including such former strongholds of worker organizing as Chile, Argentina, and Brazil. Successful unions such as the Sindicato Unido, a sugar workers union in the Dominican Republic, have been destroyed. Its leaders disappeared and its funds were impounded. Under martial law in the Philippines strikes are illegal and union activities are under tight surveillance. Arrest, torture, and harassment of union leaders is continual. But it is not only the well-known repressive governments that use their power to break strikes. Sugar workers in the All Trinidad Sugar Estate and Factory Workers Trade Union are well organized and have been able to push the wages of sugar workers up to $10 a day. But the government, which runs the sugar industry, used police to try to break a long strike in 1975. They failed, but in Guyana, where there is also a strong union, the government, despite socialist rhetoric, used army personnel and police to break a similar strike.

What about the peasants? Most of the human energy expended in the world is still in the form of sowing, tilling, and reaping by small agricultural producers, who, as Teodore Shanin of the University of Manchester puts it, ''with simple tools and the help of their families produce for their own consumption and for the fulfillment of obligations to the holders of political and economic power.'' The role of the peasant around the world, as we have seen, is steadily being eroded by the advance of the international market economy. But the millions that remain still have a crucial role to play in feeding the rest. If there is one observation about the contemporary world that unites Marxists and non-Marxists, it is that peasants are the most exploited people in the world. Keeping food prices down is government policy everywhere, but especially in countries that are selling a low-wage labor force. Farmers are subsidizing industrial workers around the world. As a result peasants often do not have enough to eat. They must walk miles for drinkable water. Millions work days that make factory workers' hours look like a banker's schedule. At the end of those days they sprawl on the floor of their hut with their wife and the six or seven children—or if they are lucky they all clamber into a single bed, leaving the floor to the sheep. There is neither electric light, toilet, nor ready source of water. Marxists talk of the surplus value that is extracted from this extraordinary labor, which provides the calories to feed the workers who produce the commodities that enrich the capitalists. Non-Marxists, such as Michael Lipton of Sussex University, talk of the "urban bias" that is common to virtually all governments (including some that are believers in Marxism-Leninism), under which the cities are developed at the expense of the countryside and those who live and work in it. Why do peasants who still outnumber everybody else put up with it?

It is a mistake to think that peasants are always passive. The twentieth century has witnessed a series of peasant wars—in Mexico, Russia, China, Vietnam, and elsewhere. In every case, as Eric Wolf has shown in his *Peasant Wars of the Twentieth Century,* some great external event has mobilized the peasants—usually a national rebellion against foreign domination which produced an unnatural, often temporary, alliance of countryside and city. But usually peasants are opponents rather than vehicles of revolutionary change. The repression of peasants in the efforts to "modernize" the agricultural sector from Stalin's war on the "kulaks" to the excesses of the North Vietnamese land reform in the 1950s represent some of the blackest chapters in socialist history. The reasons why peasants are slow to move from the recognition of injustice when it develops, have been analyzed well by Wolf. Peasants, for the most part, work alone. They compete with one another, particularly for scarce credit, so that they are slow to cast their individual lot with their neighbors. They work too long and hard to have the leisure for political plotting. They must respond to the rhythms of nature or they will have nothing to eat. As long as the peasant stays on the land, there are traditional cushions against disaster—rich relatives, the family hoard—but when they move out they face disaster. Then, too, peasant interests, as Wolf point out, "often cross-cut class alignments. . . . A peasant may be at one and the same time owner, renter, sharecropper, laborer for his neighbors and seasonal hand on a nearby plantation. Each different involvement aligns him differently with his fellows and with the outside world."

Drawing on his study of villages John Berger has given us a powerful insight into peasant consciousness. The peasant traditionally thought of his obligation to the landlord or feudal chief as "something which had to be endured before the struggle for survival opened." It was either a natural duty or an inevitable injustice, but it was part of the rhythm of life. The peasant believes, not in the myth of progress, which underlies the modern urban culture and is the spur to political struggle, but in the myth of the Golden Age. "The peasants imagines an unhandicapped life, a life in which he is not forced to produce a surplus before feeding himself and his family, as a primal state of being which existed before the advent of injustice." His dream then is to return to that life.

Obsessed with the challenge of survival, peasants are suspicious of all sorts of innovation, whether it is a new piece of machinery or a new political movement. The farmer's world is beset by continuous and often capricious changes of nature. All this produces an understandable resistance to man-made changes. But despite this culture of survival, as Berger calls it, peasants as a class are in the process of being wiped out anyway. In 1894, Engels predicted that capitalist production would destroy the peasant economy "as a steam engine smashes a wheelbarrow." Now there are no more peasants in Britain except for a few in Scotland and Ireland; in France 150,000 leave the land each year. In the U.S. the tiny fraction of the population that produces food for the rest grows steadily smaller. Throughout the Third World the exodus from the countryside gathers force year by year.

4.

The Global Factory cannot function without a new international economic order. The question is what kind of new order? On August 15, 1971, President Nixon broke the basic rules of the existing order when he unilaterally devalued the dollar, imposed a surcharge on imported goods, and closed the "gold window." Creditors with billions of unwanted dollars could no longer exchange them for gold. The Bretton Woods system that came into being at the end of World War II had broken down. Since then a worldwide struggle has been in process to determine what will take its place.

The old order reflected the preeminent power of the United States and the confidence of its leaders that in a world without borders American multinational corporations would reign supreme. It was a world based on the ideology of liberal trade. Franklin Roosevelt's Secretary of State Cordell Hull had the traditional American gift for making commercial self-interest sound like an international crusade. A tireless foe of protectionism, Hull worked to open up the world for American goods. "When goods move, soldiers don't" was his favorite aphorism. At the Bretton Woods Conference of 1944 were born three institutions to realize the American dream for the postwar world, the International Monetary Fund, the World Bank, and the foundation for an international trade organization that came to be known as GATT. Under the economic order established at Bretton Woods the largest expansion of world trade in history occurred. The rules laid down by the three institutions forced a lowering of trade barriers throughout the capitalist world. The socialist countries refused to join the system, and the Soviet Union set up a rival system, COMECON. The dollar was the world currency, and the job of the World Bank and the International Monetary Fund was to see that Europe and Japan had enough of them to buy American goods.

In the first postwar generation some stunning changes occurred. Europe and Japan recovered and began to earn enormous quantities of dollars for their exports. The problem now was not the lack of dollars in the hands of potential buyers of American goods but the "dollar overhang." The U.S. exported capital in the form of foreign investment, aid, and huge overseas military expenses, and in the process lost most of its gold. More than 100 nations were created out of the old colonial empires, and these too entered the world trading system. They became increasingly dependent, as we have seen, on foreign oil and imported food, but they lacked the dollars to buy them. The International Monetary Fund was not originally intended to solve liquidity problems of nonindustrial countries but to help the industrialized nations to recover. In the 1970s, however, a big increase in loans to Third World countries took place. By 1975 the outstanding debt of the non-oil-producing countries of the Third World was $141 billion.

More than a third of this amount, which is staggering, given the small gross national product of these countries, is supplied by private multinational banks. The exponential growth of foreign operations of U.S. banks is one of the important phenomena of the 1970s. In 1965 there were 11 U.S. banks operating branches overseas. By 1975, 125 banks had 732 branches in 59 countries. Some 40 percent of the profits of the top 5 U.S. banks are derived from overseas. (For Chase Manhattan Bank in 1976 foreign lending operations were the source of 78 percent of its profits.) U.S. Government policy has favored the increasing use of multinational banks rather than public lending institutions to deal with the financial crisis of the developing countries. Bankers are worried about the cumulative debt of the Third World. Zaire's debt is 72 percent of its gross national product; Somalia's indebtedness exceeds its gross national product by a considerable amount. To prevent the possibility of a chain reaction of bank failures due to the default on these large loans, the International Monetary Fund polices domestic economies of debtor nations by imposing austerity measures as a condition of further financing —usually tight money policies, wage controls, import restrictions, reduction of social services, and devaluations of currency. Private banks base their determination of the creditworthiness of poor countries on the IMF seal of approval. Thus the power of the international financial institutions, public and private, is political as well as economic. The poor countries see themselves becoming ever more dependent upon world trade for their basic resources, food and fuel, and for exporting their own natural resources and manufactured goods. The ground rules of world trade produce ever greater inequality because of three basic facts of international life. The industrial nations are in a position to keep the prices of commodities low and manufactured goods high. They are unwilling to give special concessions to Third World countries that would enable them to overcome the inherent inequality that stems from lack of capital, technology, and experience. They refuse to permit the transfer of technology except under terms that perpetuate dependence.

This then is the backdrop for the struggle to reshape the international economy. The principle issue is whether the present system dominated by the industrial countries will be marginally changed to keep pace with the economic and political developments of the 1970s or whether a new order with significantly more political power for the poor countries will be created. The positions put forward by the industrial nations, many of which were developed by the Trilateral Commission, a private group that included President Carter and leading members of his Administration, are designed to preserve the existing order. The New International Economic Order proposals are intended to produce a new balance of power. (Whether the specific proposals would actually accomplish this is another matter.)

At the center of the conflict is the role of the multinational corporation. As the economic writer Jeremiah Novak has shown, there have been two schools of thought ever since World War II about what should be the building blocks of the world political economy—the multinational corporation or the nation-state. That is the core issue in the current debate on the new international economic order. John Maynard Keynes's proposal at Bretton Woods, which was rejected by the United States, was built around a central bank much less subject to American control than the present IMF and World Bank and with far greater resources and he called for a truly international currency instead of the dollar. Nations in need of foreign exchange could get it from the bank in the form of overdrafts. They would not need to attract private capital. Thus they could choose their economic strategy—socialism or capitalism or something in between. They could preserve the option to pursue full employment policies. The system that was adopted instead made the penetration of the multinational corporations into the Third World inevitable, for instead of an ample public source of foreign exchange the only option was private capital. This meant that Third World economies were integrated into a world economy dominated by a few rich countries and lubricated by the multinational firms.

Once this happened, countries lost the power to plan their own economies. Creditors set the limits. To plan a full employment economy became extremely difficult because the conditions imposed by the International Monetary Fund excluded it. Providing a hospitable climate for foreign investment capital has been a condition of receiving short-term assistance for meeting balance of payment deficits, but the spiral of debt and the influx of job-destroying technology that accompanies the arrival of the multinationals vitiate the possibility of making job creation and the alleviation of poverty the national priority.

The Global Factory needs a new set of supranational institutions to keep functioning. Everyone agrees on this. The instability of the industrial world stems in large measure from the failure of traditional fiscal and monetary policy of every nation-state to deal with the new global economy. Because tax laws and the powers of central banks stop at the national frontier, multinational corporations can easily frustrate them. They confound tight money policies by borrowing abroad. They upset currency controls by speculating against the dollar. They undercut the taxing authority by arranging their affairs so as to have their profits show up in Panama or other tax havens. The need to restore some sort of international order is obvious to everyone, including the multinationals. The Trilateral Commission proposals, which represent the point of view of the corporate leaders of the U.S., West Europe, and Japan, from whose ranks the organization is heavily recruited, call for a strengthened IMF to act as a central bank and banker of ''last resort'' and for an international currency.

The poor nations want a greater role for public lending institutions as an alternative to private capital and more controls on multinationals. Above all, they want the voting power to reflect the distribution of world population, not the concentration of the world's wealth. There is an enormous irony, as some Third World economists point out, in the separation of long-term development and short-term balance of payments financing. The World Bank is engaged in a campaign to finance ''basic needs'' in poor countries, loans to help the rural poor, and to provide basic requirements such as clean water and housing. But across the street the International Monetary Fund is imposing conditions that frustrate all such goals.

At the center of the debate is the legitimacy of the corporation and the legitimacy of the state. Both are in trouble. The multinational corporations are the principal planners of the resource systems we have been considering. They are the developers and distributors of energy, the miners and transporters of minerals, the sellers and distributors of food, fertilizer and tractors, the organizers of water use, and the managers of the international labor market. In all these activities they are locked into complex and changing relationships with government—sometimes as adversaries, more often as joint venturers—for, increasingly, governments everywhere, now including China, depend upon the giant corporations for essential resources. In the 1960s the euphoria of corporate spokesmen was stunning; "Working through great corporations that straddle the earth," declared George Ball, chairman of Lehman Brothers International, "men are able for the first time to utilize world resources with an efficiency dictated by the objective logic of profit." For Jacques Maisonrouge of IBM the great case for multinationals is that they use world resources "with a maximum of efficiency and a minimum of waste . . . on a global scale."

But all sorts of evidence has come to light to challenge corporate dogma. The World Bank released a mass of figures that showed that the poor were getting relatively poorer, not richer, in the countries where the multinationals were most active. Price gouging, manipulation of transfer pricing, interference in local politics as evidenced by ITT's celebrated efforts against Allende, bribery of local officials, and growing awareness of the inappropriateness of expensive and complex technology in poor countries—all contributed to the image of the imperial corporation serving its own interests at the expense of every country it touched. Far from being an efficient organizer of world resources, the corporation appeared exceedingly wasteful. Why was the flying of parts around the world to save labor costs and tariff duties "efficient" if it required extravagant use of finite resources more precious than money? Was the massive output of goods from the Global Factory "efficient" if the goods were beyond the reach of most people and did not fill the most basic human needs?

The myth of the market could not withstand even a cursory examination. In the classic economic models, ideal countries known as "A" and "B" would theoretically both gain in exchanges conducted through multinationals. But in the real world of "unequal exchange," there flow all sorts of unhappy economic consequences, such as income inequality, debt, and inflation. The myth of the market presupposes something close to perfect information on both sides, but the corporations have vastly superior knowledge about market conditions around the world, technological developments, resource reserves, and other crucial facts that enable them to buy cheap and to sell dear. The largest purchaser and processor of cocoa in the world, for example, controls 30 to 40 percent of the world market and is the publisher of principal information on future supply and demand. As the economist Gerald Helleiner puts it, "Its advance knowledge of prospects enables it to derive speculative gains in commodity markets and immeasurably strengthens its bargaining capacity. That its forecasts influence the market has been statistically demonstrated."

Finally, the market myth presupposed arm's-length buyers and sellers, but the multinational buys from and sells to its own controlled subsidiaries, and to a great extent the market is bypassed. Thus in 1976 at least 45 percent of total U.S. imports came from overseas firms that were related to the importing firm. The prices are administered by corporate bureaucrats, and the transactions are planned as completely as if the bureaucrats sat in government offices. The difference is the planning criteria. Government bureaucrats take as their guiding star notions of "national interest," strategies for political survival, and, not uncommonly, the condition of their personal portfolios. Corporate bureaucrats think about how to make the firm bigger and more profitable.

But the 1970s was hardly a decade of glory for the nation-state either. Bloody military dictatorships took over presidential palaces throughout the Third World. The "new majority" was far from a tyranny, as Ambassador Daniel P. Moynihan charged at the U.N., since it had little real power, but its spokesmen sometimes talked wildly in public forums, and the poor nations seemed hopelessly divided, authoritarian, and corrupt. Finance ministers from starving African countries would invite World Bank officials to their magnificent homes to dine on truffles and caviar flown in from Paris. The new paternalism of the World Bank, which had dramatically shifted its rhetoric and, to a lesser extent, its lending patterns, emphasized the reactionary role of national sovereignty in poor countries. The local government was the problem, not the solution. To help the people the local elites had to be outwitted, circumvented, or bludgeoned. Why make transfers of capital and technology to poor countries when the only recipients of the largesse will be corrupt officials? Why agree to lower tariffs for Third World goods when the result will be to take from the poor in rich countries (by creating unemployment) to give to the rich in poor countries?

This in essence was the ideological counterattack mounted in the West against the New International Economic Order. It was accompanied by a strategy for dividing the Brazils, Irans, and Koreas from their poorer brothers of the "fourth world" or even the "fifth world." The ideological counterattack was powerful because to a certain extent it was based on fact. It was persuasive to the elites in rich countries because it offered the justification for keeping the present economic order essentially untouched. From the point of view of the world's desperate majority, however, the position of the West was a disaster. The paternalist rhetoric was accompanied by an unyielding position on every important economic issue dividing the rich and the poor nations.

There is no hope of developing economic policies to avoid the world employment crisis unless public authorities have the power to pursue full employment strategies and the power to participate in developing the terms under which they will relate to the world economy. It is simply not true that the more trade there is, the richer everyone becomes. It obviously depends upon terms and conditions of trade. Because of the unique role of the dollar and the unique power of its economy and military machine, the United States was until recently the only nation free to pursue its own national economic policies irrespective of the effects on other nations. Autarchy is neither practical nor desirable. Even a huge country like China cannot stay completely self-reliant forever. But there is a wide variety of terms and conditions on which disparate geographic units can relate to the world economy. The welfare of people who live there can be served only if there is public governance of local resources by officials who derive their legitimacy and authority from the people they serve.

The culture of corruption, which has been used so effectively to discredit the aspirations of the Third World, flourishes in economies still in the shadow of colonialism. The Idi Amins, Bokassas, and Mobutus are put into power and maintained in power by foreign governments and corporations. To expect enlightened and saintly leaders to emerge overnight from 400 years of imperial rule is to hold societies without experience in running their own affairs for hundreds of years to a higher standard than we hold ourselves. The emergence of honest patriotic leaders is indeed the crucial need of developing countries. The industrial nations cannot recruit them, but when they emerge, as they often have, they can support them by creating an international environment in which they can survive.

The restructuring of the world economy to permit the participation of a majority of the world population as producers and consumers involves painful choices. To achieve full employment may require greater protectionism, at least temporarily. For many countries, including the United States, there ought to be a greater emphasis on developing a national market and domestic industry. Keynes understood the importance of national self-reliance. In 1933 he wrote:

> I sympathize therefore with those who minimize rather than maximize economic entanglements between nations. Ideas, knowledge, art, hospitality, travel—these are the things that of their nature should be international. But let goods be homespun whatever it is—and above all, let finance be national.

The rise of the Global Factory has had devastating impacts upon workers in the United States and other industrial countries. There are, according to union estimates, 165,000 unemployed U.S. textile and apparel workers and another 150,000 who are "underemployed." Real wages for industrial workers declined in the U.S. in the mid-1970s. Industrial unions have lost ground. The strike is an increasingly ineffective weapon against multinational firms that can and do shift production abroad in response to militant labor demands. The "world car" is assembled in no single country. Production of components can be switched from factory to factory, a strategy for controlling labor costs and weakening labor's power. The threat of leaving the country is sufficient on occasion to induce unions to take what amounts to wage cuts. Despite organized campaigns to spread unionism in the South, the proportion of U.S. factory workers organized in unions has declined. The ability of unions to organize internationally and to mount transnational operations against the multinationals has not been impressive. Language barriers, lack of money, and preoccupation with pressing problems at home all conspire to keep organized labor from developing a global reach of its own.

The loss of power at the bargaining table leads to a loss of political power. Organized labor barely succeeded in electing a Democratic president pledged to an anti-unemployment policy in 1976. The unions failed to secure the passage of the Labor Law Reform Bill, which might have reversed the erosion of their bargaining power.

In Europe the power of unions grew impressively in the early 1970s, but it crested and declined as the decade ended in recession and mounting inflation. In 1974 the British coal miners had ousted the Conservative Government and negotiated a "social contract" with the Labour Government, which had little in it for employers. The Italian unions were militant. The German unions had negotiated a form of "codetermination" in which workers were sharing in a variety of company decisions, and annual wage increases were up to 17 percent. The Swedes were considering legislation that encouraged worker ownership of companies. But, as the decade ended, the Social Democrats lost power in Britain, Holland, and Sweden and the Communists suffered setbacks in Italy and France. In Japan the trade unions lost ground.

As long as one part of the world labor market can be played off against the rest, the bargaining power of workers everywhere suffers. It is in the interests of U.S. workers, as Walter Reuther used to argue, to join forces with workers in such places as Taiwan or Ireland to press for eventual equalization of wages and working conditions across the world. It is a commendable but utopian goal in the present international order.

In the meantime, the burdens caused by the dramatic shift in world production cannot be allowed to fall on U.S. workers in shoes, textiles, and other industries that can no longer operate profitably in the United States. Protectionism is inefficient since tariffs make goods artificially expensive. It can only be a temporary solution, but it is an essential one. The long-term solution is a restructuring of U.S. industry to make products for which the comparative advantage still resides here—new energy technologies and sophisticated products designed to meet basic needs. Operating across the whole U.S. economy are industries that make noncompetitive, wasteful, or dangerous goods, from tobacco to aircraft carriers. A national commitment to industrial conversion and the research and development to make it possible is, as we have seen, a necessity for achieving substantial energy savings. It is equally indispensable for building a full employment economy and for restoring productivity and competitive power to U.S. industry in a world no longer subject to American control.

Corporations can outplan governments because multinationals have huge advantages in exploiting both space and time. The mandate of government stops at the national frontier, but corporations operate globally. In democracies, governments plan in the full glare of publicity; corporations plan in secret. Corporate executives, in theory, at least, can plan years ahead of governments that are supposed to be regulating them because by and large their leadership has been more stable. Henry Ford II outlasted six postwar Presidents of the U.S.; chief executives come and go at GM and most of the other top corporations by way of a decorous process that must be the envy of both the Kremlin and the Democratic party. But the guiding star by which they plan—capital accumulation through profit maximization—leads to concentration of power without responsibility. The Global Factory creates certain incentives that stimulate production—chiefly, acquisitiveness and competitiveness—but the incentives it kills—caring, frugality, and concern about social consequences—are the ones needed for global survival.

CHAPTER XI

The Politics of Survival

1.

THE NEW IDEOLOGIES of scarcity are indebted to the dismal teachings of Malthus and Ricardo, but they embrace two insights from our own time that have completely transformed contemporary judgments about the sufficiency of resources. One is customarily expressed in a cliché of the 1950s, "the revolution of rising expectations"; the other in the inevitable 1970s word *interdependence*.

Malthus said that demand for resources would exceed supply because of the population explosion. Contemporary ideologues of scarcity are Malthusians, but the problem, as they see it, is worse than Malthus predicted. It is not only that the absolute numbers of mouths to feed multiplies, but that certain mouths that used to be content with a little now demand more. Consumption increases because ever-increasing numbers of people make ever-increasing demands for forms of development that take ever greater quantities of natural resources. Millions of people in the former colonial appendages who had no role whatever in the global distribution of resources now demand a role, or, more accurately, politicians and generals of the Third World demand such a role in their name. Put simply, the rich now face the prospect of scarcity because the poor are demanding a different division of the pie.

Interdependence, a favorite word of recent years which means that everything is related to everything else and in some way is limited thereby, is defining a new reality, both physical and political. Interdependence in the days of John F. Kennedy used to mean, as the President once put it, "the burden will be completely on us"; the American debt to the rest of the world was barely acknowledged. Dependency ran one way only. But in the 1970s the steep rise in cost of imported oil, the growing dependency on imported minerals, and the enormous importance of foreign markets to the U.S. economy dramatized how crucially dependent the U.S. has become upon the rest of the world.

The rediscovery of biological dependence was even more unsettling. After 400 years of illusions of God-like power, man had learned enough about the natural environment to realize that he was a creature. Every increase in wealth carried with it ecological costs. Industrial pollution killed a certain but unknown number of human beings every year. The timber of the Amazon that seemed there for the taking was in fact a snare; massive deforestation in Brazil would deplete the oxygen supply and even threatens to crack the Arctic ice cap and bring ruinous floods to the hemisphere. Human beings everywhere are part of interconnected ecosystems in which changes in one part are transmitted to the whole.

Thus, officials at the Three Mile Island nuclear plant liked to point out after the famous accident in 1979 that the radiation levels in Harrisburg after an atmospheric explosion of a nuclear bomb in China the year before were almost fifty times higher than after the local leak. Increasingly sophisticated technology seemed to be leading not to orderly growth but to an inevitable tyranny of disorder. One technical solution gave rise to three new technical problems. Cost now became the limiting factor in fulfilling the dream of abundance. Even when the economic limits to growth were overcome, social limits intervened. Automobiles with engines capable of reaching speeds of 90 miles an hour crept bumper to bumper along the Los Angeles freeways at 12 miles an hour. Social institutions seemed to follow the same laws of entropy as physical organisms.

It is ironical that the rediscovery of limits coincides with two of the most audacious technological feats in human history. One is genetic engineering, the sudden glimpse of a power to shape the very stuff of life. The other is the colonization of space. These breakthroughs encourage new fantasies of power, but they do not break the ecological straitjacket known as the Second Law of Thermodynamics: Ever greater consumption of energy produces ever greater quantities of heat which never disappear but must be counted as a permanent energy cost. Since accumulation of heat can cause ecological catastrophe, these costs limit man's adventure in space as surely as on earth. Under the banner of "grow or die" industrial capitalism produced a highly complex civilization, but the drive to accumulate now threatens to destroy society. Clearly, human survival requires new ways of thinking and a new sorting of values.

From different perceptions of scarcity flow different political prescriptions. At the root of the global struggle for resources is the primal fear Lyndon Johnson expressed to the troops in Vietnam: "There are three billion people in the world. They want what we have." The specter of the hungry mob supports Hobbesian politics, a world of struggle over inadequate resources that cries out for Leviathan, the authoritarian state that can keep minimal order. The Malthusian fantasy offers an alternative to the Leviathan state. There is no need for a civil authority to regulate scarce goods, because Nature, cruel only to be kind, periodically thins the surplus population by famine.

Thomas Robert Malthus, a mathematician who took the cloth, concocted his famous theories by mixing biology and arithmetic. "Fixed laws of nature" decreed that human beings, because of their sinful appetites, would reproduce faster than their food supply and would fall prey to famine, "the most dreadful resource of nature." His notions of biological determinism were an antidote to the unbounded optimism of the eighteenth-century rationalists. Godwin and Condorcet, for example attributed the misery of the world to human institutions and looked forward to a day when "there will be no war, no crimes, no administration of justice, as it is called, and no government." The rationalists promoted the unsettling idea that private property had something to do with human unhappiness, and Malthus was most eager to demonstrate instead that poverty was part of the divine order. Tinkering with human institutions would not eliminate it, and the clumsy efforts of the tenderhearted would imperil the whole human race. To raise the wages of the poor was sheer idiocy, for every man thinking himself rich would "indulge himself in many hours or days of leisure . . . and in a short time not only the nation would be poorer, but the lower classes themselves would be much more distressed than when they received only eighteen pence a day."

2.

How little ideas of economic scarcity have changed! Malthus borrowed most of his from Richard Cantillon, an Irish currency speculator who inspired the Physiocrats, and from Adam Smith, who himself vacillated between celebration of abundance through pure capitalism and worry over the proclivities of monopolists for marketing scarcity. Plato and the ancient Chinese philosopher Mencius had expressed concern over the destruction of the earth by the deforestation and overgrazing of their day. Aristotle traced "civic dissension and wrongdoing" to the poverty created by unrestricted reproduction. In the early Christian era Tertullian welcomed wars, plagues, and famines because they "serve to prune away the luxuriant growth of the human race." In today's world the heirs of Malthus preach what they call "lifeboat ethics," claiming the same monopoly on realism that fortified the dismal preacher when he pronounced his death sentence for the poor. To explain natural selection Darwin borrowed Malthus' notion that population expands at a geometric rate while food supply grows at an arithmetic rate. Only the fittest survived in the struggle of the many over the inadequate food supply. Nature "red in tooth and claw," according to Herbert Spencer and his conservative acolytes, regulated the excess population, and the winners in the permanent contest for survival were the custodians of the best genes of the race. The process could be assisted by sensible policies of eugenics, and the Malthusians of our day are always passionate about birth control and some are intrigued by genetic engineering. The most radical philosophical implication of the Malthusian myth is that human beings must adjust one way or another to the immutable stinginess of nature. Within the tradition coexist uneasily the heirs of the Fabian eugenicists, who believe that the most damaging blows to civilization are struck in bed; Indira Gandhi's army of social reformers, who forcibly sterilized 8 million Indians; and, in its most malignant form, the Hitlerian ideologues who arranged for the extermination of "useless breeders."

The prophets of abundance have been fighting the Hobbs-Malthus tradition for more than 300 years. Man need not be remade to fit nature's straitjacket, for the triumph of technology offers the possibility of conquering nature. Human institutions can be created to temper the struggle for the earth. The most famous exponent of such views is Karl Marx, who believed in "the necessity of bringing a natural force under the control of society . . . of appropriating or subduing it on a large scale by the work of the human hand. . . ." Man's nature is to be productive. Only through mass production can scarcity be eliminated, and only by conquering scarcity can justice be achieved. In a Malthusian struggle over limited resources, the exploiters triumph over the exploited; only an abundant society can be a classless society.

The historic role of capitalism, according to Marx, is to lay the foundations for abundance. For this reason there is an ambivalence running through his writings about whether the capitalist passion to master nature is progressive or reactionary. Note this passage from the *Grundrisse*, an early work:

> For the first time, nature becomes purely an object for humankind, purely a matter of utility; ceases to be recognized as a power for itself; and the theoretical discovery of its autonomous laws appears merely as a ruse so as to subjugate it under human needs, whether as an object of consumption or as a means of production. In accord with this tendency, capital drives beyond national barriers and prejudices as much as beyond nature worship, as well as all traditional confined, complacent, encrusted

satisfactions of present needs, and reproductions of old ways of life. It is destructive towards all of this, and constantly revolutionizes it, tearing down all the barriers which hem in the development of the forces of production, the expansion of needs, the all sided development of production, and the exploitation and exchange of natural and mental forces.

The contemporary apostles of abundance through mastery of nature are as likely to be found at the chamber of commerce as at the Central Committee of the Soviet Communist party. Neither seems willing to recognize that technology itself, no matter who controls it or in whose interests it is allegedly used, sets limits for society. Machines determine the physical environment and the nature of politics. Capitalist and socialist views of the uses of abundance are noticeably different. Socialists call for abundance for the many rather than the few. Moreover, the relationship between man and man is theoretically different under capitalism and socialism, but the relationship between man and nature is essentially the same.

Attitudes toward scarcity and abundance do not break down according to traditional ideological divisions. Conservationists and antigrowth ideologues often appear conservative because they despair of making the pie big enough to render redistribution painless, and except for a few symbolic "life-style" changes they show no enthusiasm for cutting themselves smaller slices. They invite the poor countries to remain peasant societies to keep world pollution levels down. On the other hand, the most ardent capitalists make the same optimistic assumptions about salvation through technology as do leaders of the socialist world. Herman Kahn, who specializes in positive thinking about modern capitalism, predicts for his corporate clients a new golden age of consumption. Andrei Gromyko asserts that mankind "is not threatened by energy strangulation." Science has "by no means had its final say." *Sotsialisticheskaya Industriya* sounds like the Atomic Industrial Forum when it tells its readers that chemical fuels will last 150 years and nuclear fuels substantially longer. The dangers of nuclear energy, despite some devastating accidents that appear to have occurred in the USSR, are accepted as the price of progress. To accept limits of growth doctrines, Soviet leaders argue, would mean the "perpetuation of [capitalism's] economic advantage over the rest of the world."

Neither Soviet leaders nor U.S. corporate leaders can accept the implications of the Malthusian tradition. Particular scarcities, to be sure, offer political opportunities. For capitalist managers controlled scarcity disciplines the market, justifies high prices, and solidifies monopolistic power. But all this, though widely known, is unmentionable in polite political discourse. For communist state bureaucrats local or temporary scarcities permit certain interests in the society to be advanced ahead of others. Scarcity in one commodity or another is a planning instrument. That is not public knowledge either.

Scarcity in general is quite another matter. The notion of systemic limits is threatening to capitalists and socialists alike. Capitalism requires the unrestricted right to turn public resources into private wealth. Capitalist competition compels the participants to place the interests of the firm ahead of city, state, or country. Built into the incentive system is the notion that the welfare of civilization depends upon the output of a few hundred such firms and that anything done to slow the stream of goods or the profits earned thereby is impoverishing.

The legitimacy of the Soviet state and other socialist regimes depends upon delivering the promise of equality, but an equality of abundance, not poverty. Therefore the race to appropriate from nature and to produce for people must continue unabated. Shortages, according to Soviet ideology, are a product of a "private enterprise system of management with its uncontrolled development of production" and can be avoided by sensible socialist planning. A socialist society that had attained affluence might well have a different ideology, but this cannot be proved on the basis of our experience so far.

Both modern capitalism and modern socialism see expanded production as the answer to human happiness. The Keynesian revolution was based on the notion that the cause of poverty was not scarce supply but insufficient demand. (Keynes himself, it should be noted, predicted that in time his most brilliant insights would become not only obsolete but "dangerous.") Increasingly, the goods produced by capitalist factories and socialist factories are the same, and the ideological debate focuses on narrow technical questions about whether the planning function should be vested in firms or vested in the state. The more profound distinction between stimulating production through moral incentives (propaganda, education, emulation, etc.) or material incentives is becoming blurred as socialists have come to place greater emphasis on the latter.

Planners in companies and planners in states behave essentially alike in one respect. Natural resources for the next generation and the air and water for this one tend to be counted as free goods. The economic value of the next generation's copper, oil, or water is for practical purposes discounted to zero in market economies. State planners work in five-year frameworks, ten at the most, and hence make the same sacrifice of resources in favor of productivity. Marx said that capitalists live by the maxim "*Après nous le déluge*" as they maximize short-term gains at the expense of posterity. A "rational miser," as Marx called him, the capitalist's lifetime goal is to leave his children property even if it means robbing them of clean air and water. But for Marx productivity is what gives meaning to life; man becomes, in C. B. MacPherson's phrase, the "infinite consumer." His disciples in power do not show much sensitivity to the basic needs of posterity.

The Marxist concept of abundance is a product of the Enlightenment. Francis Bacon's faith that experimental science could now make "the effecting of all things possible" was echoed in Descartes' call to man to cut loose his "childish" dependence upon authority and tradition. No laws not of his own making constrained him. The illusion of limits could be transcended. The era of technological hubris coincided with the era of fossil fuel consumption. In just 300 years a huge chunk of the geological capital of the ages was consumed as if it were an ever-growing annuity guaranteed until the end of time. If Marx had predicted the end of scarcity in the midst of carboniferous capitalism and before the twentieth-century gushers had come in, it is hardly surprising that his modern disciples should resist the notion of natural limits.

The idea of a slow-growth "steady state" economy is threatening to socialism for two principle reasons. One is that countries that experiment with Marxism-Leninism are poor, and they are not enthusiastic about maintaining a steady state of poverty. The other is that without the myth of abundance, distributive justice becomes impossible without massive coercion. The promise of equitable sharing of future abundance is much less disturbing than the threat to redistribute existing finite resources. Within the socialist movements of Europe, therefore, including both the Eurocommunists and the Social Democrats, an ideological debate about growth is gathering force. The fundamental philosophical choice—can human beings dominate nature or are they limited by nature—now divides both capitalism and socialism. It may well be the issue on which a true "convergence" of the market economies and the centrally planned economies takes place.

3.

Both capitalism and socialism must confront the "tragedy of the commons" noted first by the nineteenth-century Malthusian William Forster Lloyd and elaborated in our day by Garrett Hardin. The problem has been summarized by William Ophuls:

Men seeking gain naturally desire to increase the size of their herds. Since the commons is finite, the day must come when the total number of cattle reaches the carrying capacity; the addition of more cattle will cause the pasture to deteriorate and eventually destroy the resource on which the herdsmen depend. Yet, even knowing this to be the case, it is still in the rational self-interest of each herdsman to keep adding animals to his herd. Each reasons that his personal gain from adding animals outweighs his proportionate share of the damage done to the commons, for the damage is done to the commons as a whole and is thus partitioned among all the users. Worse, even if he is inclined to self-restraint, an individual herdsman justifiably fears that others may not be. They will increase their herds and gain thereby, while he will have to suffer equally the resulting damage. Competitive overexploitation of the commons is the inevitable result.

Overcoming scarcity for individuals thus produces a common scarcity for all—the ecological deterioration of the oceans, rivers, farmlands, and forests on which everyone is dependent. Cassandras and Panglosses propose different political solutions to this dilemma of human shortsightedness. The latter tend to minimize the problem, assuming that growth in the end will yield enough for all and that the next generation of technology will correct the mistakes of the last one. Panglossianism leads to a politics of interest-group conflict and muddling through—in short, what we now have in the United States. The Cassandras wisely reject such faith, but their Malthusian analysis leads them to reject democracy too. Garrett Hardin, asserting that "injustice is preferable to total ruin" proposes a regime of "mutual coercion." Despairing of human altruism to subordinate the quest for personal enrichment to the common good, the heirs of Hobbes have seized upon the dangers of ecological catastrophe to legitimate the modern-day Leviathan.

The contemporary Malthusians come to support authoritarianism reluctantly. But human survival requires restraint of individual appetites. The Trilateralists warn of an "excess of democracy" leading to an irresponsible press, a collapse of authority, and a crippling of government. The "crisis of democracy," according to the Trilateralists, stems from its ungovernability. The answer is more control, more "consensus," and less freedom of the news media and other private interests to subvert the common good.

Both the neo-Malthusians and the Trilateralists, who seek to combine a growth ethic with a Malthusian analysis, resort to a variety of privilege-protecting images to dramatize the need for authoritarian government. One is "spaceship earth." It gives an accurate notion of the hermetic character of the life-support systems on which all beings are dependent and of the limited space available to us. But it gives a most misleading and dangerous impression that there is a pilot who is or should be in charge. The all-wise and all-knowing captain who knows where the spaceship is heading or how to take it there does not exist, but incompetence has never been a disqualification for the ambitious. Similarly, the "lifeboat ethic" poses the problem of sharing world resources in terms that make it easy for the rich. A gentle shove, and those who were doomed to die anyway because of their history of reckless reproduction, will make it possible for the rest to survive in comfort. A more appropriate image, as some have pointed out, is the luxury liner.

The ever-rising demands of ever more visible hungry masses disturb the well-established privileged order of the rich and powerful nations. "Triage" is another image, one borrowed from the First World War. The world is divided into the obvious survivors, those hovering on the brink of life and death who are not yet beyond hope, and the "basket cases" to be abandoned. Since there is a certain obstinacy in human nature which keeps people from sacrificing their lives to the greater good to the extent required, individual freedom must be limited in the interest of "more precious freedoms."

Lifeboat ethics have a long heritage. The rich habitually confuse their own acquisition programs with the common good and numb whatever residual feelings of empathy they may retain with stern judgments about the depravity of life's losers. Poverty is a sign of God's disfavor, a badge of laziness, a consequence of incontinence, or a natural disaster beyond all human control. The world is divided into a few engines and many wagons. The wagons would make no progress at all unless the engines raced ahead. Extra wagons slow the train and must be detached. In the name of the lifeboat ethic, wages are cut, strikes are outlawed, food subsidies abandoned, and health and welfare programs for the poor scrapped.

Privilege-protecting myths are justified in the name of global planning. In a hierarchic world where everyone knew his place these myths produced an imperial order. They enabled certain races and peoples to organize the world economic system by sheer rapacity and ingenuity. These were the survival values as long as the frontier seemed open. Greed was the key to justice. Reckless acquisition meant economic growth, and economic growth was necessary for equitable distribution. As the pie grew, more and more was available for the less rapacious and the less ingenious. But in a time of a resource squeeze confidence in future rewards and future justice wanes and the struggle intensifies. The temptation to write off the "unproductive" and the losers becomes irresistible.

However, there are now hundreds of millions of men, women, and children without money or the hope of making money for themselves or anyone else. Abandonment of this huge population is no longer a practical survival strategy for the rich, because the costs of such a monumental human sacrifice are prohibitive. The destruction of human life on such a scale degrades the political and psychological basis of all human existence.

This devaluation process is already advanced. In the industrial West we often note that "life is cheap" in the Orient or other exotic places, which is a way of saying that the death rate is high and people seem to be stoical about it. But the two world wars that decimated Europe and brought catastrophe to Asia were planned in the industrial capitals. The bullets and the bombs that have caused 25 million casualties in the generation since World War II were aimed at targets in poor countries, but they were made in the rich countries.

In the U.S. the annual 50,000-plus highway deaths are accepted as the price of progress. Individual comfort and idiosyncrasy are valued more than preservation of life. The attempt to curb the carnage of the autobahns in West Germany by imposing a speed limit was defeated by asserting an inalienable "freedom to speed." In the United States the effort to curb the "Saturday night specials" habitually used to dispatch husbands, wives, schoolboys, taxi drivers, liquor store owners, and bridge partners has been blocked by a powerful lobby that thrives on a similar set of beliefs. Child abuse, a bureaucratic euphemism for the murder and mutilation of children by parents, has shown a dramatic increase in recent years. Keeping the cities ablaze with light powered by nuclear generators is valued more than the thousands who are fated to die from radiation-induced cancers.

Mounting street crime testifies to the process of devaluation of human life that is under way everywhere. Warfare has arrived at a wholly new stage. There is continuous warfare of the government against the population as in Cambodia, Idi Amin's Uganda, and Argentina, Uraguay, and El Salvador. Nuclear war strategy is now concerned with the survival of missiles rather than people, and victory is determined by a body count. (The crown goes to the side that loses a few million less than the enemy.)

The three traditional impulses for protecting human life have been deadened by progress. One is religious. The obligation to respect the individual is derived from a duty to a supreme being or supernatural source. There is a transcendent value to each soul. Despite revivals of religious sentiment in our time, the centuries-long process of secularization continues. The religious commandments in the Old and New Testament that worshipping God requires ministering to the poor and the helpless have lost much of their force.

The second impulse for valuing life is based on community, the traditional obligations to family and village. Each individual had a duty to protect the other members of the community; each in turn expected protection and support from the rest. Village culture should not be idealized. Treating children as property, abandoning babies on hillsides, and murdering them with impunity are traditions too. But in the traditional family it was not the rule for children to become alienated and for parents to be abandoned when they became old. When family and community structures break down, as is happening everywhere in the wake of industrialization, the only social institutions that automatically value individuals as more than consumer or worker lose their power to protect.

The third impulse for valuing human beings is economic. Workers are paid enough to keep them strong enough to man the machines and to reproduce the next generation of workers. But the worldwide explosion in the labor market means that while certain people are valued because they are needed, huge numbers are not. As workers become increasingly replaceable, their social value declines and, as we have seen, they are treated accordingly.

4.

The lifeboat ethic is undermining the legitimacy of the nation-state itself. That process was already well under way before the resource squeeze began. Territorial empires like the United States and the Soviet Union are becoming ungovernable. The traditional function of the nation-state, territorial defense, can no longer be performed by any national state, however powerful. One hundred nuclear bombs falling on either country would kill at least 35 million people, according to the Department of Defense, and destroy perhaps two-thirds of the industrial capacity. Neither country has the technological means to prevent many times that number of bombs from landing on their targets. As we have seen, national governments are unable to regulate the most important economic units operating within their territory. Multinational corporations can evade taxes, speculate against the national currency, despoil resources, frustrate a national employment policy, and governments can do little about it, for their mandate stops at the water's edge or the national frontier, and corporations escape into a world market of their own making where no government operates.

Even when it could no longer defend its own people, the nation-state continued to attract allegiance because it could organize society within a vast territory and infuse it with purpose, usually killing one group of foreigners or another. It could be an arbiter of competing interests and a mollifier of class and regional conflict. But in an age of scarcity these functions become more difficult. The Southwest resists "subsidizing" the Northeast with controlled natural gas prices. South Carolina resists being the repository of nuclear wastes from generators that light up the cities of the East and Middle West. California talks about "self-sufficiency." Because the Federal Government has failed to develop a plan for the economic integration of the nation on terms that appear equitable to the various regions, the nation is already in an advanced state of dissolution. Regional and local loyalties are becoming more intense, and antipathy to central authority is rising everywhere. The current bad repute of "big government" is due to its distance and to its insensitivity to local concerns.

The nation-state is caught in the middle. It is neither large enough to plan on a global scale, where that is needed, as in environmental controls and resource allocation, nor small enough to be accountable to people where they live. As a consequence, separatism is a worldwide phenomenon. In the United States much of what we call "national" is a facade. Neither political party has a national program. Each is a loose coalition of local duchies which rises like a phantom every four years to elect candidates for high office. Allegiance to these "national" parties has declined sharply. The national purpose that once united class and region —manifest destiny, cold war, the American Dream—has become elusive.

The conservative columnist Kevin Phillips attributes the prolonged paralysis of leadership to the resurgence of "tribalism and balkanization" in America. The "Eastern Establishment" no longer has a near monopoly on high office. The last three elected Presidents have been from the Sun Belt, but they have found the country ungovernable. None succeeded in carrying through a major domestic program. Each spent time making and unmaking foreign commitments, ordering weapons, and performing other tasks more amenable to Presidential initiative than solving the energy or water crisis in the U.S. or resurrecting the decaying cities.

Growing parochialism in the United States takes many forms. It almost invariably involves the distribution of resources. "The Northwest is poised for a regional civil war—an interstate battle over the allocation of low-cost federal power," Dixy Lee Ray, the governor of Washington, told Congress. Idaho has accused Washington of seeding Idaho clouds and diverting the rain across the state border. The governor of Hawaii wants a constitutional amendment permitting a state to block the influx of new residents. Geographic, economic, and ethnic splintering has overwhelmed the myth of the melting pot.

Easy assimilation of successive waves of immigrants rests on the promise of abundance. In a time of scarcity the welcome mat is rolled up. The waves of immigration continue, but social attitudes harden. There is a counterattack on black-white integration from many quarters. The race theories of Schockley that put the blame for the plight of blacks on nature instead of human institutions, the legal attacks on compensatory measures favoring blacks, such as quotas, and the abandonment of a national goal to integrate housing—all have helped to build up the formidable barriers that still divide the races in the U.S. White upper-middle-class families are reclaiming the central city in the major metropolitan areas. The result is a new traffic pattern that symbolizes the deepening division of the country. In the morning, whites (and a handful of blacks) drive from their downtown duplexes to the suburban headquarters of the major firms. Blacks are bused from the ever-growing Paris-like belt of workers' suburbs that ring the older cities to sweep the floors and wash the dishes downtown. In the evening the pattern is reversed. Institutionalized injustice of this sort is a time bomb, for the metropolitan centers are still predominantly occupied by a black and Latin population cut off from the American Dream.

Separatism is even more advanced elsewhere. The Great Russians who run the Soviet Union are about to become an ethnic minority. The demands for cultural autonomy and the stirrings of ancient nationalist movements—Ukrainians, Latvians, Uzbeks, and many others—are creating what CIA analysts believe is the number one problem for the Soviet leadership. In Canada, Quebec flirts with independence. There are separatist tendencies in mineral-rich Alberta. In 1977, according to one poll, half the population of Scotland favored independence. The Scottish Nationalists lost ground in the 1979 elections, but the issue of Scottish separatism still strongly persists. More than 10 percent of the Welsh, despite centuries of British rule, want a separate or autonomous Wales. There are significant separatist movements that are pulling at the French nation too. In August 1977, Corsican nationalists blew up a television station, leaving two-thirds of the island without programs from Paris. Similar movements exist in Brittany, Alsace, and the Occitan region in southern France.

The Samis (Laplanders) are struggling to maintain a separate culture in the arctic reaches of Norway, Sweden, and Finland. In Japan the descendants of the ancient Ainu people put up signs periodically demanding a separate republic. In Spain there are significant divisions according to language; about 25 percent speak Catalan, Gallego, or some tongue other than Castilian, the official "Spanish." As in India, parts of the Middle East, and Africa, separate languages form the core of separate cultural identities and resistance to the dominant national or international culture. The Kurds, the South Moluccans, the Pashtuns, and the inhabitants of Shaba province in Zaire have succeeded in giving their independence movements international visibility by acts of terrorism or civil war.

The integration of the world through products, advertising, and media transmissions of the multinational corporations is no doubt the prevailing cultural trend of our age. But there is a powerful counter force resisting this process which appears to be gathering steam. The drive to protect separate cultural identities is profoundly related to resource questions. Where there is a strong separatist movement it usually turns out that the area from which it springs possesses an important resource on which the larger political unit from which it seeks to disengage depends. Thus the Scots believe that the North Sea oil is theirs. Birmingham and Manchester pipe cheap water from Wales, paying less for it than do the Welsh. The inhabitants of Shaba, where Zaire's cobalt and copper are concentrated, are no more eager to be exploited by corrupt officials from an alien tribe posing as the "national government," than they were to hand over their patrimony to the Belgians. The less able or willing the national authorities are to integrate cultural or ethnic minorities on an equitable basis, the more the need for cultural identity and the desire to control local resources reinforce each other. The promise of governments to create an affluent society that embraces the whole national territory is losing credibility everywhere. Even where cultural differences are minor, resource development is creating tensions. In Australia the resource-rich states (Queensland and Western Australia) are heavily controlled by foreigners and the minerals are destined for export, a reality that is sharpening political conflict between these states and the others.

The myths of scarcity of the last 300 years all lead to a dead end. Malthus' world order regulated by famine is as hopeless a prospect as a world order guided by Adam Smith's invisible hand. Neither can work in a planet soon to receive its 6 billionth soul. The cultural and economic integration of the world has proceeded to the point where masses of people cannot be easily abandoned. The winners pay heavy costs for the suffering of the losers whether they realize it or not.

The global struggle that stretches across the world—from the Sandinistas' fight against Samoza in Nicaragua to the liberation movements of Africa—is a fight for redistribution of power and resources. Between nations and within nations the perception of scarcity leads to naked class war. The pressure for a more equitable distribution of world resources is intensifying, and so is the resistance. The costs of class warfare are enormous for all sides. The rich resist transfer payments when they are obvious, such as unemployment benefits, welfare checks, and commodity price supports for poor countries. But in a world of permanent class struggle, the costs of maintaining islands of affluence are escalating. To support the military and police, there is a steady drain of money, oil, copper, manganese, cobalt, and other resources. The defense of privilege now requires a style of life that robs it of its pleasures. Double locks, armed guards, and a healthy fear of kidnapping and assassination are the rewards of achievement almost everywhere. Moreover, the poor extract public money in all sorts of hidden ways. In Washington, D.C., for example, the abandonment of the "unproductive" poor has spawned a large population of isolated and demoralized teenage women without a role in society except to produce babies who might love them and make them feel important. These thirteen- and fourteen-year-old mothers are giving the nation's capital the distinction of having one of the highest infant mortality rates in the industrial world. Premature babies born to poorly nourished mothers extract from society far more money than decent education, prenatal care, or job opportunities would have cost, for it is easy to spend more than $100,000 in the weeks of elaborate care needed to keep a small baby alive. One of the meanings of "interdependence" is that it is hard to abandon people without paying for it.

The regulation of the marketplace works no better than Malthus' reaper. On a global scale, as we have seen, there is no necessary scarcity of any of the resources we have been discussing. Our investigation of the five global resource systems arrives at the same conclusion as the studies of Wassily Leontief for the U.N.; the RIO project of another Nobel laureate, Jan Tinbergen; the Bariloche Foundation project; and others. Theoretically, there are ample resources in the world to support a decent life for the predicted global population of the year 2000, but not to support lopsided opulence or continual ecological plunder. Yet scarcity is real because the control of resource systems is planned in such a way that much of the world does not have enough. For those without adequate jobs or money, and that may soon be close to a majority of the global work force, the market is almost irrelevant. Companies and countries that control resources worry more about short-term glut than long-term scarcity. In the interests of maintaining their hold on the elements of power, companies delay development of new resources and divert old resources, not to where they are most needed, but to where the most promising profits can be expected.

Are there principles for organizing the world resource systems other than Malthusian warfare against the surplus population or renewed technological assault on nature? The present planning system embraces both principles. The global trend is to combine the drive for indiscriminate industrialization with the politics of austerity. The pessimism of the Malthusians has a good deal of dreary evidence to support it, but ideologies of abandonment should evoke the deepest suspicion. They are myths for the rich wrapped in the intimidating mantle of science. Proclaiming the inevitability of disasters that will strike others serves to protect privilege and to make the struggle for justice seem futile. Indeed, the fatalism of the Cassandras is another form of *"Après moi le déluge."* Tired intellectuals tend to confuse the end of the Affluent Society with the end of civilization. Every age is faced with the same Faustian temptation. You can purchase privilege-protecting order at the price of freedom. At the first intimations of scarcity the privileged declare the obsolescence of democracy because a system of distribution of scarce resources which would suit the majority would threaten the good life of the comfortable.

Scarcity is a product of political and economic organization. It is an inevitable consequence of the present planning system. The process of developing and distributing energy, minerals, food, water, and human energy is substantially guided by global corporations and government bureaucracies. Each operates under a set of incentives that encourage maldistribution of wealth and ecological insult.

The choices seem clear. The present planning systems can continue in effect. The result will be growing scarcity, creating severe social dislocation in the industrial world and starvation and mass unemployment in the rest of the world. Against this background of social disorder the escalating arms race is likely to produce a nuclear war.

The alternative is to recognize that peace and prosperity for rich and poor alike require a new planning system operating on different incentives and rooted in a set of survival values that fit this age, rather than the age of capitalist accumulation through which we have just come. Instantaneous, revolutionary transformation of the world order is out of the question, but rapid evolution of a survival strategy is both essential and possible.

The bedrock principle for evolving a survival strategy is that every person born has political and economic rights and has a vested right to a decent minimal share of world resources by virtue of having been born. The explicit purpose of the global resource systems is to serve the world population, and that must mean *everybody* on earth. There is no alternative to making human rights truly universal, for there is no middle position that permits dividing humanity into superior races and inferior races, productive individuals and nonproductive individuals, the lucky and the unlucky. The genocidal mind-set threatens the survival of the whole human race, for it is subject to no natural limits. The inevitable result is Hobbesian war. The unequivocal acceptance of the notion of minimum rights attaching to each individual at birth provides the essential framework for voluntary control of population. Only human beings with a sense of their own value and a minimum sense of security can make responsible decisions about how many children to have.

The second survival principle is the protection of communities. This would require shifting our definition of economic health from one that emphasized the "balance" of the world economy or the national economy to one that insisted that the communities where people actually live be in balance and not be mere appendages of distant economies beyond their control. Economists and government officials who listen to them usually measure progress by such gross and aggregate indicators as the volume of world trade, the rise in the gross national product, or the improvement of per capita income. It is assumed that if the United States as an economic unit is doing well, prosperity will automatically trickle down to Youngstown, Detroit, and Kansas. But we know this it is not so, and because it is not so, the political cohesion of these larger units is strained.

Interdependence of one sort or another in the contemporary world is unavoidable, but the modes of interdependence are the products of one sort of planning or another. A rational planning system should start with the goal of community health—physical, economic, and spiritual. (Whether the relevant community for planning purposes is a city or a neighborhood, or a consortium of geographically separated population centers, depends upon the local circumstances.) The purpose of planning should be to enable a given population to develop a balanced and secure economy within which to achieve the quality of life they want. The idea that certain cities, regions, or countries must be abandoned for the greater good of the world economy is unacceptable. The goal ought to be maximum self-reliance of those communities large enough to survive economically and small enough to accommodate some form of face-to-face politics. Autarchy is neither possible nor desirable, but for many cities in the U.S. and for virtually all Third World countries the present modes of interdependence result in an automatic resource drain. To develop new modes of interdependence it is necessary in many cases to disengage sufficiently from the world economy or the national economy to change the terms of future integration.

To increase the self-reliance of local economies—within the United States and within the rest of the world economy—it is necessary to change trade policies that preserve inequalities. The New International Economic Order proposals represent a modest effort to do this, and the theory behind them at least ought to be embraced in the interest of world stability. Within the United States the same efforts to protect the integrity of local economies and to restore the power of such communities to plan their own future should be encouraged. Locally raised tax money should be used to develop community-based energy systems, development banks, and other institutions to revitalize local economies. National policy should be designed to enable communities throughout the nation to undertake a variety of such initiatives.

In the United States, we could start by redefining "national security" to make the security of local communities a prime national goal. The safety of nuclear plants, mines, and factories, for example, should be the responsibility of local residents. They have a much greater incentive to avoid an accident than either the collection of executives halfway across the country who represent the "owner" or the corps of Washington-based inspectors from the regulating agencies. Individuals derive their sense of personal security in large measure from the security that their city or town can provide. National security has little meaning if the local economy cannot provide jobs; if food, shelter, energy, health care, and transportation are not available at prices people can afford; and if people are afraid to walk the streets. Local communities can no longer be at the mercy of distant boards of directors who decide when to move in and when to move out. Companies must be required to give notice, to nego-tiate the terms under which they leave, to bear a fair part of the cost of the dislocation they have caused. When a company decides to leave, the city ought to be eligible for federal funds with which to buy the facility and to convert it into an enterprise that can employ its citizens and fi-nance essential public services.

The key to democratic planning is democratic control of capital. If the capital in the hands of multinational corporations and banks is flowing to the international money markets instead of such priority investments as solar energy, low-cost housing, and other crucial public needs, it is nec-essary to exert greater public control to create new markets. The self-serving system of private planning and public anarchy must be replaced by new mechanisms for gaining better public control of the capital re-sources of the nation. This can be done within a democratic political system and a truly mixed economy in which a variety of forms of public governance of resources coexist with a strong competitive free market.

The problem with present planning systems, public and private, is that accountability is weak. Private planning systems in the global corpora-tions operate on a set of narrow incentives that frustrate sensible public policies such as full employment, environmental protection, and price stability. Public planning is olympian and confused because there is nei-ther a clear consensus on social values nor political priorities. To accom-plish anything, explicit choices must be made, but these choices can be made effectively only with the active participation of the people most directly involved. This, not nostalgia for small-town times gone forever, is the reason that devolution of political power to local communities is a political necessity. The power to plan locally is a precondition for sensible integration of cities, regions, and countries into the world economy.

The process of planning priorities, of deciding what should be pro-duced, of envisioning a decent physical environment, can take place only on a human scale. In his book *The Breakdown of Nations*, Leopold Kohr, anticipating E. F. Schumacher, makes an impressive historical argument that bigness leads to various forms of social breakdown. It is now clear that the sheer size of corporations and government bureaucracies has weakened the underpinnings of liberal capitalism.

Democracy is under severe attack at the very moment when gathering evidence suggests that popular participation is a survival value. Major structural changes cannot take place in any country without the mobilization of the whole people. The solution of the energy crisis in the U.S., for example, requires a degree of public understanding and participation which our political institutions do not know how to achieve. Mobilization by propaganda and mass manipulation does not work in the long run, because communitarian values cannot be built with totalitarian techniques. Eventually the cynicism, fear, and apprehension stimulate a reversion to individualism, personal isolationism, and self-protection.

As crucial as democratic values are for survival, ideological attacks are being mounted against them on the Right and on the Left. In every industrial democracy business leaders are questioning the compatibility of "one man, one vote" and capitalist productivity. A less "permissive" political system is needed, they say, to overcome the social paralysis and deadlock which is destroying the economic system. The liberal Left too wonders how the requirements of political and ecological stability can be reconciled with democracy. Robert Heilbroner reluctantly concludes that the complexity and intractability of the overriding global problems—pollution, famine, war—may mean that abandonment of democracy is the price of survival. George Rathjens, a professor of political science at the Massachusetts Institute of Technology and an expert on nuclear arms, thinks a "radical change in our whole life style, meaning the surrender of most democratic values and the addition of rather brutal methods," may offer the only hope of averting nuclear war by 1999. Such views have provided the ideological rationalization for dictatorships, Left and Right, around the world.

Whether the redistribution of power, the precondition of the redistribution of resources, can occur without a huge escalation of revolutionary warfare is dubious. Yet the prospects of such warfare are so horrendous that there is a strong interest shared by the powerful and powerless alike to navigate the transition to a new global order by less violent, more evolutionary strategies.

One such strategy involves the development of new forms of popular participation appropriate to different cultural traditions, and different economic and political systems. The eighteenth-century political structures in the United States, the old-fashioned parliamentary democracies of Europe, and the one-party state are all inadequate for democratic resource planning. The process of developing new institutions is a long one, and it takes different shapes in different societies. But the process can evolve from a world consensus that political participation is not only a fundamental human right but one that is inextricably connected to the achievement of basic economic rights.

The choice is more democracy or much less. The effective participation of people in making the decisions that most directly affect them is the precondition for economic, political, and spiritual liberation. Until people can play a direct role themselves in shaping their own physical and economic environment they are not fully alive. When masses of people come to see themselves as either extensions of machines for making things they can never have, or as surplus population, they lose the incentive to create. They lose and the world loses immense resources—imagination, creativity, love, and power. There are stories from many parts of the world that corroborate one simple idea. Where peasants in Latin America have been able to organize farms in such a way that they can control what is grown, how it is grown, and how it is shared, productivity increases and many of the pathologies associated with "development" disappear. When workers share not only in the proceeds of the assembly line but in the decisions concerning its operation and, ultimately, what is produced, the alienation that now threatens productivity in every industrial country begins to dissolve and the passion for living returns. The most impressive achievement of socialist societies is that thousands who lived rote lives under the old regime are now awake.

A world facing class warfare on a scale that threatens the whole human family can find stability only by embracing the goals of justice and equality. The way *not* to get redistributive justice, as politicians of austerity like to point out, is by keeping the present system functioning with massive welfare payments.

Social relationships change when the majority is able to exert *effective* demand. Before they can get their fair share of resources, they must have the power of entitlement. That is something that is usually fought for, not given.

Political participation can take many different forms. Consultation before decisions are made builds community more effectively than opportunities for ratification after the fact. Most elections are votes of confidence or no-confidence and have little discernible impact on specific decisions. For most people in the world their connection to the productive order is tenuous; they can lose their land or their job on a moment's notice. They live at the mercy of economic and political decisions over which they have no control. In such conditions of insecurity it is not surprising that peasants overplant and overgraze and that millions of tons of good soil are washed away through erosion and forests are hacked away for firewood.

The sense of stewardship which is essential for conserving and renewing resources grows out of a sense of belonging. If each family is only for itself or each nation only for itself, the prevailing ethos is "Take what you can while you can." Where there are stable communities, agricultural practices tend to be more careful. Traditional peasant societies in many cultures practice conservation for self-preservation. But when the old society is disrupted and an intruding culture brings in new values that are the antithesis of traditional values, peasant communities dissolve. Those who come to preach "efficiency" in agriculture arrive with machines that rip forests to shreds, pave over rich soil, and flood the land with expensive and nutritionally wasteful packaged food.

In the U.S. the appeal to conserve goes unheeded because it runs counter to the basic ideology of the country: Consume more. The economy depends upon it. A pious message from the President is no match for the hundreds of millions of dollars of advertising designed to stimulate consumption. The example of turning off a light or two in the White House makes little impression on those who pass by the world headquarters of global corporations in the heart of Manhattan all ablaze twenty-four hours a day.

Stewardship is a survival value for the human race, for unless each generation is willing to limit its share of resources, it is sentencing the next generation to deprivation and increasing misery. Stewardship does not mean zero growth for the world economy. The debate about when or whether to arrive at a "steady state" economy has clouded the issue. In order for the planet to achieve a certain stability some parts of the world economy must grow at a faster rate than others. It is obvious that the nonindustrial world must use far more natural resources than in the years of colonial exploitation and that the industrial nations, the U.S. in particular, must limit their consumption. It is inconceivable that 250 million Americans can continue to consume a third of the most crucial resources in a planet of 6 billion people. The monopoly of sophisticated technology in the hands of the rich nations must be broken in the interests of a minimum world order.

Stewardship requires a capacity to feel the pain and to share the joy of people who live at a great distance. People do not practice conservation unless they see a compelling purpose and can envision the flesh-and-blood beneficiaries of their sacrifice. Would it make a difference if Americans could imagine how electricity in a Peruvian village transforms lives of drudgery and how far the wasted wattage of the average American could go to lighting that village? (By wasted wattage I mean not only individual carelessness but each citizen's share of the much larger amounts wasted by the industrial and commercial system.) Our educational establishment inoculates us against empathy. The survival values our society prizes are individualist. We are trained to be cerebral, thick-skinned, and obsessed with ourselves. These are not the survival values of a world of scarcity.

Stewardship implies a rational system of sharing not only across distance but across time. When people were tied to particular plots of land it was easier to feel part of the rhythm of the generations. The son, the grandson, and the great-grandson would be tilling the same land in the same way. But with these ties broken, where are the roots of obligation to posterity? There is a weakening of the sense of tradition, of participating in a chain of being. Tycho Brahe, the astronomer, said he spent his life counting stars so that posterity would have fewer to count. That sense of building a future over centuries eludes modern men and women. In a world built on exchange relationships it is hard to see what posterity has to give me to compensate for my limiting my share of resources. Why then should I care? For some there is a religious injunction. The only secular answer is that without a sense of the future, living loses its meaning. The lack of connectedness to the future (as well as the past) reveals itself in the special restlessness that permeates industrial culture. Without seeing ourselves as trustees of the natural order for something beyond ourselves, there is no answer to the inescapable human question: Why am I here?

The process begins by a gradual overcoming of the self-protective ignorance that isolates us from the majority of people of the world and a growing awareness of the needs, fears, and hopes that bind all humanity. Developing harmonious human relationships and a harmonious relationship with nature go hand in hand. Both are requirements for survival of the human race. Surely, the continuation of the present competitive assault on the natural order will bring chaos, deprivation, and quite possibly the death of everything. However, no new relationship with nature is possible without a new stage in human relationship rooted in the most basic survival values of all: sharing and cooperation. The point has been made in a thousand ways throughout history.

There is a storehouse of human wisdom about the relationship between the social order and the natural order to be found in those universal myths that Carl Jung called the "collective unconscious" of the race. The simplest stories told again and again in many different guises express the deepest insights culled from thousands of years of collective experience. Someone unlocks the secret of abundance by sharing a little of nature's bounty with a stranger. It is the New Testament story of the feeding of the 5,000 with a few loaves and fishes. It is the tale from Greek mythology of the miraculous pitcher; a poor couple share their bit of milk with the stranger and the pitcher flows forever. The tale is retold in a bit of folklore from Brittany as the miraculous fish. In the Tibetan tale "The Story of Two Neighbors" a poor man helps a young sparrow with a broken leg and is rewarded with a kernel of grain that becomes a harvest of jewels. His rich neighbor learns the secret and looks for a sparrow of his own to help. Finding none, he creates a charitable opportunity for himself by shoving a sparrow out of the nest and fixing its broken leg. His reward is a kernel that yields not jewels but a process server who levies on all his lands and cattle.

The secret of survival in the coming lean years lies somewhere in these mythic shadows. The most basic human need of all is the need to be human, which, in an age of scarcity, means being in psychological and biological harmony with the rest of creation. The task of politics is to give expression to these yearnings so that institutions can be created to enable people to do what they know they must.

Notes and Bibliography

Chapter II
Oil: Enought for What?

The literature of oil is immense. The best summary of alternative projections of supply and discussion of energy alternatives can be found in the report of the Subcommittee on Energy and Power of the House Interstate and Foreign Commerce Committee, *Project Interdependence U.S. and World Energy Outlook Through 1990,* Washington, D.C.: GPO, Nov. 1977. MIT Workshop on Alternative Energy Strategies, *Energy: Global Prospects 1985–2000,* New York: McGraw-Hill, 1977, was a major effort to arrive at an international consensus of supply and demand and evaluation of energy alternatives. It was largely dominated by the petroleum industry, and the report reflects this bias. M. King Hubbert's famous predictions on the energy shortage can be found in "The Energy Resources of the Earth," *Scientific American,* Sept. 1971, pp. 61–70. There are scores of updated estimates. The best places to look are *Oil and Gas Journal,* World Bank publications, and such other publications as *Business Week, Forbes,* and the *Economist,* which give accounts of oil finds and disappointments.

The classic account of the political role of oil is Robert Engler, *The Politics of Oil,* New York: Macmillan, 1961. His *Brotherhood of Oil: Energy Policy and the Public Interest,* Chicago: University of Chicago Press, 1977, brings the story up to date. It includes a detailed account of the recent involvement of political figures with the oil industry. John Blair, *The Control of Oil,* New York: Random House, 1976, is the best of many books on the impact of oil on the U.S. economy and includes detailed studies of the techniques for controlling the supply and the price. Carl Solberg, *Oil Power,* New York: Mason Charter, 1976, contains excellent discussions of the sociology of the automobile, and I have drawn heavily from it. See also Robert Stobaugh and Daniel Yergin, "The End of Easy Oil," in Stobaugh and Yergin, eds., *Energy Future: Report of the Energy Project at the Harvard Business School,* New York: Random House, 1979.

Oil company profits are now widely reported. Cover stories on the petroleum industry in *Time, Business Week,* and other magazines are commonplace. They are a good source for tracing shifting oil company attitudes toward government.

The involvement of OPEC in the U.S. economy is also well reported. See Craig S. Karpel, "The Petro Industrial Complex," *Penthouse,* July 1978, pp. 76–149, and his "Ten Ways to Break OPEC," *Harper's Magazine,* Jan. 1979, p. 65.

An excellent summary of energy alternatives is to be found in Steven Schneider, "Common Sense About Energy: Part 1—Where Has All the Oil Gone?," Jan./Feb. 1978; "Part 2—Less Is More: Conservation and Renewable Energy," Mar./Apr. 1978, *Working Papers for a New Society*.

For a discussion of exponential growth see Hubbert, *op. cit.*, and Lester Brown, *The Twenty-Ninth Day,* Worldwatch Institute, New York: Norton, 1978.

Chapter III
Oil: The Politics of Transition

The story of the development of Middle East oil by the major oil companies has been told in Leonard Mosley, *Power Play,* New York: Random House, 1973, a readable account that borrows from the pioneering work of Robert Engler, *The Politics of Oil,* Chicago: University of Chicago Press, 1967, originally 1961; and in Benjamin Schwadran, *Middle East, Oil and the Great Powers,* 3rd ed., New York: Wiley, 1973. Carl Solberg's *Oil Power,* New York: Mason Charter, 1976, has further information and an excellent bibliography on this period. For a picture of the pre-OPEC world oil market, see John Blair, *The Control of Oil,* New York: Random House, 1976; M.A. Adelman, *The World Petroleum Market,* Baltimore: Johns Hopkins University Press, 1972; and the staff report of the Subcommittee on Monopoly of the Select Committee on Small Businesses, U.S. Senate, 82nd Cong., 2nd Sess., Washington, D.C.: GPO, 1952, Committee Print no. 6. For an account of the OPEC success, see Anthony Sampson, *The Seven Sisters,* London: Hodder & Stoughton, 1975, which is also a readable account of the origins and development of the oil giants. Still fascinating is Ida Tarbell's classic muckracking work, *History of the Standard Oil Company,* New York: McClure, Phillips, 1904. The arrangements for controlling Iranian oil are described in Senate Subcommittee on Multinational Corporations, *The International Petroleum Cartel, the Iranian Consortium and U.S. National Security.* Hearings before the Subcommittee on Multinational Corporations of the Committee of Foreign Relations, U.S. Senate, 93rd Cong., 2nd Sess., *Multinational Corporations and U.S. Foreign Policy,* pt. 7, Washington, D.C.: GPO, 1974.

See also Edith T. Penrose, *The Large International Firm in Developing Countries: The International Petroleum Industry,* Cambridge, Mass.: MIT Press, 1968.

On the links between Saudi Arabia and the U.S. economy, articles appear regularly in such publications as *Business Week, Forbes,* and *Fortune.* Here are a few: "Saudi Arabia: Jittery and Rich in a Sea of Oil," by Jack Anderson, *Parade Magazine,* July 16, 1978; "Oil, No Salvation for the Saudis as World Economies Slow," *Business Week,* June 18, 1979; Thomas Ferris, "Riding the Saudi Boom," *New York Times Magazine,* Mar. 25, 1979, p. 23.

A popular account of Middle East money is Michael Field, *A Hundred Million Dollars a Day,* New York: Praeger, 1976. The role of the Marshall Plan in converting Europe to oil is told in Carl Solberg, *Oil Power,* New York: Mason Charter, 1976, ch. 7. There is an enormous literature on the impact of the oil prices on the world economy. Most of it reflects the business cycle, sounding the note of alarmism or complacency as growth rates dictate. See the Trilateral Commission reports *Energy: A Strategy for International Action*, 1974 and *Energy: The Imperative for a Trilateral Approach* and *Energy: Managing the Transition*, 1978; Jahangir Amuzegar, "OPEC and the Dollar Dilemma," *Foreign Affairs*, July 1978; and Walter J. Levy, "Oil Policy and OPEC Development Prospects," *Foreign Affairs*, winter 1978–79.

Useful information on comparative U.S., European, and Japanese imports, conservation efforts, and alternative energy development can be found in the Trilateral Commission report *Energy: Managing the Transition*, 1978.

Louis Turner and his colleagues at the Royal Institute of International Affairs have written several unpublished papers on the integration of the Middle East into the world petroleum economy. Some material is in his *Oil Companies in the International System*, Royal Institute of International Affairs, London: Allen & Unwin, 1978. For a good journalistic account of the thinking of the oil technocrats see George Goodman's (Adam Smith's) article "Arabs, Their Money . . . and Ours," *The Atlantic*, Feb. 1978, p. 33–44. Two other sources on the role of Saudi Arabia and Iran in the oil economy are the *Geopolitics of Energy*, by Melvin A. Conant, director, reprinted for the U.S. Senate Committee on Interior and Insular Affairs, Jan. 1977 (a committee print, GPO, 95th Cong., 1st Sess., Energy Publication 95-1); and the publications of the Middle East Research and Information Project in Washington, D.C. See especially Report no. 20, "Middle East Oil and the Energy Crisis," Sept. 1973; Report no. 26, "Saudi Arabia: Bullish on America," Mar. 1974; Report no. 37, "Iranian Nationalism and the Great Powers," May 1975; Report no. 40, "America's Shah, Shahinshah's Iran," Sept. 1975; Report no. 42, "Development in the Middle East," Nov. 1975; and Report no. 43, "Land Reform and Agribusiness in Iran," Dec. 1975. For a brief account of the 1953 coup against Mossadeq, see my *Intervention and Revolution: The United States in the Third World*, rev. ed., New York: New American Library, 1972, ch. 10.

Chapter IV
Energy: What Is to Be Done?

The best short statement of the transitoriness of fossil fuels is in M. King Hubbert, "The Energy Resources of the Earth," *Scientific American*, Sept. 1971, pp. 61–70. The discussion of natural gas in the text relies heavily on U.S. Bureau of Mines, *Mineral Facts and Problems*, Washington, D.C.: GPO, 1977; Carl Solberg, *Oil Power*, New York: Mason Charter, 1976, ch. 8; Bethany Weidner, "What Natural Gas Shortage?," *The Progressive*, Apr. 1977, p. 19; Barry Commoner, *The Politics of Energy*, New York: Knopf, 1979; and Steven A. Schneider, "Common Sense About Energy: Part 1—Where Has All the Oil Gone?," Jan./Feb. 1978; "Part 2—Less Is More: Conservation and Renewable Energy," Mar/Apr. 1978, *Working Papers for a New Society*.

Alcohol fuels are discussed in Fred Cook, "Gasohol—A 100 Proof Solution," *The Nation*, vol. 228, Apr. 21, 1979, pp. 417, 432–36; and in a forthcoming book by Hal Bernton from which most of the historical material in the text is taken. The wood-burning economy is discussed in two excellent pamphlets from Worldwatch Institute, Washington, D.C.: Erik Eckholm, "The Other Energy Crisis: Firewood," *Worldwatch Paper 1,* Sept. 1975; and his "Planting for the Future: Forestry for Human Needs," *Worldwatch Paper 26,* Feb. 1979, Washington, D.C. The depredation of the Amazon is chronicled in Norman Lewis, "The Rape of Amazonia," *Observer Magazine,* Apr. 22, 1979; and in William Flanagan, "The Richest Man in America Walks to Work," *New York Magazine,* Nov. 28, 1977; Norman Lewis, "The Rape of Amazonia," *Observer Magazine,* Apr. 22, 1979; and "Daniel Ludwig's Floating Factory," *Time,* June 19, 1978.

The discussion of coal was based on U.S. Bureau of Mines, *Mineral Facts and Problems, op. cit.;* Robert L. Galloway, *A History of Coal Mining in Great Britain,* New York: A.M. Kelley, 1968; Steven A. Schneider, *op. cit.;* Robert Engler, *The Brotherhood of Oil: Energy Policy and the Public Interest,* Chicago: University of Chicago Press, 1977; Report of Office of Technology Assessment, *The Direct Use of Coal; Prospects and Problems of Production and Consumption,* Washington, D.C.: GPO, 1979; Barry Commoner, *The Poverty of Power: Energy and the Economic Crisis,* New York: Bantam, 1976; James S. Cannon, *Mine Control: Western Coal Leasing and Development,* New York: Council on Economic Priorities, 1978; and Congressional Research Service, *Project Interdependence: The U.S. and World Energy Outlook Through 1990,* Washington, D.C.: GPO, Nov. 1977.

For energy company profits, see Anne Witte, "Profits and Politics," *People and Taxes,* vol. 7, no. 11, Nov. 1979.

There is a considerable literature on nuclear safety. The best summary statement is in Barry Commoner, *op. cit.* For the industry response to critics see publications of the Atomic Industrial Forum, and the series in *Fortune* in 1978–79. The publications of the Union of Concerned Scientists have stood the test of time. See especially *The Nuclear Fuel Cycle: A Survey of the Public Health, Environmental, and National Security Effects of Nuclear Power,* Cambridge: MIT Press, 1975. Also, Sheldon Novick, *The Electric War: The Fight Over Nuclear Power,* San Francisco: Sierra Club Books, 1976. On the economics of nuclear energy see Richard Barber and Associates, *ERDA-52, Lesser Developed Countries' Nuclear Power Prospects 1975–1990: Commercial, Economic and Security Implications,* Washington, D.C., Aug.–Sept. 1975; and House Committee on Government Operations, *Nuclear Power Costs,* Apr. 1978; Charles Komanoff, *Power Plant Performance: Nuclear and Coal Capacity Factors and Economics,* New York: Council on Economic Priorities, 1976. The story of the uranium cartel and the wave of lawsuits it spawned is told in Anthony J. Parisi, "The Great Uranium Flap," *New York Times,* Sunday, July 9, 1978. For further information on ethical and political implications of nuclear energy, see Christian Hohenemser, Roger Kasperson, and Robert Kates, "The Distrust of Nuclear Power," *Science,* vol. 196, Apr. 1, 1977; Christian Hohenemser, "The World-Wide Debate over Nuclear Power: The Real Issues Are Values and Ethics," *Science Forum,* Aug. 1976, p. 52; Sen. Mike Gravel, "Plutonium Recycle: The Civil Liberties View," *Civil Liberties Review,* p. 42; "Energy and Labor in the Consumer Society,"

Washington, D.C.: Environmentalists for Full Employment, July 1976; National Council of Churches of Christ (New York), Policy statement on *The Ethical Implications of Energy Production and Use,* adopted May 11, 1979; Alvin Weinberg, "The Age of Substitutability," *Science,* Feb. 20, 1976, pp. 683–89; "The Maturity and Future of Nuclear Energy," *American Scientist,* vol. 64, Jan. 1976, pp. 16–21; Mark Hertsgaard, "Trading in Nuclear Futures," *Mother Jones,* June 1979; and report prepared by Pan Heuristics for U.S. Arms Control and Disarmament Agency, *Moving Towards Life in a Nuclear Armed Crowd?,* Dec. 4, 1975, rev. ed., Washington, D.C., Apr. 22, 1976. On technical issues relating to proliferation, see the report of the Comptroller General, *An Evaluation of the Administration's Proposed Nuclear Non-Proliferation Strategy,* Washington, D.C.: GPO, Oct. 4, 1977.

On renewable energy sources the basic theoretical work is Amory Lovins, *Soft Energy Paths: Toward a Durable Peace,* copyright by Friends of the Earth, New York: Ballenger, 1977. See also Barry Commoner, *op. cit.* There is a growing literature on solar energy: Richard Munson, "Ripping Off the Sun," *The Progressive,* Sept. 1979; "The Coming Boom in Solar Energy," *Business Week,* Oct. 9, 1978, p. 88; Denis Hayes, "Energy: The Case for Conservation," *Worldwatch Paper 4,* 1976; Hayes, "Nuclear Power: The Fifth Horseman," *Worldwatch Paper 6,* 1976; Hayes, "Energy: The Solar Project," *Worldwatch Paper 11,* 1977; Hayes, "The Solar Energy Timetable," *Worldwatch Paper 19,* 1978, all Washington, D.C.: Worldwatch Institute; Arjun Makhijani, "Solar Energy and Rural Development for the Third World," *Bulletin of Atomic Scientists,* June 1976, p. 14; Skip Laitner, *The Impact of Solar and Conservation Technologies Upon Labor Demand,* paper presented to the Conference on Energy Efficiency, Washington, D.C., May 20–21, 1976; Gene Marine, "Here Comes the Sun," *Ramparts,* Mar. 1974; Barry Commoner, "Energy and Jobs," *Canadian Labour,* Mar. 1978; U.S. Department of Energy, *The Great Adventure: A Report on the Ten Regional Public Hearings on Solar Energy for the Domestic Policy Review,* Washington, D.C.: GPO, Oct. 1978; *Jobs and Energy,* Washington, D.C.: Environmentalists for Full Employment, spring 1977; Trilateral Commission Paper 18; *Energy: Managing the Transition;* Council on Environmental Quality (Washington, D.C.), *The Good News About Energy 1979;* and *Creating Solar Jobs: Options for Military Workers and Communities,* a report of the Mid-Peninsula Conversion Project, Mountain View, Cal., Nov. 1978; Council on Economc Priorities, *Jobs and Energy: The Employment and Economic Impact of Nuclear Power, Conservation, and Other Energy Options,* New York, 1979.

Chapter V
Minerals: The Rocks of Civilization

The excellent publications of the Bureau of Mines of the U.S. Department of Interior Washington, D.C., are as good a place as any to begin research on minerals. The bureau prepares an analysis, called *Mineral Facts and Problems,* of each important industrial mineral. It is updated periodically, and chapters on specific minerals are published separately. Most of the analysis of reserves, resources, environmental costs, and structure of the metals industries were found there. Two other Bureau of Mines publications should also be consulted: *Mineral Industry Surveys* and *Mineral Commodity Summaries*. The latter is updated annually and contains the latest information on reserves, prices, and similar matters.

The Bureau of Mines publications contain fascinating historical notes about each metal. But most of the historical references in the chapter come from two major sources: Fernand Braudel, *Capitalism and Material Life 1400–1800*, New York: Harper & Row, 1967; and Lewis Mumford, *Technics and Civilzation*, New York: Harcourt, Brace & World, 1934. Mumford's subsequent work *The Myth of the Machine*, Vol. I: *Technics and Human Development*, 1967, and Vol. II: *The Pentagon of Power*, 1970, New York: Harcourt, Brace & World, develops some of these same themes. The bibliography to *Technics and Civilization* is a doorway to a world of forgotten scholarship. Charles Booth's 17-vol. *Life and Labour in London*, ca. 1902, New York: A.M. Kelly, 1969; E.C. Eckel, *Coal and Iron War: A Study of Industrialism, Past and Future*, New York, 1920; Thomas A Rickard, *Man and Metals: A History of Mining in Relation to the Development of Civilization*, New York; Arno Press, ca. 1932, 1974.

The special issue of *Science* of Feb. 20, 1976, is the best comprehensive discussion of the problems of mineral exhaustion, pollution control, possibilities of recycling and substitution, and evolution of national policy. The articles by Ableson and Hammond, Landsberg, Fried, Boyd, Huddle, and Cook were particularly useful. John Tilton's *The Future of the Nonfuels Minerals*, Washington: Brookings Institution, 1977, is most valuable for its economic analysis of mineral scarcity.

One of the most sophisticated statements of the "limits to growth" argument is Fred Hirsch's *Social Limits to Growth*, Cambridge, Mass: Harvard University Press, 1976. For the argument for limits to growth argument see Wilfred Beckerman, *In Defense of Economic Growth*, London: Jonathan Cape, 1974. The quintessential Panglossian view of scarcity is Herman Kahn's *The Next 200 Years: A Scenario for America and the World*, for the Hudson Institute, New York: Morrow, 1976.

The most famous Cassandra-like analysis of minerals scarcity is *The Limits to Growth*, the 1974 Club of Rome report by Donella Meadows *et. al.*, New York: University Books, 1974. It has been somewhat unfairly attacked as a result of the popularization of its findings; although the methodology is questionable, the idea of limits is not. See H. S. D. Cole *et al.*, *Models of Doom: A Critique of the Limits of Growth*, New York: University Books, 1974, for a detailed critique. Wassily W. Leontief's study for the United Nations, *The Future of the World Economy*, New York: Oxford University Press, 1977, is more optimistic and more convincing. The model of the world economy by the Bariloche Foundation in Argentina is an interesting effort to assess the supply of world resources assuming a more rational and less unjust pattern of distribution. Its findings are encouraging. See also Jan Tinbergen, *Reshaping the International Order*, New York: Dutton, 1976. For an informed mainstream view of the scarcity issue, see Edward Mason's "Natural Resources and Environmental Restrictions to Growth," *Challenge*, Jan./Feb. 1978, p. 14.

Two texts I found helpful were G. J. S. Govett and M. H. Govett, *World Mineral Supplies: Assessment and Perspective*, New York: Elsevier Scientific Publishing Co., 1976; and Charles Park, *Affluence in Jeopardy: Minerals and the Political Economy*, San Francisco: Freeman, Cooper, 1968. Each combines geological, economic, and some historical information. The Govetts' book is detailed and includes a large bibliography of scientific papers. James F. McDivitt, *Minerals and Men: An Exploration of the World of Minerals*, for Resources for the Future, Baltimore: Johns Hopkins University Press, 1965, is also a valuable survey.

There is a vast literature on the seabed. For a popular account of ocean mining see A. S. Loftas, *The Last Resource: Man's Exploitation of the Oceans*, Chicago: Regnery, 1970. The legal literature is considerable. There is a good account of the negotiations and legal issues in Jonathan I. Charney, "The International Regime for the Deep Seabed; Past Conflicts and Proposals for Progress," *Harvard International Law Journal*, winter 1976, pp. 1–50. See also Jack N. Barkenbus, "How to Make Peace on the Seabed," *Foreign Policy*, vol. 25, winter 1976–77, pp. 211–20. The Comptroller General report "Deep Ocean Mining—Actions Needed to Make It Happen," Washington, D.C.: GPO, June 28, 1978, describes the exploration activities of companies, the economic problems of seabed mining, and environmental issues, and makes recommendations for federal policy. On space mining see "Mining the Apollo and Amor Asteroids," *Science*, July 22, 1977, p. 363. For a debate on the political, social, economic, and psychological implications of space colonies see Stewart Brand, ed., *Space Colonies*, A Co-Evolution Book, Sausalito, Cal.: Whole Earth Catalog, 1977. Gene Bylinsky's two-part series in *Fortune*, "Industry's New Frontier in Space," Jan. 29, 1979, p. 71, and "Space Will Be the Next Construction Site," Feb. 26, 1979, p. 63, describes the technological possibilities of locating metallurgical activities in space.

Works on specific metals and their peculiar economic behavior include The Economist Intelligence Unit, *The London Metals Exchange*, Tonbridge, Eng.: Whitefriars Press, 1958; J. W. F. Rowe, *Primary Commodities in International Trade*, Cambridge: Cambridge University Press, 1965; and Cheryl Payer, ed., *Commodity Trade of the Third World*, New York: Wiley, 1975, especially the discussion of zinc by Ian M. Robinson and of copper by David N. Waite; John Deverell and the Latin American Working Group, *Falconbridge: Portrait of a Canadian Mining Multinational*, Toronto: James Lorimer, 1975; and Jamie Swift and The Development Education Centre, *The Big Nickel: Inco at Home and Abroad*, Kitchener, Ont.: Between the Lines, 1977. The last two are critical accounts of the nickel industry's operations in Canada and contain a good deal of information about the industry culled from diverse sources. Harvey O'Connor's *The Guggenheims: The Making of an American Dynasty*, New York: Arno Press, 1976 (originally 1937), includes a rich historical account of the copper industry in America. For a case study of the copper industry in Chile and bauxite mining in Jamaica, see Norman Girvan, *Corporate Imperialism: Conflict and Expropriation*, New York: Monthly Review Press, 1976.

For a discussion of the inequities of commodity pricing, see Orlando Letelier and Michael Moffitt, *The New International Economic Order*, Washington, D.C.: Transnational Institute, 1977; Michael Moffitt, *Derailing Development*, Washington, D.C.: Institute for Policy Studies, 1978; John W. Sewell and the Staff of the Overseas Development Council, *The United States and World Development, Agenda 1977,* New York: Praeger, 1977; Zuhayr Mikdashi, *The International Politics of Natural Resources,* Ithaca, N.Y.: Cornell University Press, 1976; Harold J. Barnett and Chandler Morse, *Scarcity and Growth: The Economics of Natural Resources Availability,* Baltimore: Johns Hopkins University Press, 1963; International Economic Studies Institute, *Raw Materials and Foreign Policy,* Washington, D.C., 1976, a report that is unsympathetic to the Third World positions on commodities.

Among the many journals devoted to the minerals economy which have been most helpful to me have been *Metals Bulletin,* a weekly account of news of the industry; *Materials and Society,* a bimonthly journal that tries to integrate technical, political, and economic analyses of the minerals world; *Chemical and Engineering News* (see especially the article by Will Lepkowski entitled "Politics and the World's Raw Materials," June 4, 1977); *Business Week* (see especially the article "Now the Squeeze on Metals," June 2, 1979); and *Science.* Legal and political as well as technical problems of satellite photography can be found in *Photogrammatic Engineering and Remote Sensing,* Journal of the American Society of Photogrammetry (see esp. vol. 42, no. 2, Feb. 1976).

Chapter VI
Food: Sowers, Reapers, Ranchers, and Eaters

Forecasts of the world food crisis abound. Most of the issues are well discussed in the May 9, 1976, *Science,* a special issue, totally devoted to food (see especially the article by Thomas Poleman, "World Food: A Perspective," p. 510). These official forecasts are useful: *Alternative Futures for World Food in 1985—Vol. 1, World GOL Model Analytical Report,* Foreign Demand and Competition Divisions of the Economics, Statistics and Cooperative Service, USDA, Foreign Agricultural Economic Report No. 146, Washington, D.C.: GPO, Apr. 1978. Pierre R. Crosson and Kenneth D. Frederick, "The World Food Situation: Resource and Environmental Issues in the Developing Countries and the U.S.," *Resources for the Future,* Washington, D.C.: Johns Hopkins University Press, 1977.

The analysis of Mexico's food import requirements by the International Monetary Fund was obtained by the New International Economic Order Project of the Institute for Policy Studies.

For analyses that concentrate on the physical causes of underproduction and maldistribution of food, Lester R. Brown, *The Twenty-Ninth Day,* Worldwatch Institute, New York: Norton, 1978; and Erik P. Eckholm, *Losing Ground: Environmental Stress and World Food Prospects,* New York: Norton, 1976. Both researchers are members of the Worldwatch Institute, Washington, D.C., which has produced extremely useful studies of a variety of resource issues treated in this book.

Dan Morgan's pioneering study of the grain companies, *Merchants of Grain,* New York: Viking, 1979, was the principal source for the discussion in the chapter. The hearings before the Senate Subcommittee on Multinationals, *Multinational Corporations and United States Foreign Policy—International Grain Companies,* Washington, D.C.: GPO, June 18, 23, and 24, are also useful. Good theoretical discussions of food power are to be found in Peter Wallenstein, "Scarce Goods as Political Weapons: The Case of Food," *Journal of Peace Research,* vol. 13, no. 4, 1976; and Lester Brown, "The Politics and Responsibility of the North American Breadbasket," *Worldwatch Paper 2,* Washington, D.C.: Worldwatch Institute, Oct. 1975. An excellent review of U.S. experience is to be found in *Use of U.S. Food for Diplomatic Purposes—An Examination of the Issues,* Congressional Research Service report prepared for the House Committee on International Relations, Washington, D.C.: GPO, Jan. 1977.

Solon Barraclough, director of the United Nations Research Institute for Social Development, has devised a methodology for looking at the world food system and is sponsoring empirical studies in several countries; this methodological framework is outlined in the institute's project proposal, *Food Systems and Society,* Geneva, July 1978. The research of the institute emphasizes economic and institutional problems of food production and distribution. Effective popular versions of some of these ideas are to be found in Susan George, *How the Other Half Dies,* Montclair, N.J.: Allanheld, Osmun, 1977; Susan George, *Feeding the Few: Corporate Control of Food,* Washington, D.C.: Institute for Policy Studies, 1979; Frances Lappé and Joseph Collins, *Food First: Beyond the Myth of Scarcity,* Boston: Houghton Mifflin, 1977; and Frances Moore Lappé and Joseph Collins, *World Hunger: Ten Myths,* San Francisco: Institute for Food and Development Policy, May 1979.

For medical information on the baby's need for trace metals, see "The Role of Zinc and Other Trace Metals in Pediatric Nutrition and Health," by K. Michael Hambidge, M.D., *Pediatric Clinics of North America,* vol. 24, Feb. 1, 1977, pp. 95–106. For a discussion of the politics of famine, see Robert J. Ledogar, *Hungry for Profits: U.S. Food and Drug Multinationals in Latin America,* New York: Idoc-North America, 1975; Jack Shepard, *The Politics of Starvation,* New York: Carnegie Endowment for International Peace, 1975; Elie A. Shneour, *The Malnourished Mind,* Garden City, N.Y.: Doubleday Anchor Books, 1974; Ronald Sider, *Rich Christians in an Age of Hunger,* New York: Paulist Press, 1978; and Institute of Nutrition of Central America and Panama, *Fincas—A Study of Factors Which Influence Fetal Growth and Subsequent Child Development,* Guatemala City: NCAP, 1978.

For further material on the food population issue, one should consult Lester Brown, *The Twenty-Ninth Day,* Worldwatch Institute, New York: Norton, 1978, and the references listed there. Climatic effects on food are well summarized in Stephen H. Schneider, *The Genesis Strategy,* New York: Delta, 1976.

For a discussion of the plight of small farmers in America and the ecological problems associated with agribusiness, see Michael Perelman, *Farming for Profit in a Hungry World,* Montclair, N.J.: Allanheld, Osmun, 1977. For an official view on agribusiness, see Clifford M. Hardin, "Foreword," in U.S. Department of Agriculture, Contours of Change, *The Yearbook of Agriculture,* Washington, D.C.: GPO, 1970. Thorstein Veblen's 1923 "The Independent Farmer," in Max

Lerner, ed., *The Portable Veblen,* New York: Viking, 1948, offers many insights about the position of small farmers which are still relevant. For a discussion of food and the energy crisis, see David Pimentel *et al.*, "Food Production and the Energy Crisis," *Science,* vol. 182, Nov. 1973. Perelman, *op. cit.*, contains an extended discussion of the efficiency of large- versus small-scale farming. See also Irving Hoch, "Returns to Scale in Farming: Further Evidence," *American Journal of Agricultural Economics,* vol. 58, no. 4, Nov. 1976.

The classic history of food systems is Fernand Braudel's *Capitalism and Material Life, 1400–1800,* New York: Harper & Row, 1973. Useful articles are to be found in Elborg Forster and Robert Forster, eds., *European Diet from Pre-Industrial to Modern Times,* New York: Harper & Row, 1975. The new role of the soybean is discussed in Folke Douring, "Soybeans," *Scientific American,* vol. 230, no. 2, Feb. 1974; and Richard Rhodes, "A Bean to Feed the World?," *The Atlantic,* Jan. 1975, pp. 38–43. *The Proceedings of the World Food Conference of 1976,* July 1, Iowa State University, Iowa State University Press, 1977, contains the Rivera study of Philippine rice farmers mentioned in the text and much other useful information. Marvin Harris, *Cows, Pigs, Wars and Witches: The Riddles of Culture,* New York: Random House Vintage Books, 1974, is an entertaining, provocative, and insightful exercise in anthropological speculation about why certain peoples eat or refuse to eat certain foods.

Chapter VII
Water: The Springs of Life

The strategic role of water in the rise and fall of empires is summarized in H. R. Vallentine, *Water In the Service of Man,* Baltimore: Penguin, 1967. The classic statement of the theory of "hydraulic despotism" is to be found in Karl Wittfogel, *Oriental Despotism: A Comparative Study of Total Power,* New Haven: Yale University Press, 1957. Further historical material, particularly relating to the United States, is included in Jim Wright's readable and informative *The Coming Water Famine,* New York: Coward, McCann, 1966.

The U.S. Water Resources Council has published a detailed analysis of present and projected water use which shows the relative use of water by households, farms, factories, and energy producers: U.S. Water Resources Council, *Nationwide Analysis Summary,* Washington, D.C.: GPO, Sept. 1977. There is a large literature on water problems of underdeveloped countries. Robert I. Saunders and Jeremy J. Warford, *Village Water Supply: Economics and Policy in the Developing World,* published for the World Bank by Johns Hopkins University Press, Baltimore, 1976, is a good place to start. See also S. K. Krishnaswami, "Health Aspects of Water Quality," *American Journal of Public Health,* vol. 61, no. 11, 1971, pp. 2259–68; Arthur A. Maass and David J. Major, "The Objectives of Water Policy and Related Institutional Problems," United Nations Panel of Experts on Water Resource Development Policies, Buenos Aires, June 1970; Arthur A. Maass *et. al., Design of Water-Resource Systems,* Cambridge, Mass.: Harvard University Press, 1962.

The Interfaith Center on Corporate Responsibility, 475 Riverside Drive, New

York, N.Y. 10027, has documentation from several countries on the effects of infant formulas in underdeveloped countries. See also *Sojourners,* Sept. 1978.

On U.S. water policy, an excellent source is Gilbert F. White, *Strategies of American Water Management,* Ann Arbor: University of Michigan Press, 1969. See also Charles C. Bradley, "Human Water Needs and Water Use in America," *Science,* vol. 138, Oct. 1962, p. 490; Arthur A. Maass, *And the Desert Shall Rejoice: Conflict, Growth and Justice in Arid Environments,* Cambridge, Mass.: MIT Press, 1978; Symposium on water resources management in a changing world, a collection of articles in *Natural Resources,* Oct. 1976, pp. 737–974; John C. Pierce and Harvey Doerksen, *Water Politics and Public Involvement,* Ann Arbor, Mich.: Ann Arbor Science Publishers, 1976.; John A. Ferejohn, *Pork Barrel Politics,* Stanford, Cal.: Stanford University Press, 1974. On current water quality problems, see "Water: The Next Resource Crisis?," *Nation's Business,* Sept. 1977; "Some Water Is Hardly Fit to Drink," *Changing Times,* Mar. 1978.

Arthur Morgan, *Dams and Other Disasters: A Century of the Army Corps of Engineers in Civil Works,* Boston: Porter Sargent, 1971, is a passionate and informed account of a century of mischief making by the dam builders of the Army Corps of Engineers. For other views on dams see John McPhee's *The John McPhee Reader,* William L. Howarth, ed., New York: Random House, 1977, especially the chapter "Encounters with the Arch Druid," which brilliantly captures the feelings and arguments of dam enthusiasts and dam haters. For more on dams and their effects, see Gilbert White, *op. cit.;* "Mighty Rivers, Dusty Ground," *The Atlantic,* Apr. 1978, p. 53; George Sibley, "The Desert Empire," *Harper's Magazine,* Oct. 1977, pp. 49–68; and "Carter's Water Projects: Pork Barrel Sellout?," *Outdoor Life,* Nov. 1977.

On iceberg towing see Kendrick Frazier, "Is There an Iceberg in Your Future?," *Science News,* vol. 112, Nov. 5, 1977, p. 298; Col. Roy Thompson, "Water as a Source of Conflict," *Strategic Review,* vol. 6, spring 1978, p. 62. On water conflicts, there is a huge international law literature. For a technical background on the U.S.–Mexico water dispute, see Francisco Tomargo and Robert Young, "The Colorado River Salinity Problem in Mexico," *Journal of Natural Resources,* Jan. 1978; John Neary, "The Great Southwest Water War," *Saturday Review,* Sept. 3, 1977, pp. 19–22. For a discussion of water problems in California, see U.S. Department of Interior, "Westside Study Report on Critical Water Problems Facing the Eleven Western States," Washington, D.C., 1974; and the *Special Task Force Report on the San Luis Unit,* Central Valley Project, California, published in Washington, D.C.: GPO, 1978, U.S. Department of the Interior, Bureau of Reclamation; John Wesley Powell, *Report on the Lands of the Arid Regions of the United States,* 1877.

Chapter VIII
Scarce Resources and the New International Military Order

A study of the theory of imperialism should begin with J. A. Hobson, *Imperialism: A Study,* London: Allen & Unwin, rev. ed., 1902; and V. I. Lenin, *Imperialism,* New York: International Publishers, 1939. See also my *Roots of War:*

The Men and Institutions Behind U.S. Foreign Policy, New York: Penguin, 1973, ch. 8. Walter Millis, ed., *The Forrestal Diaries,* New York: Viking, 1951. The writings of Haushofer, Kjellen, and Mackinder have been gathered in Andreas Dorpalen, *The World of General Haushofer: Geopolitics in Action,* New York: Farrar & Rinehart, 1942, and the quotes in the text are from this valuable collection.

For historical accounts of the importance of minerals and resources in the development of recent U.S. foreign policy, the works of Gabriel Kilko are recommended, especially his *Roots of American Foreign Policy,* Boston: Beacon Press, 1969; and (with Joyce Kolko) *The Limits of Power: The World and U.S. Foreign Policy 1945–1954,* New York: Harper & Row, 1972. For a somewhat different interpretation see my *Intervention and Revolution: The United States in the Third World,* rev. ed., New York: New American Library, 1972.

On the new world military order see Istvan Kende, "Dynamics of Wars, of Arms Trade and of Military Expenditures in the Third World 1945–1976," *Instant Research on Peace and Violence,* Helsinki: Tampere Peace Research Institute, 1977, vol. 2, pp. 56–67; Johan Galtung, who conducts peace research for the U.N., counts 114 wars in the Third World during these years and gives the figure of 25 million killed. See *Sojourners,* Aug. 1979, p. 7.

On the role of resources in the new international military order see Malvern Lumsden, "Global Military Systems and the New International Economic Order," and Helge Hveem, "Arms Control Through Resource Control: The Link Between Military Consumption of Raw Materials and Energy and the Disarmament Question," both in *Bulletin of Peace Proposals,* vol. 9, no. 1, 1978; Michael T. Klare, *Supplying Repression,* Washington, D.C.: Institute for Policy Studies, 1978; Barbara Rogers, "Namibia's Uranium" (unpublished study sponsored by Washington Office on Africa); Michael T. Klare, "The Political Economy of Arms Sales," *Bulletin of Atomic Scientists,* Nov. 1976.

The best account of world military expenditures are the periodic reports of Ruth L. Sivard, "World Military and Social Expenditures 1977," Washington, D.C. The figures in the text are from a report of Feb. 1978. See also General Accounting Office report *Military Sales: An Increasing U.S. Role in Africa,* Apr. 4, 1978; and Guy J. Pauker, *Military Implications of a Possible World Order Crisis in the 1980's,* Washington, D.C.: The Rand Corp., 1977.

Numerous articles have appeared in magazines speculating on the use of military power to obtain access to Middle East oil. See, for example, Miles Ignotus, "Seizing Arab Oil," *Harper's Magazine,* Mar. 1975, p. 45. But two careful studies highlight the limits of foreign military operations to assure access to Middle East oil: Maj. Daniel W. Christman and Maj. Wesley K. Clark, "Foreign Energy Sources and Military Power," *Military Review,* Feb. 1978.

The inside account of U.S. covert operations in Zaire is in John Stockwell, *In Search of Enemies,* New York: Norton, 1978. For changing perceptions of U.S. military power in the business world, see the cover story "The Decline of U.S. Power," *Business Week,* Mar. 12, 1979, pp. 36–96. The evasion of the Rhodesian boycott by Mobil is described in *The Oil Conspiracy,* Center for Social Action of United Church of Christ, New York, June 21, 1976. The material on the Philippines is from an unpublished government report by J. Nicanor Perlas III, a former Filipino official. Some of the information has been published by Friends of the Filipino People, Washington, D.C.

Chapter IX
Multinational Corporations and the World Employment Crisis

Books on multinational corporations appeared in great numbers in the early 1970s. In Richard Barnet and Ronald Müller, *Global Reach: The Power of the Multinational Corporations,* New York: Simon & Schuster, 1974, a long note section contains a comprehensive list of books and articles published before the middle of 1975. See also J.-J. Servan-Schreiber, *The American Challenge,* London: Hamilton, 1968 (tr. by Ronald Steel); Raymond Vernon's *Storm Over the Multinationals: The Real Issues,* Cambridge, Mass.: Harvard University Press, 1977; and C. Fred Bergsten, Thomas Horst, and Theodore H. Moran, *American Multinationals and American Interests,* Washington, D.C.: Brookings Institution, 1978. The Vernon book is a defense of multinationals in the form of a critique of the critics. There is useful information in it, but it skirts the principal issues. For a review see my "Vernon: Storm over the Multinationals: The Real Issues," *Harvard Law Review,* vol. 91, no. 5, Mar. 1978. For another view of issues of multinationals and development, see Mary E. Jegen and Charles K. Wilbur, eds., *Growth with Equity: Strategies for Meeting Human Needs,* New York: Paulist Press, 1979. The Bergsten, Horst, Moran book presents interesting material on labor and tax issues, and the authors try to take what they term a moderate position between the "sovereignty at bay" (Vernon) school and the "global reach" school on multinationals. My own impartial view is that they have not succeeded.

The most important new empirical work has been the Max Planck study cited frequently in the text. Otto Kreye *et al., World Market-Oriented Industrialization of Developing Countries: Free Production Zones and World Market Factories,* Max Planck Institute (forthcoming). See also "Free Trade Zones and Industrialization of Asia," *AMPO Japan-Asia Quarterly Review,* Tokyo: Pacific-Asia Resources Center, 1977; and Mary Kaldor, *The Disintegrating West,* New York: Hill & Wang, 1978, especially the chapter "The Corporation and the State," which contains important insights. A series of articles in business publications document the changes in international production discussed in the text, especially the rise of Third World multinationals and the increasing competition among U.S., European, and Japanese companies. For information on changes in international production, see "When Poor Countries Turn the Tables in World Trade," *U.S. News & World Report,* Oct. 16, 1978; Herbert E. Meyer, "Those Worrisome Technology Exports," *Fortune,* May 22, 1978, pp. 106–9; "Microcomputers—Big Profits from Tiny Chips," *Dollars and Sense,* no. 34, Feb. 1978, p. 4; Washington *Post* series by Dan Morgan on rubber, Mar. 7–8, 1979; and *Business Week,* June 13, 1977, p. 88, on migrant labor. For a positive outlook on contributions of multinationals, see David Blond, "The Future Contribution of

Multinational Corporations to World Growth—A Positive Appraisal," *Business Economics,* May 1978; "Why Foreign Companies Are Betting on the U.S." *Business Week,* Apr. 12, 1976; "The Multinationals: No Strings Attached," *Foreign Policy,* no. 33, winter 1978–79, pp. 121–34; and Raymond Vernon, "Storm over the Multinationals, Problems and Prospects," *Foreign Affairs,* vol. 55, Jan. 1977, pp. 243–62. For a negative outlook on the contributions of multinationals, see "Multinationals at Bay," *Saturday Review,* vol. 3, Jan. 24, 1976, p. 12. See also "The Relative Sizes of U.S. and Foreign-based Multinationals," *New International Realities,* vol. 1, July 1976, pp. 11–16; also, rev. ed., *ibid.,* vol. 3, winter 1978, pp. 16–24; "The 500 Largest Industrial Corporations Outside the U.S.," *Fortune,* Aug. 14, 1978; Sanford Rose, "Why the Multinational Tide Is Ebbing," *Fortune,* Aug. 1977, p. 111; and "Nestle at Home Abroad," *Harvard Business Review,* vol. 54, Dec. 1976, pp. 80–88. For information on the global car, see Gerald R. Rosen, "The Auto Clash Goes Global," *Dun's Review,* vol. 111, Apr. 1978; "National Journal Special Issue on the Automobile," *National Journal,* vol. 8, no. 1, Jan. 3, 1976; and "To a Global Car," *Business Week,* Nov. 20, 1978, p. 102.

For a description of working conditions in the export platforms, see *The U.S. and South Korean Textiles: A Closely Woven Fabric,* Philadelphia: American Friends Service Committee, July 1978, p. 1, and the references cited there; "America's Sweatshops in the Sun," *American Federationist,* AFL–CIO, May 1978, p. 17; "American Boom in Mexico," *Dun's Review,* Oct. 1978, p. 119; and Susan Rifkin, "Five U.N. Agencies Back the Third World Against Multinational Corporations," *Far Eastern Economic Review,* Jan. 12, 1979. The June Nash essay, "Women in Development: Dependency and Exploitation," appeared in *Development and Change,* vol. 8, no. 2, Apr. 1977.

The International Labor Office projections on world unemployment are found in the *Year Book of Labour Statistics 1978,* Geneva: ILO, 1978; "World Job Crisis—The Worst Is Yet to Come," *ILO Information,* vol. 6, no. 3, 1978; *Development Forum,* vol. 6, no. 8, Sept. 1978. See also, Ho Kwon Ping, "The Plight of the Absolute Poor," *Far Eastern Economic Review,* Sept. 1, 1978, p. 95, for a discussion of "absolute poverty" in Asia; P. Hasan, "Growth and Equity in East Asia," *Finance and Development,* June 1978, vol. 15, no. 2, p. 29; and "Needed: 120,000 New Jobs a Day," *Development Forum,* vol. 6, no. 8, Sept. 1978.

For a discussion of the rise of Third World multinationals see Hugh D. Menzies, "U.S. Companies in Unequal Combat," *Fortune,* Apr. 9, 1979; David A. Heenan and Warren J. Keegan, "The Rise of Third World Multinationals," *Harvard Business Review,* Jan./Feb. 1979; Lawrence G. Franko, "Multinationals: The End of U.S. Dominance," *Harvard Business Review,* Nov./Dec. 1978, pp. 93–101; and Bill Kazer, "Taiwan's Bittersweet Success," *Far Eastern Economic Review,* Nov. 24, 1978.

The decline of U.S. industrial innovation and productivity has been widely discussed. "The Decline of U.S. Power," *Business Week,* Mar. 12, 1979, pp. 36–96; "Machine Tools Lose an Export Edge," *Business Week,* Feb. 5, 1979; and Eli Ginzberg, "The Job Problem," *Scientific American,* vol. 237, Nov. 1977, pp. 43–51.

Chapter X
The Internationalization of Labor: Jobs and the New Economic Order

A good introduction to the role of slavery and indentured servitude is Kingsley Davis' article "The Migrations of Human Populations," in *The Human Population*, San Francisco: W. H. Freeman, 1974, pp. 53–68. Much of the analysis of this chapter is drawn from Harry Braverman, *Labor and Monopoly Capital*, New York: Monthly Review Press, 1974, which is the best empirical and theoretical account of labor as a commodity. The International Labor Organization periodically publishes world unemployment figures. The projections quoted in the text are found in *ILO Information* (see especially *ILO Information*, vol. 6, no. 3, 1978); *Development Forum*, vol. 6, no. 8, Sept. 1978; *Year Book of Labour Statistics 1978*, Geneva: International Labor Organization, 1978. For an analysis of the ideologies underlying employment statistics, see James S. Henry, "Lazy, Young, Female and Black: The New Conservative Theories of Unemployment," *Working Papers*, May/June 1978, pp. 55–65.

On the U.S. labor market, see Richard B. Freedman "Discussion Paper No. 626," Harvard Institute for Economic Research, June 1978 (unpublished); Eli Ginzburg, "The Job Problem," *Scientific American*, Nov. 1977, pp. 43–51; "The Nation's Science and Engineering Manpower Resources 1974," *Science Resource Studies Highlights*, June 29, 1976; Richard C. Edwards, Michael Reich, and David Gordon, eds., *Labor Market Segmentation*, Lexington, Mass.: D. C. Heath; *Proceedings of World Employment Conference*, Geneva, June 1976.

The discussion of the steel industry draws on an analysis in the world shift in production in "Steelyard Blues: New Structures in Steel," vol. 13, no. 1, Jan./Feb. 1979, *NACLA Report on the Americas*.

On job auctions and regional labor shortages, see Franz Serdahely, "184,000 Reasons Why Your Taxes are Staggering," *Philadelphia Magazine*, Dec. 1978, p. 138; "More Jobs than Workers," *Dun's Review*, Mar. 1978, p. 70.

On the effects of microprocessors on European employment, see Kathleen Newland, "Global Employment and Economic Justice: The Policy Challenge," *Worldwatch Paper 28*, Washington, D.C.: Worldwatch Institute, Apr. 1979.

There is a huge literature on migrant workers. See Zafer Ecevit and K. C. Zachariah, "International Labor Migration," in *Finance and Development*, Dec. 1978, p. 32; "How Europe Handles Its Migrant Workers," *Business Week*, June 13, 1977; Fred Halliday, "Migration and Labor Force in the Oil Producing States of the Mid East," *Development and Change*, vol. 8, no. 3, July 1977, pp. 266–81; and Martin Godfrey, "The International Market in Skills," *Development and Change*, vol. 6, no. 4, 1974, p. 5.

An exciting account of peasant ways of seeing is to be found in John Berger's "Towards Understanding Peasant Experience," *Race and Class*, no. 4, spring 1978, p. 345. Eric C. Wolf, *Peasant Wars of the Twentieth Century*, New York: Harper Colophon Books, 1969, is the classic in the field. See also Michael Lipton, *Why the Poor Stay Poor: Urban Bias in World Development*, Cambridge, Mass.: Harvard University Press, 1977; Teodor Shanin, "The Peasants Are Coming!

Migrants Who Labor, Peasants Who Travel and Marxists Who Write," *Race and Class*, vol. 19, no. 3, 1978; and Peter Waterman, "Workers in the Third World," *Monthly Review*, vol. 29, Mar. 1977, pp. 50–64.

On the New International Economic Order, a good introduction is Orlando Letelier and Michael Moffitt, *The New International Economic Order*, Washington, D.C.: Transnational Institute, 1977; Howard M. Wachtel, *The New Gnomes: Multinational Banks in the Third World*, Washington, D.C.: Institute for Policy Studies, 1975; Jeremiah Novak, *The International Economic Order* (forthcoming); Gerald Helleiner, "World Market Imperfections and the Developing Countries," *Overseas Development Council Occasional Paper No. 11*, May 1978.

Chapter XI
The Politics of Survival

The classic works on scarcity are Thomas Malthus, *An Essay on Population*, reprint of 6th ed., London: Ward, Lock, 1826; David Ricardo, *Principles of Political Economy and Taxation*, Everyman's ed., London, 1926; and John Stuart Mill, *Principles of Political Economy*, Ashley ed., London: Longmans, Green, 1929. The standard economic analysis of scarcity is to be found in Harold J. Barnett and Chandler Morse, *Scarcity and Growth: The Economics of Natural Resource Availability*, Baltimore: Johns Hopkins University Press, 1963. An engaging account of economic ideas is presented in Guy Routh, *The Origin of Economic Ideas*, New York: Random House, 1975. William Ophuls, *Ecology and the Politics of Scarcity*, San Francisco: Freeman, 1977, is a stimulating discussion with a good bibliography. Harrison Brown, *The Challenge of Man's Future*, New York: Viking, 1954, is still a major contribution. See also Kenneth Boulding's article "Is Scarcity Dead?," *Public Interest*, vol. 5, fall 1966, p. 36.

On the limits imposed by ecology, see Eugene P. Odum, *Fundamentals of Ecology*, 3rd ed., Philadelphia: Saunders, 1971; and Howard T. Odum, *Environment, Power and Society*, New York: Wiley, 1971.

The influential pessimistic works of the 1970s were Robert Heilbroner, *An Inquiry into the Human Prospect*, New York: Norton, 1974; Donella H. Meadows et al., *The Limits to Growth: A Report for the Club of Rome's Project on the Predicament of Mankind*, New York: University Books, 1974; Rufus Miles, *Awakening from the American Dream*, New York: Universe Books, 1976; Fred Hirsch, *Social Limits to Growth*, Twentieth Century Fund, 1976; Lester R. Brown, *The Twenty-Ninth Day*, New York: Norton, 1978. For an antidote to the new Malthusianism, see articles by Jeremiah Novak, "In Defense of the Third World," *America*, Jan. 21, 1978; "A New Perception of World Hunger," *America*, May 13, 1978; "World Hunger: Other Perceptions," *America*, June 24, 1978; "Beyond North and South: The Second Coming of the World Economy," *Worldview*, Mar. 1978; "An Overview of the Need for Structural Change in International Economic Institutions," testimony before the Subcommittee on International Development and Subcommittee on International Economic Policy and Trade, Sept. 20, 1978. See also Herman Kahn, *The Next 200 Years: A Sce-*

nario for America and the World, for the Hudson Institute, New York: Morrow, 1976. Soviet versions of Panglossianism are described in these articles: Daniel S. Papp, "Soviet Scarcity: The Response of a Socialist State," *Social Science Quarterly,* vol. 57, no. 2, Sept. 1976, p. 350; and Daniel Papp, "Marxism-Leninism and Natural Resources," *Resources Policy,* June 1977.

The lifeboat ethic is preached in Garret Hardin, "The Tragedy of the Commons," *Science,* vol. 162, Dec. 13, 1968, pp. 1243–48; *Exploring New Ethics for Survival,* New York: Viking, 1972; and most explicitly in Hardin's "Lifeboat Ethics: The Case Against Helping the Poor," *Psychology Today,* vol. 8, Sept. 8, 1974, p. 38. For a different perspective and critique see Ronald Sider, *Rich Christians in an Age of Hunger,* New York: Paulist Press, 1978. For the possibilities of abundance through sharing, see Peter Kropotkin, *Fields, Factories and Workshops,* New York: Greenwood Press, 1978 (Copyright 1901); Murray Bookchin, *Post Scarcity Anarchism,* Berkeley, Cal.: Ramparts Press, 1971; E. F. Shumacher, *Small Is Beautiful,* New York: Harper & Row, 1973; Leopold Kohr, *The Breakdown of Nations,* New York: Dutton, 1957; Lewis Mumford, *The City in History: Its Origins, Its Transformations and Its Prospects,* New York: Harcourt, Brace & World, 1961; Lewis Mumford, *The Myth of the Machine,* New York: Harcourt, Brace & World, 1967; Karl William Kapp, *The Social Costs of Private Enterprise,* Cambridge, Mass.: Harvard University Press, 1950; Edward Mishan, *Technology and Growth: The Price We Pay,* New York: Praeger, 1970.

For an account of contemporary separatism in America see Kevin Phillips, "The Balkanization of America," *Harper's Magazine,* May 1978, p. 37.

The literature on community self-reliance and community protection is growing. See, for example, Gar Alperovitz and Jeff Faux, "An Economic Program for the Coming Decade," *Democratic Review,* Nov. 1975. See also Stephen Michaelson, "Community Based Development in Urban Areas," in Benjamin Chinitz, ed., *Central City Economic Development,* Cambridge, Mass.: ABT Books, 1979, pp. 124–29.

The growing attack on democracy can be found in an influential book by Michel Crozier, Samuel P. Huntington, and Joji Watamki, *The Crisis of Democracy,* Trilateral Report Triangle Paper. Leonard Silk and David Vogel, *Ethics and Profits,* New York: Simon & Schuster, 1976, contains an interesting collection of statements by corporate leaders questioning "one man, one vote" democracy. See also Peter Steinfels, *The Neo Conservatives: The Men Who are Changing America's Politics,* and my own "The Crisis of the Corporation," TNI Pamphlet 3, Washington, D.C.: Institute for Policy Studies, 1975.

For the beneficial effects of participation in agriculture, see Solon Barraclough, *op. cit.,* and Erik Eckholm, "The Dispossessed of the Earth: Land Reform and Sustainable Development," *Worldwatch Paper 30,* Washington, D.C.: Worldwatch Institute, June 1979.

Myths that touch on scarcity, abundance, and sharing can be found in *Folktales of All Nations,* F. H. Lee, ed., New York: Coward, McCann, 1932; *Folktales of Greece,* Georgios A. Megas, ed., Chicago: University of Chicago Press, 1970; *100 Armenian Folktales,* Susie Hoogastan-Villa, ed., Detroit: Wayne State University Press, 1966.

For two accounts of scarcity and its effect on planning, see L. D. Nelson and Julie A. Honnold, "Planning for Resource Scarcity: A Critique of Prevalent Proposals," and Denton E. Morrison, "Growth, Environment, Equity and Scarcity," both in *Social Science Quarterly,* vol. 57, no. 2, Sept. 1976. A broader view of scarcity and its place in various ideologies can be found in Immanuel Wallerstein, "The Rise and Future Demise of the World Capitalist System: Concepts for Comparative Analysis," *Comparative Studies in Society and History,* vol. 16, 1974. See also Robert W. Cox, "Ideologies and the New International Economic Order: Reflections on Some Recent Literature," *International Organization,* vol. 33, no. 25, spring 1979; B. Bruce Briggs, "Against the Neo-Malthusians," *Commentary,* July 1974; Michael Zimmerman, "A Comparison of Marx & Heidegger on the Technological Domination of Nature," *Philosophy Today,* 1979, p. 99; and David Harvey, "Population, Resources and the Ideology of Science," *Economic Geography,* vol. 50, 1974, pp. 256–77.

Index

337